*THE PARANOID STYLE
IN AMERICAN DIPLOMACY*

Stanford Studies *in* Middle Eastern
and Islamic Societies *and* Cultures

THE PARANOID STYLE IN AMERICAN DIPLOMACY

Oil and Arab Nationalism in Iraq

Brandon Wolfe-Hunnicutt

STANFORD UNIVERSITY PRESS
Stanford, California

Stanford University Press
Stanford, California

© 2021 by the Board of Trustees of the Leland Stanford Junior University. All rights reserved.

No part of this book may be reproduced or transmitted in any form or by any means, electronic or mechanical, including photocopying and recording, or in any information storage or retrieval system without the prior written permission of Stanford University Press.

Printed in the United States of America on acid-free, archival-quality paper

Library of Congress Cataloging-in-Publication Data

Names: Wolfe-Hunnicutt, Brandon, author.
Title: The paranoid style in American diplomacy : oil and Arab nationalism in Iraq / Brandon Wolfe-Hunnicutt.
Other titles: Stanford studies in Middle Eastern and Islamic societies and cultures.
Description: Stanford, California : Stanford University Press, [2021] | Series: Stanford studies in Middle Eastern and Islamic societies and cultures | Includes bibliographical references and index.
Identifiers: LCCN 2020044695 | ISBN 9781503613829 (cloth) | ISBN 9781503627918 (paperback) | ISBN 9781503627925 (ebook)
Subjects: LCSH: Iraq Petroleum Company—History. | Petroleum industry and trade—Government policy—Iraq—History. | Arab nationalism—Iraq—History. | United States—Foreign relations—Iraq. | Iraq—Foreign relations—United States. | Iraq—Politics and government—1958–
Classification: LCC E183.8.I57 W65 2021 | DDC 327.730567—dc23
LC record available at https://lccn.loc.gov/2020044695

Cover design: Rob Ehle and Kevin Barrett Kane
Cover photos: Burning off natural gas from the oil fields in Rumaila, southern Iraq. Middle East. Robert Burch / Alamy Stock Photo. Date palm silhouette, 123rf.com.
Typeset by Motto Publishing Services in 10.5/14.5 Brill

Contents

	List of Maps and Illustrations	vii
	Cast of Characters	ix
	Introduction	1
1	The Rise and Fall of the Hashemite Monarchy	9
2	The Free Officers' Revolution	30
3	The Emergence of OPEC	60
4	The Overthrow of Qasim	85
5	The Rise and Fall of the Ba'th	110
6	The Emergence of the Iraq National Oil Company	135
7	The Arab-Israeli June War	162
8	The Return of the Ba'th	187
9	The Nationalization of the IPC	204
	Conclusion	225
	Acknowledgments	229
	Notes	233
	Index	295

Maps and Illustrations

MAP 1. Sykes-Picot Agreement, 1916	xv
MAP 2. Iraqi Oil Industry Operations, 1953	xvi
MAP 3. Iraqi Economic Activity, 1978	xvii
FIGURE 1. Oil majors organizational chart, 1952	19
FIGURE 2. Free Officers 'Abd al-Karim Qasim and 'Abd al-Salam 'Arif, 1958	47
FIGURE 3. Yarmouk housing complex, Baghdad, 1965	64
FIGURE 4. Al-Rasheed Street, 1961	65
FIGURE 5. Abdullah Tariki, 1961	68
FIGURE 6. President Qasim and aides, 1963	111
FIGURE 7. US embassy in Baghdad, 1955	112
FIGURE 8. Arab world leaders at Luxor, 1964	136
FIGURE 9. Khair el-Din Haseeb, 1957	140
FIGURE 10. Khair el-Din Haseeb, 1964	148
FIGURE 11. Baghdad financial district, 1959	149

Cast of Characters

IRAQI POLITICAL LEADERS

'Abd al-Ilah (1913–1958). Regent and adviser to King Faysal II, 1939–58.

Salih Mahdi 'Ammash (1924–1979). Ba'thist Minister of Defense, 1963. Minister of the Interior, 1968–70. Ambassador to the Soviet Union (1971–74), France (1974–76), and Finland (1976).

'Abd al-Salam 'Arif (1921–1966). Early Free Officer and key organizer of the 1958 Free Officers' Revolution. Broke with Qasim in support of Nasser. Appointed President by the Ba'th in 1963 and remained in power until his death.

'Abd al-Rahman 'Arif (1916–1982). Brother of 'Abd al-Salam and President of Iraq, 1966–68.

Ahmad Hasan al-Bakr (1914–1982). Early Free Officer and key organizer of the 1958 Free Officers' Revolution. Joined the Ba'th Party in 1959. Prime Minister, 1963. President, 1968–79.

Mustafa Barzani (1903–1979). Founder of the Kurdish Democratic Party and leader of the Kurdish nationalist movement.

'Abd al-Rahman al-Bazzaz (1913–1973). Prominent lawyer, educator, and politician. Ambassador to Britain in 1963 and to the United Arab Republic, 1963–64. Secretary General of OPEC, 1964–65. Prime Minister, 1965–66.

Faysal ibn Husayn al-Hashemi (1855–1933). King of Iraq, 1921–33.

Muhammad Hadid (1906–1999). Prominent industrialist and organizer of Jam'at al-Ahali (the "Ahali Group") in the 1930s. Finance Minister, 1958–63.

Sa'dun Hammadi (1930–2007). President of the Iraq National Oil Company, 1968–74. Oil Minister, 1970–74.

Nasr al-Hani (1917–1968). Ambassador to the United States, April 1964–June 1967. Ambassador to Lebanon, 1967–68. Foreign Minister, July 1968.

Khair el-Din Haseeb (1929–). Key architect of the IPC nationalization strategy as Governor of the Central Bank of Iraq, 1963–65, and a member of the Iraq National Oil Company Board of Directors, 1967–68.

Sassoon Hasqail (1860–1932). Member of the Ottoman Parliament and Chair of the Ottoman Budget Committee, 1908–18. First Iraqi Minister of Finance, 1921–25.

Saddam Hussein (1937–2006). Ba'th Party organizer, 1960s. President of Iraq, 1979–2003.

'Abd al-Fattah Ibrahim (1906–?). Social and political theorist and founder of Jam'at al-Ahali (the "Ahali Group") in the 1930s. Oil adviser to Qasim, 1958–63.

Adib al-Jadir (1927–2019). Director General of Oil Affairs, 1958–59. Minister of Industry, 1963–65. A member of the Iraq National Oil Company Board of Directors, 1967–68. Minister of Industry, 1968.

Rashid 'Ali al-Kaylani (1892–1965). Prime Minister, 1933. Leader of 1941 Nationalist revolt against the British.

Fadl 'Abbas al-Mahdawi (1915–1963). President of the Higher Military Court (the "People's Court," which prosecuted Ba'thist opponents of President 'Abd al-Karim Qasim's government, 1959–63. Executed along with President Qasim during the Ba'thist coup of 1963.

'Abd al-Karim Qasim (1914–1963). President of Iraq, 1958–63. Leader of the 1958 Free Officers' Revolution and President of Iraq, 1958–63. Executed during of the Ba'thist coup of 1963.

'Ali Salih al-Sa'di (1928–1980). Ba'th Party General Secretary, 1960–63. Deputy Prime Minister, 1963.

Nuri al-Said (1888–1958). Defense and Foreign Affairs Minister, 1920s and 1930s. Frequent Prime Minister from the late 1930s until the 1958 Free Officers' Revolution.

Jallal Talabani (1933–2017). Leader of the Kurdish nationalist movement. Split with Mustafa Barzani and the Kurdish Democratic Party to found the Patriot Union of Kurdistan in 1975.

Hardan al-Tikriti (1925–1971). Ba'thist Commander of the Air Force, 1963. Minister of Defense, 1968–70. Vice President, 1970.

'Abd al-'Aziz al-Wattari (1930–?). Minister of Oil, 1963–65.

Tahir Yahya, (1913–1986). Organizer of the 1958 Free Officers' Revolution. Nasserist Prime Minister, 1963–65, 1967–68.

REGIONAL POLITICAL LEADERS

Gamal Abdel Nasser (1918–1970). Leader of the Egyptian Free Officers that overthrew the Egyptian monarchy in 1952. President of the Republic of Egypt, 1954–70. Leader of the pan-Arabist movement of the 1950s and 1960s.

Muhammad Reza Pahlavi (1918–1980). Shah (king) of Iran, 1941–79. Leader of the opposition to the pan-Arabist movement of the 1950s and 1960s.

Faysal Ibn 'Abd al-Aziz al-Sa'ud (1904–1975). Saudi crown prince, 1953–64. Effectively overthrew his brother King Saud in a 1962 palace coup. King of Saudi Arabia, 1964–75. Leader of the opposition to the pan-Arabist movement of the 1950s and 1960s.

Abdullah Tariki (1917–1997). Saudi Oil Minister, 1961–62. Co-founder of OPEC in 1960 and frequent adviser to the Iraqi government in the 1960s.

AMERICAN OFFICIALS AND ADVISERS

James Akins (1926–2010). First Secretary of US Embassy in Iraq, 1961–65. Director of the State Department's Office of Fuel and Energy, 1969–72. Ambassador to Saudi Arabia, 1973.

McGeorge Bundy (1919–1996). National Security Advisor, 1961–66.

Miles Copeland (1919–1991). CIA Arabist, 1947–57.

James Critchfield (1917–2003). CIA Near East Division Chief, 1959–69.

Roger Davies (1921–1974). State Department Arabist, 1946–74.

Allen Dulles (1893–1969). Director of the CIA, 1953–61.

John Foster Dulles (1888–1959). Secretary of State, 1953–59.

James Forrestal (1892–1949). Secretary of Defense, 1948–49.

W. Averell Harriman (1891–1996). State Department adviser, 1940s–1960s.

Richard Helms (1913–2002). Director of the CIA, 1966–1973. Ambassador to Iran, 1973–76.

John D. Jernegan (1911–1981). Ambassador to Iraq, 1958–59. State Department Arabist, 1960s.

Henry Kissinger (1923–). National Security Advisor, 1969–75. Secretary of State, 1973–77.

Robert Komer (1922–2000). National Security Council member, 1950s–1960s.

William Lakeland (1923–2015). Political officer in the US Embassy in Baghdad, 1960–64. State Department Arabist, 1964–68.

Walter J. Levy (1911–1997). Oil industry expert and State Department adviser.

Roy Melbourne (1904–2007). State Department political officer and diplomat. US chargé d'affaires, Baghdad, 1962–63.

William Rogers (1913–2001). Secretary of State, 1969–73.

Kim Roosevelt (1916–2000). CIA Near East Division Chief, 1950–57.

Walt W. Rostow (1916–2003). National Security Advisor, 1961–69.

Robert Strong (1915–1999). Ambassador to Iraq, 1963–67.

Phillips Talbot (1915–2010). Assistant Secretary of State for Near Eastern Affairs, 1961–65.

Nicholas Thacher (1915–2002). State Department Arabist and diplomat. First Secretary of US Embassy in Baghdad, 1956–58.

EUROPEAN POLITICAL LEADERS

Anthony Eden (1897–1977). Conservative British Prime Minister, 1955–57.

Charles de Gaulle (1890–1970). French general officer and anti-Fascist resistance leader (1940–45). President, 1959–69.

Nikita Khrushchev (1894–1971). Soviet Premier, 1953–64.

Alexi Kosygin (1904–1980). Soviet diplomat, 1960–80.

Harold MacMillan (1894–1986). Conservative British Prime Minister, 1957–63.

Enrico Mattei (1906–1962). Italian anti-Fascist resistance leader, member of parliament, 1948–53, and ENI chairman, 1953–62.

Harold Wilson (1916–1995). Labour Party Prime Minister of Britain, 1964–70.

OIL COMPANIES
Corporate Sectors

Majors. General term for the seven large vertically and horizontally integrated international oil companies: BP, Shell, Exxon, Mobil, Chevron, Texaco, and Gulf. Also known as the "Seven Sisters."

Independents. General term for the international companies that emerged as significant competitors to the majors in the 1950s and 1960s.

Domestics. General term for the domestic American oil and gas industry that was in direct competition with both the major and independent international companies.

Standard Oil Company. Originally founded by John D. Rockefeller in Ohio in 1870, the Standard Oil Company soon formed a trust that dominated national and international oil markets. In 1911, the Standard Oil Trust was broken into thirty-four regional companies, following a Supreme Court ruling which found that the trust constituted an illegal monopoly.

The IPC and Its Constituent Firms

Iraq Petroleum Company (IPC). Consortium composed of BP, Shell, Exxon, Mobil, CFP, and Partex. Originally known as the Turkish Petroleum Company, 1914–28. Nationalized by the Iraqi government, 1972–75.

British Petroleum (BP). Originally a British venture known as the Anglo-Persian Oil Company, 1908–33. The British government acquired a controlling interest in the firm in 1914. Known as the Anglo-Iranian Oil Company, 1933–54. Known as BP since 1954. At the conclusion of the 1928 Red Line Agreement, it held a 23.75 percent interest in the IPC.

Compagnie Françoise des Pétroles (CFP). CFP was a French investment group formed in 1924 to hold French shares in the IPC. The French government acquired a controlling interest in the firm in 1931. At the conclusion of the 1928 Red Line Agreement, the firm held a 23.75 percent interest in the IPC.

Exxon. Standard Oil of New Jersey was the largest of the companies to emerge from the 1911 breakup of the Standard Oil Trust. Originally marketed as Esso (S.O.), the firm became known as Exxon in the early 1970s. In 1999, it merged with Mobil to form ExxonMobil. At the conclusion of the 1928 Red Line Agreement, it held an 11.875 percent interest in the IPC.

Mobil. Standard Oil of New York was one of the companies to emerge from the 1911 breakup of the Standard Oil Trust. The firm became known as Mobil in the 1950s. In 1999, it merged with Exxon to form ExxonMobil. At the conclusion of the 1928 Red Line Agreement, it held a 11.875 percent interest in the IPC.

Partex. Portuguese holding company for Armenian businessman Calouste Gulbenkian. At the conclusion of the 1928 Red Line Agreement, it held a 5 percent interest in the IPC.

Shell. Originally a British-Dutch venture known as Royal-Dutch Shell formed in 1907. At the conclusion of the 1928 Red Line Agreement, it held a 23.75 percent interest in the IPC.

Other Regional Firms

Arabian American Oil Company (Aramco). Consortium composed of Exxon, Mobil, Chevron, and Texaco. Acquired extensive concessionary rights in Saudi Arabia between 1932 and 1948.

ENI—Ente Nazionale Idocarburi (ENI). Italian state-owned company organized for the express purpose of competing with the majors.

Entreprise de Recherches et d'Activités Pétrolières (ERAP). French state-owned company formed in 1965 for the express purpose of competing with the IPC for an Iraqi concession.

Iraq National Oil Company (INOC). Iraqi state-owned oil company formed in 1964.

National Iranian Oil Company (NIOC). Iranian state-owned oil company formed in 1954.

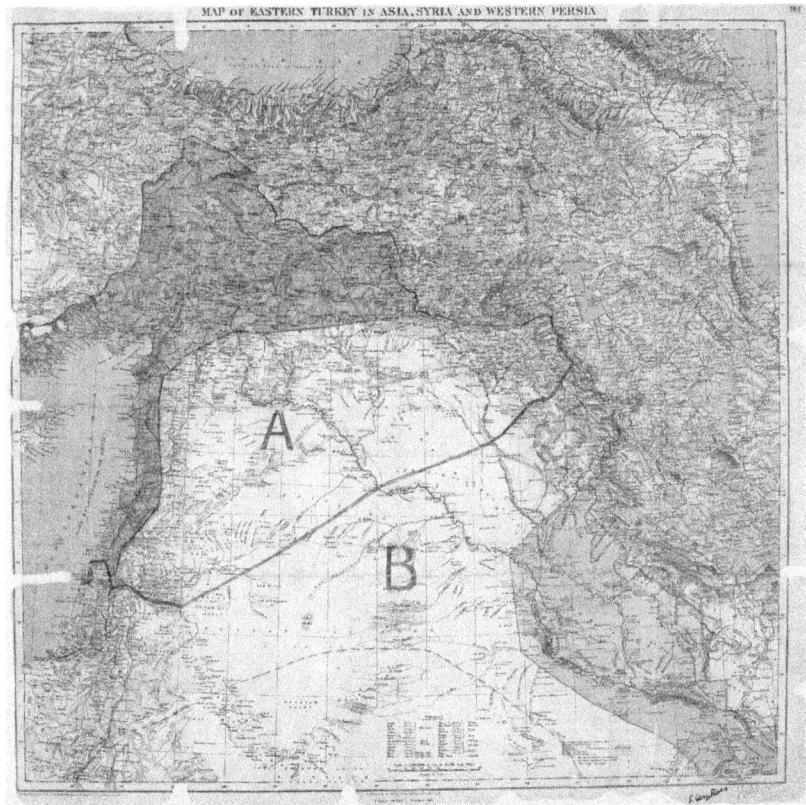

MAP 1. Sykes-Picot Agreement, 1916. The map shows the British-French wartime agreement for the division of Ottoman territory into respective British and French spheres after the war. Source: UK National Archives, MK1/426.

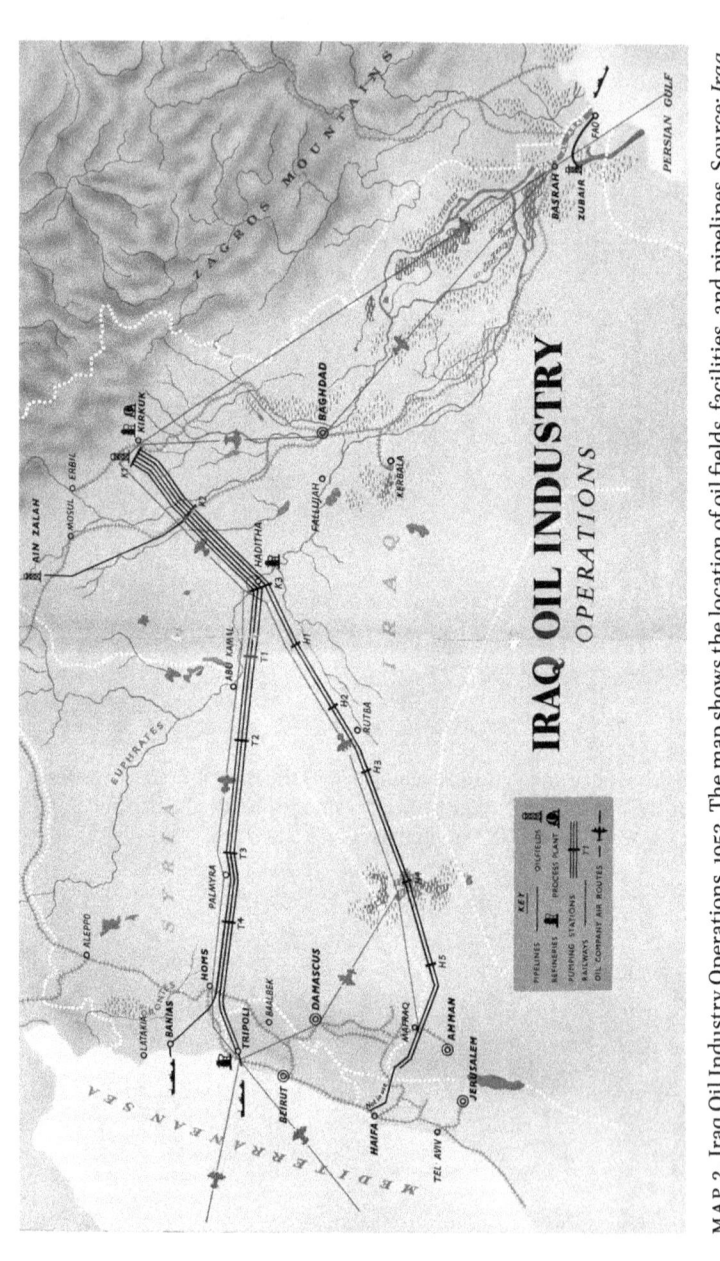

MAP 2. Iraq Oil Industry Operations, 1953. The map shows the location of oil fields, facilities, and pipelines. Source: *Iraq Today*, Directorate-General of Propaganda, Baghdad, 1953, courtesy of Perry-Castañeda Library, University of Texas, Austin.

MAP 3. Iraqi Economic Activity, 1978. The map, created by the CIA, shows expanded oil industry operations after the nationalization of the Iraq Petroleum Company. Source: Central Intelligence Agency, Map 503930 1978, courtesy of the Perry-Castañeda Library, University of Texas, Austin.

*THE PARANOID STYLE IN
AMERICAN DEMOCRACY*

INTRODUCTION

AROUND MIDNIGHT ON JULY 14, 1958, THE AMERICAN STATE DEpartment received a telegram from the US embassy in Iraq explaining that earlier that day Iraqi soldiers had arrested a number of Americans staying at the New Baghdad Hotel.[1] One of those arrested was Eugene Burns of Sausalito, California. Burns was a Moscow-born AP reporter and nature writer in Baghdad promoting the Holy Land Foundation, a nonprofit group with the stated purpose of improving US–Middle East relations.[2] Burns was also rumored to be the CIA station chief in Baghdad.[3] Another of those arrested was George Colley, Jr., of San Francisco. Colley, president of the overseas division of the Bechtel Corporation, was in the country to "inspect oil company projects."[4] A third was Robert Alcock, an industrial engineer from Los Angeles, who was in the country meeting with Colley without the official knowledge of either the State Department or the government of Iraq.[5] The fourth was Jose Carabia, a Cuban-born "collector of orchids for the New York and Missouri botanical gardens, in Iraq as an 'expert on plants of the Bible.'"[6] After being arrested at the hotel, the Americans, with about ten other foreigners, were loaded onto military vehicles that were headed for the Ministry of Defense. En route to their destination, an angry mob surrounded the vehicle and dragged the Americans into the street. Burns, Colley, and Alcock were beaten and stabbed to death. Carabia escaped to tell the tale.[7] Despite a determined search by Iraqi authorities, the bodies of the dead Americans were never recovered. Most likely they had been buried in a "common grave" with about fifteen Iraqi casualties of the revolution.[8]

The three dead Americans were among the estimated thirty people who were killed in what became known as Iraq's Free Officers' Revolution.[9] The revolution had begun in the early morning hours when a column of rebel tanks burst through the gates of the Royal Palace and seized King Faysal II, along with several of his family members, advisers, servants, and guards. The group was immediately dragged into the courtyard and executed by firing squad. A second unit of rebel soldiers deployed to the residence of Prime Minister Nuri al-Said. The prime minister momentarily escaped, but was captured the next day while trying to flee the country dressed as a woman. Nuri was immediately shot dead and buried, only to have his corpse disinterred by an angry mob so that it could be dragged through the streets of Baghdad, hung from a lamppost, burned and mutilated, and ultimately, repeatedly run over by municipal buses until, according to a Western observer, "it resembled *bastrouma*, an Iraqi sausage meat."[10]

American newspapers represented the three Americans killed in Iraq as tragic victims of a senseless mob. Tragic as their individual fates might have been, the history recounted in this book suggests that something more was at work in the streets of Baghdad in July 1958 than simply the random violence of an Iraqi crowd. Bechtel was not just any international firm—it occupied a central node in the structure of the world economy.[11] Bechtel had been founded by Warren A. Bechtel and George Colley in 1906 to construct a thirty-six-mile rail link connecting Sunol to Oakland, California.[12] By 1912, the firm had landed its "first big job"—a 106-mile rail line through the rugged Eel River Canyon, in northern California's Mendocino County.[13] By the 1920s, it would be one of the country's largest construction and engineering firms. In 1937, it merged with the Consolidated Steel Corporation to form the Bechtel-McCone Corporation, which expanded beyond pipe and rail construction to engage in petrochemical processing and the construction of oil refineries. During World War II, it moved into shipbuilding and soon became one of the country's largest defense contractors and a leader in the field of nuclear energy production. By 1950, company co-founder John McCone was undersecretary of the US Air Force. At the time that George Colley's son George Jr. was slain in the streets of Baghdad in July 1958, McCone headed the US Atomic Energy Commission (AEC), which regulated the production of civilian nuclear energy. Three years later, McCone was made director of the Central Intelligence Agency.

To disentangle the various strands that came together in the New Baghdad Hotel in July 1958, this book examines the history of one of the firms with which Bechtel did business—the Iraq Petroleum Company (IPC). The history of this consortium of international oil companies offers a unique lens through which we can view a number of social and political processes of world historical significance. By examining the history of the Iraqi effort to nationalize the IPC, from the beginning of that effort in the 1920s through its successful conclusion in the 1970s, we gain an understanding of the relationship between business and government as the system of imperial rule fell into a terminal crisis. We get a sense of how the Americans sought to prop up and defend the IPC and other imperial structures built by the British. And we learn of the political and economic strategies employed by Iraqi nationalists to overcome the legacies of colonialism.

I examine the history of the IPC nationalization from three distinct perspectives: the oil company officials who sought to defend their business interests in Iraq, the Iraqi state-building class that carried out the nationalization, and the American diplomats who sought to mediate between the two contending sides. To access oil company perspectives, I utilize the private archives of the Iraq Petroleum Company—a consortium of multinational firms that was formed in the immediate aftermath of World War I. To access the perspectives of the Iraqi state-building class, I read US and oil company records "against the grain," and supplement these documents with Iraqi memoirs and oral history interviews with Khair el-Din Haseeb, of one of the key players in the drama. To access US diplomatic perspectives, I engage with the official records of the State Department.[14]

Drawing on these sources, I advance three main arguments. First, I contend that the unique features of the IPC consortium rendered it particularly vulnerable to eventual nationalization. I show that this consortium, composed of firms registered in Germany (for a time), Britain, France, the Netherlands, Portugal, and the United States, was largely the creation of a dying British Empire. It was the very weakness of the British Empire that accounted for the consortium's heterogeneous origins and the business rivalries among its constituent firms. At the end of World War I, the British were not, on their own, able to exercise sole control over the Iraqi oil industry, and so they had to allow other interested parties to share in the country's production. But this mix of corporate interests created political vulnerabilities that Iraqi oil nationalists were able to exploit in their own drive to gain control over the industry.

Second, I assert that Iraq's state-building class, over the course of roughly three generations, overcame tremendous obstacles to marshal the force necessary to expropriate the property of some of the world's richest and most powerful corporations. These obstacles arose from a variety of sources. When the consortium first began to take shape, "Iraq" did not yet exist as an independent nation-state. At the time, on the eve of World War I, Iraq was still under Ottoman rule, divided into three distinct *vilayets* (provinces). After the war, Iraq was integrated into the structure of British imperialism as a League of Nations' "mandate state"—a kind of halfway house between direct colonial administration and full national sovereignty. Iraqi state-builders had to overcome this lack of administrative capacity and construct national institutions and establish global relationships that would allow the government to operate a wholly nationalized industry. The key turning point in the history of this state-building process was the 1958 Iraqi Free Officers' Revolution, which swept away the vestiges of the semi-sovereign monarchy and replaced it with an independent republic.

Third, I show how the Iraqi oil nationalization effort, and especially the 1958 revolution, exposed critical contradictions and vulnerabilities in the logic and structure of American power. In seeking to mediate between the largely British-run oil company and Iraqi nationalists, American policymakers found themselves trying to serve several masters at once. The United States had long championed the right of national self-determination over colonial rule—at least rhetorically. And so the US owed a measure of support to Iraqi nationalists. The United States was also in a close geopolitical alliance with the British, first against Germany in the two World Wars, and then against the Soviet Union in the Cold War. And so the US owed a measure of support to British imperialists. The United States was also the corporate headquarters of the world's largest energy companies—companies that wanted to make money in the Middle East. And so the US owed a measure of support to American oil giants that were invested in the IPC. But as the decades wore on, still more claimants appeared. By the end of the 1960s, new actors were in a position to make compelling demands on the American state. Domestic American oil and gas companies, the Israel lobby, and major defense contractors all developed interests in Iraq that ran counter to the preferences of the IPC. In seeking to satisfy all of these constituencies, the US government satisfied none.

Business rivalries within the oil industry, Iraqi nationalism, and American diplomatic equivocation all fused in the early 1970s to produce a successful nationalization that would have major repercussions for the region and the world. The US government, rent by competing demands and preoccupied with a world full of trouble—from Vietnam to Berkeley—stood paralyzed as Iraqi oil nationalists advanced methodically toward their goal of nationalizing the industry. The IPC, which had long depended on diplomatic and political support—first British and then American—was suddenly left to contend with the Iraqi nationalists on its own. The Iraqi Ba'th Party—an Arab socialist party that conspired to seize power in the late 1960s—skillfully took advantage of favorable world trends to bring to fruition what had been building for nearly a century. In the wake of Iraq's bold action, producer-state control would become the industry norm by the end of the 1970s. In the pages that follow, I trace this grand arc as it circumscribed some of the most significant developments in the global history of the twentieth century: the decolonization of Asia and Africa, the US Cold War with the Soviet Union, and the rise of sovereign petrostates in the Middle East.

In developing the above arguments I contribute to three broad fields of knowledge. With respect to international political economy, this book adds to the ongoing critique of what is sometimes called the "oil scarcity myth." In short, the oil scarcity myth holds that oil supplies are scarce and access to them is insecure, and that to secure necessary supplies of a vital resource, the US government must support the operations of private American oil companies operating in the Middle East. According to this view, private oil companies serve as a kind of public policy instrument securing a public good. Recent scholarship by Robert Vitalis, Timothy Mitchell, and Roger Stern turns this long-familiar story on its head.[15] The core proposition of this new scholarship is that oil supplies (from the Middle East or elsewhere) are neither scarce nor insecure. On the contrary, the major problem afflicting the industry from its inception has not been scarcity but superabundance, due to the vast quantity of naturally occurring oil deposits and the economic tendency toward industrial overproduction.[16] When a large number of firms compete to meet a finite demand, prices and profits fall. In extremis, prices fall below the cost of production and some firms are ruined.

New histories of oil, recognizing this tendency toward overproduction, focus on the actions of states, and the US state above all others, to stabilize prices and profits by "producing scarcity."[17] In the strong version of this argument, it is the state that serves the firm (not the other way around) in the firm's ceaseless quest for private accumulation. While this book demonstrates the extent to which the US state helped the IPC to hold down production in Iraq so as to stem the tide of overproduction that riddled the industry in the 1950s and 1960s, it also shows that the US state was not the "unified and coherent" actor that political scientists might theorize.[18] Rather, the US state was an arena of competition in which different interest groups vied for influence over the policymaking process.[19]

The second broad field to which this book contributes is Iraqi history. Empirically, it documents the virtually unknown history of the "Al-Haseeb group," which engaged in a broad struggle to defend what historian Christopher Dietrich describes as the principle of "natural resource sovereignty."[20] This group sought international recognition, through the United Nations and other agencies of global governance, of the permanent right of postcolonial states to unilaterally expropriate private property and abrogate existing contracts—such as the oil concession agreements in force in Iraq and across the broader region.

At the heart of the struggle for natural resource sovereignty was the "unequal exchange thesis." This thesis, intellectually rooted in the developmental economics of Raúl Prebisch's groundbreaking *The Economic Development of Latin America and Its Principal Problems (1949)*, introduced the concepts of core, periphery, and underdevelopment.[21] According to this thesis, the oil concession agreements of the early twentieth century were concluded among parties of unequal power and served to enshrine the advantages of the powerful over the powerless. The agreements were structured in such a way that the value of the raw materials exported from former colonies declined faster than the value of finished goods imported into those former colonies. The only way to break the pattern of underdevelopment and equalize the terms of trade was to abrogate existing contracts and bring the country's natural resources under public control.

In seeking to redress the economic injustice of the existing oil concession in Iraq, Iraqi nationalists were also engaged in a process of imagining a secular, democratic, and multiethnic conception of national identity. Scholars have long noted the "resource curse" of oil—the ways in which the existence of an oil industry in a postcolonial society undermines secular and democratic values and institutions. Clearly, IPC management and hiring practices hardened ethnic and sectarian identities in Iraq, but sometimes overlooked is the extent to which oil nationalism offered a unifying theme in Iraqi history. I show that oil concerns, and specifically the imperative of confronting foreign-owned companies, played an important role in bringing about moments of broad national reconciliation and multiethnic and multireligious harmony among Iraqis. In so doing, this book helps to illuminate the material analog to what historian Orit Bashkin describes as "the other Iraq."[22]

American diplomatic history represents the third broad field to which this book contributes, building on the long and venerable tradition of critique in the spirit of William Appleman Williams.[23] In the 1950s, Williams, a former naval officer turned diplomatic historian at the University of Wisconsin–Madison, offered a broad conceptual framework, not only to make sense of American diplomatic history but also to synthesize a great many disparate strands of American historiography.[24] Central to this concept was the idea of American empire as a "way of life"—something more closely approximating a religion than a mere political and economic system.[25] At the heart of this spirit of American imperialism was the idea that an "open door" to the markets and resources of the world represented a kind of Balm of Gilead to cure any and all ailments afflicting American society.

For Williams, it was not the practical necessity of capital expansion that best explained the history of American imperialism but rather a larger *weltanschauung* that located the sources of and solutions to American social problems in the world at large.[26] The value of this interpretive framework is its emphasis on economic themes, including the more spiritual dimensions of the private enterprise system.[27] By viewing US-Iraqi relations through this economic lens we are able to see a number of relations that might otherwise remain out of sight. We see economic interests nestling within the rhetoric of national security. We see pronouncements about human rights and democracy as swords of empire cutting down actual Middle Eastern democrats. And we see multinational oil corporations exercising a certain "business privilege" to unduly influence American foreign policy.[28] But we also see these oil majors as just one set of interests vying for influence over US foreign policy. Other concentrations of economic power—from the oil majors' domestic and international competitors, to defense contractors, to the Israel lobby—all were jockeying for position within the arena of struggle that is the American state. In this pursuit of power, government offices and budget shares are the prizes. The policy outcomes that emerge from this process cannot be rationally deduced from *a priori* principles (about democracy, or Communism, or the Anglo-Saxon race, or whatever else), but rather reflect the larger balance of political forces at any given time. In offering this more dialectical approach to the study of American foreign policy, this book adds to the ongoing effort to transcend what are sometimes called "the myths of empire."[29]

To transcend these myths of empire and arrive at a more complete understanding of America's role in Iraq, it is necessary to step back and situate the 1958 Free Officers' Revolution within a broader regional historical context. This in turn will allow us to make sense of two crucial, interrelated developments: the political movements that led to the overthrow of the Hashemite monarchy, and the American perception that this overthrow represented a grave threat to US interests in the region.

Chapter 1

THE RISE AND FALL OF THE HASHEMITE MONARCHY

IN THE LATE 1950S, AMERICAN POLICYMAKERS IN THE DWIGHT D. Eisenhower administration were at a loss to devise an appropriate policy response to the dynamics of decolonization across Asia and Africa. In Iraq, those dynamic processes entailed the emergence of a state-building class, the elaboration of nationalist doctrines of natural resource sovereignty, and the formation of vast popular movements against British imperialism. The course and outcome of the two World Wars accelerated these processes. Before those wars, the British Empire was the hegemonic center of the capitalist world system. By the end of those wars, the empire was teetering on the verge of bankruptcy. Despite this precipitous decline, Iraq at midcentury remained squarely within a British sphere of interests—not a formal colony, but not truly sovereign either.[1]

The United States was not yet a major player in the region. Its policy was to support Britain's traditional hegemonic role.[2] But though they viewed those decolonizing dynamics from afar, American policymakers saw them as deeply threatening to their sense of national economic and security interests. The final collapse of British imperial authority in Iraq, signaled by the 1958 Free Officers' Revolution, produced a security dilemma for American policymakers. To understand why those dynamics were so unsettling to the United States, it is first necessary to understand the regional context in which the Iraqi Free Officers' Revolution was able to prevail over the country's British-backed Hashemite monarchy.

THE HASHEMITE MONARCHY

The Hashemite monarchy drew its name from Faysal ibn Husayn al-Hashemi—a direct descendant of the Prophet Muhammad and the leader of the storied Arab revolt against the Ottoman Empire during World War I.[3] Faysal's father, Husayn, was the sharif of Mecca, an Ottoman title denoting authority over the Hejaz region of the Arabian Peninsula where the holy cities of Mecca and Medina are located. Before the war, Husayn sought British support for an independent caliphate in Mecca.[4] After the Ottomans entered the war on the side of Germany, British officials offered vague promises of support for Arab independence after the war, if Husayn would fight with the British against the Ottomans. In accordance with these promises, Husayn declared a revolt in June 1916, and dispatched his sons Faysal and 'Abd Allah to organize a rebellion of Arab nationalist officers in the Ottoman army. The nationalist officers, mainly from Iraq and Syria, had sought independence before the war and rallied to the "Sharifian cause."

The British then deployed covert agents (T. E. Lawrence the most famous among them) to Arabia to coordinate and supply the forces of Faysal and 'Abd Allah.[5] The Arab army proved effective in harassing Ottoman supply lines, and by war's end, Faysal's forces had occupied Damascus. In Damascus, Faysal set up an administration to govern his nascent Arab Kingdom.[6] The British, along with the French, initially appeared willing to recognize Faysal's claim to Arab independence. As the war ended in November 1918, the British and French issued a joint statement pledging their commitment to the "establishment of governments and administrations deriving their authority from the initiative and the free choice of the native populations."[7] But this pledge contradicted the terms of the secret Sykes-Picot Agreement. According to the terms of Sykes-Picot, reached in May 1916, French and British officials would partition the Arab territories of the Ottoman Empire among themselves after the war. Mesopotamia was to fall under British control, Syria and Lebanon under French control. Palestine was to be an Anglo-French condominium with British control over the port to Haifa. (See Map 1: Sykes-Picot Agreement.) By the end of the war, British forces were in control of Iraq, Syria, and Palestine, while the French occupied Lebanon. Faysal and his Syrian administration, composed mainly of Iraqi officers, remained in Damascus under British protection, but in September 1919 the British withdrew from Syria, leaving Faysal to contend with the French on his own.[8]

Aware of Franco-British machinations, and the consequent precariousness of his situation, Faysal sought to consolidate his government in Damascus by organizing a Syrian General Congress. At the congress, held in Damascus on March 8, 1920, delegates declared constitutional monarchies in Syria and Iraq with Faysal and 'Abd Allah on their respective thrones.[9] The British and French responded to the assertion of Arab independence in Iraq and Syria with a conference of their own. At San Remo, Italy, in April, French and British diplomats formalized a version of the Sykes-Picot Agreement. In accordance with the 1919 Treaty of Versailles's provision for "advanced nations" to govern territories "inhabited by peoples not yet able to stand by themselves under the strenuous conditions of the modern world," the newly created League of Nations awarded mandates to the French to govern Syria and Lebanon, and to the British to govern Mesopotamia, Palestine, and Transjordan.[10]

The League of Nations' patronizing language about peoples not yet ready for self-government was deeply offensive to Iraqis, who had a long history of regional autonomy under the Ottoman system.[11] Iraqis immediately rose in arms against the British assertion of mandate authority. Prominent Shi'i Ayatollah Muhammad Shirazi had already declared British civil administration in Iraq unlawful in early March. Shi'is, composing roughly half the population and concentrated mainly in the southern part of the country, demonstrated *en masse* against the British occupation. After being met with force, mass peaceful demonstrations escalated into armed attacks on British authorities. The Shi'i rebellion was soon joined by Sunni Arabs in the center of the country, who composed about 20 percent of the population. By July, the entire lower and middle Euphrates region was in rebellion. In the north, Kurdish tribesmen, who also composed about 20 percent of the population, took advantage of British preoccupation with the rebellion in the south to seize control of local villages and towns.[12]

While the British deployed thousands of colonial Indian soldiers to suppress the rebellion in Iraq, the French moved against Faysal's government in Damascus. On July 24, the French defeated Faysal's Arab army at the Battle of Maysalun and deposed his nascent regime.[13] As Sharifian officers were expelled from Syria, they rallied to the cause in Iraq in the hope of "establishing the kind of government in Baghdad that the French were forcing them to abandon in Syria."[14] By October, the British largely succeeded in suppressing the Iraqi uprising, but only at considerable expense, including the lives of some six thousand Iraqis. In the years to come, the uprising, known as the *Thawrat al-'Ishrin*, or Revolution of 1920, emerged as a key symbol of anti-British Iraqi nationalism.[15]

The strength of the uprising in Iraq, and an equally assertive "Quit Mesopotamia" campaign in the British press and parliament, compelled the British to devise a new approach to governing Iraq.[16] Since first entering the country in 1914, the British had sought to impose direct colonial rule on Iraq following the Indian model and administered by the India Office. Some within the imperial bureaucracy, intelligence agent Gertrude Bell in particular, recognized the need to accommodate nationalist opinion in Iraq. But it was not until after the 1920 uprising that Britain formally adopted a new policy. Rather than trying to administer Iraq through the Indian Office, Colonial Secretary Winston Churchill formed a new Middle East Department to oversee a transition to a system of indirect rule through an Arab head of state. For Churchill, the idea was to "maintain firm British control as cheaply as possible."[17] The most expedient means to this end was to declare a constitutional monarchy in Iraq and install an Arab king.

The most likely candidate for the throne in Iraq was either Faysal or 'Abd Allah. Of the two, British officials perceived Faysal to be the more "pliant instrument." Whereas 'Abd Allah had responded to the Battle of Maysalun by rallying his forces in the Syrian desert and threatening to retake Damascus, Faysal had sought British protection in Palestine and then in London. As the British considered Faysal for the role of Iraqi king in December 1920, he offered assurances that if given the position he would make no effort to recover Damascus.[18] These assurances made Faysal acceptable to British policymakers. The fact that he belonged to a well-known family, had a reputation for tolerance in matters of religion, and had reigned briefly in Syria convinced the British that Iraqis would accept him as well.[19] The decision was formalized at the Cairo Conference in April 1921. To mollify 'Abd Allah, the British, at that same conference, declared the Emirate of Transjordan and placed him on the throne there.

THE IRAQ PETROLEUM COMPANY

British interests in Iraq (and by extension, Faysal) were based largely on oil considerations.[20] Iraq had long been known to possess huge quantities of oil. In 1899, the Ottoman government granted a German investment firm, Deutsche Bank, an exclusive concession to produce and sell Iraqi oil resources. Two years later, German geological surveyors found that the Mosul region was sitting atop "a veritable 'lake of petroleum' of almost inexhaustible supply."[21] This German interest in Iraqi oil compelled the British to begin exploring for oil in neighboring Iran. At the time, Germany and Britain were engaged in the imperial rivalry and arms race that ultimately culminated in the outbreak of World War I. In an effort to outflank the Germans, the British, in 1901, acquired an oil concession covering southern Iran, from that country's ailing Qajar monarchy. In 1907, British engineers struck oil at Masjid-i-Suleiman near the border with Iraq. Soon thereafter, British investors formed (what eventually became known as) the British Petroleum Company (BP) to produce and market Iranian oil.[22]

BP's success in producing oil in Iran, and Britain's escalating rivalry with Germany, spurred further British efforts to secure the oil resources of Iraq. As part of the Anglo-German arms race, Winston Churchill, as first lord of the admiralty (the top civilian post for the British Royal Navy), implemented a naval modernization program by converting the British fleet from older coal-powered vessels to newer, faster, and more powerful oil-fueled ships.[23] While the Royal Navy undertook this naval conversion program, it looked to the BP as a source of future supply.[24] It therefore supported BP in an aggressive campaign to gain control of the German oil concession in Iraq, which Deutsche Bank had yet to develop. Deutsche Bank's failure to develop its Iraqi concession, in turn, led the Ottoman government to consider competing offers from BP and Royal Dutch Shell (Shell), the latter at that time the world's second-largest oil company (just behind the American giant Standard Oil).

Between 1912 and 1914, an Ottoman Armenian businessman named Calouste Gulbenkian reconciled competing interests in Iraq by forming a new consortium known as the Turkish Petroleum Company (TPC).[25] This new consortium reflected Britain's ascendant position in Iraq. According to terms concluded in March 1914, BP controlled 50 percent of the TPC, while Deutsche Bank and Shell each controlled 22.5 percent of the company. The remaining 5 percent of the company remained with Gulbenkian, or "Mr. Five Percent" as he became known. Three months later, the British government invested £2.2 million in BP, making the British government the majority shareholder in BP and a minority shareholder in the TPC.[26] However, the TPC agreement was concluded on June 28, 1914—the very day on which Austrian Archduke Franz Ferdinand was assassinated, catalyzing the series of events that culminated in the outbreak of World War I. With the Ottomans entering the war on the side of Germany in October, the British Custodian of Enemy Property seized control of the German shares in the TPC, and a final resolution of the competing interests would have to await the outcome of the fighting.[27]

After the war, when French and British officials met at San Remo, French diplomats demanded a share of the TPC in exchange for recognizing British claims to the oil-rich province of Mosul. According to the Sykes-Picot Agreement, Mosul was to lie within the French sphere of influence. However, at San Remo, French diplomats agreed to cede Mosul to Britain in exchange for the British transfer of the German shares in the TPC to the Compagnie Françoise des Pétroles (CFP), a new state-directed firm created for the express purpose of holding French shares in the TPC.[28] This agreement satisfied French demands, but led Walter Teagle, the president of Standard Oil of New Jersey (Exxon), the world's largest oil company, to demand that the "open door" principle be applied to Iraq.[29] According to this principle, American investors were to be given unrestricted access to the markets and resources of the world without regard for colonial preferences or spheres of interest.[30] Eager to retain American support for British foreign policy in the region, the British accommodated these demands and allowed Exxon, along with another American firm, Standard Oil of New York (Mobil), to buy into the consortium.[31] The negotiations were long and complex, but by 1928 an agreement was reached in which BP, Shell, CFP, and the American companies (Exxon and Mobil, incorporated as a joint venture known as the Middle East Development Company) each held 23.75 percent of the company, while Gulbenkian retained the remaining five percent. The following year, the TPC changed its name to the Iraq Petroleum Company.[32]

Left out of these agreements were the government and people of Iraq. In 1922, as the world's leading oil companies negotiated among themselves for the right to exploit Iraq's oil wealth, Sassoon Hasqail, Iraq's first finance minister, challenged the legality of the 1914 TPC concession. The scion of a prominent Jewish banking family in Baghdad, Hasqail had served as a high official in the former Ottoman government and was an inheritor of centuries-long Iraqi administrative traditions. He now sought to bring that civil service experience and expertise to bear on the management of Iraq's natural resources. In his negotiation with the companies, he argued that the TPC's 1914 agreement had not been ratified by the Ottoman parliament and was therefore legally invalid. He demanded a renegotiated concession in which the Iraqi government would have the right to purchase a 20 percent ownership stake in the consortium, and in which Iraqis would be included on the company's board of directors in London and trained for management positions in Iraq. Hasqail also demanded that the IPC's concession be limited to the area immediately surrounding Kirkuk so that other areas of the country could be opened up to a competitive bidding process.[33]

In presenting Iraq's demands to the companies, Hasqail put forward a powerful legal argument that would in time transform the international political economy of natural resources. But in 1922, Hasqail was in no position to compel the consortium to accept any of his demands, and none were included in a 1925 revision to the original 1914 concession agreement.[34] For having placed the interests of the Iraqi people over the preferences of imperial Britain, Hasqail was removed from his post and his services were never again consulted.[35]

Because Hasqail was excluded from Iraq's government, Iraq's abundant human and natural resources were integrated into the world economy on terms entirely dictated by the British. One result was that the Iraqi economy remained highly dependent on the financial health of the capitalist West. The financial virus that attacked metropolitan capitals in October 1929 soon infected the colonies. As the crash of the stock markets in London and New York set off a global economic slump that severely depressed demand for oil from Iraq or anywhere else for the next decade, the IPC laid off the vast majority of its Iraqi labor force and went to great lengths to ensure that Iraqi oil did not make it to world markets. These delaying tactics went so far as "the drilling of shallow holes on locations where there was no danger of our striking oil," as one internal company memo explained.[36] A subsequent internal communication described the companies' strategy in rather frank terms: "We are not actuated by a hell for leather rush to find oil; we want to set up a convincing window dressing that we are working the concession."[37] The extent to which the company went in order to maintain the appearance of developing its concession indicates that while the prevailing balance of power between the government of Iraq and the IPC clearly favored the company, the IPC could not simply disregard Iraqi government concerns. As an Iraqi nationalist movement gathered strength over the course of the 1930s, the company would be forced to take those concerns ever more seriously.

WORLD WAR II AND THE RASHID 'ALI COUP

The IPC's disinterest in developing its oil concession contributed to the rise of anti-British nationalist sentiments at all levels of Iraqi society. This included the armed forces. During the mandate period, which formally ended in 1932 when Iraq was admitted to the League of Nations as a sovereign member, Faysal established the institutions of a modern state, including a parliament and a cabinet of ministries.[38] But most of Faysal's state-building efforts were focused on developing a strong army and air force that could effectively wrest tax revenue from the countryside. As a result, the army, in particular a group of four army colonels (known collectively as the "Golden Square"), came to exert a powerful influence in Iraqi politics. Their influence increased after the death of Faysal in 1933. The crown then passed to Faysal's brother Ghazi, who sympathized with and patronized anti-British nationalist army factions.

In 1939, King Ghazi was killed in a car accident. Iraqi nationalists suspected the "accident" to be the work of British agents in collaboration with Nuri al-Said, a former Sharifian officer who had become the dominant political figure in Iraq's parliament, and was infamous as Britain's main conduit of influence in the country.[39] With the death of King Ghazi, formal power passed to the king's four-year-old son, Faysal II. Given Faysal II's immaturity, Nuri selected Prince 'Abd al-Ilah, Ghazi's 26-year-old cousin and brother-in-law, to act as the king's regent until the king came of age. While King Ghazi had harbored strong anti-British views and patronized Arab nationalist groupings in the military, Nuri and 'Abd al-Ilah saw their interests as tied to those of Britain and excelled at exploiting the networks of British patronage.

The conflict between Arabs and Jews in Palestine, and Britain's harsh suppression of the Palestinian Arab Revolt of 1936–39, exacerbated anti-British sentiments in Iraq. The economic dislocations that attended the onset of the World War II further inflamed these sentiments. In August 1939, as Britain mobilized for war against Germany, it enacted the Emergency

Powers Defence Act, which subjected the "sterling bloc" (countries that tied the value of their currency to the British pound) to strict capital and import controls.[40] As a member of the sterling bloc, Iraq experienced rampant inflation and critical food shortages, with foodstuffs and shipping capacity requisitioned for the war. In April 1941, the British established the Middle Eastern Supply Centre, a regional economic planning agency based in Cairo, to "ease civilian hardships caused by Allied impositions" and stabilize the regional war economy.[41] But by this time a powerful nationalist movement had formed in Iraq.

In the context of growing anti-British sentiment, the Golden Square colonels began seeking an alliance with Germany as an alternative to Britain. By this point, Germany had a strong influence in the country through its ambassador, Fritz Grobba—a sophisticated diplomat who spoke Arabic and Turkish and had purchased the Arabic newspaper *al-'Alam al-'Arabi* (*The Arab World*) to propagate anti-British Nazi propaganda.[42] Grobba's notions of ethnic nationalism did not go unchallenged. Before the war an Iraqi intelligentsia had taken to print media to articulate a secular, democratic, and pluralist vision of Iraqi national identity (see below).[43] But as the war approached, the space for democratic engagement closed down and many of Iraq's leading officers adopted a strongly pro-German and anti-British worldview. This was especially the case after al-Hajj Amin al-Husayni, the grand mufti of Jerusalem, fled British arrest in 1937. After fleeing to Beirut, al-Hajj Amin took up residence in Baghdad in 1939, where he circulated pro-German, anti-British propaganda.[44]

British concern about German influence in Iraq was exacerbated by France's fall to the Nazis in May 1940. The fall of France left Syria and Lebanon, which were still French mandates, under Axis control. The situation deteriorated still further when Italy joined the war on the side of Germany the following month. In response to the Italian declaration of war against Britain, Britain instructed the government of Iraq to break diplomatic relations with Italy. The prime minister at the time, Rashid 'Ali al-Kaylani, came under intense pressure from the nationalist colonels to refuse the British request. Rather than immediately complying with Britain's instructions, Rashid 'Ali sought an alliance with Germany against Britain. The Germans were preoccupied with an invasion of the Soviet Union and did not reciprocate the Iraqi overture, but by November the British had lost patience with Rashid 'Ali and demanded his resignation. Rashid 'Ali dragged his feet, but eventually agreed to step down by the end of January 1941.

Rashid 'Ali's supporters within the officer corps, however, refused to accept the British diktat. Instead, on April 1, they stormed the Royal Palace in an effort to arrest 'Abd al-Ilah and reinstate Rashid 'Ali. The regent fled to the US legation (the United States did not have a formal embassy in Iraq until 1948), whereupon US resident minister Paul Knabenshue smuggled him out of the capital to the safety of the British Royal Air Force headquarters at the Habbaniyya airbase, just west of the city.[45] The regent thus survived the incident, but his position remained tenuous. Rashid 'Ali, reinstated in the prime minister's office, deposed the regent and appointed a distant relative in his place. Rashid 'Ali, still trying to mediate between the British above him and the colonels below him, complied with a British request to land troops in Basra on April 7, but the colonels rebelled. Iraqi forces surrounded the Habbaniyya airbase and refused to allow the British access to Iraqi airspace. The British showed little patience with the intransigence of the colonels. British forces immediately opened fire on Iraqi positions surrounding Habbaniyya, routed Iraqi forces, and occupied the capital. Rashid 'Ali and al-Hajj Amin escaped to exile in Egypt; the colonels were tracked down and hanged one by one.[46] Rashid 'Ali, for his part, would not return to Iraq until after the 1958 revolution.

With the suppression of the "Rashid 'Ali coup," the British restored 'Abd al-Ilah to the regency and Nuri al-Said to the premiership. But the episode made the crown prince and premier "so odious among the people that, regardless of what they did afterwards, they were never able to command public confidence. Their image as servants of foreign interests and the impression that the British were in the background of their actions and policies simply would not wash," as the great Iraqi historian Hanna Batatu explained.[47]

OIL AND THE COLD WAR

The 1941 Rashid 'Ali coup demonstrated the vulnerability of the Hashemite regime during WWII. After the war, the British made a concerted effort to stabilize the power of the monarchy. British efforts were made easier by a massive increase in demand for oil to fuel postwar economic reconstruction

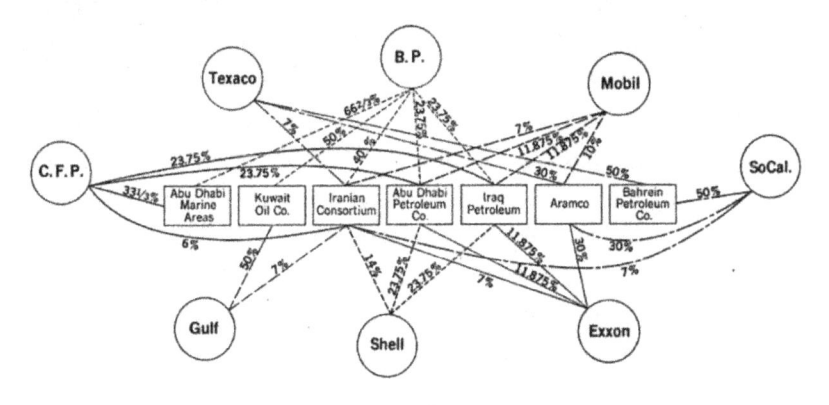

Ownership Links Between the Major International Oil Companies (Including Compagnie Française des Pétroles) and the Major Crude-Oil Producing Companies in the Middle East

FIGURE 1. Oil majors organizational chart, 1952. The chart shows the interlocking ownership and management agreements among the major oil companies operating in the Middle East. Source: US Senate, *Subcommittee on Multinational Corporations Hearings*, Part V, 1974, p. 290.

in Europe and Asia. This allowed for a general increase in Middle Eastern oil production. To serve this demand, major new fields were developed in Bahrain, Saudi Arabia, and Kuwait, and production in Iraq and Iran was expanded. Pipelines were constructed or expanded, linking those fields to the Persian Gulf and Mediterranean coast. US antitrust laws were waived to allow for a series of new mergers and acquisitions that had the effect of concentrating approximately 90 percent of globally traded oil under the control of seven highly integrated multinational companies.[48] These trends toward consolidation in the industry ultimately culminated, between 1944 and 1948, in the merger of Chevron, Texaco, Exxon, and Mobil to form Aramco, which held exclusive rights to what the State Department described as "the greatest material prize in world history"—the oil fields of Saudi Arabia—and would soon become "America's single largest private overseas investment."[49]

The postwar oil boom coincided with, and was supported by, the onset of the Cold War. As part of the American strategy of Soviet containment, the United States unveiled the Marshall Plan for European economic recovery in June 1947. The plan allocated $13 billion in economic aid to European states that agreed to exclude Communists from their governments and that supported American foreign policy globally.[50] As part of this program, the Marshall Plan subsidized the conversion of European industrial plants from reliance on coal energy produced domestically to oil imported from the Middle East.[51] As a result, a full 10 percent of the total Marshall Plan aid was channeled into purchasing oil produced in the Middle East by American companies.[52]

According to the architects of the Marshall Plan, US economic aid would inoculate Europe against Communist subversion, provide profit-making opportunities for American oil companies abroad, and increase revenues to oil-producing states, which would, in turn, obviate any need for direct US foreign assistance.[53] The United States was particularly interested in the use of private oil revenue as an alternative to US foreign aid after the government of Venezuela, between 1943 and 1947, demanded an even 50 percent of the total oil revenue produced in the country.[54] To avoid the risk of outright nationalization, the State Department encouraged the companies operating in Venezuela to accept this arrangement.[55] After a right-wing coup brought a business-friendly regime to power in November 1948, the companies acceded to the terms of the 50–50 profit sharing formula in Venezuela.[56]

Fifty–fifty profit sharing in Venezuela compelled Saudi Arabia to demand the same terms. As in Venezuela, the State Department pressed American companies to accept these terms. In December 1950, Aramco reluctantly agreed, but insisted that it be allowed to deduct royalties paid to Saudi Arabia from its US income tax. The Truman administration agreed, and as a result, Aramco's US income tax fell from $50 million in 1950 to $6 million in 1951. At the same time, royalties to Saudi Arabia increased by a similar amount.[57] After an IRS audit ruled in Aramco's favor, tax-deductible profit sharing was institutionalized throughout the region.[58] However, the British management of BP, which was only sharing 17 percent of oil revenue with the government of Iran, was initially unwilling to accept these new terms.[59] The conflict over revenue sharing in Iran then escalated into a much more fundamental dispute over the terms of the BP concession that ultimately culminated in Iran's May 1951 nationalization of BP and all of its assets in Iran. Iran's nationalization of BP, in turn, gave rise to an oil crisis in which British warships blockaded the Iranian coastline to enforce an international embargo against the purchase of nationalized Iranian oil.[60] To support these efforts, the United States waived antitrust laws and allowed American oil companies to coordinate production increases elsewhere to offset the loss of Iranian oil.

The disruption of Iranian oil production due to the US-backed British blockade proved a boon to Iraq, where much of the increase to compensate for the loss of Iranian production was concentrated. Whereas Iraq produced only 5 percent of regional production in 1948, by 1953 that figure jumped to 27 percent.[61] To ensure the stability of that production, and avoid a replay of the nationalization crisis in Iran, the IPC, in August 1951, concluded a major revision to the terms of its concession. In addition to increasing Iraqi production from 6.4 million tons in 1950 to 18 million tons by 1952, the IPC agreed to adopt the 50–50 profit-sharing formula with the Iraqi government.[62] This new agreement increased the Iraqi share from $1.75 to $5.50 per ton.[63] With increased production, and an increased share of the profits, oil's share of total government revenue jumped from less than 10 percent in 1950 to more than 60 percent by 1952.[64] At the same time, the IPC agreed to minimum production and revenue guarantees, the appointment of Iraqis to the IPC's board of directors, and to undertake a dramatic expansion of the country's production infrastructure, including new refineries to serve domestic Iraqi needs as well as new and expanded pipelines linking Iraqi oil fields to the Mediterranean and the Gulf. (See Map 2: Iraqi Oil Industry Operations, 1953.)

THE OPPOSITION PUBLIC SQUARE

As part of the 1951 agreement, the British formed an Iraqi Development Board to channel increased oil revenue into development projects that would reinforce political stability in the country. The board, composed of Iraqi ministers and advised by British economic and technical experts, made notable gains in the field of education. The increased oil revenue financed thousands of new primary and secondary schools.[65] These investments, intended to stabilize the country's politics, had the opposite effect. Iraq had previously been the site of a vibrant and sustained program of mass education, primarily due to the efforts of Sati' al-Husri—Iraq's first director general of education from 1921 to 1927.[66] A former Ottoman administrator and theorist of education, Husri sought to develop a national education system that would militate against the sectarianism engendered by British colonialism.[67] Toward this end, he devised a secular and nationalist Arabic-language curriculum that insisted on providing an equal education to all Iraqis without regard to tribe, sect, or gender. Only in this way could Iraq's multitude of cultural traditions be fused together into a nationalist movement powerful enough to evict the British Empire from the region. In the 1920s, Husri took advantage of British preoccupation with other matters, mainly oil and the suppression of tribal rebellions, to secure substantial resources for the Ministry of Education.[68] These investments went a long way toward creating a broadly shared sense of Iraqi national identity, and ultimately cut against the thrust of British imperialism.

The British, having rejected the principle of secular democracy, sought to make Iraqi society "legible"—that is, governable—by conceptualizing that society in terms of discrete and hermetically sealed tribes and sects.[69] This same logic was appealing to the British-installed King Faysal, who, in 1927, dismissed Husri from his post and brought in education advisers from the United States. These advisers, the so-called Monroe Committee led by Paul Monroe from Columbia University's Teachers College, brought a model of education to Iraq that was based on racially segregated US institutions—and the Tuskegee Institute in particular.[70] Instead of giving all Iraqis the same education, Iraqi Christians would be given a Christian education, Iraqi Kurds a Kurdish education, Shi'is a Shi'ite education, and so on. Moreover, Arab boys would be trained in the arts of manual labor, while Iraqi girls would be given less education, and what education they received would be more focused on childrearing and homemaking.

Despite British and American efforts to impose sectarianism on the country, a vibrant "opposition public square" emerged in Iraq, in which an Iraqi intelligentsia composed of journalists, educators, religious scholars, poets, novelists, and others developed a powerful theory of secular democracy as the alternative to colonialism.[71] One of the most significant theorists of this secular and democratic worldview was 'Abd al-Fattah Ibrahim. Ibrahim had studied at the American University in Beirut, and then at Columbia University in the 1920s, before returning to Iraq to help found the Ahali Group (*Jama'at al-Ahali*)—an organization of public intellectuals committed to building social democracy in Iraq in the early 1930s.[72] In his 1939 book *Introduction to Sociology* (*Maqaddima fi'l ijtima*), Ibrahim developed a theory of populist democracy (*dimukratiyya sha'biyya*) that he contrasted with a faux or "capitalist democracy" that he had observed in the United States.[73] Whereas capitalist democracy served only a tiny and elite fraction of society, Ibrahim envisioned a democracy that gave free and equal representation to all. According to Ibrahim, democracy was a concept with both "political and social implications."[74] A truly democratic state, he insisted, would guarantee as rights of citizenship free education, free health care, minimum wages, and shelter fit for human habitation. A state that failed to secure these rights for all of its citizens could not be considered truly democratic.

Writing against the backdrop of Fascism's triumph in Europe, and Europe's effort to export that ideology to Iraq and larger region, Ibrahim eviscerated the intellectual foundations of ethno-nationalism. In contrast to European notions of racial purity, Ibrahim articulated a pluralist theory of culture in which national identity would be based not on language, ethnicity, or religion but rather on a shared commitment to a set of democratic principles: universal human rights to include economic rights, freedom of speech and religion, open and transparent political parties, and free and fair elections.[75]

The hard political realities of World War II left little space for Ibrahim's secular, democratic, and socialist vision to flourish. The war brought the Rashid 'Ali revolt and renewed British occupation. After the war, Nuri al-Said consolidated increasingly despotic powers in his own hands. In response to Nuri's British-backed authoritarianism, the Communist Party of Iraq (CPI) emerged as the most important organization advancing a secular and socialist vision for Iraqi society. The CPI had been secretly organized in the 1930s in response to the Great Depression. By the 1940s, though still illegal, it had evolved into a mass political party drawing support from a religiously and ethnically diverse social base. The key figure in the party's expansion in these years was Yusuf Salam Yusuf, a charismatic and dynamic Assyrian Christian known as Comrade Fahd.[76] Despite Nuri's police-state restrictions, Fahd made a concerted effort to build a mass base for the party by organizing peasant leagues and oil, railway, and port worker unions. Peasants and workers in the north were predominantly Kurdish, while peasants and workers in the south were predominantly Shi'i. This regional pattern necessitated an explicitly anti-sectarian organizational strategy. Moreover, much of the party's urban intelligentsia leadership was Christian or Jewish. For all of these reasons, the Communist Party emerged as the most popular force of secular opposition to British imperialism over the course of the 1940s.[77]

CPI opposition to the British was soon joined by the emergence of the still infinitesimal *Ba'th* (Renaissance) Party. The Ba'th was established in Syria 1947 as an anti-imperialist, socialist, and pan-Arabist party. In 1952, it opened a branch in Iraq. Though the party was tiny, with no more than three hundred members, it pursued a vanguard strategy focused on co-opting the armed forces.[78] A third significant opposition group emerged after the 1952 Egyptian Free Officers' coup that overthrew the British-supported monarchy and brought Colonel Gamal Abdel Nasser to power in Cairo: the Iraqi Free Officers. This secretive group of midlevel officers was modeled on the Egyptian Free Officers Club and took inspiration from Egypt's example of ousting a British-backed monarchy. This was especially the case after Nasser successfully withstood the combined Israeli, French, and British invasion of Egypt during the 1956 Suez War.

THE SUEZ WAR AND THE EISENHOWER DOCTRINE

The emergence of powerful nationalist movements opposed to Britain's continued role in the region after WWII presented a dilemma for American policymakers. American officials who thought about Iraq and the larger region were of many minds with regard to the question of how to respond to the rising force of Arab nationalism and the corresponding decline of British influence. One current of thought, strongly influenced by the experience of the New Deal, held that an integrated program of regional economic development modeled on the Marshall Plan represented the best guarantor of political stability, and the best bulwark against the encroachment of Soviet influence.[79] This current of thought envisioned massive capital assistance for large-scale development projects modeled on New Deal initiatives such as the Hoover Dam and Tennessee Valley Authority. Policymakers adhering to this New Deal worldview saw the vestiges of a dying British imperialism as a source of instability, and for that reason an obstacle to US interests. From this perspective, colonialism was a spent force. The contest was now between nationalism and Communism, and it was incumbent upon the United States to embrace moderate Arab nationalists so as to avoid a radicalization of regional politics that would redound to the benefit of the USSR and its local allies.

By the late 1940s, however, with the onset of the Cold War, the New Deal was in retreat in American politics.[80] Whereas New Dealers envisioned large-scale development projects as a solution to regional political problems, President Truman's eventual Point Four program of development assistance, unveiled in January 1949, ruled out a large-scale, Marshall Plan–style capital investment and included only modest "technical assistance."[81] Rather than viewing Communist movements as a response to colonialism and economic underdevelopment, this more conservative current of thought viewed regional events through an "invariably distorting lens of Cold War geopolitical strategy that saw the Kremlin as the principal instigator of global unrest."[82]

By the late 1940s, the Cold War perspective was hegemonic within the US government, especially after the Eisenhower administration took office in January 1953.[83] To counter the perceived Soviet threat to the region, the Eisenhower administration envisioned a relatively close alliance with Britain and organized a regional treaty alliance known as the Baghdad Pact.[84] The United States initially tried to persuade Egypt to join the organization, but Nasser refused to enter a military alliance that included Britain.[85] Rather than joining the Baghdad Pact, which took effect in February 1955, Nasser traveled, in April of that year, to Bandung, Indonesia, to participate in a summit of twenty-nine Asian and African nations. At the conference, China's Zhou Enlai rallied delegates against the threat of the French-Indochina War (1945–55) escalating into a regional war that would pit China against the United States. The assembled nations further expressed opposition to colonialism and demanded inclusion in and reform of United Nations structures of global governance.[86]

By September of that year, Nasser had responded to a major French-Israeli military buildup, and the US refusal to supply similar weapons to Egypt, with a major arms agreement with the Soviet Union through Czechoslovakia. The Eisenhower administration attempted to persuade Nasser to cancel the agreement by promising to provide Egypt with a $56 million loan to help finance a planned Aswan Dam project that was to provide hydroelectrical power to the Nile River Valley.[87] But when Nasser refused to cancel the Soviet arms agreement, the Eisenhower administration delayed and then, on July 19, 1956, abruptly canceled the loan offer. The following week, on July 26, Nasser responded by nationalizing the French- and British-owned Suez Canal Company, proclaiming that he would use Suez Canal shipping tolls to finance the project without US or Soviet assistance.[88]

The nationalization of foreign interests touched a kind of livewire in American foreign policymaking. It was the nationalization of BP that compelled the Eisenhower administration to covert action in Iran in 1953. And it was the nationalization of the United Fruit Company that compelled the Eisenhower administration to covert action in Guatemala in 1954. Now, in July 1956, Nasser had nationalized the company that managed passage of two-thirds of the world's daily oil shipments. On August 1, US secretary of state John Foster Dulles met with British prime minister Anthony Eden and assured the prime minister that "a way had to be found to make Nasser disgorge what he was attempting to swallow."[89] Dulles also warned against taking military action against Egypt, but Eden and the British interpreted this to be mere pro forma moralistic and legalistic rhetoric for public consumption, and assumed that Dulles was in favor of belligerent action.[90]

Believing that when push came to shove they would have US backing, the British then began meeting in secret with France and Israel to plan a military invasion that would overthrow Nasser and restore the Suez Canal Company. The British found very willing accomplices in France and Israel. Within Israel, Defense Minister Moshe Dayan had been advocating war with Egypt since the conclusion of the Soviet arms deal of the previous December.[91] However, Israeli prime minister David Ben-Gurion restrained Dayan and other Israeli hawks until he could secure the support of France—at the time, Israel's most important military ally.[92]

France, for its part, had reasons of its own to favor the overthrow of Nasser. Not only had Egypt nationalized French shares in the Suez Canal Company and threatened the French client and ally in Israel, but Nasser was supporting Algerian rebels, who had been waging a war of independence against French colonial authority since November 1954. As Egypt integrated Soviet arms deliveries in the spring of 1956, France grew increasingly alarmed that these arms would make their way into the hands of the Algerian rebels. France therefore joined the conspiracy to topple Nasser through military action.[93] Dulles continued to warn against using military force to resolve the crisis, and sought to mediate between the contending parties to reach a negotiated solution. But just as had been the case in Iran in

1953, the British believed that "the Americans often went along when others took the initiative."[94] The British-French-Israeli conspiracy was formalized with the Protocol of Sèvres on October 24. Five days later, Israel invaded Egypt, and on October 31, Britain and France joined the war by launching airstrikes on Egyptian positions in the Canal Zone, and landing paratroopers shortly thereafter.

The invasion of Egypt put the Eisenhower administration in an awkward position.[95] The invasion began less than a week before a US presidential election and at the very moment that the Soviets had sent troops into Hungary to suppress an uprising against Communist rule. In the heat of a presidential campaign, Eisenhower could not condemn Soviet aggression in Eastern Europe while appearing to condone Israeli-French-British aggression in the Middle East. Worst of all, Eisenhower feared that the appearance of US support for naked aggression against a popular Arab leader would drive the "whole Arab world" into the arms of the Soviets.[96] Eisenhower therefore demanded an immediate ceasefire, and revoked US oil and financial assistance to Britain until it complied.[97] Under intense US pressure, and faced with dwindling supplies of oil and gold, Britain finally backed down and withdrew in early December. With the withdrawal of Britain, Israel and France soon followed suit.

Nasser's ability to withstand the tripartite invasion elevated his already larger-than-life stature in the region.[98] As the British withdrew and a wave of popular enthusiasm for Nasser rose throughout the region, Dulles met with Prime Minister Eden and lamented the fact that the British "had not managed to bring down Nasser."[99] The president likewise expressed concern that Nasser was beginning to "believe that he can emerge as a true leader of the entire Arab world," and that he was working to create an "Arab 'bloc' extending from Pakistan to Dakar."[100] In the months ahead, the Eisenhower administration, therefore, endeavored to succeed where the British, French, and Israelis had failed. Toward this end, the president, in January 1957, proposed a new "Eisenhower Doctrine" for the region. According to this proposal, the United States would counter Nasser's Egypt by arming conservative Arab states aligned with the US in the Cold War. In an effort to persuade a reluctant Congress to provide military and economic aid to Egypt's regional enemies, Eisenhower modeled his initiative on the Truman Doctrine and called for US assistance to any Arab state resisting "overt armed aggression from any nation controlled by International Communism"—a tendentious reference to Egypt.[101]

THE END OF THE OLD REGIME IN IRAQ

Hashemite Iraq, under the leadership of Prime Minister Nuri al-Said, was the prime beneficiary of the Eisenhower Doctrine. In the wake of the Suez War, the United States looked to Iraq's Nuri al-Said as a regional counter to Nasser.[102] The strategy was not without its appeal. Nuri had been a leading figure in Iraqi politics since the state's founding. He held near dictatorial powers within Iraq and harbored ambitious visions of leading a pan-Arab federation of his own.[103] But the effort to cultivate Nuri as a counter to Nasser backfired dramatically. Indeed, Nuri's alignment with the Eisenhower Doctrine brought all of Iraq's leading opposition groups—the Communists, Ba'thists, and Free Officers—together to form a unified National Front in February 1957. Despite ideological differences among the three groups—the Communists sought mass mobilization from below to restructure Iraqi property relations, while the Ba'thists sought to cultivate the organic unity of an Arab society free of class divisions, and the Free Officers fluctuated between the two poles—Nasser was hailed by all three as a potent symbol of revolutionary nationalism. As Nasser's image was paraded through the streets of Baghdad, Nuri was denounced as a lackey of American imperialism.[104]

The response to the Eisenhower Doctrine was similar throughout the region. In February 1958, Egypt and Syria joined their two countries to form the United Arab Republic (UAR)—a merger that left Syrian sovereignty in the hands of Nasser.[105] In March, Yemen joined the UAR. That same month, Saudi Arabia's King Saud was effectively replaced by his brother Faysal, after Cairo's Voice of the Arabs broadcast credible allegations that Saud was conspiring with the CIA to assassinate Nasser and dissolve the UAR.[106] And in May, Lebanese Nasserists staged an uprising against the CIA-backed regime of President Camille Chamoun, who was seeking an unconstitutional second term in office.[107]

It was against this backdrop of popular enthusiasm for Nasser that the coup in Iraq unfolded. On the night of July 13–14, Nuri sent Iraqi forces into Jordan to defend Jordanian King Husayn against a possible Nasserist coup. However, rather than proceeding to the Jordanian border as ordered,

Brigadier General 'Abd al-Karim Qasim, the 45-year-old commander of the Twentieth Brigade and the most senior Iraqi Free Officer, directed 'Abd al-Salam 'Arif, a 36-year-old colonel, to lead a column of Iraqi tanks into the Iraqi capital. On orders from Qasim, 'Arif quickly secured all major intersections and government installations. 'Arif himself seized control of the Baghdad Radio transmitter to announce the dissolution of the monarchy, while rebel units were dispatched to the Royal Palace and the prime minister's residence to complete the coup. The rebels met very little resistance, and within an hour, the Hashemite monarchy came to an end in a hail of gunfire. The body of the king was withheld from the public, but the bodies of Nuri (who was captured the following day) and 'Abd al-Ilah, the most prominent symbols of the old order, were paraded through the streets of Baghdad.

In the aftermath of the coup, the US ambassador to Iraq, Waldemar J. Gallman, reflected on the significance of Nuri's murder:

> From my personal experience and observation covering these past four years in Iraq, I would say that with the murder of Nuri, illiberal as he may have at times been in dealing with domestic issues, Iraq sacrificed her best leader toward an eventual life of dignity and decency and her strongest bulwark against recurrent chaos, if not savagery. A number of well-placed and knowledgeable Iraqis have been quoted to me within the past few days as having said, in effect, that within ten years at the most a monument would be erected in Baghdad to Nuri.
>
> I hope, in fact I believe, they are right.[108]

No monument to Nuri was ever erected in Baghdad. But the ambassador was correct that the overthrow of the old regime opened a particularly violent period in the history of Iraq. US paranoia about the implications of the coup for Western oil interests contributed a great deal to the violent convulsions that rocked Iraqi politics in the years ahead.

Chapter 2
THE FREE OFFICERS' REVOLUTION

THE 1958 IRAQI FREE OFFICERS' REVOLUTION WAS A WATERSHED event. The overthrow of the Hashemites forced the Eisenhower administration to fundamentally rethink its strategic approach to the Arab world. The basic foreign policy objectives in the region remained unchanged. The United States still sought to maintain private industry control over regional oil fields, and it still sought to contain the spread of Soviet influence in the Arab world. But the question of how best to secure these objectives was a matter of fierce internal debate that pit John Foster Dulles, the secretary of state, against his brother Allen, the director of the CIA. Foster (as he was commonly known) had been the architect of the Eisenhower Doctrine. According to this strategic concept, formed in the immediate aftermath of the 1956 Suez War, Nasserist pan-Arabism was the greatest threat to American regional interests. To contain this threat, the US would supply military and economic assistance to Nasser's regional rivals—most notably, Iraq. However, with the overthrow of the Hashemites, that strategic approach lay in tatters, and policy space opened for Allen to propose new ideas. Whereas Foster had long tended toward taking a hard line against Nasser as a "witting or unwitting Soviet proxy," Allen had more "sympathy for the devil" and had long sought ways in which the US and Egypt could cooperate on intelligence matters.

Foster, as the older brother and senior figure in government, dominated the policymaking process in the years leading up to the 1958 coup. But the overthrow of the Hashemites roughly coincided with the decline and ultimate failure of Foster's health. With Foster's departure from government in early 1959, opportunity arose for Allen's more conspiratorial approach. Allen concluded fairly quickly after the 1958 coup that the emerging Iraqi regime was far more radical and threatening than was Nasser's Egypt, and resolved to find ways for the United States and Egypt to work together to contain the Iraqi revolution. By early 1959, the Eisenhower administration, led by Allen Dulles and the president himself, had decided that it might be good policy to "help Nasser take over in Iraq." Over the course of that year, the CIA began putting the pieces in place to do just that.

CRACKPOT REALISM AND THE CULT OF COVERT ACTION

To understand how and why the Eisenhower administration became engaged in an effort to aid the Nasser takeover in Iraq, it is helpful to briefly examine the evolution of American intelligence policy in the period leading up to the 1958 revolution. Intelligence is simply politically or strategically relevant information. However, the term is often meant to imply information that one government (or other political entity) seeks to keep secret, and that another seeks to uncover.[1] The United States first developed a peacetime intelligence agency with the National Security Act of 1947. This landmark piece of legislation was part of the fundamental reorganization of the American state at the start of the Cold War. Michael J. Hogan describes it with "only some exaggeration" as the "Magna Charta of the National Security State."[2] It established the Office of the Secretary of Defense, the Joint Chiefs of Staff, the National Security Council (NSC), the Central Intelligence Agency (CIA), and a series of subsidiary boards and agencies tasked with mobilizing and coordinating munitions, scientific research, and other national resources.

The reorganization of the armed forces was first proposed by General of the Army George C. Marshall in 1943. Marshall's plan sought to unify the various branches of the military under a single, civilian-led department of defense. His proposal, submitted to Congress in 1944, emphasized efficiency, accountability, and the elimination of redundancies in the defense budget. However, Marshall's proposal encountered fierce resistance from Secretary of the Navy James V. Forrestal, a former Wall Street banker who joined President Roosevelt's cabinet in 1944. In place of Marshall's emphasis on centralized authority, Forrestal preferred more "corporative schemes in which responsibility was shared among government agencies and between public and private leaders."[3] Between 1944 and 1947, Forrestal drew on contacts in the media to mobilize an intense public relations campaign in support of an alternative proposal that would preserve the navy's autonomy (and budget) against Marshall's drive for centralization. Forrestal's alternative proposal also included the creation of a central intelligence agency to assume the functions of the wartime Office of Strategic Services (OSS), and a national security council to coordinate policy planning and implementation. Marshall took particular exception to these proposals. He warned that these new agencies would be endowed with "almost unlimited" power and would reduce the president and secretary of state to "automatons" under the control of anonymous, unelected national security managers.[4] Wyoming senator Edward V. Robertson was even more outspoken in his opposition to the proposed National Security Act. On the Senate floor he described the proposed CIA as a potential "American Gestapo," and the proposed NSC as a "Frankenstein monster." "We must not let our fear of Communism," he warned, "blind us to the danger of military domination."[5]

Marshall and Robertson lost, and Forrestal won. Congress approved the bill on a simple voice vote (that is, by affirmation without a roll call record of yeas and nays), and on July 26, 1947, the president promptly signed the National Security Act into law. The bill went into effect in September when Forrestal was confirmed as the first secretary of defense. "Frankenstein" was alive. However, so too was resistance to Forrestal's new and expansive concept of "national security." This was particularly true among the uniformed military, including Rear Admiral Roscoe H. Hillenkoetter, the first director of central intelligence (1947–50). Hillenkoetter was especially anxious over a provision within the National Security Act that authorized the CIA to "perform such other functions and duties related to intelligence affecting the national security as the National Security Council may from time to time direct."[6] It was unclear what these other functions might entail, and Hillenkoetter was reluctant to use the CIA to intervene covertly in the domestic political affairs of other countries. According to the CIA's legal counsel, the agency had no authority to conduct such operations.[7]

To overcome what he saw as Hillenkoetter's "timidity," Forrestal prompted the efforts of his young protégé George Kennan. A former diplomat in the Moscow embassy that Forrestal had brought to Washington to disseminate anti-Soviet views, Kennan soon developed a plan for a "covert 'guerrilla warfare corps'" to carry out "political warfare operations" against the Kremlin.[8] On the basis of Kennan's proposal, Forrestal then led, in November 1947, the NSC in expanding the mandate of the CIA: "The National Security Council . . . has determined that . . . the foreign information activities of the U.S. Government must be supplemented by covert *psychological operations.*"[9] Six months later, the CIA's mandate was expanded still further: "The National Security Council . . . has determined that . . . the overt foreign activities of the US Government must be supplemented by *covert operations.*"[10] By "covert operations," the NSC meant activities "which are so planned and executed that any US Government responsibility for them is not evident to unauthorized persons and that if uncovered the US Government can plausibly disclaim any responsibility for them." This was to include

> propaganda, economic warfare; preventive direct action, including sabotage, anti-sabotage, demolition and evacuation measures; subversion against hostile states, including assistance to underground resistance movements, guerrillas and refugee liberation groups, and support of indigenous anticommunist elements in threatened countries of the free world.

This provision constituted the legal foundation for what a US Senate investigation later described as the "doctrine of plausible deniability."[11] The CIA would henceforth be authorized to engage in any number of subversive and paramilitary activities without ever being asked to publicly account for its decisions. Here was a secret, unaccountable instrument of seemingly limitless potential. The CIA, not unlike Tolkien's "One Ring," offered its bearer a cloak of invisibility.[12] Under the guise of "national security," one could see all without ever being seen.

The allure of the CIA's cloak of invisibility proved irresistible to all who encountered it. One such figure was Allen Dulles. Dulles first embarked on a career in intelligence during WWI, when he enlisted in the clandestine services of the State Department. Owing to patrician family connections—his uncle was Robert Lansing, the secretary of state to President Woodrow Wilson; his grandfather, John Watson Foster, had been secretary of state to President Grover Cleveland (1892–93); his brother John Foster was a partner at Sullivan & Cromwell, a high-powered Wall Street law firm specializing in international business law—Dulles rose to become the chief of the State Department's Office of Near Eastern Affairs by 1922.[13] In this capacity he had brokered the entry of Exxon and Mobil into the IPC consortium. In 1926, Allen Dulles left the State Department to join Sullivan & Cromwell, where Foster would soon be made senior partner. Allen remained at Sullivan & Cromwell until the outbreak of WWII, when he joined the OSS as a covert agent in Europe and managed to recruit a Nazi spy ring known as the Gehlen Organization into American intelligence operations.[14]

After the war, Allen returned to Sullivan & Cromwell but still felt called to state secrecy and international intrigue. It was he who, in February 1948, met with Secretary of Defense Forrestal to recommend the expansion of the CIA's authority to include covert operations. In Allen's mind it was not enough for the CIA to simply analyze the world. The CIA had to be prepared to use intelligence-gathering networks to actually shape the course of world events. It was on the basis of this policy recommendation that the NSC, in June 1948, approved policy directive 10/2—the document that authorized the CIA to engage in "covert operations."[15] Allen's ideas melded with those of Forrestal. In their February meeting, Forrestal asked Allen to "conduct of formal review of the CIA's first-year record, to be presented in January 1949." Both Forrestal and Allen believed that New York governor Thomas Dewey would be elected president in November, and both were angling for positions in an anticipated Dewey administration. Allen's review (known as the Dulles-Jackson-Correa Report) was to serve as a kind of resume in support of his bid to be made director of central intelligence (DCI), the highest-ranking position within the CIA.[16] However, Allen's ability to divine the course of future events fell short. In November 1948, Truman won a surprise victory over Dewey, and Allen's prospects of being made DCI evaporated. More problematic still was the demise of Forrestal, Allen's most important patron in Washington.

For some time, Forrestal had been obsessed with what he saw as a Communist danger to American "national security."[17] But that anti-Communism was soon fused with an anti-Zionism that would prove his undoing. Such a fusion was a function of Forrestal's Wall Street background. In the 1930s, Forrestal, as a senior partner with the Wall Street law firm Dillon, Read & Co., had brokered the merger that constituted the nucleus of the Aramco consortium in Saudi Arabia.[18] As secretary of the navy during WWII, Forrestal negotiated long-term naval supply contracts with that same consortium.[19] After the war, as the first secretary of defense, Forrestal believed it imperative that the United States take care not to antagonize the Arab states in which his former corporate clients had business interests.[20] If the US were to lose the "goodwill of the Arabs," Forrestal warned the House Armed Services Committee in January 1948, *"access"* to Middle East oil supplies would be put in jeopardy. Should the Arabs choose to withhold their oil from the world market, the US military would be left unprepared, the Marshall Plan would fail, the anti-Soviet coalition would crumble, and American automakers would have to convert to making "four-cylinder" engines within ten years.[21]

Of particular concern to Forrestal was the UN partition plan for the Palestine Mandate.[22] Forrestal opposed the UN's plan to partition the mandate into separate Arab and Jewish states for fear that it would provoke a backlash from Saudi Arabia. According to Forrestal, the US-allied absolute monarchy in Saudi Arabia might be so moved by concern for Palestinians displaced by the new state of Israel that it would withhold oil exports from the world market in retaliation. Forrestal, therefore, became an outspoken opponent of the Truman administration's decision to immediately recognize the new state of Israel in May 1948. As the presidential election of 1948 approached, Forrestal became embroiled in a bitter public fight with Zionist donors to the Truman campaign.[23] To add insult to injury, Forrestal was soon replaced as secretary of defense by Louis Johnson, a Democratic Party operative with no experience in defense or national security issues who had only gained the position by bundling Zionist campaign contributions during the 1948 election.[24]

By the time of his replacement as secretary of defense, however, Forrestal's mental state had declined markedly. He became convinced that a Zionist-Communist conspiracy had infiltrated the US government at its highest levels and that he was being targeted because of his efforts to alert the public to the danger. He therefore refused to resign his office and launched an anti-Zionist campaign in the press. After months of controversy, Forrestal was physically removed from office and admitted against his will to a psychiatric ward of the Bethesda Naval Hospital in nearby Maryland in May 1949.[25] At Bethesda, Forrestal received extensive psychiatric treatment, but his demons would not abate. At approximately 2 a.m. on May 22, 1949, "Forrestal walked into the kitchen, took the sash from his bathrobe, tied one end to the radiator and the other around his neck, and went through the window, falling to his death on a third-floor passageway thirteen stories below."[26] As it turned out, bearing the "One Ring" could make one quite ill.

Forrestal had been the main architect of the CIA and the larger national security state of which it was an integral part. After his death, Allen Dulles became the most significant figure shaping American intelligence policy. Like Kennan, Allen had been a protégé of Forrestal and had been an informal adviser to the CIA since 1949. In January 1951, he was brought into the agency as deputy director of operations. This put him in charge of covert operations, but his ultimate ambition to be made DCI would have to await a shift in the political winds in Washington. That shift, which occurred in 1952, first brought Allen's brother Foster to power. The rise of Foster, in turn, opened the door for Allen.

Foster was, by the late 1940s, a prominent figure within Republican Party politics. Although he had spent most of his career on Wall Street, Foster did have government experience during WWI. At the same time that Allen had joined the State Department's clandestine services (in 1916), Foster took a leave from Sullivan & Cromwell to advise the State Department on the terms of the postwar settlement. After playing a prominent role in shaping the "peace to end all peace" at Versailles, Foster returned to Sullivan & Cromwell where he made a fortune brokering business deals between the United States and Germany. In the 1930s, he remained personally close to the German regime, believing Nazism to be a necessary bulwark against Bolshevism.[27] As the US considered entry to WWII, Foster did pro bono legal work for the "America First Committee," which opposed US intervention.[28] With the defeat of Nazi Germany and the onset of the Cold War, Foster became an enthusiastic proponent of Henry Luce–style "American globalism," believing it to be the only remaining force capable of turning back the rising tide of Bolshevism. Foster was a key foreign policy adviser to Dewey's 1948 campaign and expected to be made secretary of state after the election. After his electoral loss, Dewey was not in a position to make Foster secretary of state, but he did, in 1949, appoint Foster to a vacant Senate seat from New York. However, electoral politics was not Foster's forte. Foster's business ties to the Nazi Germany proved a major liability as he campaigned for the special election, and he was defeated handily by his Democratic opponent in November.[29] Allen had also gone 0–1 in electoral politics when he failed to win the Republican nomination to represent New York's 16th Congressional District in 1938.

The political fortunes of the Dulles brothers improved dramatically with the election of Dwight D. Eisenhower in 1952. Shortly after Eisenhower announced his intention to run for president, Foster met with him to share his foreign policy views.[30] These included the idea, publicized with great fanfare in a May 1952 article in *Life*, that Truman's policy of Soviet Containment was soft on Communism and that what was needed was a policy of "Rollback" in which the United States would "liberate" peoples suffering under the yoke of Communist rule.[31] Eisenhower was, at this point, locked in a bitter nominating contest with Ohio senator Robert Taft, who represented the more conservative western wing of the Republican Party. Foster's hardline anti-Communist views were more closely associated with the Taft wing of the party, and Eisenhower met with Foster, in large part, to inoculate himself against attacks from the right.[32] After the election, to appease that same conservative base, Eisenhower selected Foster to serve as secretary of state. Foster, in turn, recommended his brother Allen for DCI—a recommendation that Eisenhower accepted at the end of January 1953.[33]

Upon taking office, Eisenhower intentionally crafted a public image of himself as little more than the "golfer in chief." He studiously avoided partisan politics and controversial issues and gave the impression of leaving the heavy lifting of public policy to practical men drawn from the world of business, and from Wall Street in particular.[34] There was a certain element of affect in this presentation. Historians have long since demonstrated that Eisenhower, far from being a passive chief executive whose administration was dominated by subordinates, used the bellicose rhetoric of Foster and the covert methods of Allen instrumentally to advance shared political and economic objectives.[35] There was indeed a kind of division of labor within the Eisenhower administration—Foster did the loud talking, Allen did the quiet walking, and the president presented an amiable face to the public.

The problem, however, was that Eisenhower's reliance on Foster's bellicose rhetoric to define American national interests, and Allen's covert methods to pursue and defend those interests, quickly yielded what many saw as an out-of-control intelligence apparatus. This was particularly so because the 1950s proved to be a crucible of global political and economic change. As European empires broke down and new states emerged, covert action became not just a cloak of invisibility but a "silver bullet" that could bring down any and all of the assorted monsters lurking in the dark corners of the postcolonial world. There developed in the Eisenhower years a kind of "cult of covert action" in which the invisible hand of the CIA took on almost magical properties to solve complex problems in what was becoming known as the "Third World."[36]

Adherence to the "cult of covert action" produced a strong tendency to overstate Soviet intentions and capabilities, and to respond to all "Soviet threats," real and imagined, with CIA intervention.[37] Hence it was the Dulles brothers in 1953 who conspired to overthrow Mossadegh after his government nationalized BP—a firm the Dulles brothers had represented while at Sullivan & Cromwell—and in 1954 conspired to overthrow Jacobo Arbenz in Guatemala after his government passed legislation threatening to the United Fruit Company—another major multinational that the Dulles brothers had represented while at Sullivan & Cromwell. In viewing threats to Sullivan & Cromwell clients as part of a global Communist conspiracy directed by the Kremlin, the Eisenhower administration engaged in what the sociologist C. Wright Mills described as "crackpot realism":

> These men have replaced mind with platitude, and the dogmas by which they are legitimated are so widely accepted that no counter-balance of mind prevails against them. Such men as these are crackpot realists; in the name of realism they have constructed a paranoid reality all their own; in the name of practicality they have projected a utopian image of capitalism.[38]

According to Mills, the reality upon which the realist school of international relations had been founded was, in fact, simply a paranoid fantasy.

While Mills, a dissident intellectual at Columbia University (1946–62), was outspoken in his critique of what he described as "the Power Elite" running American government and society in the 1950s, the sense that American intelligence capabilities had grown out of control was much broader than that. In 1955, English novelist Graham Greene published *The Quiet American*, a cautionary tale about the unintended consequences that could flow from well-groomed American intelligence operatives, wholly lacking in self-awareness, intervening in the domestic politics of postcolonial societies.[39] As Greene observed, the intellectual detachment and patrician insulation against the human consequences of one's decisions that was typical of American covert agents quickly gave way to a brutalism of action that was matched only by a certain creativity of mind in which virtually anything could be rationalized. Greene's novel, a US best-seller in 1957, was so biting that Edward Lansdale, a former Madison Avenue advertising executive turned architect of some of the CIA's most outlandish covert operations, felt compelled, in 1958, to commission an adaption of Greene's novel as a major motion picture starring film legend and decorated WWII hero Audie Murphy.[40] However, in the version commissioned by the CIA, the moral of the story is inverted: Greene's ultimately murderously duplicitous "quiet American" is transformed into an heroic action-intellectual ready to roll up his sleeves and do what must be done to turn back the tide of global Communism.[41]

In their different ways, Mills and Greene both registered a powerful critique of American society in the 1950s. Mills looked at how American power was constituted at home, while Greene explored how that power was abused abroad. But this critique was not simply confined to the realm of American civil society or popular culture. On the contrary, even within the halls of government in Washington there was a growing sense that something was amiss with America's intelligence agencies. In 1952–53, Republican senator Joseph McCarthy leveled accusations that the CIA had been infiltrated by Communist agents.[42] At the same time, Democratic senator Mike Mansfield renewed concerns, originally raised in 1947, that in the CIA, the United States had created a global "Gestapo" force of virtually unchecked authority.[43] To rein in potential intelligence abuses, Mansfield proposed a bill that would establish congressional oversight for the CIA.[44]

Senator Mansfield's intelligence reform bill was ultimately rejected by a vote of 59 to 27. But in response to the growing sense of concern over the CIA, President Eisenhower, in late 1955, established a formal covert action review committee known as the President's Board of Consultants on Foreign Intelligence Activities. In the summer of 1956, this advisory committee, composed of veterans of the intelligence establishment, conducted an exhaustive review of US covert operations and produced a highly critical study known as the "Bruce-Lovett Report."[45] The report condemned what it saw as "the increased mingling in the internal affairs of other nations of bright, highly graded young men who must be doing something all the time to justify their reason for being."[46]

The report merits quotation at length for what it reveals regarding official anxiety over US intelligence capabilities and practices:

> Busy, moneyed and privileged, [the CIA] likes its "King Making" responsibility (the intrigue is fascinating—considerable self-satisfaction, sometimes with applause, derives from "successes"—no charge is made for "failures"—and the whole business is very much simpler than collecting covert intelligence on the USSR through the usual CIA methods!). . . .
>
> Should not someone, somewhere in an authoritative position in our government, on a continuing basis, be counting the immediate costs of disappointments, . . . calculating the impacts on our international position, and keeping in mind the long range wisdom of activities which have entailed our virtual abandonment of the international "golden rule," and which, if successful to the degree claimed for them, are responsible in a great measure for stirring up turmoil and raising the doubts about us that exist in many countries of the world today? What of the effects on our present alliances? What will happen tomorrow?

Co-author Robert Lovett later recalled the concern that animated their report:

> What right do we have to go barging around into other countries, buying newspapers and handing money to opposition parties or supporting candidates for this, that or the other office? . . . The idea of these young, enthusiastic fellows possessed of great funds being sent out in some country, getting themselves involved in local politics, and then backing some local man and from that starting an operation, scared the hell out of us.[47]

In its last written report to the Eisenhower administration, the Bruce-Lovett committee raised grave concerns about the entire enterprise of covert operations:

> We have been unable to conclude that, on balance, all of the covert action programs undertaken by CIA up to this time have been worth the risk or the great expenditure of manpower, money and other resources involved.

In addition, we believe that CIA's concentration on political, psychological and related covert action activities have tended to detract substantially from the execution of its primary intelligence-gathering mission. We suggest, accordingly, that there should be a total reassessment of our covert action policies.[48]

There was a growing sense in and out of government that with the CIA, the United States had created a monster. That sense would be confirmed time and time again in Iraq in subsequent years.

AMERICAN SPIES IN ARABIA

As damning as the Bruce-Lovett findings appear, the possibility exists that the report itself was part of a subtle influence campaign. Both Bruce and Lovett were deeply experienced in the dark arts of information warfare—and it is possible that their report was part of an effort by an anti-Nasser faction within the Eisenhower administration to discredit a rival pro-Nasser faction.[49] Whether or not this was the intended effect of the committee and its report, it was the practical outcome. The study was conducted and the report authored against the backdrop of the 1956 Suez Crisis, and at a moment of extreme tension among policymakers over the appropriate direction for US foreign policy with regard to Nasser and the Middle East. This tension even divided the Dulles brothers. Allen saw in Nasser's brand of Arab nationalism a kind of "Third Force" that was equally opposed to both Soviet Communism and European colonialism.[50] Even after Nasser's 1955 Czech arms deal, Allen argued in the NSC that the United States might still "do business" with him, as Nasser represented a "wave of the future."[51] Allen was overruled by Foster, who seized on the Soviet supply as irrefutable proof that Nasser was a Communist agent. Rather than continuing to seek accommodation with Nasser, as Allen's CIA had been since the early 1950s, Foster advocated an anti-Nasser strategy known as Project OMEGA.[52] By criticizing these "bright, highly graded young men" who were "mingling in the affairs of other nations," Bruce-Lovett may have been issuing a subtle critique of Allen and the CIA Arabists that Foster Dulles saw as too smitten with Nasser.[53]

The anti-Nasser sentiment animating Project OMEGA, the Baghdad Pact, and (perhaps) the Bruce-Lovett Report culminated in the Eisenhower Doctrine of January 1957. This effort to isolate and contain Nasser's regional influence was, in turn, highly controversial within the CIA. Nasser had outlawed the Egyptian Communist Party and was engaged in a sustained purge of Egyptian Communists. Allen Dulles and many within CIA and other intelligence agencies, therefore, saw Nasser as the principal bulwark in the region against the spread of Communist ideology in the region.[54]

Shortly after the Eisenhower Doctrine was announced, the CIA's long-time station chief in Damascus, Miles Copeland, "resigned" from the agency to open a political consultancy business in Beirut with his longtime CIA collaborator, James Eichelberger.[55] Copeland's departure was followed shortly thereafter by the "resignation," in December 1957, of Kermit ("Kim") Roosevelt, the grandson of former president Theodore Roosevelt and director of covert operations for CIA's Near East division since 1949. After "leaving" the CIA, Kim Roosevelt took a highly paid position as vice president of Gulf Oil, but both he and Copeland remained "loyal alums" of the CIA in the sense that they continued to receive funds, provide analysis (as we will see in this chapter), and perform certain "other tasks" for the agency.[56]

The departure of Copeland and Roosevelt from their official positions was indicative of a more general changing of the Praetorian Guard at the CIA. The clearest indication of this shift occurred in early 1958, when Allen Dulles chose not to replace Kim Roosevelt with Archie Roosevelt, the CIA's Beirut station chief and the longest-serving and most-experienced covert operative in the region (and Kim's cousin). Rather than promoting Archie, Dulles sent him to Madrid, and placed authority for Middle East operations under the control of Norman Paul, a man about whom little is known and less is written.[57] Archie was not happy with the decision: "Imagine sending me to one of the few countries where I don't speak the language . . . I've spent so much of my life studying the Middle East—what do I know about Spain?"[58]

Archie's exile to Spain, as part of the more general purge of Arabists in the CIA and State Department associated with the Eisenhower Doctrine, put the United States in an awkward position from which to respond to the Iraqi coup. Indeed, the coup caught the CIA by surprise and was a major source of embarrassment for Allen Dulles.[59] He remained the nation's top spy chief, but increasing authority over the agency began to shift to Richard Bissell, the CIA's deputy director of plans.[60] The coup in Iraq therefore transpired during something of an interregnum in American intelligence policy. This interregnum, and the scandals that proceeded it, did not, however, impinge on what a US Senate investigation later described as the

CIA's "institutionalized capacity" for covert action—to include assassination attempts against foreign leaders. Indeed, this institutionalized capacity played a decisive role in shaping the American response to the Free Officers' coup in Baghdad.

EISENHOWER, THE DULLES BROTHERS, AND THE PARANOID STYLE

The military coup in Iraq came as a surprise to the Eisenhower administration.[61] But perhaps it should not have. Political officers in the US embassy in Baghdad had been warning for nearly a decade that the monarchy was resting on dangerously unstable foundations.[62] Nuri and the regent were deeply despised for their adherence to the Baghdad Pact and for their indifference to the unmet social needs of ordinary Iraqis. The failure of the old regime to recognize and accommodate popular unrest worried some State Department officials. These officials advocated distance from British policies in the region and embraced nationalist demands for political reform and economic development. But the notion of recognizing the legitimacy of nationalist demands was antithetical to the paranoid mindset of the Eisenhower administration. From the perspective of the official mind in Washington, the problem was Communism, and dealing with Communism required a firm hand. The very factors that estranged Nuri's government from the Iraqi people—its "long history of successfully ordering the government's coercive apparatus, specifically the secret police, to muzzle the press, crack down on underground movements, and repress different uprisings"–were the very factors that endeared it to Washington, and to John Foster Dulles in particular.[63]

American "imperial anxiety" over the course of events in Iraq was apparent in the Dulles brothers' initial responses to the coup.[64] On July 14, as events were still unfolding, Allen Dulles explained in a briefing to the NSC:

> If the Iraq coup succeeds it seems almost inevitable that it will set up a chain reaction which will doom the pro-West governments of Lebanon and Jordan and Saudi Arabia, and raise grave problems for Turkey and Iran.
>
> The Soviet Union will undoubtedly welcome these developments and do what it feels it safely can without direct involvement in overt hostilities to support this chain reaction.[65]

However, Allen's take was rather restrained when compared to that of his brother. In response to Allen's comments, Foster called for the immediate landing of US troops in Lebanon, where the major oil companies had substantial investments in the pipeline terminals that shipped oil from Kirkuk and the Persian Gulf to European markets, and where the CIA was running an influence campaign to "elect" President Camille Chamoun to an unconstitutional second term in office.[66] The next day, the president, on the advice of Foster, ordered 3,500 marines into Lebanon, while the UK parachuted two battalions into Jordan on July 17.[67]

As US Marines waded ashore on the beaches of Beirut, Foster outlined the rationale behind the US intervention:

> In Secretary Dulles' view, *the real authority behind the Government of Iraq was being exercised by Nasser, and behind Nasser by the USSR.* It was not yet clear whether this tutelage would result in overt anti-Western action. The British were deeply concerned over the situation in Iraq and were equally concerned over Kuwait, which has close ties with Iraq. If the oil fields of Iraq and Kuwait fell under hostile control and if the conditions for the sale of oil were altered (that is, if oil prices were increased), the financial impact on the United Kingdom might be catastrophic. Secretary Dulles explained that the United Kingdom obtains oil cheaply and uses it to bolster sterling, and that any material alteration of that situation would seriously affect the United Kingdom's financial posture. The British were frantically seeking to effect arrangements which would *insure their continued access to the oil of the area.*[68]

In presenting the "real authority" in Iraq as "being exercised" by the USSR, and in presenting the coup as a threat to American oil interests, Foster engaged in what can be described as a "paranoid style" in American diplomacy—that is, diplomacy conducted in a "style of mind" characterized by a "sense of heated exaggeration, suspiciousness, and conspiratorial fantasy."[69]

The notion that the coup in Iraq threatened the "continued access to the oil of the area" was particularly at odds with the facts. This is because *access* to Middle East oil was never truly at issue in the late 1950s. Not only had Qasim, on July 18, taken to Baghdad Radio to announce the IPC operations would remain unaffected by the change in government, but the critical "national security" concern with regard to Middle East oil in the summer of 1958 was not the threat of too little supply but rather the problem of endemic global overproduction.[70] The Soviets had recently embarked on what the Eisenhower administration described as a "Soviet oil offensive." Soviet oil production had doubled between 1955 and 1960, and by 1958 the Soviets were competing aggressively to supply an increasing share of Western markets (see chapter 3).[71] Contrary to nightmare scenarios of the Soviets "seizing control" of Middle Eastern oil fields and denying Western consumers access to a critically needed source of energy, the Soviet Union was "threatening" Western oil interests by supplying Western markets with low-cost oil.[72]

At the same time the Soviets were competing aggressively to supply Western oil markets, a new category of "independent internationals" had entered the Middle East hoping to compete with the established majors. Over the course of the 1950s, they moved aggressively into the Middle East, most notably in Libya, where by 1959 seventeen different companies worked eighty-four separate concessions.[73] To protect domestic American oil companies (including the private investments of Treasury Secretary Robert Anderson) from a flood of low-cost oil from the Middle East and North Africa, the Eisenhower administration had, in 1957, imposed voluntary import controls to limit how much Middle Eastern oil American companies could dump on American markets.[74] When these voluntary controls proved inadequate, President Eisenhower established mandatory import quotas based on Oil Import Administration demand forecasts. According to the president, the executive measure was necessary as "crude oil and the principal crude oil derivatives and products are being imported in such quantities and under such circumstances as to threaten to impair the national security."[75]

Given the actual balance of forces in the global oil industry, Foster's dire warnings of an oil supply cutoff might be interpreted as consistent with what journalist I. F. Stone described as his penchant for carefully contrived anti-Communist sermons revealing the workings of a deeply "cynical" mind:

> His prevarications are so highly polished as to be aesthetically pleasurable.... Dulles is a man of wily and subtle mind. It is difficult to believe that behind his unctuous manner he does not take cynical amusement in his own monstrous pomposities. He gives the impression of a man who lives constantly behind a mask.[76]

In a similar vein, British double agent Kim Philby once observed that "John Foster Dulles needed Communism the way that Puritans needed sin."[77] In this sense, Foster's response to the Iraqi coup should be seen as an effort to rhetorically mobilize the specters of "global Communism" and an "oil supply cutoff" in support of the notion that the United States had to "do something." What that something was, beyond deploying marines to Lebanon, was not entirely clear to Foster.[78]

Foster's lack of useful ideas, combined within his declining health, contributed to his marginalization in the policymaking process. Foster had been hospitalized with stomach cancer during the Suez War. By the time he returned to office in early January 1957, he had become the target of increased criticism from Congress and the press as the architect of a reckless foreign policy that was sowing chaos from the Suez to Hungary. His rhetoric of "liberation" had proved hollow in Budapest (where the Soviets crushed a CIA-backed uprising in 1956), and even Allen, who had always been deferential to his older brother, began to challenge Foster's assertions that all manifestations of global political unrest were the work of Soviet Communist agents.[79] Allen understood the necessity of engaging in this kind of hyperbolic rhetoric to move public opinion and the Congress, but he expressed increasing concern about actually believing it. It appeared that Foster's carefully calibrated cynicism was giving way to sincere delusion.

Foster's paranoia never reached the dimensions of Forrestal, but the tendency to believe in the monsters of one's own conjuring could be quite strong. In the aftermath of the Iraqi coup, in between hospital stays, he seemed to grow increasingly lost in the labyrinth of his own mind. Unable to distinguish between actually existing Soviet foreign policy and the overheated rhetoric that had launched his political career, Foster grew less and less relevant to the making of American foreign policy. While President Eisenhower and Allen Dulles responded to the Iraqi coup by adjusting US foreign policy in the region and looking for opportunities to collaborate with Nasser against actually existing Arab Communism, Foster remained dogmatically wed to his view of Nasser as little more than a "Soviet proxy." That interpretation, always a stretch, became completely untenable in the weeks and months following the Iraqi coup.

THE US IN THE ARAB COLD WAR

Within weeks of the coup, it became clear that while the Iraqi Free Officers were inspired by their Egyptian counterparts, Iraq's revolutionaries were neither unified nor Egyptian-directed.[80] On the contrary, the issue of *wahda*, or political union, with the United Arab Republic quickly emerged

FIGURE 2. Free Officers 'Abd al-Karim Qasim and 'Abd al-Salam 'Arif, 1958. Source: Burt Glinn, Magnum Photos. Reprinted with permission.

as a point of bitter contention between General Qasim and Colonel 'Arif. Just days after the revolution, 'Arif traveled to Damascus to meet with Nasser and the leaders of the Syrian Ba'th Party, where he proclaimed his support for "Unity Now." The following week 'Arif returned to Iraq with Ba'thist leaders Michel 'Aflaq and Fu'ad al-Rikabi, and the three began touring Iraqi cities giving speeches praising Nasser and promoting the cause of pan-Arab unity.[81] Although the Iraqi Ba'th party was still at this time a miniscule political grouping with no more than a few hundred members, its calls for pan-Arab unity attracted a strong following among Sunni military officers, and it proved capable of mobilizing large crowds behind 'Arif.

Qasim, on the other hand, had resisted calls for immediate union and proposed instead a looser form of association. The Iraqi leader had no intention of yielding to either Nasser or 'Arif. But the conflict between Qasim and 'Arif was not simply personal. It was rather rooted in a deep-seated tension in Iraqi society between *wataniyya* and *qawmiyya*—two competing notions of national identity.[82] The former presupposed national solidarity on the basis of the Iraqi nation-state, the latter on the basis of tribal, ethnic, religious and linguistic associations. In practical terms this was debate between Iraqism (Iraq as the state of its citizens) and pan-Arab nationalism (Iraq as an unnatural truncation from the organic unity of Arab society). Of the two, Iraqism had a strong following on the left. Kurds, Shi'is, Christian, Jews, and other religious and ethnic minorities constituted the majority of the Iraqi population, and among these groups there was strong opposition to merging Iraq's sovereignty into a larger pan-Arab federation that would be dominated by Sunni Arabs.[83] As the Ba'th emerged to give voice to the demand for pan-Arab unity, the Iraqi Communist Party emerged as the strongest force of opposition to joining the UAR.

As 'Arif and the Ba'thists grew more assertive in their calls for immediate union, Qasim grew increasingly reliant on Communist support. On August 1, just two weeks after the revolution, Qasim allowed the Communist Party to form its own militia—the People's Resistance Force (PRF)—as an Iraqist counter to nationalist groupings within the army. The tension between Qasim, supported by the Communists, and 'Arif, supported by the Ba'th, continued to mount over the summer and culminated in Qasim's dismissal of 'Arif as deputy prime minister at the end of September. 'Arif was then dispatched to Bonn as the Iraqi ambassador to Germany. 'Arif initially resisted his new position, but eventually departed the country in mid-October. Two weeks later he returned in secret and began plotting an Egyptian-backed coup that would have overthrown Qasim and brought Iraq into the UAR. Qasim discovered 'Arif's plot and had him arrested and jailed. A special military tribunal presided over by Col. Fadl 'Abbas al-Mahdawi, the highest-ranking pro-Communist official in Qasim's government, sentenced 'Arif to death, but the sentence was never carried out and 'Arif would reemerge two years later to resume his efforts.[84]

The split between Qasim and 'Arif confounded the Eisenhower administration's analytical categories for making sense of political events in Iraq. The Eisenhower Doctrine, which pledged to defend conservative monarchies (such as the now-defunct Iraqi Hashemites) from Nasser's Egypt (which it described as a "state controlled by International Communism") was still the official policy of the United States. But as Nasser increased his repressive efforts against Communists in the UAR at the same time that Qasim increased his reliance on the Iraqi Communist Party, American policymakers became increasingly aware of the need to devise a new approach to the region. Under pressure from lower levels of the State Department, the

Eisenhower administration adopted NSC policy directive 5820/1 in early November. This directive repudiated the Eisenhower Doctrine's facile formulation of Egypt as a "state controlled by International Communism," and recognized the need to engage more constructively with Nasser, and associate US policy "more closely with the aims and aspirations of the Arab people."[85]

By "associat[ing] itself more closely with the aims and aspirations of the Arab people," the NSC meant the overthrow of the government of Iraq. At least this is how it looked from Baghdad, where Qasim suspected that the United States was working with Egypt against him.[86] The Iraqi leader based his suspicions of US motives on the failure of the US embassy to inform him of a plot organized in early December by Rashid 'Ali, the former general who led the short-lived "Iraqi Revolt" of 1941. The British embassy, by contrast, seeing Nasser as a bigger threat than Qasim, had the same information and took it to the Iraqi government.[87] Qasim's sense of American motives was essentially on the mark. Although Qasim could not have been aware of the deliberations between the US embassy and the State Department, he was likely aware that on December 3 an Iraqi officer "who claimed to represent a 'free officers movement'" approached the US embassy seeking US support for a coup against Qasim.[88] The unnamed officer may have been dispatched by Qasim himself to test American motives and US embassy officials acknowledged that he may have been an agent provocateur. "The embassy was," nonetheless,

> impressed by his sincerity and proposed to check him out. If [*text not declassified*] story was essentially correct, the Embassy thought that the coup could prove a crucial turning point in Iraq's history and perhaps a watershed in stopping Communist advances in the Arab world. Should [*text not declassified*] prove out, the Embassy recommended giving him and his colleagues limited support. If the coup was successful, it recommended providing the new government generous assistance.

Secretary Dulles, who shared the British aversion to Nasser, rejected the embassy's call for support of the planned operation, and Ambassador Gallman met with Qasim to deny any US involvement in the plot.[89] But the Iraqi leader remained convinced that the US was attempting to subvert his regime.

The day after Gallman met with Qasim to deny US involvement in the Rashid 'Ali plot, acting secretary of state Christian Herter replaced Gallman with John D. Jernegan as the new ambassador to Iraq, and dispatched William Rountree, the assistant secretary for Near Eastern and South Asian Affairs, to the region to meet with Arab leaders including Nasser and Qasim. Both moves, the replacement of the ambassador and the dispatch of the assistant secretary, portended closer cooperation between the United States and Egypt with regard to Iraq, as envisioned by NSC 5820/1.[90] And indeed, the Rountree mission proved an important turning point in US-Iraq relations. After meetings in Lebanon and Jordan, Rountree traveled to Cairo where he met privately with Nasser on December 15.[91] In their meeting, Nasser emphasized his concern over Communist influence in the region and issued what Rountree understood to be a "thinly-veiled invitation to collaborate on Iraq."[92] The following day, Rountree traveled to Baghdad to meet with Qasim. Rountree had a very different reception in Iraq. Whereas his reception in Cairo had been orderly and cordial, he was met at the Baghdad airport by Communist demonstrators shouting "Rountree go home!" On the way to the Iraqi capital, Rountree's limousine was pelted by garbage and rocks, smashing the windshield, and Iraqi troops had to be called in to disperse the crowd.[93] While meeting with Qasim, "Mr. Rountree found the building filled with machine guns, all pointed in his direction," and Qasim reiterated his accusation that the US was working to foment a coup against his government.[94]

As Rountree returned from the region, the NSC met in Washington to consider the extent to which the US should "seek an area of mutual accommodation with Nasser regarding Iraq."[95] It was particularly interested to learn if there were "military or political figures available in Iraq who could work with the US and UAR in such a situation." In response to these questions, Rountree composed a memo arguing that Qasim was "a dupe or willing tool of the Communists," and that Nasser was the "only acceptable source of outside support left to Iraqi Nationalist elements who may wish to move against the present regime."[96] The following day, on December 23, the NSC met to further consider the matter. In the meeting, Rountree, now returned from Iraq, recounted his discussions with Nasser and Qasim and recommended that exploring an area of mutual accommodation with Nasser would be "thoroughly consistent with our objective of denying the area to Soviet domination."[97] Rountree explained, "There is a conflict of interest between the UAR and the Soviet Union," and expressed satisfaction that Cairo was "at last prepared to do something about Communism in the UAR," as "the Arabs are becoming aroused to the real danger, i.e., to the fact that that it is not colonialism but Communism." The president then expressed satisfaction with Rountree's analysis and voiced his support for working with Nasser to contain Communist influence in Iraq.

The Eisenhower administration's new pro-Nasser policy line was codified at a meeting of the NSC on January 15. In the meeting, John Foster Dulles, who briefly returned to duty, expressed apprehension about working with Nasser, whom he continued to regard as a Soviet proxy. His brother Allen, on the other hand, took heart in the fact that

> Nasser was a kind of conspiratorial fellow. Accordingly, it might be useful to send a lower level envoy to talk over matters with him frankly. The President concluded the discussion by stating his view that this seemed to be a case of whether we decided to support a baby-faced Dillinger [Nasser] or an Al Capone [Qasim].[98]

For his part, the president sided with Allen over Foster. When put in terms of Dillinger versus Capone, the president noted, "It might be good policy to help the UAR takeover in Iraq," and he recommended providing Nasser with "money and support" toward this end.

Over the coming weeks and months, the United States moved into increasingly close alignment with Egypt with regard to Qasim and Iraq. This shift into tacit alignment with Egypt was made easier by the incapacitation of Dulles. In February, the ailing secretary of state was again hospitalized for cancer treatment. He still sought to direct American policy from his hospital bed, but by the time he stepped down in April, Foster was a mere shadow of the "monster" he had once been. Within a month, he was dead. His final words, according to his brother:

> Would this nation of ours and our allies ever thoroughly understand the scope of the peril, the unchanging goals of communism and its subtle and subversive techniques to accomplish them? The tempo of the action changed but the threat was constant, the advance and then the retreat, the probing now here, now there, each weakness of the Free World tested, its strong points bypassed.[99]

THE SPECIAL COMMITTEE ON REGIME CHANGE

The American shift toward a policy inimical to Qasim's regime, and its tacit support for Egyptian efforts to bring it down, accelerated in early 1959. A major catalyst in this direction was a failed military uprising in Mosul in March of that year. The revolt, in which pan-Arabist officers backed by Egypt planned to seize the Mosul garrison while army intelligence chief Rif'at al-Hajj Sirri arrested Qasim in Baghdad, was discovered and preempted by the People's Resistance Force.[100] In a panic, Brigadier Nazim al-Tabachali and Colonel 'Abd al-Wahhab al-Shawwaf launched the uprising prematurely. Qasim responded by deploying the Iraqi air force to bomb rebellious units while Communist militias killed hundreds of nationalist partisans in nearly a week of bloodshed. In the aftermath of the failed uprising, pan-Arabist officers were purged from the army and government, while Communists were rewarded with high-level posts within the regime. For the first time in its history, the Communist Party was allowed to organize in the open, and the ranks of the party and its militia swelled dramatically.[101]

American policymakers looked with grave concern at the unfolding events in Iraq. On the Senate floor, Allen Dulles described Iraq as "the most dangerous spot on the globe."[102] Behind closed doors, the United States intensified its effort to help the Nasser "takeover." In an April 1959 meeting of the NSC, Eisenhower agreed that the situation in Iraq was dire, and that if the US was "really going to undertake to save Iraq, we should have to begin to do so now."[103] Toward this end, the NSC formed a "Special Inter-Agency Working Group" to monitor the situation closely for the "purpose of determining what the U.S. Government either alone or in concert with others, can do [*1 line of source text not declassified*] to avoid a Communist takeover in Iraq."[104] This special working group followed events very closely over the course of 1959, and soon developed a detailed plan for assisting nationalist elements committed to the overthrow of Qasim.[105]

The NSC's special working group laid out details of the plan to topple Qasim in a September 1959 study, "Preventing a Communist Takeover in Iraq."[106] The study described Qasim as a "madman" increasingly beholden to the Communists, and warned that if the US did not act, Iraq would become a Soviet satellite.[107] It called for covert assistance to Egyptian efforts to topple Qasim, and "grooming political leadership for a successor government to Qasim." The report proposed several potential successors to replace

Qasim. At the top of the list was Rashid 'Ali al-Kaylani. At the same time, it recommended seeking out "other Army leaders" or "a Moslem divine" to lead a new regime. "As a last resort," it recommended setting up a "self-styled free Iraqi government" to request "open military intervention" on the part of the Egyptian and/or Jordanian armies.[108]

One foreign service officer who was especially taken with the committee report was William Lakeland, the officer in charge of Iraqi-Jordanian affairs at the State Department.[109] Lakeland was particularly inclined toward collaboration with Nasser owing to a close personal relationship with the Egyptian leader. Lakeland was an Arabic linguist and Foreign Service officer who first arrived in Egypt in 1951, on the eve of the Egyptian revolution. While in Egypt, Lakeland became acquainted with legendary Arabist diplomat and scholar Richard P. Mitchell, who, in turn, introduced Lakeland to Muhammad Hasanayn Haykal, an important confidant to Nasser. After Egypt's 1952 revolution, Haykal introduced Lakeland to Nasser, and for a time, Lakeland hosted weekly meetings with Nasser and other leading Egyptians at his apartment on the Nile.[110] Between 1954 and 1957, he was posted to Aden, Saudi Arabia, and Yemen, before returning to Washington to work in the State Department's Office of Near Eastern Affairs. From Washington, Lakeland looked with great favor on Nasser's effort to take over in Iraq. In response to the committee report, Lakeland concluded that Qasim was a "weak reed on which to base our policy.... We should look ahead; chances for a stable Iraq diminishing under Kassem. Ought to be looking for alternatives."[111]

By the fall of 1959, it was becoming increasingly clear that the most likely alternative to Qasim was the Ba'th. On October 1, the NSC met to discuss endemic coup plotting in Iraq. Allen Dulles noted rumors of an Egyptian-backed plot to assassinate Qasim within "the next two months," and advised that the US begin contingency planning in the event of a protracted struggle between nationalists and Communists.[112] The following week, on October 7, a young Saddam Hussein took part in a Ba'thist-organized assassination attempt against Qasim.[113] The attempt failed, but Qasim suffered a gunshot wound that left him hospitalized for more than a month. Saddam and his fellow assassins escaped to Cairo where they enjoyed Nasser's protection for the remainder of Qasim's tenure in power. As of yet, there is no evidence of US involvement in the assassination plot, but the brazen attempt clearly brought the Baʿth to the attention of the CIA as a group that could potentially stage a successful coup d'état.[114]

Some members of the special working group, especially representatives from the CIA, expressed growing interest in the Baʿth and its effort to topple Qasim.[115] In December, the CIA procured a highly alarmist Special National Intelligence Estimate that stressed the Communist threat to Iraq and expressed cautious optimism regarding the prospects for a nationalist coup.[116] Two weeks later, Allen Dulles dispatched James Critchfield, a CIA station chief in Europe who has spent the last eleven years recruiting and directing the former-Nazi spy ring known as the Gehlen Organization, to Cairo to serve as the CIA's new Near East and South Asia division chief. Critchfield would hold this position for the next ten years. It appears that Normal Paul continued to direct CIA planning in Washington, but it was Critchfield who would direct operations on the ground in the region.[117]

Not everyone in Washington shared the CIA's alarmism. Nicholas Thacher, a former embassy officer in Baghdad (1956–58) who, in 1958, moved to the Department of Near Eastern affairs in Washington, was particularly outspoken in his dissent.[118] He complained the CIA's estimate "overplayed" Qasim's dependence on the Communists, and "underplayed [Qasim's] own highly developed sense of self-preservation which ... will incline him to stop Communist inroads on his own power before the relationship has shifted to one where he is subservient to the Communists."[119] Others in the State Department shared this more sober assessment and warned against intervening too directly in Iraqi political affairs: "Nationalism, whether of the domestic Iraqi type or the Pan Arab variety, will do a better job of opposing communism if it is unhampered by recognized ties with foreign, particularly Western, elements."[120]

Despite State Department calls to maintain a "hands-off" approach, the CIA proffered two concrete proposals to bring about regime change in Iraq—most likely part of a still-classified "Project Clean Up."[121] The proposals themselves, identified only as "Proposal I and II," remain classified, but State Department records show that on January 12, the NSC authorized "expanded activity suggested by the CIA."[122] Details remain classified, but marginal notes at the bottom of one NEA document indicate that the CIA envisioned "utilizing Nasser's capabilities in the Baʿth situation."[123]

Shortly after the CIA devised Project Clean Up, the State Department received a secret air pouch from the US embassy in Beirut containing a report authored by Miles Copeland and James Eichelberger, the former CIA agents who had "resigned" in 1957 over their opposition to the Eisenhower Doctrine. Now established in Beirut and operating a political consultancy firm known as "Copeland & Eichelberger," they advocated an Egyptian-backed coup in Iraq.[124] The report, authored in February 1960, reiterated the same theme present in the "Preventing a Communist Takeover" study from the previous September. Copeland and Eichelberger criticized the State Department's hands-off approach and sought to elucidate the "reality of Communism in Iraq."[125] They claimed that Communists had "infiltrated both the government machinery and the military" and that it was only a matter of time before Qasim succumbed to Communist pressure. They rejected the State Department's characterization of Qasim as a "crafty fox" capable of "balancing political forces in Iraq." In their view, Qasim was a "madman." They warned that if he remained in power, it was "probable that Iraq will increasingly become a Communist agency in the Middle East through which the Soviet Union can promote its strategic objectives in the area without assuming direct responsibility."

Copeland and Eichelberger also assessed the prospects for a Nasserist and/or Baʿthist-led coup d'état. In contrast to the NEA's claim that "the best hope for solution in Iraq lies with Iraqis themselves," Copeland and Eichelberger contended:

> Apparently, *nobody* of any significance in Iraq thinks there is any chance whatever of stopping the Communists through the *internal* mobilization of non-Communist elements. All apparently feel that the real choice before them is between accommodation with the Communists *or* the elimination of Communists *through external intervention*. [Emphasis mine.]

Rather than relying on internal Iraqi forces, Copeland and Eichelberger endorsed the idea of providing covert assistance to Nasser's efforts to overthrow Qasim.

THE MYSTERY OF THE POISONED HANDKERCHIEF

Given the limits of available documentation, we know very little about US covert operations in Iraq in the early 1960s. What we do know is alarming. We know that many years later, in the mid-1970s, in the face of a broad national crisis over the definition of US national intelligence and surveillance powers, Frank Church, a populist Democratic senator from Idaho, launched a wide-ranging Senate investigation of CIA practices in light of public allegations that the CIA had participated in the September 1973 coup d'état against Chilean president Salvador Allende. Over the course of 1975–76, Church, as chairman of the Senate Foreign Relations Committee, presided over classified committee hearings, subpoenaed documents, and ultimately published fourteen separate volumes detailing various aspects of American foreign policy and intelligence practices. One of these reports was the *Interim Report: Alleged Assassination Plots Involving Foreign Leaders*.[126] The *Interim Report* did not investigate US covert operations in Iraq, instead focusing on allegations of US involvement in assassination plots in the Democratic Republic of Congo (1960–61), Cuba (1960–65), the Dominican Republic (1960–61), Vietnam (1963), and Chile (1970). But in the course of investigating a "generalized assassination capability" within the CIA, it did make passing reference to a covert operation in Iraq.

The report described the operation in a long footnote on page 181:

> In February 1960, CIA's Near East Division sought the endorsement of what the Division Chief called the "Health Alteration Committee" for its proposal for a "special operation" to "incapacitate" an Iraqi Colonel believed to be "promoting Soviet bloc political interests in Iraq." . . . The approved operation was to mail a monogrammed handkerchief containing an incapacitating agent to the colonel from an Asian country. [CIA science adviser Joseph] Scheider testified that, while he did not now recall the name of the recipient, he did remember mailing from the Asian country, during the period in question, a handkerchief "treated with some kind of material for the purpose of harassing that person who received it."[127]

The Church committee did not look further into the case and provided little additional detail. And owing to the paucity of documents, the case has elicited little attention from scholars. Even the identity of the CIA science adviser identified in the footnote has evaded close scrutiny. Who was Joseph Scheider, and where did he get the authority to poison an Iraqi colonel?

"Joseph Scheider" was an alias for Sidney Gottlieb, the so-called "Dark Sorcerer" of the CIA.[128] Gottlieb was an American chemist recruited into the CIA by Allen Dulles in 1951 to develop a new program in "mind control" research.[129] For more than ten years, Gottlieb directed the program, dubbed MK-ULTRA, as it established a global network of CIA black sites where classified human experiments were performed.[130] The most notorious of these sites were directed by former Nazi doctors recruited into the CIA to continue their research on so-called "expendables"—captured Soviet agents or unreliable Eastern Bloc defectors.[131] Others were more innocuous "pads" in Greenwich Village and San Francisco, where prostitutes lured unsuspecting members of the criminal underworld into a controlled environment where the effects of sex and drugs on human consciousness could be intensively studied.[132] Still other sites included places like Stanford University, where MK-ULTRA-funded science performed LSD experiments on willing college students such as a young Ken Kesey in 1959.[133]

By the time that Qasim came to power in Iraq in 1958, Gottlieb was operating as a "field agent" specializing in the manufacture and delivery of poisons and other materials for use in efforts to assassinate foreign leaders (exploding cigars and the like).[134] The Iraqi colonel identified in the Church committee report was just one of many foreign leaders that the US targeted for assassination in these years. But who was he, and why was he targeted for assassination?

Without access to a fuller array of documents, we can't know for certain exactly who Gottlieb was targeting in Iraq, but historian Nathan Citino offers a compelling argument that the target of the operation was most likely Fadl 'Abbas al-Mahdawi, the Iraqi colonel that presided over Qasim's *Mahkamah al-'Askariyah al-'Ulya al-Khassah (Special High Military Court)* that had tried and convicted pan-Arab nationalists such as Rashid 'Ali and 'Abd al-Salam 'Arif. Citino bases this conclusion on an exhaustive analysis of the twenty-two-volume Arabic transcript of the court's proceedings that was published by the Iraqi Ministry of Defense between 1958 and 1962.

Citino's conclusion is eminently plausible. Al-Mahdawi did indeed fall quite ill in early 1960, and he did indeed suffer a "terminal illness before a firing squad in Baghdad (an event we had nothing to do with) not very long after our handkerchief proposal was considered," as Gottlieb described the event to the Church committee.[135] But the most powerful piece of circumstantial evidence pointing to al-Mahdawi as the target of the operation was his ideology. Although he was not a member of the Iraqi Communist Party, he was sympathetic toward the movement, and "American officials used his prominence at any given moment as a barometer of communist influence on Qasim.... Bombastic and theatrical, a butcher's son lacking in formal legal training, al-Mahdawi presided over quintessential show trials in which he baited and abused witnesses in between giving speeches from the chair."[136] While American officials dismissed their import, Citino shows that al-Mahdawi's speeches defined and communicated to "Iraqi audiences a modern, socialist vision of *wataniyya* nationalism. In this vision, Iraq would be an independent, multiethnic republic friendly toward but not subservient to the Soviet Union."[137]

Al-Mahdawi's vision of "multiethnic republic" clashed violently with the American vision of world order in the 1950s.[138] At home, Americans were rent by the notion of equal citizenship without regard to color. The idea that the United States would allow a pro-Soviet multiethnic republic to emerge in Iraq was simply beyond the pale. In trying to poison the Iraqi colonel, the CIA was in fact "killing hope" for secular pluralism in Iraq and the wider region.

THE CIA'S RATIONAL PURSUIT OF AN IRRATIONAL END

The CIA's poisoned handkerchief operation represented the logical conclusion of the basic premises put forward by James Forrestal in his initial proposals for the CIA. Surely, Forrestal's anti-Zionism alienated important Democratic Party donors and led to his ultimate downfall. But Forrestal's larger vision of the world—sans the anti-Zionism—was not his alone. His larger anti-Communist and authoritarian philosophy of government was institutionalized in the aftermath of World War II. It was Forrestal who prevailed over George C. Marshall in laying the institutional foundations for American postwar diplomacy. It was Forrestal who had brought Kennan and the Dulles brothers into the inner circles of government. It was the *USS Forrestal* that carried US Marines ashore in Lebanon in July 1958, that supported a CIA-backed coup d'état in Brazil in 1964, and that launched airstrikes against Vietnam in 1967. To this day, CIA and academic biographers write glowingly, if tragically, about Forrestal's legacy. The US Department of Energy is currently housed in the James B. Forrestal Building in Washington, DC.

The American spies in Arabia, from Kermit Roosevelt to Sidney Gottlieb, were simply following orders that originated in the dark recesses of James Forrestal's Cold War–addled mind. Men like Roosevelt were asked to find Communists and men like Gottlieb were asked to make them disappear.

And so that's what they did. The handkerchief operation seems not to have come off as planned. But that was hardly the first or last covert operation the CIA would launch in Iraq. Ironically, the failure of the handkerchief operation almost guaranteed that similar such operations would be conducted in the future. In the grand tradition of failing upward, Gottlieb was soon promoted within the agency. By the mid-1960s he had graduated to upper management of the CIA, and in 1973 he retired as one of the agency's most decorated officers.[139] At each station in this upward climb, Gottlieb, and those like him, were awarded with more authority and a larger, highly classified budget. With such power, who could but use it?

Chapter 3
THE EMERGENCE OF OPEC

IN HIS CLASSIC 1965 STUDY, *THE ARAB COLD WAR*, MALCOLM Kerr observed that 'Abd al-Karim Qasim "presided over a strange regime that drifted in a twilight zone between Communism and a shapeless anarchic radicalism, resting on no visible organized support and held together largely by the bafflement of all potential challengers of the 'Faithful Leader' in seeking an appropriate ground on which to confront him."[1] Kerr's observation is not without considerable insight. Qasim excelled in politics by keeping his opponents off-balance. But as baffling as they might appear, Qasim's maneuvers may have involved more foresight and coordination than many have been willing or able to discern then or since.

Almost immediately following the CIA's poisoned handkerchief operation in early 1960, Qasim initiated a dramatic turnabout in Iraq's relationship to the United States. He signaled his displeasure with the quality of Soviet military imports, cracked down on the Iraqi Communist Party, and reached out to Washington for military and economic aid. As this chapter will show, policymakers in the Eisenhower administration interpreted this as a great if largely unheralded victory in the Cold War. It seemed only to validate and legitimize the kind of covert activities that Sidney Gottlieb and the CIA had undertaken in Iraq. From Washington, it appeared that the CIA's covert methods had successfully contained Soviet influence in Iraq.

But Qasim's very apparent break with the Communists was only an initial movement in a coordinated campaign to nationalize the Iraqi oil industry.

Qasim's campaign to nationalize the IPC displayed such strategic brilliance that one wonders if the fracas with the Americans at the New Baghdad Hotel, simultaneous with the physical destruction of the Hashemite monarchy, was in fact all part of a larger design. Was the new leader laying the groundwork from the start? Was he looking at the example of Iran and saying to the Americans: How are you going overthrow me without a king, a prime minister, or a CIA station? It was, after all, in Abbasid Iraq that the game of chess was perfected. Perhaps Qasim drew on that heritage in devising his approach to oil.

Whatever the origins of Qasim's strategy, by early 1960 that strategy entailed entering a new level of international cooperation with other oil-producing states. If the initial daring movement into Baghdad required steely nerves, tight operational security, and an impeccable sense of timing, this movement out of Baghdad into the larger world would require a different and more diplomatic skill set. Qasim had these skills as well and he used them to forge the international cooperation that would ultimately give rise to OPEC—the Organization of Petroleum Exporting Countries—and help to lay the institutional foundation for the eventual nationalization of the IPC. And though it would not become apparent for some time, the emergence of OPEC in Baghdad in September 1960 exposed a deep rift in Washington over the direction of American foreign oil policy in the Middle East. Qasim would not live to see it, but it was that rift that would ultimately prove critical to the eventual success of the effort to nationalize the IPC.

QASIM'S MOVE TO THE COLD WAR RIGHT

The CIA's 1960 poisoned handkerchief operation, and the larger Project Clean Up of which it was likely a part, represented a clear case of paranoid statecraft. Covert agents like Miles Copeland and James Eichelberger systematically overstated the threat of the Iraqi Communist Party coming to power in Iraq. And though they presented their opinions as facts, the reality in Iraq was quite different. Qasim was not a Communist stooge, and the influence of the Communist Party in Iraq was severely circumscribed by Qasim's own well-trained sense of self-preservation. No secret methods were required to discern this. Open-source intelligence made it plain, and many in the State Department understood it perfectly well.

In their effort to push back against hyperbolic representations of Qasim's Iraq as a "state controlled by International Communism," State Department analysts pointed to a large body of evidence that CIA agents like Copeland and Eichelberger were unwilling to countenance. They pointed to internal political dynamics in Iraq that did not conform to a bipolar vision of the world. Indications that the Communist Party was in no position to seize power in Iraq had been apparent for some time. One clear example was Qasim's response to violence that erupted between Kurdish Communists and their wealthier Turkoman and Arab neighbors in Kirkuk in July 1959.[2] Rather than supporting the Communists, Qasim deployed government forces to quell the violence. He then seized on the bloodshed in Kirkuk as an opportunity to move against the party. He castigated the Communists as the aggressors and used the press to sensationalize reports of Communist atrocities. In the aftermath of Kirkuk, he closed down the PRF (the Communist militia that had crushed the nationalist revolts in Mosul and Kirkuk), arrested a large number of Communist partisans, and purged the armed forces, peasant leagues, and trade unions of Communist influence. Qasim's drive against the left was interrupted by the Ba'th's October 1959 assassination attempt that hospitalized Qasim until mid-January. When he emerged from the hospital, Qasim resumed and accelerated the anti-Communist campaign. He soon promulgated a new Law of Associations that outlawed the Communist Party and dismissed additional Communist and pro-Communist ministers from this government.[3] Al-Mahdawi remained in his position as head of the Special Military Court, but the scope of the trials was severely circumscribed.

This sequence of events offered the State Department a powerful set of arguments with which it could push back against the CIA's drive for covert action. Qasim exploited the State Department's credulity brilliantly. Perhaps getting word from someone in the American embassy that the CIA was out to get him, Qasim put out a quiet entreaty to Washington. In February 1960, just as the handkerchief operation was being approved, Qasim appointed a new moderate figure named Hashim Jawad to serve as foreign minister, with the understanding that Jawad would exclude Communists from the ministry and reorient Iraqi foreign policy away from the Soviet Union.[4] Little is written about Hashim Jawad (not be confused with Ba'th

Party organizer Hazim Jawad), but the American embassy in Baghdad took his appointment as a very good sign.

Shortly after Jawad's appointment, ʻAli Haidar Sulaiman, the Iraqi ambassador to the US, met with Christian Herter, who had recently replaced the late John Foster Dulles as secretary of state. The meeting proved pivotal. Sulaiman was a relatively conservative figure who had been a fixture of the old Hashemite order in Iraq.[5] At the time of the 1958 coup, he had been Iraq's ambassador to West Germany. But as Qasim sought to improve ties to the West, he made Sulaiman the Iraqi ambassador in Washington. When they met in February 1960, Sulaiman assured Herter that the "Communist movement was dead in Iraq."[6] Qasim had simply used Communist support to consolidate his regime against his pan-Arabist challengers. But now that the pan-Arabist threat appeared vanquished, Qasim was focused on the "art of government" and in need of "competent administrators and economic technicians." Toward the end of February, Ambassador Jernegan confirmed that the "trend toward improved relations with the US . . . seems to be accelerating rapidly."[7] In early March, Jernegan reported with much satisfaction that Qasim no longer felt it "necessary to take steps demonstrating 'withdrawal' from contacts and associations with the west."[8] Qasim was instead interested in technical and economic assistance agreements with the West that would allow him to move forward with an ambitious development agenda that he had set forth upon coming to power. Developments were so positive from Washington's perspective that Eisenhower disbanded the NSC's special working group on Iraq and began exploring avenues for technical and economic cooperation with the "present regime."[9]

WINDS OF CHANGE IN THE WORLD OF ARAB OIL

Qasim's softened line toward the United States was indeed part of a more general pattern. By early 1960, he was fairly secure in power. Both the Communists to his left and the Baʻthists to his right appeared to have been checked, and he seemed to have a fair amount of room to maneuver in the middle. And once the basic task of seizing control of the coercive instruments of government was complete, the more long-term challenges of promoting balanced economic development came to the fore. Qasim had signaled his ambitions in this direction as part of his consolidation of power. In October 1958, he inaugurated a far-reaching land reform program that broke

FIGURE 3. Yarmouk housing complex, Baghdad, 1965. Photo by Latif al-Ani of the Yarmouk neighborhood in Baghdad constructed in the Qasim period. Source: Latif al-Ani courtesy of The Arab Image Foundation. Reprinted with permission.

up large landholdings and distributed them to formerly landless peasants in twenty-to-forty-acre plots.[10] Not only did this break the political power of the rural landlords, which had been a key pillar of the Hashemite order, but it also built a loyal base of support for Qasim among the rural poor.[11] Another immediately popular measure was the construction of Madinat al-Thawra, a modern public housing project in Baghdad for recent immigrants from the countryside.[12]

As popular as Qasim's development measures were, they required money. At the time, Iraq remained dependent on the IPC for more than 60 percent of government revenue.[13] And if Qasim was going to successfully meet the

FIGURE 4. Al-Rasheed Street, 1961. Photo by Latif al-Ani of al-Rasheed Street in central Baghdad. Source: Latif al-Ani courtesy of The Arab Image Foundation. Reprinted with permission.

demand of a restless population, he would have to wrest more income from the oil companies.[14] However, attempting to extract concessions from the oil companies was a dangerous business. In Iran at the beginning of the decade, the effort to increase the rates of taxation on the oil companies escalated into the nationalist movement that brought Mohammad Mossadegh to power. Mossadegh then led a complete nationalization of the Iranian oil industry, to which the British and Americans responded by placing an embargo on Iranian nationalized oil.[15] The loss of oil revenue fatally weakened Mossadegh's government and left it vulnerable to a British- and American-backed coup d'état.

The ghost of Mossadegh hung over Qasim's every initiative. Avoiding the fate of Mossadegh would require a great deal of cooperation among oil-producing states. The United States and Britain had been able embargo Iranian production only because the companies had an integrated management structure that could easily offset the Iranian production decrease with production increases elsewhere (see earlier fig. 1). However, the prospect of forging cooperation among oil-producing states in the region, let alone the world, was quite daunting.[16] Even though the world's largest concentration of oil reserves were located in the Middle East, major oil-producing states were widely distributed around the globe. Beyond the Middle East, there were major production centers in the United States, Soviet Union, Latin America, and Indonesia. And with the exception of the Soviet Union, the vast majority of those oil operations were under the management control of the "Seven Sisters"—the cartel comprising the world largest companies: Exxon, Mobil, Chevron, Texaco, Gulf, BP, and Shell.

Qasim's demands were national, but the companies were global. To rectify this imbalance, Qasim lent force to a movement to politically unify countries in the global South that, like Iraq, depended on oil production for the lion's share of their government revenue. In 1955, Ahmad Sukarno, the nationalist leader of the similarly situated oil-producing state of Indonesia, organized the Asian-African Conference in Bandung, at which this kind of cooperation was a major item on the agenda.[17] In attendance at the summit was a high-profile Arab delegation that included Gamal Abdel Nasser as well as Abdel Khalek Hassouna, the Egyptian secretary general of the Arab League. Nasser and Hassouna were deeply impressed by the summit's call for economic cooperation among postcolonial states. Upon their return from the summit, Nasser and Hassouna met with Mohammad Salman, an Iraqi engineer with expertise in oil affairs. Salman then agreed to lead a new Petroleum Bureau of the Arab League, and spent the next two years traveling among Arab capitals conducting an exhaustive comparative analysis of the various oil concession agreements then in force.

Salman found the oil concession agreements in the Middle East shared a number of common features that precluded a sustained program of economic development.[18] Among such common features were the following: the duration of many of the agreements was sixty years or more; the concessions covered the entirety of the state's territory, which precluded industry competition; companies were not required to actually produce oil from discovered fields, which allowed them to capture and hold oil-producing lands, not for the purpose of selling the oil but rather to prevent upstart competitors from doing so; producing states were completely excluded from the ownership and management structures of the companies; rates of taxation could not be amended as rates of production or profitability changed; and legal disputes between the company and the state were to be resolved through international arbitration, not in a local court of law. Salman presented his findings in a final report to an assembly of the Arab League in April 1957. The assembled delegates supported Salman's conclusions and agreed to form a permanent Arab Oil Congress to meet periodically to coordinate efforts to revise individual concessions.

Although delayed by the Iraqi Revolution and subsequent rivalry between Egypt and Iraq, the first meeting of the Arab Oil Congress was eventually held in Cairo in April 1959. The meeting brought together for the first time the leading figures that would shape the oil politics of the region—and the world—for the next decade. Salman was the main organizing force behind the group.[19] But he was joined by a young progressive reformer named Abdullah Tariki, who was then the Saudi director general of petroleum and mineral resources.[20] Tariki would become the most famous Arab oil expert of his generation.

Born into a modest family in Nejd in 1919, Tariki demonstrated exceptional intelligence from an early age and was selected to receive formal education in Cairo, and then in the United States. After receiving a MA in petroleum geology from the University of Texas–Austin in 1947, he worked as an oil regulator for the Texas Railroad Commission and then at Texaco before returning to Saudi Arabia in 1953. This was a fortuitous time to arrive in Saudi Arabia. 'Abd al- Aziz, the first king of Saudi Arabia, died in November of that year. The decline and death of the king opened a power struggle between the new king, Saud, and his ambitious younger brother Faysal. At the same time, long-suffering oil workers organized a massive strike wave that rocked Saudi oil fields for months.[21]

In the highly charged atmosphere of the early 1950s, Saud brought reformers into his government, including the 35-year-old Tariki, who became the country's first director general of petroleum affairs. This was a subcabinet-level position that audited oil revenues for the Finance Ministry.

FIGURE 5. Abdullah Tariki, 1961. Co-founder of the Organization of Petroleum Exporting Countries (OPEC). Source: James Burke, Getty Images. Reprinted with permission.

The appointment of Tariki was just the beginning of a reformist wave. That wave gained momentum in the wake of the Suez War. In 1958, while the Free Officers' Revolution took hold in Iraq, a Nasserist Free Princes' Movement emerged in Saudi Arabia in which a group of liberal reformers within the royal family called for constitutional reform, political cooperation with Egypt, increased wages and benefits for workers, and greater state control over oil company operations.[22] To accomplish this last objective, the Free Princes invested a great deal of hope in the considerable talents of Abdullah Tariki. The 1959 Arab Oil Congress offered Tariki the first opportunity to demonstrate that talent on the world stage.

As the summit approached, the companies expressed a great deal of alarm. The companies had gotten hold of an advance copy of the speech that Tariki planned to give and understood that the kind of producer-state cooperation that he was proposing presented a dire threat to their interests. In March, Exxon's representative warned the State Department that the "sanctity of contracts" was in danger and that if the summit were allowed to go forward and succeed, the whole system of private enterprise would be thrown into disorder.[23]

The companies knew their business well, and the conference did not disappoint. Both Salman and Tariki gave rousing addresses calling for revisions to the concessionary system in the region. But it was Frank Hendryx, an American legal adviser to Tariki, who generated the most controversy. Shielding Tariki from the political heat of the opinion, Hendryx launched a frontal assault on the legal basis of the existing concessions throughout the region.[24] He decried the existing agreements as little more than colonial charters that had be invalidated by the legal principle of *rebus sic stantibus*—roughly, by right of changing circumstances. The concessions had been signed by unequal parties before conditions of true sovereignty pertained. The governments in question were now internationally recognized as sovereign and retained the sovereign right to amend or abrogate existing international agreements. He called on the companies to immediately relinquish areas not under current development so that producing states might open those areas to a competitive bidding process. If the companies were not willing to relinquish nonproducing fields, Hendryx argued that the oil-producing states should resort to their sovereign authority: "An oil-producing nation, by the laws of civilized nations, may clearly, in a proper case, modify or eliminate provisions of an existing petroleum concession which have become substantially contrary to the best interests of its citizens."[25]

The 1959 conference proved a major turning point in the history of world oil. At its conclusion, Qasim effected a fundamental reorganization of Iraq's institutional structure with regard to oil. Most significantly, he elevated the profile of moderate and liberal reformers grouped around Muhammad Hadid in the Ministry of Finance. Educated at the American University of Beirut and the London School of Economics (under prominent socialist Harold Laski), Hadid had been a prominent industrialist and one of the founders of the Ahali Group with 'Abd al-Fattah Ibrahim in the 1930s.[26] In the 1940s, he was a founder of the moderate socialist National Democratic Party and went on to (very briefly) serve as minister of supply for the monarchy. After the revolution, Qasim made him minister of finance. This was a particularly important position because, at the time, Iraq did not have a separate ministry of oil. Oil affairs were handled instead by the Finance Ministry's Office of Petroleum Affairs. For the post of director general of petroleum, Hadid selected his Ahali ally Ibrahim, the social theorist who had articulated a populist theory of democracy in his 1939 book, *Introduction to Sociology (Maqaddima fi'l ijtima)*.[27]

In the wake of the Cairo oil summit, as Qasim prepared to engage the oil companies, he turned increasingly to Hadid.[28] Based on advice from Hadid (and behind Hadid, Ibrahim), Qasim created a separate Oil Ministry, and selected Mohammad Salman to serve as Iraq's first minister of oil.[29] In the months ahead, Hadid and Salman, with broad philosophical guidance from Ibrahim, began laying the groundwork that would revolutionize oil politics in the region.

THE RISING FORCE OF DOMESTIC AMERICAN OIL AND GAS

Frank Hendryx, an American lawyer representing Arab oil nationalists at the 1959 Arab Oil Congress, posed a political and legal dilemma for the US State Department. In critiquing the legal foundations of the existing concessions as mere colonial charters, Hendryx pointed to a significant contradiction and vulnerability in American foreign oil policy. Since the era of the great oil deals of the late 1940s, American foreign oil policy had rested on a few foundational assumptions. The first was the desirability of US foreign direct investment in Middle Eastern oil production. As we saw in chapter 1, it was believed that this prolific source of reserves could provide a low-cost sources of fuel for the postwar reconstruction of Europe and Asia. A second—that the exploitation of foreign oil would conserve US oil supplies for use in a time of national emergency. A third—that oil revenues accrued in oil state treasuries would provide a source of development capital, obviating the need for US foreign aid. This set of assumptions undergirded what oil historians call the postwar petroleum order. Left out of this order, however, were the interests of a set of politically powerful domestic American oil and gas producers who were the natural competitors of the international majors that did business in the Middle East.

When the majors spoke of conserving American oil reserves, domestic producers heard only that their freedom to drill would be circumscribed. The idea of buying cheap oil from "Moslem Arabs" rather than higher-priced American oil produced by hardworking, patriotic, Christian "roughnecks" was simply anathema.[30] While George Marshall and George Kennan set up the institutional foundations of the petroleum order, domestic oil and gas cried bloody murder. These domestic producers had a powerful advocate in the US Department of the Interior, which issued licenses to drill for oil and gas in the wide-open spaces of the American West.

In the language of political science, Interior was "captured" by the very industrial interests it was charged with regulating.[31] As a consequence, Interior never bought into the Cold War concept of the majors as quasi-public utilities providing a public good. Whereas the majors, with the support of the State Department, looked to the Middle East as the source of critical raw materials for an integrated world economy, Interior had resisted the shift in the "center of gravity of world oil" from the Gulf of Mexico to the Persian Gulf in the 1940s.

Rather than acquiring and defending concessions to produce oil abroad, Interior looked to the subsoil resources of the American West and saw a future of "American Energy Independence."[32] The oil and gas resources located under American soil (tar sands and shales, natural gas, etc.) were not of the kind located in the Middle East, but in 1947 the Department of the Interior called for a new "Manhattan Project" to develop a synthetic fuels industry and build an infrastructure to market these abundant resources.[33] From this standpoint, investing in the technology to transform matter appeared a safer bet than forging stable relationships with "medieval kingdoms" half a world away.

Interior's Manhattan scheme was no idle threat. There was in fact a large and well-organized domestic constituency behind it. And that domestic constituency had no difficulty generating public antipathy for the machinations of the big international firms. This is because "Standard Oil" occupied a special place in the pantheon of American corporate goblins. No firm piqued populist rage quite like Standard. While the origins of this rage were rooted in the dynamics of late nineteenth-century industrialization in the United States, it continued unabated through World War II.

During the war, members of Congress complained that Standard was overcharging for fuel deliveries to the military. After the war, the Federal Trade Commission (FTC) launched an investigation of the same with regard to fuel deliveries to Europe as part of the Marshall Plan.[34] Using the power of subpoena, the FTC in 1949 produced a four-hundred-page classified report, *The International Petroleum Cartel*, which documented a "series of agreements among the seven largest oil companies in the world to divide markets, to distribute on a quota basis, [and] to fix prices and to control the production of oil throughout the world." According to the US Department of Justice, "These agreements are in violation of the antitrust laws of the United States."[35] To defend itself against these charges, the major companies (Exxon, Mobil, Chevron, Texaco, Gulf, BP, and Shell) retained the services of Sullivan & Cromwell, at which the Dulles brothers were still senior partners.[36]

Sullivan & Cromwell was initially able to stall the investigation, but in August 1952 John Sparkman, the Democratic candidate for vice president and the chair of the Senate Small Business Committee, which was highly sympathetic to domestic American competitors to the major internationals, released the FTC's report to the public.[37] During the 1952 presidential election campaign, Truman and Sparkman presented themselves as populist opponents of "Big Oil," and the threat of criminal prosecution against the major companies helped reinforce that theme.[38] However, after the election, in one of his last acts as president, Truman intervened to block the Justice Department from filing criminal charges against the companies. On January 12, 1953, he instructed the attorney general to "terminate" the "pending grand jury proceedings," and file instead a civil suit (which would have only limited powers of subpoena and would not carry criminal penalties).[39] However, two weeks later, the Eisenhower administration took office and chose to establish a special cabinet commission to advise the president on the proper course of action with regard to the case.[40] To head this new commission the president appointed incoming secretary of state John Foster Dulles, who had just stepped down as senior partner in the law firm representing the companies.

Not unsurprisingly, Dulles soon concluded that "the enforcement of the Antitrust laws of the United States against the Western oil companies operating in the Near East may be deemed secondary to the national security interest."[41] This led to the first in a series of "consent decrees" (formal agreements between the Justice Department and the offending companies), which effectively granted the companies explicit authorization to collaborate in opposition to producer-state demands. But even with consent decrees, the Justice Department's civil case remained pending (though inactive), and the threat of renewed antitrust action was a constant source of concern for the companies.[42] This was especially the case as John Foster Dulles began to fade from the scene in Washington.

Dulles had been a stalwart champion for the companies. But as his health declined and his bombastic anti-Communist rhetoric became cumbersome, Eisenhower began looking in another direction for counsel. Increasingly, this search narrowed to his longtime friend Robert Anderson, an independent oilman from Texas. Born the son of a humble farmer in Burleson in 1910, Anderson earned a law degree from the University of Texas in 1932 and soon entered the state legislature as a New Deal Democrat.[43] During WWII, Anderson served as an aide to the secretary of the army. In this capacity he met Eisenhower, who in 1954 appointed him to serve as deputy secretary of defense. In 1955, Anderson left the government to form Ventures, Ltd., a holding company for mining interests throughout the American West, but he continued to serve as a trusted personal adviser to President Eisenhower. So close did he become to the president that in January 1956 Eisenhower, with the support of the CIA, appointed him to carry out a highly sensitive "crypto-diplomatic" mission to negotiate a peace agreement between Egypt and Israel.[44]

Anderson's venture into Arab-Israeli crypto-diplomacy was a failure (in the sense that war broke out shortly thereafter), but his work with Ventures paid off handsomely. In 1956, he purchased large tracts of oil-bearing lands in Louisiana and Texas. As the ink dried on the purchasing contract, Anderson came back into government as Eisenhower's treasury secretary in 1957. In this capacity, Anderson sounded the alarm about the threat to American "national security" (and the value of his own oil-bearing lands) posed by the flood of cheap Middle Eastern oil flowing into the US economy.[45] To contain this threat, Anderson advocated a regime of oil import quotas that would protect domestic oil and gas producers from international competition. To this end he helped organize an intergovernmental Special Committee to Investigate Crude Oil Imports. After an exhaustive study of the threat that foreign oil posed to the domestic oil and gas industry, the Special Committee recommended a set of voluntary import quota controls.[46] After voluntary import controls failed to stem the tide of Middle Eastern oil flooding

US markets, the president imposed a mandatory import quota system by executive order in March 1959.

The oil import quota scheme adopted in 1959 allowed Robert Anderson to earn windfall profits from his oil investments in Texas and Louisiana.[47] The sale of those lands was just one in a long series of shady business dealings that would eventually land Anderson in a federal penitentiary for banking and tax fraud.[48] We will visit another of those shady business deals in chapter 7, but before the fall came the pride, and in the late 1950s, Anderson could not have been more proud. That pride was not Anderson's alone. On the contrary, it was shared by two of the most powerful figures in Washington, House majority leader Sam Rayburn and Senate majority leader Lyndon B. Johnson, both of Texas.[49] Johnson in particular had risen to national leadership by aggregating political contributions from Texas-based oil and gas firms—Brown and Root, in particular—into a national political machine that could influence election outcomes throughout the country.[50]

Johnson's pride took on increased significance as the 1960 US presidential election approached, for which he was a leading contender for the Democratic Party nomination. And just as Johnson geared up for the presidential run, the Justice Department began to once again take up the FTC's suspended antitrust case against the majors. In April 1960, lawyers for the companies met with Attorney General William Rogers to request renewed assurance against this threat of antitrust prosecution.[51] The attorney general then brought the matter before the National Security Council.[52] At the meeting, the State Department's Office of Near Eastern Affairs (NEA) strenuously defended the companies. According to its analysis, any new antitrust action would have serious and "unfavorable repercussions on U.S. relations in the NEA area."[53]

> In Saudi Arabia for example, the affirmation that the four stock-holding companies of Aramco were charged by the U.S. Government with conspiracy involving restraint of trade and monopolistic practices would provide substantial support to elements in that country which have been pressing for Arabization of the company on integrated lines. While this might not lead immediately to nationalization of the company or cancellation of the concession, it would certainly upset seriously the relations of the company with the Government and strain U.S. Government relations with the

Saudi Government. It is reasonable to expect this would be accompanied by a chain effect bringing into question the equity of petroleum concession terms generally.

The NEA's analysis was quite remarkable. The Justice Department's mere suggestion that the American companies were engaged in a criminal "conspiracy involving restraint of trade monopolistic practices" was incendiary. While it might not lead immediately to nationalization, it raised the "question of the equity of petroleum concession terms generally." And from the State Department's standpoint, the "equity" of existing petroleum concessions was a stone best left unturned.

Given what the State Department regarded as threats to "American private and public interests," its analysts recommended that the "NSC declare a national security interest" in shielding the companies from antitrust prosecution. Free Trade was all well and good. Just not when defeating Communism was at issue. The NSC could brook no argument with the logic of the State Department. It agreed and ultimately ruled that moving forward with the FTC case would result in serious harm to American national security interests.[54] The NSC ran through the whole catalog of horrors that might or would ensue if the FTC insisted on going forward with the case. A few of those potential horrors are particularly noteworthy in light of subsequent events:

> (1) There might result a reduction in the U.S. control over the supply of oil for U.S. and Free World needs....
> (4) The movement to nationalization might be encouraged in several ways....
> (7) The proposed [case] would provide propaganda ammunition to leftists, nationalists and the Soviet Union for undermining and discrediting the prestige of the United States Government as well as its companies.

The "mights" were pretty bad. The United States might lose control over supply and nationalization might be encouraged. But the final "would" was the worst. How could an agency of the US government contemplate providing "propaganda ammunition to leftists"?

Just as had been the case in 1953, the NSC intervened to block the FTC case from moving forward. But those who knew the industry best were becoming increasingly aware that the majors' once unassailable position was vulnerable to challenges springing from several directions, and the State Department would not be able to fend off those challenges indefinitely.

THE SOVIET-ITALIAN CONNECTION

While the State Department was defending the majors from the threat posed by domestic oil and gas, a new threat to the majors emerged from an unexpected direction: Italy. There Enrico Mattei, a towering figure in Italian politics, mounted a spirited campaign to break the power of what he coined the "Seven Sisters cartel." A leader of the Italian anti-Fascist resistance during WWII, he was appointed by the Italian government to preside over AGIP (Azienda Generali Italiana Petroli) after the war. AGIP was an Italian state-owned oil company formed in the 1920s for the express purpose of breaking up the monopoly over the Italian energy market then held by Exxon and Mobil.

Under Mattei's leadership, AGIP discovered and developed massive oil and gas fields in Italy's northern Po Valley that allowed the company to make a serious play for international markets. With an aim to build AGIP into a major to rival the American giants, Mattei in 1953 organized ENI—Ente Nazionale Idocarburi—"a sprawling conglomerate, with a total of thirty-six subsidiaries ranging from crude oil and tankers and gasoline stations to real estate, hotels, toll highways, and soaps."[55] To expand beyond the Po Valley and establish a truly global company, ENI aggressively pursued a position in the consortium that emerged in Iran in the wake of Mossadegh's overthrow.

The Americans weren't having it. Mattei was already using his formidable position in Italian politics to erect protectionist measures restricting the ability of the American majors to operate in Italy.[56] If Mattei succeeded in establishing a direct relationship with a Middle Eastern supplier, he would have a foothold on the "greatest material prize in world history." Denied in 1954, Mattei kept at it. Probing at the periphery of the Seven Sisters' dominance, he conspired with Algerian rebels against French rule, won concessions to drill in India, Egypt, Tunisia, Morocco, Somalia and the Sudan, and in August 1957 struck a landmark deal with the shah's Iran. The agreement allowed ENI to explore for oil in regions of the country not covered by the existing concession. The difference in this agreement was its shattering of the 50–50 profit-sharing formula then the norm in the industry. Instead of demanding half of the total profits, Mattei offered Iran 75 percent of the total. Mattei saw the majors 50 and raised them to 75.[57]

The State Department was not happy. According to its analysis, the foolhardy agreement was indicative of the "aggressive character of Mattei." The Iranian gambit was just the latest act in a long-term rivalry with American oil giants with whom "he has successfully fought for some years." Having beat the majors in Italy, Mattei was now "trying to force his way into Middle Eastern oil production either through new concessions or participation in existing companies."[58] Defying the majors in Italy was one thing. Undercutting the majors in Iran was another altogether. In December 1958, Mattei took it to a whole new level by traveling to Moscow and Beijing to negotiate long-term oil agreements with the major Communist powers.[59] By 1960, Mattei was supplying half the Italian market with oil imported from the Soviet Union and poised to begin reselling that oil throughout Western Europe.[60] In November 1960, he "negotiated a five-year deal with Russia involving $100 million in bilateral trade," and provided "engineering service for the construction of a the new crude pipeline system behind the Iron curtain aimed at Western Europe."[61]

The threat of a Soviet oil pipeline aimed at Western Europe represented a major threat to the major oil companies. In response to the Soviet-ENI deal, Exxon and Mobil executives called on the NSC to voice their displeasure with the Italian statesman. In their meeting, Wolf Greeven, Exxon's regional coordinator for Europe, made it clear that "the first step in a solution to the problem of Soviet oil would be to find some method of controlling Mr. Mattei." At the heart of the problem, according to Greevan, was "Mattei's impressive political strength in Italy," as "most Italians [were] glad to get cheaper petroleum products," and cared little that it was Communist oil they were consuming.[62]

For more than two years the US State Department pleaded with Mattei to cease his dangerous liaison with Soviets, but Mattei insisted that "that he was buying Soviet oil because it was the cheapest he could get. It was his duty to provide Italy with the cheapest possible sources of energy."[63] What happened next is a matter of great speculation. In October 1962, Mattei was traveling on a private plane that was brought down by explosives packed behind the instrument panel.[64] The explosion and crash killed Mattei, the pilot, and an American journalist for *Time* magazine (and rumored CIA agent) named William McHale.⁶⁵ Many years later, a Mafia informant, Tommaso Buscetta, testified in an Italian court that the "mob—acting for a U.S. gangster under the pay of oil multinationals—was responsible for his death."⁶⁶ The full story of Mattei's "last flight" may never be known. But whether or not the CIA was involved in his death, the assassination had the effect of protecting the majors from a significant threat to their interests, and indicated the high stakes of international oil politics in the early 1960s.

THE ORGANIZATION OF PETROLEUM EXPORTING COUNTRIES

The fates of Mossadegh and Mattei demonstrated the precariously high stakes of international oil politics. But despite the dangers, Qasim, over the course of 1960 and 1961, took dramatic steps in the direction of oil nationalization. When Qasim emerged from his hospital stay and resumed regular negotiations with the IPC over perennial issues of revenue accounting, he took an increasingly firm position in asserting Iraq's sovereign right to tax the IPC parent companies. After conducting an exhaustive study of comparative export tolls, Oil Minister Salman concluded that the IPC was substantially underpaying Iraq for oil exported from the al-Faw terminal. Qasim, with the support of both Salman and Hadid, then announced a unilateral increase in Iraqi export tolls to bring them into closer alignment with regional averages.⁶⁷

While the companies, on one level, regarded Qasim's toll increase as a simple matter of tax accounting, they were also aware that Qasim's actions represented an infringement upon the sanctity of contracts as a legal principle. Moreover, such a unilateral toll increase threatened to open the door to greater state control over IPC operations, which would have implications for the business interests of IPC parent companies around the world. Qasim was only worried about Iraq. But the companies saw themselves as managing a very delicately balanced system of global supply and demand. Seemingly minor adjustments at the margins could have major ripple effects elsewhere in the world. To strangle Qasim's oil initiative while it was still in the cradle, the IPC responded to the toll increase with an immediate and dramatic cut in production and export from Iraq's southern oilfields.⁶⁸ Qasim decried the production cut as an affront to Iraq's sovereign right to tax and threatened to take further unspecified "retaliatory measures."

In the face of Iraq's threat to retaliate, the companies agreed to restore production. But less than one month later, Exxon, the largest and most aggressive of the IPC partners, announced a drastic and unilateral 7 percent reduction in "posted prices"—that is, the official price upon which rates of taxation were based. A cut in posted prices was a direct assault on the source of revenue upon which oil-producing states depended, and it was immediately perceived as such. Within the industry, and even within certain elements of Exxon itself, the move was perceived as a reckless and foolhardy assault upon the stable company-government relations that had prevailed worldwide for more than a decade. Arthur Proudfit, the Exxon CEO in Venezuela, refused to implement the new price structure—even going so far as threatening to resign if Exxon's board of directors in New York insisted on going through with it. Proudfit, along with the executives of other major companies, worried that a unilateral reduction in prices would wreck their relations with host governments. Harold Snow, BP's vice chairman, was reportedly "brought to tears" by the news of Exxon's decision, and BP chairman Maurice Bridgeman took the rare step of issuing a public statement denouncing the cut.[69] John Loudon of Shell described the cut as a "fatal move."[70] Howard Page of Exxon warned that all "hell would break loose."[71]

Exxon ultimately agreed to exempt Venezuela from the price reduction, but still applied it to all of its Middle Eastern suppliers. In this case, the "old hands" of the industry were proven correct. Within hours of the announcement, Abdullah Tariki was on the phone with Juan Pablo Pérez Alfonzo, the Venezuelan oil minister, discussing plans to move forward with the oil agenda outlined at the Arab Oil Conference of the previous April. Tariki and Alfonso then asked Qasim to host the meeting, which was scheduled to begin on September 10. Given that the meeting was organized on short notice in response to the immediate problem of the August price reductions, the agenda was quite limited. Unlike the 1959 Arab Oil Conference, there was no discussion of the legitimacy or legal status of existing concession agreements. On the contrary, all that was decided was to form a new permanent body—OPEC—to work collectively to restore the August price levels. The founding members of the organization were Iraq, Iran, Saudi Arabia, Kuwait, and Venezuela, but membership would remain open to "any country with a substantial net export of petroleum," and the headquarters would be based in Geneva, a neutral city upon which all parties could agree.[72]

Although the agenda for the Baghdad Oil Conference was quite limited, the broader theme of resource sovereignty was rejoined at the second Arab Petroleum Conference held in Beirut the following month. At the conference, Abdullah Tariki, who had recently been made a cabinet minister—Saudi Arabia's first minister of oil—emerged as the leading voice in opposition to the existing concessionary order. He reprised the arguments of Hendryx regarding the sovereign right to tax and he cited a recent study by the Arthur D. Little accounting firm to argue that the companies had employed "accounting tricks" to "swindle" producing governments out of more than $5 billion in tax receipts over the past several years. Given the manifest bad faith of the companies, Tariki demanded that the producing governments take direct control over all production and pricing decisions by adopting a program of phased nationalization.[73]

The companies immediately recognized the gravity of what had taken place in Baghdad and Beirut in the fall of 1960 and appealed directly to the State Department for help. In October, Exxon met with the State Department to warn of the new producers' association. If the proposed "international prorationing scheme" was successful, the companies would "no longer be able to manage their business in a normal way," and the producing governments would "take over the determination of oil prices, the amounts of oil to be produced, and the destination of oil shipments."[74] Given this threat, Exxon "hoped the U.S. Government would use its influence in urging the OPEC countries to go slowly in completing the OPEC organization and implementing its program." Exxon also wanted the US and British governments to devise a unified policy in opposition to OPEC. But on this occasion, neither the State Department nor any other part of the US government chose to take any action at all.

Rather than clearly signaling US opposition to OPEC as a violation of free market principles, the Eisenhower administration appeared somewhat ambivalent toward the new organization. In contrast to the majors' alarmism, the Eisenhower administration shared the perspective of Sam Falle, the British ambassador in Iran, that the formation of OPEC could actually prove to be fortuitous to Western economic interests. Given the conservative political orientation of most of the states involved, Falle believed that OPEC might come to play a moderating role in world oil politics. He was particularly heartened by the inclusion of Iran and the exclusion of Egypt.[75] As he explained in a note to the British Foreign Office,

> I do not think that the establishment of O.P.E.C. need necessarily be to the long-term detriment of the oil companies. It could indeed become a useful

forum for producing countries to discuss their problems on an economic basis, devoid of politics and polemics . . . I understand that considerable time at the recent Baghdad conference was spent by several of the more sensible and moderate representatives educating the Iraqis about the oil business . . . The object of all concerned in the business was to sell oil at the best price the world market could bear, and in this the producing countries and the companies had a common interest.

Given this potential harmony of interests, Falle warned the companies against adopting a confrontational stance toward the new organization. Such a confrontation could only bring about greater unity among oil producers and "make it difficult to play producers off each other, as they [the companies] did so successfully at the time of Dr. Mossadeq."

The Eisenhower administration shared the basic premises of Falle's analysis. Eisenhower was well aware of the fate that befell Mossadegh after he nationalized Iranian oil and was quite confident that none of the OPEC states were eager to reproduce that experience. Eisenhower was similarly confident that the companies' bargaining position vis-à-vis host governments was so overwhelmingly favorable to the companies that any producer-state challenge would be positively suicidal.[76] In a September 20 NSC meeting, "The President said that as far as the Middle Eastern countries in the new Organization were concerned, anyone could break up the Organization by offering five cents more per barrel for the oil of one of the countries."[77] Thinking of Iran and Saudi Arabia in particular, the president believed that the loyalties of oil-producing states could be purchased rather cheaply.

The question of Middle East oil was put to more formal study in a December 1960 National Intelligence Estimate (NIE).[78] The conclusions of the NIE were pretty much the same. It found that "surplus producing capacity" would continue to characterize the world oil picture for the foreseeable future. The companies would continue to face pressure to afford producing governments a greater share of total revenue, and that "greater participation by local governments in the management of the oil companies is likely," but it did not believe "that large-scale nationalization of industry facilities is probable." Nor did it believe that "the USSR will be able to upset the preponderant position of the Western companies or destroy the present overall pattern of the Middle East oil industry. Even a Communist takeover in one of the producing countries would not necessarily result in a refusal to sell the country's oil to the West."

THE LIMITS OF AMERICAN OIL INTELLIGENCE

The Eisenhower administration's refusal to take the majors' dire warnings about the formation of OPEC seriously is significant for a number of reasons. The first is that it points to a fundamental ambivalence in American foreign oil policy. On the one hand, as we have seen, the State Department and NSC had demonstrated a certain willingness to intervene to protect the majors from antitrust prosecution by the Justice Department. And on balance in the Eisenhower years, the administration was sympathetic to the majors' desire to concentrate production in the Middle East where production and transport costs were lowest. But as we have also seen, the Eisenhower administration, and Eisenhower in particular, had a certain sympathy for Robert Anderson and the plight of domestic American oil and gas producers threatened by the majors' low-cost Middle Eastern production. The official American response to the formation of OPEC conveyed this sense of ambivalence. The United States was sympathetic to the majors, but only to a degree.

The limits of Washington's sympathy for the oil majors, apparent in Eisenhower administration's nonchalant response to the emergence of OPEC, became increasingly clear over the course of the Democratic presidential administrations of the 1960s. Although it was no more than coincidence that OPEC was formed just one month after the Democratic Party selected Lyndon Johnson for its vice presidential nominee in the 1960 election, both developments were reflective of a seismic, if still subterranean, shift in the global balance of power among major, independent, and domestic oil firms. The majors were a declining force, while the independents and domestics were rising. And nothing illustrated the rise of domestic American oil and gas, in particular, as dramatically as the ascendance of Lyndon Johnson. As biographer Robert Caro explains, Johnson was the very "embodiment" of the "new economic forces"—the oil, gas, and defense interests—"that surged out of the Southwest in the middle of the twentieth century [to exert] immense influence [over] America's politics, its governmental institutions, [and] its foreign and domestic policies."[79] Johnson had been a competitor to John F. Kennedy for the Democratic nomination in 1960, and would have much preferred to win the office outright, but though he did not win the nomination in 1960, he would soon find himself just a heartbeat away.

Another point of significance regarding the National Intelligence Estimate, specifically regarding its final conclusion about the threat of a Communist takeover in an oil-producing country, merits special emphasis. The notion that a Communist takeover in Iraq would be economically insignificant stands in stark contrast to much received wisdom regarding American foreign policy in the Middle East during the Cold War. While American foreign policy was largely predicated on the notion that it was necessary to take extraordinary, sometimes covert, action to "ensure the flow of oil to the West," the NIE, when forced by circumstance to confront the possibility, acknowledged there was no supply threat. The danger was entirely imagined.

In the late 1940s, the companies had promoted the "decisive weapon" theory of oil.[80] According to that strategic concept, the fate of the Free World rested on the control of oil. If the Soviets gained that control, they would be able to deny oil shipments to the West, and perhaps the sky itself would fall. But as we have seen, the Soviet Union in the 1950s was far more interested in selling oil to the capitalist West than in restricting oil sales to the capitalist West. Clearly, the oil majors and their advocates had exaggerated the Soviet threat so as to advance their own economic interests. And clearly, they had exaggerated their own necessity in delivering those oil supplies to the capitalist West. But just because the oil companies were lying did not make them wrong.

The oil companies excelled at one thing: making money hand over fist. They understood their business interests far better than the Eisenhower administration did. The oil companies had very good reason to fear OPEC. The Eisenhower administration, blinded by the arrogance of covert action, overlooked the threat of OPEC entirely. Eisenhower believed he could throw a nickel at Saudi Arabia or Iran, and the interests of Western oil companies in the region would be secure. But in coming to this conclusion, he underestimated Qasim and the larger cause of resources sovereignty that Qasim led. Contrary to his frequent portrayal as a kind of erratic "madman," Qasim skillfully navigated the shoals of Iraqi domestic politics and harnessed the international winds of change in the 1950s to carry through broadly shared national objectives. These winds of change blew from several directions. From the south, a rising generation of nationalist oil experts arose to challenge the oil companies' monopoly on technical knowledge. From both the (Soviet) east and the (Euro-American) west, new commercial competitors emerged to challenge the oil companies' near monopoly on oil global production and marketing.

Policymakers in the Eisenhower administration had difficulty reading the direction of the political winds blowing across the Middle East. They did not recognize that Qasim was at the forefront of a global movement to decolonize the world economy. The Kennedy administration that took office in January 1961 shared this blindness, but would soon be in for a political education.

Chapter 4
THE OVERTHROW OF QASIM

IF QASIM'S MOVES AGAINST THE COMMUNISTS IN 1960 WERE intended to open space for him to mount a challenge to the IPC, then the formation of OPEC was an important development in that process. American policymakers, first in the Eisenhower administration and then in the Kennedy administration that followed, were slow to recognize the import of this development. The balance of supply and demand in the world oil market was so much more favorable to consuming nations than producing nations that American policymakers did not believe that Iraq, or any other producing state, would be in a position to threaten the interests of the major multinationals for some time to come. This sense of security with regard to oil issues was part of a broader feeling of confidence about America's role and position in the world in this period. In many ways, the incoming administration of John F. Kennedy embodied this sense of confidence and optimism.

Central to the ethos of the Kennedy administration was the idea that the United States had achieved "the end of ideology"—in the sense of having arrived at the best conceivable form of organizing a government and society.[1] There was no longer any need to debate how a government *should* be organized or the purposes to which it *should* be committed. As the United States entered the 1960s, there was a nearly all-pervasive sense among policymakers that the horrors of Fascism and Communism were self-evident, and nothing more was required than to find the best systems administrators to implement that liberal democratic consensus both at home and around the world.

The Kennedy administration's determination to find "the best and the brightest" administrators and technicians to implement a global modernizing agenda brought a new set of advisers to the fore of American policymaking. In Iraq and the broader Middle East, these were the so-called "Arabists"—area experts mainly, though not exclusively, in the State Department who viewed events in the region through the lens of economic development rather than one of Cold War bipolarity. From the Arabist standpoint, the principal threat to American interests in the region did not stem from Communist aggression or subversion but rather from the lingering effects of colonialism. From this standpoint, the Soviet Union and its local Communist allies did not cause political instability but rather exploited legitimate grievances rooted in the vastly unequal distribution of wealth in postcolonial societies. To help those societies resist the appeal of Communism, the United States needed to help modernize the economies of those societies so that they might better redress popular grievances.

Three of the most significant Arabists shaping US-Iraqi relations in the Kennedy years were William Polk, William Lakeland, and James Akins. All three were State Department officials who advocated modernizing reforms in the Arab world. This modernizing reform went so far as to envision the Iraqi state taking a greater role in managing Iraqi oil resources and distributing the benefits of oil production more widely throughout Iraqi society. Responding to his own domestic political context, but perhaps also sensing this more flexible approach to oil, Qasim, in December 1961, promulgated the most significant oil law in the region since Mossadegh's 1951 nationalization of the Iranian oil industry. Law 80, as it was known, nationalized 99.5 percent of the IPC's concessionary area.

In promulgating such a radical act, Qasim may have overestimated the Kennedy administration's willingness to countenance reform to the regional oil order. As we will see, the oil law crossed a kind of redline in the minds of the Kennedy administration faction that adhered to traditional Cold War views. These hardliners were led by Robert Komer, an influential member of the National Security Council who was able to work behind the scenes to convince his colleagues in government that Qasim's oil law represented a dangerous flirtation with Communism. In response to what Komer presented as a clear and present danger to the security of the world's energy supply, the Kennedy administration, by the middle of 1962, committed to a policy of bringing about regime change in Iraq through covert action.

THE NEW DEAL REFRACTED THROUGH THE LENS OF MCCARTHYISM

As he left office, Eisenhower appeared satisfied with his record in the Middle East. Employing Allen Dulles's "ring of invisibility," he had removed Mossadegh from office and placed the shah firmly in power in Iran. His efforts to resolve the Arab-Israel conflict had come to naught and had indeed contributed to destabilizing US relations with Nasser, culminating in the 1956 Suez War. But after taking US-Egyptian relations to the brink in 1957–58, Eisenhower had succeeded in establishing a modus vivendi with Nasser and using that relationship (in his mind at least) to check Iraq's drift toward the Soviet orbit. As he left office, he felt American oil interests in the region were more than secure.

Elsewhere in the world the prognosis was less rosy. In Vietnam, the CIA drew a page from the Mossadegh playbook to install Ngo Dinh Diem in 1955, but by the time Eisenhower left office, Diem's regime was threatened by a Communist insurgency, as was the US-backed regime in neighboring Laos. Closer to American shores, Fidel Castro's nationalist *Movimiento 26 de Julio* had ousted the US-backed dictatorship of Fulgencio Batista in Cuba in 1959. As Eisenhower presented his farewell address warning against the "unwarranted influence of the Military-Industrial Complex," Allen Dulles's CIA was hard at work on a plan to topple Castro and restore the *ancien régime* in Cuba. These smoldering brushfires would soon grow into massive infernos that would consume much of the presidency of Eisenhower's young successor, John F. Kennedy.

But alas, there was no crystal ball in Camelot. Surveying a world in a state of high flux, John F. Kennedy entered the White House in January 1961 determined to better respond to nationalist movements in the Third World. In his effort to distinguish himself from his elder predecessor, Kennedy, on the campaign trail, argued that Eisenhower lacked the vigor and imagination to engage meaningfully with what were then known as "developing nations." Just as Republicans had lambasted Truman for "losing China" to the Communists, so too did Kennedy, during the 1960 presidential campaign, criticize Eisenhower and the Republicans for "losing Cuba."[2] In place of

Eisenhower's complacency and Eurocentric focus, Kennedy resolved to win the "hearts and minds" of nations emerging from more than a century of colonial rule. The young president not only brought renewed focus to the problems of political and economic development in the Third World but also assembled a brain trust of advisers, reared in the crucible of the New Deal on the doctrines of Keynesian macroeconomic theory, who were to implement his modernizing vision for the world.[3] Drawing on the tools of centralized economic planning and business regulation, the Kennedy administration believed it was well positioned to guide "traditional societies" through the wrenching process of "modernization."

As a presidential candidate, Kennedy called for a more "action-oriented" foreign policy, and took special aim at the "pinstriped diplomats" in Eisenhower's "ponderous" State Department.[4] As he took office, Kennedy overhauled the national security bureaucracy and concentrated power in the office of the national security advisor.[5] For that all-important post, he selected McGeorge Bundy, the dean of the Faculty of Arts and Sciences at Harvard and widely regarded as a "boy genius." Bundy's deputy was Walt Whitman Rostow, a professor of economic history at MIT. Rostow was best known for his 1960 publication, *The Stages of Economic Growth: A Non-Communist Manifesto*, a virtual how-to guide for preempting Communist revolution in the Third World.

Bundy and Rostow took a special interest in the analyses of Robert Komer. In subsequent years, Komer would become known as "Blowtorch Bob"—the chief architect of the Lyndon Johnson administration's counterinsurgency strategy in Vietnam.[6] But Komer's tenure in Vietnam (1965–67) represented the culmination of a long career in the intelligence profession. After graduating with an MBA from Harvard in 1947, Komer joined the CIA as an analyst specializing in the Middle East and South Asia.[7] As a CIA analyst, Komer advocated closer ties with Nasser. Even after Nasser's 1955 Czech-Soviet arms deal, it was Komer who prevailed on Allen Dulles to see that it was still possible to "do business with Nasser." Allen Dulles agreed with this line of analysis, but ultimately, John Foster Dulles "peed on it," in Komer's words.[8] Komer then joined the ranks of aggrieved Arabists disillusioned with Foster Dulles and the Eisenhower Doctrine. However, with the demise of Foster Dulles and the abandonment of the Eisenhower Doctrine, Komer rose to prominence as the "CIA's representative to Eisenhower's NSC."[9]

With the election of Kennedy, and the ascendance of Bundy, Komer became the key architect of the US effort to promote Nasser's regional influence. Komer's call for better relations with Nasser was supported intellectually by the analyses of William Polk, a leading historian of the Middle East at Harvard, who joined the new administration as a member of the State Department's Policy Planning Council. As an academic, Polk had developed a theory of top-down, military-led authoritarian modernization based on the career of Mehmet Ali Pasha, a nineteenth-century Ottoman military governor of Egypt.[10] As a member of the State Department, Polk provided Komer, Rostow, and Bundy with a steady stream of analyses that sought to reconcile Rostow's general theory of non-Communist modernization with the regional particularities of an Arab Middle East in which Nasser was cast as a latter-day Mehmet Ali.[11] The influence of Polk and Komer was clearly felt in a June 1961 National Intelligence Estimate that described Nasser as "the leading exponent of Arab reformism" and lauded "his demonstrated readiness to assume leadership in defending Arab nationalism against Communism. Despite his dependence on the Bloc, he is not neutral in the conflict between Arab nationalism and Communism."[12]

The Kennedy administration's faith in Nasser appeared vindicated by Egypt's role in resolving a crisis over the political status of Kuwait that emerged at the end of June 1961. The crisis began on June 25, when the British granted Kuwait formal independence. Kuwait had been a British protectorate since 1899. The British protectorate in Kuwait denied Iraq access to the deepwater Port of Shuwaikh and left Iraq with just thirty-six miles of Persian Gulf coastline. Even Hashemite leaders chafed at this situation and claimed that Kuwait was in fact an integral part of the Iraqi province of Basra. Qasim responded to the Britain's 1961 declaration of Kuwait independence by reviving Iraqi territorial claims.[13]

The Kennedy administration was initially inclined to avoid any involvement in the situation. It preferred instead to preserve the "recent favorable trend" in US-Iraqi relations and to allow "political forces among the Arabs" to resolve the issue.[14] The British, however, reacted quite strongly to the Iraqi provocation. British prime minister Harold Macmillan mobilized a force of five thousand Royal Marines to land in Kuwait to preempt any Iraqi attack, and appealed to the US for political, military, and logistical support.[15] The Kennedy administration offered very reluctant support to the British, deploying only a token naval force to the region. But when British intelligence reports of Iraqi armored units massing near the Kuwaiti border proved false, the Kennedy administration concluded that the British had overreacted and undermined broader Western interests in the region.[16]

Ultimately, Egypt joined Saudi Arabia in deploying an Arab League force to Kuwait to defend against the threat of Iraqi aggression. With the arrival of Arab troops, the British withdrew. But the quickness with which the British dispatched their gunboats only reinforced the worst stereotypes of Britain's outmoded colonial approach to dealing with the Middle East. Moreover, the successful "Arab solution to an Arab problem" further confirmed for the Kennedy administration that the US no longer needed to rely on the British to provide military protection for the region, and that the strategy of constructive engagement with Arab nationalism provided a much sounder basis for US policy in the Persian Gulf.[17]

LAW 80: QASIM'S CONFRONTATION WITH THE COMPANIES

The Kuwait crisis unfolded against the backdrop of unresolved Iraq-IPC negotiations, and the British saw the two as connected. By the summer of 1961, Qasim had taken up, in a serious way, another of Oil Minister Muhammad Salman's original 1957 recommendations: relinquishment. According to the IPC's original 1925 concession agreement, the companies held exclusive rights to extract and export all oil within Iraq's sovereign boundaries. However, the IPC was only actively producing oil from three fields: Kirkuk and 'Ayn Zalah in the north and Zubair in the south (see map 2). Under pressure from producing countries, the major companies in the region had begun to relinquish control of undeveloped concessionary areas. But not so in Iraq.

In his effort to force the companies to enter the twentieth century, Qasim demanded the immediate relinquishment of 75–90 percent of the IPC concessionary area so that those areas could be developed by a soon-to-be-formed national oil company. British economic advisers believed that Qasim had contrived the entire crisis over Kuwait as a preparatory move in an effort to nationalize the IPC. The Iranian nationalization had failed because the majors were able to boycott nationalized Iranian oil by increasing production elsewhere in the region—mainly Kuwait, which had substantial "spare capacity" (the ability to immediately increase production without investing in new infrastructure). But if Qasim took the Kuwait piece off the board, he would have a free hand in nationalizing Iraqi production without fear of an embargo offset by Kuwait's spare capacity. For the British, the entire episode underlined the "dangers of underestimating Kassem's shrewdness and single-mindedness."[18]

Qasim's willingness to press his case against the companies increased dramatically after Syrian Ba'thists broke with Nasser and withdrew Syria from the UAR in September 1961. There was always more tension between Nasser and the Syrian Ba'th than appeared on the surface.[19] The Ba'th had only invited the union with Egypt as a means of checking the perceived advance of the Syrian Communist Party. As he had in Egypt, Nasser, upon coming to power in Syria, had dissolved all parties—including both the Ba'th and the Communists. The Ba'th had been willing to dissolve their own party just to defeat the Communists. But once Nasser had effectively liquidated Communist influence in Syria, the Ba'th began to chafe under Egyptian domination and joined with the similarly disposed Syrian business class in overthrowing the UAR.

Given the apparent demise of Nasserist pan-Arabism in the region, Qasim released 'Abd al-Salam 'Arif, Rashid 'Ali, and other prominent nationalists from jail in October 1961.[20] Qasim's willingness to show mercy to his enemies distinguished him in Iraqi history. But it was also his undoing. If Qasim made one major mistake, it was to believe that the Ba'th, and other Pan-Arabist groupings, were sincere in their commitment to Arab socialism—however vaguely that might have been defined. By late 1961, Qasim believed that it would be possible to cobble together a broad national coalition united by a shared interest in nationalizing the IPC. Why hang Rashid 'Ali and 'Abd al-Salam 'Arif when you could join with them in a grand patriotic cause? But Qasim's shortcoming, admirable as it may have been, was to generalize about the behavior of others based on his own system of moral values. And Qasim, above all else, valued the welfare of the Iraqi people—and particularly the lower classes. An Iraqi of Sunni, Shi'i, Arab, and Kurdish heritage, Qasim cared little for the ethnic, religious, and sectarian categories that Western powers sought to impose on his country.[21] He lived an aesthetic life, sleeping on a cot in the Ministry of Defense and donated the entirely of his government salary to the less fortunate. While the princes of Saudi Arabia and Iran were shoveling away the riches of the nation in their own private accounts, Qasim died penniless.

This system of moral values made Qasim a unique figure in the oil politics of the region. And it drove him in his relations with oil companies as he pressed them to adhere to the sanctity of contracts by paying their fair share of taxes, and negotiating in good faith over the issue of relinquishment. The oil companies, for their part, believed themselves to occupy the commanding heights of the world economy and were in no mood to entertain the demands of this son of a peasant dressed up as a general officer and playing president of a sovereign republic. When the companies rebuffed his demands, he released transcripts of the negotiations in the Iraqi press in serialized form. When the companies proved immune to public shaming, Qasim broke off negotiations altogether. On October 11, he indicated that Iraq was no longer participating in IPC's parlor games and would instead exercise its sovereign right to unilaterally legislate changes to the IPC concession.[22] As Qasim drew this line in the sand, Abdullah Tariki's legal adviser, Frank Hendryx, came to Iraq's defense, arguing in the British press that the IPC concession was a relic of the colonial era and needed to be restructured for a postcolonial age.[23]

While the companies regarded the breakdown of Iraq-IPC negotiations, and Iraq's threats to nationalize, as worrying, the Kennedy administration still had not figured out what was going on. In late November, the State Department's division of Intelligence and Research conducted a study of the breakdown of the Iraqi-IPC oil negotiations and found that the lessons of Mohammad Mossadegh's nationalization of the Iranian oil industry ten years earlier were still too obvious for Qasim to overlook.[24] Moreover, the prevailing global supply glut remained in place and left Iraq in a particularly weak negotiating position. Increased production elsewhere in the Gulf could easily offset any interruption in Iraqi supply. At the same time, oil revenues accounted for more than half of all government revenue in Iraq. From the State Department's standpoint, any disruption of IPC operations could only result in the rapid "collapse of Qasim's government."[25]

Despite the State Department's confidence that Qasim would be careful to avoid a direct confrontation with the companies, Qasim did just that in the closing days of 1961. On December 11, he issued Public Law 80—a landmark decree that would permanently alter the oil politics of the region. The eleven-page law nullified the existing concession, which it regarded as a legally invalid agreement among unequal parties, and divided the IPC's concessionary area into two categories. The first category consisted of the forty-seven "defined districts," or individual oil extraction "points" to which the companies retained access rights. The second category consisted of all other lands, which reverted to Iraqi state control. But always merciful to his enemies, Qasim included a very generous provision in his oil law. Under Article III, the IPC could engage in free market competition with other international companies to acquire leases to access these newly reclaimed fields, which could then be jointly worked with a soon-to-be-established National Oil Company.[26] From the companies' standpoint, Qasim appeared dangerously close to dismantling the IPC's colonial monopoly and establishing a free market in Iraqi oil.

American officials were divided in their responses to Law 80. John Jernegan, the US ambassador to Iraq, saw nothing particularly objectionable in the new law. The IPC concession was generally regarded as the most unequal of all of the existing concessions in the region, and the ambassador believed it was more or less inevitable that the agreement would have to be revised. Jernegan was satisfied that Law 80 allowed the IPC to continue operation in "all the areas from which they are already producing" and expressed his hope that the IPC would respond with restraint. From the standpoint of the American ambassador, the IPC should be "prepared to accept the de facto existing situation," as there was no clear basis for any "official protest against the law."[27] As the ambassador understood it, the United States had "long since accepted the principle that governments may expropriate private property provided prompt and adequate compensation is paid. In this case, it would seem extremely difficult to formulate claims for compensation, since quantity and value of oil in ground could not be proven."[28]

While Jernegan's response to Law 80 was rather subdued, Robert Komer, whose star in Washington was rising rapidly, became much more exercised. He fumed at the State Department's traditional "hands-off" approach to Iraq and began pushing for regime change.[29] In response to Komer's call for intervention, Phillips Talbot, assistant secretary of state for Near Eastern Affairs, warned of "our lack of effective means of achieving a reversal in Iraqi policy," and argued that the US "must resist firmly all efforts to force us to undertake intervention of any type in the internal affairs of Iraq unless and until it is clear that the domestic communists stand to gain control of Iraq in absence of such intervention."[30] Talbot further warned that "to intervene ineffectively in Iraq would only serve to increase the likelihood of a situation we do not want: a communist takeover." Talbot admitted, "We cannot guarantee that Prime Minister Qassim will not prove to be another Castro," but suggested that the US should not attempt any Bay of Pigs–type action.

Komer, however, would not be deterred by the State Department's caution. In his characteristic "blowtorch" style, he waged the bureaucratic equivalent of a scorched earth campaign against the State Department. While he had once "disagreed with the conventional wisdom that the Middle East was vital to U.S. interests," and noted that "only 3 percent of the oil that the United States consumed came from the region," he now emphasized economic arguments in support of an interventionist policy.[31] In his December 29 memo to Bundy, he issued a dire warning: "If he [Qasim] can add Kuwait production (largest in ME) to that of IPC, he'll have stranglehold on ME oil." He noted that "we own 23.75% of IPC," and criticized "our tendency [to] sit back and regard IPC, Kuwait and even Iraq as UK baby." Rather than allowing the British to take the lead, he advised that the US make preparations to support a "nationalist coup [that] ... might occur at anytime."[32]

DEBATING REGIME CHANGE

In support of his campaign for regime change in Iraq, Komer pressed Bundy to secure presidential approval to get Iraq contingency planning "moving."[33] Bundy then passed the following note to the president at his winter residence in Palm Beach, Florida:

> Jernegan's message seems persuasive to Komer and me, and with your approval I would like to press State Dept for action in this direction, using your interest as a stick. I would add that Dept should of course lay out a plan for action in cooperation with British if possible, but our own interests, oil and other, are very directly involved.[34]

The State Department's Office of the Historian is silent on the president's response to Bundy's appeal. This silence is telling. Indeed the president was expert at not being present when critical regime-change decisions were being made.[35] As former OSS information agent, Harvard historian, and Kennedy propagandist Arthur Schlesinger, Jr., put it in a secret memo to the president (regarding Cuba) in April 1961:

> The character and repute of President Kennedy constitutes one of our greatest national resources. Nothing should be done to jeopardize this invaluable asset. When lies must be told, they should be told by subordinate officials. At no point should the President be asked to lend himself to the cover operation. For this reason, there seems to [be] merit in Secretary [of State Dean] Rusk's suggestion that someone other than the President make the final decision and do so in his absence—someone whose head can later be placed on the block if things go terribly wrong.[36]

Following Schlesinger's wise counsel, the archive is silent on the president's response to Komer's call for regime change. But diplomatic history, like jazz, is often about the notes that are not played. In the pregnancy of the president's silence we can discern Komer wielding presidential interest "as a stick" to beat the State Department into submission. And indeed, in the days and weeks that followed, Komer effectively melded the bureaucracy to this will.

Komer's influence was clearly felt in a January 1962 NIE assessing "the outlook for Iraq over the next year or so." The document found that "plotting is endemic in military circles and assassination is an ever-present possibility," but could not "identify any particular individuals or groups likely to bring off a successful coup."[37] While that NIE could not identify local agents likely to "bring off a successful coup," the CIA, over the course of 1962, stepped up its surveillance of Iraq and took an increased interest in Iraqi opposition groups.

In March, William Lakeland, who had recently left the NEA in Washington to serve as first secretary of the embassy in Baghdad, reported meeting with several figures from the old Hashemite regime seeking support for a pro-Western coup.[38] Lakeland was decidedly cool toward the proposal. He warned against tying American fortunes to the Hashemites and discounted the likelihood of a successful "conservative-oriented coup."

> Even if such an operation would be successfully carried out, however, it is highly questionable whether the resulting situation would be a genuine improvement from the Western point of view. We are seriously concerned about the continuing poisoning of Iraqi (and other Afro-Asian) minds which appears to be taking place and believe that this problem deserves more

serious and continuing attention in the over-all conduct of our foreign affairs. As far as Iraq is concerned, however, we are convinced the problem is essentially a long and not short-term one. Changing the structure of government, replacing one despotism with another, is hardly going to solve the problems of education and development, political responsibility and social cohesiveness which have plagued Iraq throughout its life as a modern state and which will undoubtedly be with it for decades to come. *For the West to take on any form of direct or indirect responsibility for these continuing and intractable problems without reasonable assurances of being able to devote the necessary resources to see the job through would in our opinion be irresponsible and dangerous.*[39]

Lakeland's report was likely read in at least two different ways. Officials in Washington who opposed covert intervention could focus on his warning against assuming "direct or indirect responsibility" for an operation that would, at best, have a low probability of success. Officials inclined toward regime change, on the other hand, could focus on his call to "devote the necessary resources to see the job through." It was this second interpretation that meshed more neatly with the prevailing zeitgeist in Washington. Indeed, it was essentially identical to a point that Kennedy made to Bundy shortly after the Bay of Pigs debacle in Cuba:

The British could have a nervous breakdown in the wake of Suez, the French over Algeria. They each represent six to seven percent of the free world's power—and we could cover for them. But we can't afford a nervous breakdown. We're forty percent, and there's no one to cover for us. We'd better get on with the job.[40]

The "job" to which the president referred was the assassination of Fidel Castro and the defeat of Communism in Southeast Asia. But the analysis could apply just as well (or just as badly) to the situation in Iraq.

In Iraq, James Critchfield, the CIA's director of covert operations in the region, took a particular interest in the Ba'th. As he recalled many years later:

In 1961 and 1962, we increased our interest in the Ba'ath—not to actively support it—but politically and intellectually, we found the Ba'ath interesting. We found it particularly active in Iraq. Our analysis of the Ba'ath was that it was comparatively moderate at that time, and that the United States could easily adjust to and support its policies. So we watched the Baʿath's long, slow preparation to take control. They planned to do it several times, and postponed it.

We were better informed on the 1963 coup in Baghdad than on any other major event or change of government that took place in the whole region in those years.[41]

Reflective of the CIA's growing interest in the Baʿth was the "contingency planning" carried out during the spring and summer of 1962. In May, the CIA advised that a "pan-Arab nationalist" (i.e., Baʿthist) coup was increasingly likely and that it was time to begin preparing for "early recognition of a new regime." In the event of protracted civil conflict, it found "it might be necessary to give covert support for anti-Communist elements in Iraq."[42] However, this contingency planning continued to elicit resistance from certain members of the State Department. In a June 1962 memorandum to Bundy, State Department analysts acknowledged that Qasim was a source of increasing irritation to the oil companies but insisted that it was "unlikely that Qasim will go so far as to permit control of IPC operations to be transferred from the Western companies to the Soviets or the Red Chinese."[43] The State Department warned against the potential unintended consequences of any effort to "topple Qasim" and insisted, "The answer has to come from within Iraq and the United States cannot hope successfully to manipulate the internal forces at work." In the State Department's view,

> anti-Qasim nationalist forces will become more and more troubled as Qasim pursues his course which results in isolating Iraq progressively from brother Arabs and from the Free World. Eventually, in our opinion, unless the West makes serious mistakes, such internal pressures will be created in Iraq as to force a change. That change is estimated as most likely to produce another strongly nationalistic government, but with a more balanced foreign policy.

For the State Department, the inner logic of Arab politics was on the side of the US, and any American intervention could only prove counterproductive.

The State Department's effort to restrain Komer and the CIA suffered a major setback in June 1962 when Qasim ordered the recall of Ambassador

Jernegan.[44] The immediate catalyst for the recall was the reception of Kuwait's ambassador in Washington, but the move signaled deteriorating US-Iraqi relations and represented a critical opening for Komer.[45] Two days after Jernegan's recall, Komer cited Iraq's "slow but steady swing . . . toward [the] Soviet orbit," and suggested that it was time for a new Iraq policy:

> I wonder if we shouldn't take advantage of Jernegan's return for a thoroughgoing re-appraisal of our Iraq policy. . . . Given US/UK interest in Iraq and its proximity to a floundering Iran, it seems prudent to ask ourselves again whether essentially a "wait and see" policy is still valid. It probably [is] simply because of lack of promising alternatives. But *why not at least review ways in which we might more positively influence the course of events? Would CIA have any ideas*; how about another talk with the British; indeed it might even be worthwhile to solicit UAR views. We certainly want to put ourselves in the best position to (1) react quickly to a change of regime in Iraq; (2) counter an accelerated drift toward the Bloc.[46]

Komer's circumlocution regarding whether or not the CIA might "have any ideas" calls to mind King Henry II's quarrel with a "meddlesome priest."[47] Indeed, Komer's memo represented something of a coup de grâce to the State Department. In the wake of this communication, the cautionary voices emanating from the State Department fell mostly silent. As was the case with Vietnam, its analysts fell in line out of a misguided notion of mitigating damage from within.[48]

THE ANALYTICAL DECONSTRUCTION OF QASIM'S IRAQ

The first step to implementing the policy of regime change in Iraq was the replacement of Jernegan with Roy Melbourne as the new American *chargé d'affaires* in Baghdad—that is, as the highest-ranking diplomatic official in the absence of formal diplomatic relations. Previous to the post in Baghdad, Melbourne's career in the world of intelligence and diplomacy had been extensive. He first entered the Foreign Service in 1937. During WWII he was posted to Istanbul and then Bucharest, where he compiled intelligence reports for the OSS. After the war he was posted to Rome, where he worked as a political officer in the US embassy to influence the outcome of the 1948 Italian general elections. In 1951, he was dispatched to Iran, where he spent the next three years heading the political section of the US embassy. After the overthrow of Mohammad Mossadegh, Melbourne served in various posts in Europe and Washington, including a three-year stint with Komer on the NSC staff. When he arrived in Baghdad in August 1962, he found a "familiar mixture of oil, politics, and the Russians."[49]

As Melbourne prepared to assume his new post in Baghdad, the State Department's Rodger Davies traveled to Iraq to confer with Sir Roger Allen, the British ambassador in Baghdad. The two officials met amidst increasing reports of endemic coup plotting against Qasim, and Davies sought out Allen's views on the Ba'th.[50] Davies was one of the most experienced of the State Department Arabists. After graduating from UC Berkeley with a BA in Economics in 1942, he joined the US Army, where he was recruited into a specialized training program and sent to Princeton for Arabic language training under legendary professor Philip K. Hitti.[51] After completing Arabic language training, Davies was deployed to Saudi Arabia as part of the war effort. After the war, he remained in Saudi Arabia as a vice consul for the State Department. In 1949, he moved to Syria where he served as a political officer in the Damascus embassy until 1951.[52] Davies was therefore present in Syria when the Ba'th was first organized, and he seems to have taken a shine to the party. Davies's CV then went blank for the critical period of the Mossadegh premiership, before he resurfaced in Tripoli, Libya, in 1954, where he remained until moving to Iraq at the height of the Communist ascendance in the summer of 1959. In Iraq, Davies appears to have developed ever-deeper affection for the Ba'th.

However, in his 1962 meeting with Allen, Davies found that lingering, indeed festering, Anglo-American discord over the question of Arab nationalism was as acute as ever. At the end of a dying colonialism and on the verge of a shift to a Labour government, the Conservative government in London clung to power as it clung to its implacable opposition to Nasser and the Ba'th.[53]Davies and his British counterpart met just two days after the Ba'th had called off a planned coup attempt, and Allen expressed Britain's traditional opposition to Arab nationalism, and raised questions about the competency of the Ba'thist conspirators. Allen conceded that although he did not believe it was possible to "do business" with Qasim, he did not see the Ba'th as a viable alternative. Significantly, he "could not *advocate* covert activities to subvert Qasim internally" (emphasis added). On the contrary, Allen explained, there were still "circles in London where [the] feeling persisted that there is no alternative to Qasim in Iraq." Rather than supporting the Ba'th, Allen believed that the matter should be left to the IPC. In Allen's view, the IPC should simply "keep its nerve, depend on Qassim's need for undiminished revenue and do nothing except continue production with [the] hope of riding out [the] situation until [an] eventual 'convulsion' brings about a replacement regime."[54] Davies, however, pressed Allen to think more imaginatively about what the US and the UK could do jointly to "counter pressures against us."[55]

While British support for a Ba'thist coup was less than forthcoming, the State Department appeared pleased with Davies's efforts, promoting him to deputy director of the Office of Near Eastern Affairs the following month.[56] As Davies climbed the State Department bureaucracy, the NSC and CIA moved forward on other tracks. Part of what Komer described as "putting ourselves in the best position to react to a change of regime in Iraq" would certainly entail analyzing both the strength of Qasim's domestic support base as well as the strength of Iraqi opposition groups. In terms of the strength of Qasim's support base, James Akins, second secretary of the US embassy (and perhaps one of what Lakeland described as the "CIA staff in the embassy roughly camouflaged, poorly camouflaged, as being regular embassy political officers"), composed a series of detailed political reports on the strength of Qasim's domestic support base in September and October.[57]

Akins found that Qasim retained a formidable base of support among lower-class Iraqis.[58] Qasim was particularly popular among the urban slum (*sarifa*)-dwellers and rural peasants (*fellahin*). Akins noted that the "basic wage for [urban] workers had quadrupled since the revolution," and that Qasim's literacy and land reform programs were particularly popular among the rural poor. Akins warned that Iraq's lower classes had benefited greatly under Qasim and that these elements of Iraqi society would "certainly oppose anyone who would try to take away the gains they have made."[59] In a subsequent report, Akins described Iraq's sarifa-dwellers as an "instrument of terror in a time of anarchy" and warned of a generalized class war erupting in the event of an attempted coup against Qasim.[60] In Akins's analysis, any effort to overthrow Qasim would have to move quickly to neutralize this rather formidable base of support.[61] Akins found this same class-basis for Qasim's support among the Shi'i. Despite the clerical establishment issuing a series of *fatwas* (religious decrees) forbidding Communism in 1960, Akins found that Shi'i districts were Communist strongholds where support for Qasim was relatively firm.[62] The clear implication of these reports was that in the aftermath of any coup, measures would have to be taken to neutralize these bases of Qasim's support.

At the same time that Melbourne's embassy was analyzing the strength of Qasim's support base, it also took a new interest in Kurdish opposition to Qasim's regime. Qasim had initially, upon coming to power, enjoyed relatively strong support among Iraqi Kurds.[63] Qasim's mother was Kurdish and his policies toward Iraq's Kurdish minority were rather liberal. In July 1958, Qasim promulgated a provisional constitution that guaranteed equal rights for Iraq's Kurdish citizens. Reporting from Iraqi Kurdistan, Lakeland observed in March 1961:

> Kurds in Iraq are hardly worse off than Arabs in comparable circumstances. The Kurdish peasant villager is probably somewhat better off than his Arab contemporary south of him. There are Kurdish officers in Iraq's army, Kurdish Ministers in Iraq's cabinet, Kurdish importers and exporters, Kurdish Directors General, Chiefs of Police and diplomats.[64]

Kurdish representation in Iraqi politics and society stood in stark contrast to the dominant values prevailing in the United States at that moment. While Qasim was attempting to build a broad national movement in which Kurdish citizens were an integral part, the US was plagued by deepening racial strife. At the very moment that Lakeland was commenting on the relative ethnic harmony prevailing in Iraq, African American civil rights leader Robert Williams was forced to resort to armed self-defense in his efforts to integrate North Carolina swimming pools, and American society more generally.[65]

The contrast between Qasim's effort to build a multiethnic republic, and Washington's effort to prevent the same, was an important subtext in the US-Iraqi relationship in the last days of the Qasim era. As the British had before them, it appears that in the fall of 1961, the US may have begun to exploit ethnic, tribal, and sectarian differences in Iraq as part of an effort to undermine Qasim's nationalist movement. Despite the gains described by Lakeland, Kurdish leader Mullah Mustafa Barzani began threatening a rebellion against Qasim's government in the fall of 1961—just as Iraq-IPC negotiations broke down. As the IPC moved in opposition to Qasim, Israeli and Iranian covert assistance began to pour into Iraqi Kurdistan.[66]

As Israeli and Iranian covert assistance made its way into Iraq, Kurdish representatives reached out to the US embassy for the same.[67] Available documentation is limited, but by the summer of 1962 the United States may have begun to respond favorably to these appeals.[68] In August, Turkish authorities arrested two US petty officers stationed in Turkey and charged them with smuggling arms to Iraqi Kurdish rebels.[69] The Turkish arrests were followed closely thereafter by the Iraqi arrest of two (unnamed) US Army attachés stationed in Iraq, who were charged with acting as intermediaries between a former assistant army attaché in Iraq, Lt. Col. Harry Hall, and Iraqi Kurds.[70] Qasim seized on these arrests as "proof" of Western meddling in Iraq. He accused Barzani of being an IPC "stooge," and accused the US and Britain of being complicit in the revolt.

While a complete picture of the US response to the outbreak of the Kurdish War is unavailable, it is clear that in the fall of 1962 high-profile Americans began advocating on behalf of Iraqi Kurdish rebels—including *New York Times* reporter Dana Adams Schmidt. In September, Schmidt approached the US embassy in Beirut and appealed for US support for the Kurdish insurgency.[71] Schmidt warned that the failure to support the insurgency would drive Iraqi Kurds to seek assistance from the Soviets. Whereas if the US supported the insurgency, Barzani had assured Schmidt that he would purge the Kurdish movement of Communists, cooperate with "conservative Arab Iraqi elements[,] and bring Iraq back into Baghdad Pact." Schmidt then entered Iraqi Kurdistan where he spent a month as Barzani's honored guest—and publicist.[72] Schmidt filed a series of *New York Times* articles from Kurdistan that advocated for the cause of Kurdish separatism.[73]

Available documentation does not prove conclusively that the United States provided covert assistance to the Kurds in the fall of 1962, but the documents that have been declassified are certainly suggestive—especially in light of the general US policy orientation toward Iraq during this period. Indeed, by the end of 1962, the US was increasingly well-prepared for a change of government in Baghdad. However, one final piece of planning would be required to support a successful overthrow of Qasim: securing oil company support for the project. This final piece of planning would prove very difficult.[74]

AMERICAN FEUDALISM: KENNEDYS AGAINST THE ROCKEFELLERS

Unlike Lyndon Johnson, John Kennedy did not have organic roots in the oil and gas industry of the Great American West—indeed the entirety of Kennedy's "New Frontier" political persona was invented to counteract his Boston Brahmin public image.[75] But Kennedy's antipathy for the oil majors was no less intense. Whereas Johnson's opposition to the majors was rooted in crass material self-interest, Kennedy's was rooted in family honor.

According to Kennedy speechwriter Richard Goodwin, the president's brother Bobby would, in the fall of 1965, travel to Peru as part of an effort to generate international support for a future presidential run. On that trip, the younger Kennedy brother met with a group of artists, writers, and journalists. In their meeting, the Peruvians complained about US interference in their dispute with the IPC—the International Petroleum Company of Peru—a subsidiary of Exxon. To this Bobby declared, "Well, if it's so important to you why don't you just nationalize the damn oil company?" To this the Peruvians responded that Senator David Rockefeller, grandson of the Standard Oil founder, had just been in the country to warn them that "if anyone acted against International Petroleum," US development aid would be immediately suspended. To this Kennedy responded, "Oh come on, David Rockefeller isn't the government. We Kennedys eat Rockefellers for breakfast."[76]

It would be perilous to accept the words of a Kennedy speechwriter at face value. But the Goodwin vignette about Kennedys eating Rockefellers for breakfast does indicate how the Kennedys wanted to be remembered, and it does accurately convey the spirit of the Kennedy administration's attitude in its dealing with the majors in the period leading up to Qasim's overthrow. The State Department first began feeling out the oil companies about the possibility of supporting a Ba'thist coup in Iraq at the end of October 1962. In a meeting with William Lindenmuth, a Mobil executive who oversaw US interests in the IPC consortium, the State Department's Robert Strong sought to persuade Lindenmuth that the IPC should be prepared to "to form a new, realistic sort of partnership with [a] nationalist Iraq on the assumption that there will be a 'slow transfer of ownership from the investing company to a local business entity.'"[77] However, the entire notion of a "slow transfer of ownership" was antithetical to IPC interests. Exxon was by far the most recalcitrant of the partners in this regard, but Melbourne chose to portray BP as the real villain. Drawing on his experience in Iran, Melbourne complained that it was, after all, BP

> which [had] refused to see the handwriting on the wall in Iran.... While in Iran the company argued that there were merely commercial interests [involved] in which the American government should not directly concern itself, the fact remains that after [BP] had created an impossible situation, we had to pick up the pieces. I would hate to see a repetition of this here on any comparable scale, if our strategic interests were affected, as they could be in a failure of IPC policy.[78]

Melbourne's comments are deeply revealing in that they demonstrate the extent to which there was a disjuncture between the Kennedy administration's modernizing vision for the Middle East and the IPC's sense of self-interest.

The State Department's effort to elicit greater accommodation for Arab nationalism on the part of the major companies was made infinitely more difficult by regional developments over the course of the fall of 1962. In September of that year, Yemeni nationalists launched a coup against that country's insufficiently radical Arab nationalist monarchy. The coup in Yemen quickly gave way to a civil war that pitted Egyptian-backed nationalists against Saudi-backed royalists. As the Yemeni conflict intensified, American oil companies expressed concern that the revolution in Yemen would spread to Saudi Arabia and Kuwait.

Revolution in Yemen was particularly threatening, because the Free Princes reform movement in Saudi Arabia had been under way for some time.[79] It was this reformist movement that brought Abdullah Tariki into the cabinet as Saudi Arabia's first minister of petroleum and minerals in 1961 (see chapter 3). But now, in the fall of 1962, with revolution knocking on Saudi Arabia's door, the companies leaned heavily on King Saud's brother and rival, Crown Prince Faysal, to seize power and bring an end to the reformist trend in Saudi politics.[80] In accordance with this pressure, Faysal executed a palace coup against his brother in October (although the formal title of king would not be conferred until 1964). As Faysal took power, he sent forces into Yemen and exiled Tariki to Beirut.[81]

Despite the depth of the oil companies' antipathy for Nasser, and their fear that his revolution could spread to Saudi Arabia, Robert Komer, whose influence within the Kennedy White House continued to grow, forged ahead with the policy of support for Egypt. Komer, with the support of Polk, defended Egypt's role in Yemen using the language of modernization. Just as the United States was employing the concept of "Strategic Hamlets" to bring modernity to Vietnam, so too was Egypt attempting to use military force to modernize the "most backward part of the Arab world."[82] Armed with such arguments, Komer pushed through a program of food aid to Egypt and called for prompt recognition of the new republican regime in Yemen—much to the consternation of Crown Prince Faysal, Aramco, and the United Kingdom.[83] To mollify such concerns, Komer recommended "playing both sides against the middle" by adopting a policy of "overt non-intervention to please Nasser" and a policy of "very careful covert aid to the other side" to please Faysal.[84]

In a further effort to coordinate US policy with the oil companies, the State Department called a meeting with the heads of the five majors.[85] In the meeting, Phillips Talbot and George McGhee of the State Department sought to explain the Kennedy administration's policy objectives in the region. They defended US aid to Egypt and the recognition of the new regime in Yemen and they emphasized the necessity of "introducing political change through evolutionary means so as to avoid revolution." The oil companies were, however, far from convinced. One questioned if there was any "limit to which the United States was willing to go in support of Nasser." Another charged that the US was "giving $700 million in food aid to [an Egyptian] 'police state'," while a third suggested the entire enterprise of modernizing the Middle East was dubious in value and that the US should rather be focused on supporting a Saudi regime that closely aligned with US interests in the region.

The conversation between the State Department and the majors became so bitter that George McGhee threatened to withdraw entirely US support from the Saudi royal family:

> Our interests in this matter are ... similar to those of the oil companies. We support the present Saudi regime but we must consider the possibilities should it disappear. There will always be some group wanting to sell Saudi oil to a foreign company with markets. We would still wish to maintain good relations with any successor regime and we must always look beyond the present.

The extent to which the State Department was willing to go to accommodate Arab nationalism and envision a future beyond Faysal was deeply worrying to the oil companies. At the end of January, Kermit "Kim" Roosevelt, the former CIA station chief in Beirut, and now the Washington representative for Gulf Oil, called upon the State Department to express his frustration with US policy.[86] As far as Roosevelt was concerned, the Kennedy administration's effort to woo Nasser (and by extension the Ba'th) was reckless and foolhardy. Roosevelt argued that there was "no real possibility of working with Nasser because our interests and his are simply incompatible." Roosevelt cited his own "long conversations with Nasser," in which he had "gotten Nasser to admit as much." Rather than cultivating Nasser's regional influence, Roosevelt pressed again for US support for Faysal's war in Yemen.

"REDSKINS BIT THE DUST"

Efforts to harmonize the interests of business and government remained unresolved as the Ba'th made final preparations to launch its coup. But even without oil company buy-in, the Kennedy administration continued to look favorably upon the Ba'th's drive for power.[87] In mid-December, the embassy informed the State Department that "Qasim would be overthrown by a Baathi coup within a week."[88] The embassy reiterated Akins's earlier warning that the "sarifa dwellers could be expected [to] try [to] plunder residential areas until order [is] restored" and advised that the embassy officers "procure arms . . . for [the] protection of house and family when the revolt comes."[89] The December plot was ultimately postponed, but US-Iraqi tensions continued to mount. On the last day of January, Qasim held a long press conference in which he claimed that his government had discovered a massive new oilfield in an (unidentified) part of Iraq reclaimed under Law 80. He claimed that the field was worth 17 million Iraqi dinars and that he would soon announce the establishment of a new National Petroleum Company to develop the field.[90]

As Qasim looked to the future, he described "American imperialism" as the biggest obstacle to the economic development of his country:

> You must have noted in recent days the number of imperialist networks operating in our country. They are operated by American elements and backed by American funds. But, thanks to God Almighty, we were able to contain these elements and remove them to evil places which suit evil persons like them.

He went on to claim that he possessed a dossier containing "important secrets about their oppressions in Baghdad, Iraq, and in the neighborhood of Iraq." These were the "secrets of the Baghdad Pact. They are the secrets of the imperialists in the Middle East, the methods they use to sow discord, and the targets they aim at."

According to Qasim, the Americans were motivated by something deeper than mere oil interests. Yes, they wanted to control the oil, but ultimately, it was arrogance and racism that best explained American behavior:

> I do not wish to speak about the nuclear or hydrogen bombs which America possesses. I do not wish to speak either about its arrogant suppression of freedom, the segregation existing in America, and its destruction and assimilation of the various nationalities. The Arabs, Afghans, Germans, and Indians go to America and become assimilated, forgetting their language. After one generation, they become 100 per cent American. Despite this, this oppressive State constantly hoists the flag of shamelessness by attacking our Republic and accusing it of trying to assimilate the various nationalities in it.

This insight is key to understanding what happened next. By calling out the "destruction and assimilation of various nationalities" in the US, Qasim drew a sharp contrast with what he was attempting to do in Iraq. Drawing on 'Abd al-Fattah Ibrahim's philosophy of multicultural populism, Qasim was attempting to construct a new Iraq, and a new conception of Iraqi national identity, in which the multitude of Iraqi cultural traditions would be given political representation.

The entire proposition of multicultural philosophy posed an existential threat to the organizing principle of the American state. American legal traditions had been very explicit in defining the racial basis of US citizenship.[91] And the US Constitutional order had, for nearly two hundred years, proven very resilient in defending that racial conception of citizenship.[92] Even in the face of powerful and determined social movements, the American legal system was simply unwilling to entertain the notion of equal protection under the law without respect to color. Although it is unlikely that he was aware of the specifics, Qasim called out the "arrogant suppression of freedom, the segregation existing in America," not two weeks after Alabama Democrat George Wallace was inaugurated as governor. It was in that inaugural address that Wallace made his infamous pledge to defend "segregation now, segregation tomorrow, [and] segregation forever."[93]

Qasim's embrace of a multicultural philosophy was not simply an ontological assault on the very principles of "Anglo-Saxon world order."[94] It was rather an analog to his material assault on property holdings of some of the world's largest and most powerful private corporations. A week after his speech denouncing the ideology of American imperialism, the British Foreign Office informed the State Department that "Qassim may be on the verge of adopting earlier draft law setting up National Oil Co to exploit areas taken earlier from IPC."[95] As Marx observed, ideas are a material force in history, and Qasim's ideas represented a material threat to the IPC. As this threat materialized in early 1963, Melbourne concluded that the time had come to "establish our credit with [the] anti-Communist opposition."[96]

Two weeks later, Qasim arrested Ba'th Party Army Bureau head Salih Mahdi 'Ammash and party general secretary 'Ali Salih al-Sa'di, leading others in the party to decide that the time had come to strike. In the early morning hours of February 8, 1963, Ba'thist gunmen assassinated Jalal al-Awqati, the commander of the Iraqi Air Force and the highest-ranking Communist in Qasim's government, as he exited a bakery. Simultaneous with the al-Awqati assassination, pilots loyal to the party launched air attacks on Qasim's headquarters in the Ministry of Defense. At the same time, a column of rebel tanks closed in on the Ministry of Defense compound and seized control of the Baghdad Radio control tower to announce the "14 Ramadan Revolution"—denoting the Islamic date of the coup.

As news of the coup spread across Iraqi airwaves, crowds rushed to Qasim's defense.[97] Batatu describes the scene in vivid detail:

> Simultaneous and in the same directions, poured workmen, porters, and artisans from Kifah (Old Giza) Street, and especially from 'Aqd al-Akrid [the poorer districts of Baghdad]. Waving the absurdist of weapons—mostly canes (Qasim would to the end refuse to give them firearms)—they had the appearance of sheep rushing forth highly-spirited to the shambles.[98]

The Communist Party tried to coordinate and direct this popular mobilization, but because Qasim had disarmed their PRF militia in 1959, Iraqi Communists were in no position to defend themselves, let alone the regime. Over the next three days, the party would be utterly decimated in a brutal campaign of house-to-house fighting.

As blood flowed in the streets of Baghdad, Roy Melbourne relished every detail, none more than the conduct of the Iraqi media. In his first detailed report back to Washington, he noted with satisfaction: "The coup caught programmers of Baghdad television by surprise. In their confusion, they put on an American western. While Iraqi planes were sending rockets into the Ministry of Defense, American redskins bit the dust on the screens of Iraqis' television sets."[99] Television airwaves went silent shortly thereafter and did not resume until 6:00 p.m. the next day when a "five-minute reading from the Holy Koran" came on the air. "Then there were two Felix the Cat cartoons." Then at 7:00, Baghdad TV aired a four-minute video displaying the slain bodies of Qasim, and his two close aides, leftist brigadiers Taha Shaikh al-Ahmad, the head of Qasim's security detail, and Fadhil 'Abbas al-Mahdawi, the head of the Special Military Court who had likely been the target of the CIA's 1960 poisoned handkerchief operation. "The only living person in the picture was a grinning, rather silly looking young soldier who held up Qasim's head by the hair, rotated [it] grotesquely and once, obviously on instructions, spat in the late Leader's face." Programming then returned to "Gardening in the United States" followed by the American western *Wagon Train*.

Chapter 5
THE RISE AND FALL OF THE BA'TH

SCHOLARS ARE ONLY BEGINNING TO UNCOVER THE EXTENT TO which the United States was involved in organizing the coup that overthrew 'Abd al-Karim Qasim. Similar mystery surrounds the role that the US, and the CIA in particular, played in facilitating the Ba'th's campaign of extermination directed against the Iraqi Communist Party that was an integral part of the coup. Hanna Batatu's classic 1978 study of Iraqi social and political movements was the first to assert that the CIA may have supplied Ba'thist death squads with the names and addresses of suspected Communists to be targeted for assassination.[1] While he was careful to note that CIA involvement could not be "unerringly established," he did relay a highly suggestive interview that the King Husayn of Jordan gave to the Egyptian daily *Al-Ahram* (*The Pyramids*) in September 1963:

> I know for certainty that what happened in Iraq on 8 February had the support of American Intelligence. . . . Numerous meetings were held between the Ba'th party and American Intelligence, the most important in Kuwait. Do you know that . . . on 8 February a secret radio beamed to Iraq was supplying the men who pulled the coup with the names and addresses of the Communists there so that they could be arrested and executed. . . . Yet *I* am the one accused of being an agent of America and imperialism![2]

Our understanding of the events described by King Husayn has advanced a great deal in the decades since Batatu's book was first published—mostly

FIGURE 6. President Qasim and aides, 1963. Slain bodies of Qasim (left) and aides Fadhil ʿAbbas al-Mahdawi and Taha Shaikh al-Ahmad after the February 1963 coup. Source: Bettmann Collection, Getty Images. Reprinted with permission.

thanks to the path-opening archival work of Weldon C. Matthews. But much speculation continues to swirl around this question of CIA-supplied Communist lists.

The imputation of US involvement in the campaign of assassination directed at the Iraqi Communist Party is significant because it speaks to a larger pattern in American foreign policy. The CIA had long employed the method of targeted assassination in its global crusade against Communism. In 1954, a CIA team involved in the overthrow of Guatemalan leader Jacobo Arbenz compiled a veritable "Handbook of Assassination," replete with precise instructions for committing "political murder" and a list of suspected Guatemalan Communists to be targeted for "executive action."[3] In the 1960s, the Kennedy administration made this rather ad hoc practice into a science.[4] According to its special warfare doctrines, covertly armed and trained "Hunter-Killer teams" were a highly effective instrument in the

FIGURE 7. US embassy in Baghdad. Spanish architect Josep Lluís Sert's 1955 design. Source: Josep Lluís Sert courtesy of the Frances Loeb Library, Harvard University Graduate School of Design. Reprinted with permission.

root-and-branch eradication of Communist threats in developing nations.[5] In what became known as the "Jakarta Method"—named for the systematic CIA-backed purge of Indonesian Communists in 1965—the CIA was involved in countless campaigns of mass murder in the name of anti-Communism.[6]

The employment of the Jakarta Method raised unsettling questions—both morally and pragmatically. Who could be legitimately targeted for assassination? If the cause of anti-Communism was just, could any measure in service of that cause be considered off-limits? Who ultimately bore the moral responsibility for such decisions? Moral or not, did it work? Did it render formerly recalcitrant states cooperative allies in the global war against Communism? There is no evidence that top-level policymakers grappled with these questions in any serious way. But lower down, in the bowels of the American embassy in Baghdad, these concerns were voiced. The way that they were addressed—or deferred—haunted some embassy officials for the rest of their lives. Others seem to have never lost a night of sleep thinking about it.

AFTER SUCH KNOWLEDGE: LAKELAND, AKINS, AND THE SHADOWS OF AMERICAN POWER

The question of who bore ultimate moral responsibility for the atrocities of the Ba'thist regime can be addressed from many different angles. The Iraqi side of the affair is discussed in detail below on the basis of the available archival record. But before we can engage that archival record we have to engage the historiography that shapes our interpretation of the documents found therein.[7] One of the most prominent popular accounts of the coup and the US role therein is found in journalist Said K. Aburish's *Saddam Hussein: The Politics of Revenge* (2000). He claims, "The Ba'ath-CIA conspiracy against Kassem . . . [,] led by William Lakeland who was stationed at the Baghdad embassy as an attaché, represented one of the most elaborate CIA operations in the history of the Middle East."[8] According to Aburish, Lakeland, taking direction from James Critchfield, the CIA's Near East division chief in Cairo, and working in association with *Time* magazine correspondent William McHale, compiled the lists of Communists leaders that were then supplied to the Ba'th National Guard militia, who in turn carried out the extensive and systematic purge.[9]

The sources for Aburish's account are somewhat obscure. Although Aburish does not cite it, the claim that Lakeland was working for the CIA agent may derive from the Arabic memoirs of Talib al-Shabib, who served as foreign minister for the regime that emerged from the coup. In those memoirs, Shabib described Lakeland as the "assistant to the military attaché, who was openly working for the CIA, and working to enhance the security cooperation between the US and Iraq."[10] The origins of Aburish's claim about McHale are even more obscure, and the theory is complicated by the fact that McHale was killed in the bombing that brought down Enrico Mattei's airplane in October 1962 (see chapter 3).

In 2010, Lakeland gave an oral history interview in which he addressed Aburish's claims directly.[11] He denied that he ever had any involvement with the CIA and insisted that he had, in fact, always been opposed to the "tendency to fall back on the spooky channel" that Allen Dulles had been so fond of:

> It's absolutely untrue. I was a regular Foreign Service officer and never worked for or had any position in the CIA in my whole life. In fact, generally, as a Foreign Service officer, I rather resented the use of this sort of spooky channel by some of the secretaries of state, including Mr. Dulles, who was— whose own brother, of course, ran the CIA and who was quite prone to use the CIA as a convenient way of back-channel operations and communication. Of course, he had his choices and he had the perfect right to do it as

he wished. But all my career, I just felt that this tendency to fall back on the spooky channel, so to speak, rather than doing it through the official diplomatic channel, was ill-advised, and in many cases, resulted in considerable confusion rather than clarity in the conduct of our foreign affairs.[12]

When pressed specifically about allegations that he had "masterminded" the coup against Qasim, Lakeland denied the charge categorically:

> I just have to say for the record that I first learned of this coup by—when I happened to turn on the local Baghdad radio station—TV station and came upon a scene in which some of the rebel officers were in Abd Karim Qasim's office and his body was in the chair, facing his desk, facing the camera. And they were reporting that he had been executed. And they turned his head so we could see where the bullet had gone through his temple, just so nobody would doubt the fact that he was dead. . . .
>
> I had absolutely nothing, not even advanced knowledge that this coup was taking place. And the idea that somehow or other I was the CIA agent who was masterminding this is just total fantasy. . . .

Significantly, Lakeland did not deny that the CIA was operating out of the embassy or that it collaborated with the Ba'th, but he insisted that he had no part in any of these dealings:

> Now there were CIA staff in the embassy roughly camouflaged, poorly camouflaged, as being regular embassy political officers, and that sort of thing. And they had a station chief of their own who was nominally part of my section, but in fact, of course they ran [the] show. They didn't take orders from me.[13]

He acknowledged that within official circles there was a strong current of opinion that saw the Ba'th as a "modernizing and possibly even democratizing influence" in the country and region, but insisted that he had "never personally bought that positive line towards the rising power of the Ba'th Party." From his perspective, the

> Ba'ath Party people involved were indistinguishable from what the Iraqis call and the Arabs call the mukhabarat, that is the secret service, the secret police, who were a bunch of thugs who went around knocking off people who were not in favor. . . . . I was much more inclined to feel that the

best hope for Iraq at that point really was for the old Sunni aristocracy if you want, but the Sunni solid modernizing middle class offered the best hope of a reasonable government and progress and development.[14]

What are we to make of Lakeland's recollections, refracted as they were through forty-seven years of tragic experience? Do available records allow us to assess Lakeland's account in a new light? They do. They suggest that while Aburish may have overstated Lakeland's role in the coup, Lakeland himself may have understated that role. Recall that Lakeland was the State Department Arabist who had endorsed Nasser-backed efforts to overthrow Qasim in September 1959. This fact alone calls into question the depth of his philosophical commitment to open diplomacy over covert intervention.

In 1960, Lakeland left the State Department in Washington to become the first political officer in the Baghdad embassy where he would remain for the next five years. Lakeland's record in Baghdad similarly suggests that he was more familiar with the "spooky" side of American foreign policy than he was later willing to let on. It may not be entirely inconsequential that in March 1962 Lakeland compiled a set of lists identifying the names of "known Communists" in Iraq. In the cover note, Lakeland boasted that his list constituted "a 'Who's Who' of communists and communist sympathizers active in Iraq today." He took particular pride in the fact that his list included the "the names of generally less prominent individuals, particularly university professors, writers, and merchants."[15]

There is no direct evidence that Lakeland supplied this list (or others like it) to the Ba'th with instructions to execute the named individuals. Nor is there any reason to believe that the Ba'th needed help from Lakeland or anyone in the CIA to identify Iraqi Communists. But the Ba'th's subsequent history of terrorizing suspected Communists—many of whom were simply university professors, writers, merchants, or others targeted for little more than expressing the vaguest of left sympathies—casts a somewhat jaundiced light on Lakeland's effort to compile a "Who's Who" of Iraqi Communists.[16]

Moreover, the idea that Lakeland had been completely uninvolved with the CIA, and only learned of the coup when Qassim's bullet-ridden body was displayed on Baghdad TV, sits awkwardly with contemporaneous US records. In the previous chapter we saw Lakeland reporting the intimate details of various coup plots in Iraq in 1961–62. The records from the coup period are similarly suggestive. Just four days after the coup, US *chargé* Roy Melbourne wrote to Rodger Davies, deputy director of the State Department's Office of Near Eastern Affairs, to commend the conduct of the embassy staff during the coup.[17] Melbourne drew special attention to the work of "Bill Lakeland and Art Callahan, [who] you can imagine, were right on top of events." The reference to Lakeland and Callahan in the same sentence is significant. Callahan was a long-serving CIA agent who, at the time of the coup, was the agency's station chief in Baghdad.[18] In another document, Lakeland and Callahan were described as "working as a team on the political side" during the coup. In yet another, Melbourne noted that "in Bill's case, the coup came as a certain mental release from the problems of his boy," who was suffering an illness at home in the US.[19]

Each of these discrete pieces of evidence suggests that Lakeland may have been more deeply implicated in what he would soon come to regard as the "crimes of the Ba'th" than he was later willing to acknowledge. "Memory says I did those things. Pride replies, and remains adamant, I could not have done those things. Eventually, memory yields," as Nietzsche reminds us.[20] But whatever Lakeland's association with the Ba'th, a far wider and clearer conduit of American influence with the Ba'th was James Akins, second secretary of the embassy from 1961–65.

In years subsequent to 1963, Akins made himself more available for public comment than most. Perhaps for this reason, he has largely evaded allegations of sub rosa ties to the CIA and the Ba'th. But his resume in the region suggests that he may have been one of the early and enthusiastic proponents of the party. Akins, who graduated with a degree in physics from Akron University in the late 1940s, had begun traveling in the Middle East as a member of the Quaker organization, the American Friends Service Committee, in 1950. After tracing the "path of Alexander the Great on foot," Akins landed in Beirut in 1952, where he began teaching physics and chemistry in Syria and Lebanon. The Ba'th Party was, of course, organized among college students in Syria during this period, and it is quite possible that Akins met some of its organizers or members at this point. In 1954, while teaching in Lebanon, Akins was recruited into the Foreign Service. After spending a year in Washington he was posted to Damascus in 1957. In Syria, Akins worked under Robert Strong (first secretary and then consul, 1954–58), who would be US ambassador to Iraq (1963–67) and who Lakeland later identified as the strongest proponent of the "pro-Ba'thi line" of analysis.[21]

After short postings in Madras and Beirut, Akins was made vice consul to Kuwait in 1959.[22] Two years later he moved to Baghdad, where he began compiling his dire warnings about Baghdad's sarifa dwellers constituting an "instrument of terror in a time of anarchy." It may also be significant that in May 1962 Akins compiled an addendum to Lakeland's "Who's Who" of Iraqi Communists with additional names.[23]

Also suggestive of Akins's role in the coup are his public comments many years after the fact. In a 2000 interview, he had this to say about the coup and Communist purge:

> We were very happy. They got rid of a lot of communists. A lot of them were executed, or shot. This was a great development. And things opened up in Iraq. We resumed diplomatic relations. Ultimately, we sent out an ambassador. But when did the disillusionment start? Not while I was there. I left in 1965.[24]

Four years later he offered this in another interview:

> The [1963 Ba'thist] revolution was of course supported by the U.S. in money and equipment as well. I don't think the equipment was terribly important, but the money was to the Ba'ath party leaders who took over the revolution. It wasn't talked about openly—that we were behind it—but an awful lot of people knew.[25]

Unlike Lakeland's, Akins's retrospective comments betray no regrets about what transpired in Iraq in 1963. Whereas Lakeland evinced a measure of critical self-reflection, Akins, so many years later, appeared to take continued satisfaction in the Ba'th's anti-Communist purge.

A NET GAIN FOR OUR SIDE

What really happened in Iraq in February 1963 remains shrouded behind a veil of official secrecy. Many of the most relevant documents remain classified. Others were destroyed. And still others were never created in the first place. What we do know on the basis of the record that has been made available to scholars is that US *chargé* Roy Melbourne kept very close notes of what was going on as the coup unfolded. While fighting continued at the Ministry of Defense on the night of February 8–9, a US military attaché "conducted a recon around the city" and reported in minute detail the progress of an apparently well-organized and well-executed operation.[26] The attaché described "college-aged men in green arm bands manning checkpoints at major street junctions," and was particularly "impressed by politeness, efficiency and especially by display of friendliness to Americans shown by soldiers and National Guard."[27]

Historian Weldon Matthews provides considerable insight into what was behind the National Guard friendliness to Americans: "The American relationship with militia members and senior police commanders had begun even before the February coup, and Ba'thist police commanders involved in the coup had been trained in the United States."[28] He pays special attention to the roles played by the new director general of police, General Ahmad Amin; the new commander of the mobile police, Brigadier Fadil al-Samarra'i; and the new assistant director of the general security police (unnamed in the sources). All three were graduates of the International Police Academy in Washington, DC—a Kennedy-era counterinsurgency school that trained Third World military elites in the arts of surveillance, detention, and interrogation.[29] It is perhaps not insignificant that, as part of their training, these officers interned with police departments throughout the American South at a time when Southern police departments were on the frontline of enforcing American racial segregation. Some of that police culture may have translated from Washington to Baghdad. And that shared police culture may help to explain the underlying affective bond between American counterinsurgency strategists and Ba'thist National Guard commanders.

The key conduit in that affective bond was Robert Komer. Komer embodied the Kennedy administration's fascination with counterinsurgency, and he knew how to frame that fascination within the logic of the Cold War in ways that made him very effective in shaping policy outcomes. On February 8, as the news of the coup broke in Washington, Komer composed a memo to the president that explained the coup in classic Cold War terms as a "net gain for our side." He described the coup as the work of a "moderate left but anti-communist group with good military ties." In seeking swift recognition for the new government in Iraq, he emphasized the Cold War stakes and suggested that under a Ba'thist government a new oil settlement would be forthcoming.[30]

Komer based his optimistic assessment of the new regime, at least in part, on a detailed set of personnel files provided to him on the day of the coup. Even before the full cabinet had been announced in Baghdad, Komer had a complete profile of leading figures of the new regime. Komer was particularly satisfied with the selection of General Ahmad Hasan al-Bakr to serve as prime minister. Al-Bakr was the highest-ranking Ba'thist officer in Iraq, and according to his biographic profile, he appeared to "harbor no personal ambition, and to have a deep rooted personal belief in the principles of democratic civilian government." Although he had never held office and appeared "something of a figurehead," Komer's file suggested that al-Bakr had the strength of character to "hold the new government together, and by so doing, emerge as a true prime minister."[31]

What may have been most attractive about al-Bakr's biography was that he had been recruited into the Ba'th Party by General Salih Mahdi 'Ammash, when the two were placed in a common jail cell after a failed coup attempt in September 1958. The coup attempt took place less than one month after 'Ammash returned to Iraq from the United States, where he had spent a year serving as an assistant military attaché in the Iraqi embassy in Washington. After being released by Qasim in 1961, 'Ammash continued to organize clandestinely within the military, and he headed the Ba'th Party's Army Bureau at the time of the 1963 coup. In the period leading up the coup, he was "known to be friendly to the service attachés of the US Embassy in Baghdad," and it was the arrest of 'Ammash on February 4 that triggered the coup. With the overthrow of Qasim, 'Ammash became minister of defense, where he would be in a position to reorient Iraqi arms supply agreements away from the Soviets and toward the US.

Another bright spot from Komer's perspective was the selection of Hazim Jawad to serve as the new minister of state. According to Komer's file, "Jawad's entire youth and maturity have been devoted to clandestine political activity on behalf of the Ba'th."[32] He had been involved in the Ba'th's October 1959 assassination attempt against Qasim and afterwards had escaped to Egypt. There he "received training form the UAR intelligence service in clandestine wireless telegraphy," before returning to Iraq in 1960 to coordinate "clandestine radio operations for the UAR." As we saw in chapter 2, late 1959 and early 1960 was a peak of US-UAR intelligence collaboration. It was in September of 1959 that Copeland and Eichelberger authored their report advocating US assistance for Nasserist efforts to take over in Iraq. It is quite possible that Jawad became familiar to US intelligence at that point, as a subsequent State Department cable once described him as "one of our boys."[33] By the time of the 1963 coup, Jawad was "responsible for clandestine printing and propaganda distribution operations for the BPI." In this capacity, he may have been involved in the radio transmission of Communist lists to Ba'thist kill teams.

The Komer memorandum reporting on the success of the coup was very good news from the perspective of President Kennedy. The Kennedy administration had come into office with a strong faith in and commitment to "military-Keynesian" principles of macroeconomics, in which tax cuts combined with increased defense spending were seen as a reliable way to stimulate economic growth.[34] Eisenhower, as a fiscal conservative, had sought to limit spending on the "military-industrial complex" by relying on the nuclear deterrence in dealing with the Soviets, and the CIA in dealing with the Third World. But as Kennedy entered the White House, he sought to dramatically increase defense spending as part of what he called the strategy of "flexible response."[35] The idea was to build up American ground forces so that they might more easily intervene in a land war in Asia or elsewhere. However, this increase in defense spending, coincident with a massive tax cut in January 1963, produced a growing budget deficit, which in turn placed downward pressure on the value of the US dollar.[36]

To relieve pressure on the dollar, the Kennedy administration sought to dramatically increase US military sales around the world. Toward this end, Kennedy signed the Foreign Assistance Act of 1961, which allowed the Department of Defense to sell arms on credit. To facilitate an increase in such sales, Secretary of Defense Robert McNamara established the Office International Logistics Negotiations in June 1962.[37] McNamara then put heavy pressure on the US Export-Import Bank (which facilitated US international trade) to step up financing for US arms exports. As a result of these efforts, the value of US military exports tripled between 1961 and 1964.[38]

As the Kennedy administration sought to expand US military exports, it increasingly looked to the oil-producing states of the Middle East as an emerging market. Iraq was particularly attractive in this connection. As Iraq broke with the Soviets and reoriented its weapons purchases to the West, American defense contractors stood to make a killing. In his February 8 memo to the president, Komer noted that Iraq had earned $266 million in oil revenues in 1962, and was increasingly in a position to pay in cash for American arms deliveries.[39] When the State Department pointed out that US arms sales to Iraq or other Arab states could fuel an arms race with Israel, the Department of Defense did not have to point out that an arms race was good for the arms business. By early 1963, the logic of petrodollar recycling—the use of dollar-denominated oil revenue to purchase US arms—was well established.[40] But the whole scheme rested on the Ba'th's ability to extract increased oil revenue from the IPC.

THE INTRANSIGENCE OF THE IPC

In the spring of 1963, the prospect of transforming Iraq into a significant market for the export of US arms appeared bright. Much of that optimism was based on the Ba'th's selection of 33-year-old Dr. 'Abd al-'Aziz al-Wattari to serve as the new minister of oil. According to the Komer files, al-Wattari, a graduate of the University of Texas, was a "competent technician well and favorably known to officials in the US Embassy." He was "continually helpful throughout the difficult period of the Qasim regime," and could be expected to be "friendly to the United States and moderate in his approach to negotiating with the oil industry."[41]

As al-Wattari assumed office, the embassy in Baghdad informed the State Department that the new minister could be expected to handle all outstanding oil issues on a "'commercial and economic basis' without issues being submitted to public forum."[42] The embassy did not expect al-Wattari to retract Law 80, but was confident that the law "could be subject to [a] practical application," and hoped that the IPC would extend a loan to the new regime, increase production, and quickly enter into good faith negotiations with the government over Law 80.[43]

As the new regime in Baghdad took shape, the State Department called a meeting with the heads of Exxon and Mobil. In the meeting, NEA assistant secretary Phillips Talbot tried to solicit oil company support for the Ba'th.[44] However, as had been the case in January (see chapter 3), Talbot found the companies unwilling to support a party that was doctrinally committed to Arab socialism. While Talbot emphasized the moderate character and Western training of the new oil minister, IPC management combed through Ba'th party literature and found very little difference between Qasim and the Ba'th on the question of oil.[45]

While Exxon and Mobil representatives stressed the long-term threat to their concessionary rights posed by Nasserist pan-Arab nationalism, Talbot claimed that despite the Baʿth's Nasserist rhetoric of Arab unity and socialism, they were not really socialists (more the "Scandinavian" type), and that there were deep tensions between the Nasser and the Baʿth owing to Syria's 1961 succession from the UAR.[46] The Baʿthist government of Iraq had even gone so far as to ban the public display of images of both Nasser and the new president ʿAbd al-Salam ʿArif.[47] According to Talbot, ʿArif was merely a hotheaded nationalist who had only been brought into the coup plotting at the last moment to serve as a purely ceremonial figurehead for the new regime. Throughout the conversation, Talbot emphasized the separation between Nasser and ʿArif on the one side and the Baʿth on the other.[48] Talbot attempted to seal the deal by explaining, "If the revolutionary group fully establishes itself, then for the first time there will exist a modernizing movement in the eastern part of the Arab world which will offer competition to Nasser."[49] In the months and years ahead, Talbot would be proved correct regarding subterranean tensions between Nasser and the Baʿth. But from the oil companies' standpoint, it was irrelevant as nothing was more threatening to their interests than a "modernizing movement in the eastern part of the Arab world." Whether that modernization was done in the name of Nasser or the Baʿth made no difference. In either case, oil company operations would be brought under greater Iraqi state control.

Shortly after its less-than-successful meeting with the oil companies, the State Department called a meeting with Chase National Bank for this same purpose of soliciting business support for the Baʿth. Chase was one of the world's largest banking firms and had a long history of financing major oil investments in the Middle East. However, the Chase representative proved no more eager to support Nasser's brand of pan-Arab socialism than had the oil companies. As had Talbot, the State Department's Robert Strong emphasized the theme of divisions between Nasser and the Iraqi Baʿth. He explained that while the Iraqi leaders were "proponents of statism," they were not "irrational" and would prove moderate and pragmatic in their dealings with the oil companies. The Chase representative accepted Strong's defense of the Baʿth, but shared Exxon's concern about President ʿArif. Strong emphasized the same line that ʿArif was merely a "fiery figurehead" who had been brought in to mollify Nasserists and other non-Baʿthist nationalists. But the real power in Iraq, he insisted, was with the Baʿth.[50] The Chase representative left the meeting without giving any indication that his firm intended to channel investment capital into Ba'thist-controlled Iraq.

The inability to solicit business support for the Ba'th raised grave concerns for the Kennedy administration, and foreshadowed problems for the party. From the administration's standpoint, the "most vital free world interest in Iraq" was oil. It was the "major factor which [would] permit Iraq to resist Soviet penetration," and it was "therefore in the US interest to do everything within its power to encourage both sides to reach a reasonable settlement of outstanding GOI-IPC problems."[51] However, as we have seen, the US influence with the IPC was quite limited. The day-to-day management of the company remained in BP hands, and BP was, according to Mobil representative William Lindenmuth, "influenced by Foreign Office thinking," and remained adamantly opposed to Arab nationalism and the Ba'th.[52] As they had since the emergence of Nasser's regime in the early 1950s, the British, in the final months of the Conservative government, remained convinced that the greatest threat to British regional interests did not emanate from the Soviet Union or its local Communist allies but rather from pan-Arab nationalism. British policymakers were, therefore, deeply suspicious of US links to the Ba'th—believing that the US was using these ties to displace British influence in Iraq and the wider region. From the Tory standpoint, "Americans had been in touch with the revolutionaries before the recent coup [and] were determined to hand the Middle East to Nasser on a plate."[53]

The State Department, apparently buying the representations of Exxon and Mobil, believed that British intransigence was the principal obstacle to settling the outstanding Iraq-IPC dispute over Law 80. Geoffrey Herridge, the London-based IPC managing director, certainly fit this description. But in truth, Exxon (awash in a flood of global supply) was just as opposed to a settlement in Iraq, and there were actually elements of the British group who demonstrated a willingness to compromise.[54] W. W. Stewart, the IPC's chief representative in Baghdad, held views that were much more closely aligned with the State Department. Stewart met with al-Wattari on February 12 and was particularly impressed by the new minister's belief that "oil matters should be approached from a strictly economic point of view," free of nationalist passions.[55] In their meeting, al-Wattari reassured Stewart that did he not agree with certain provisions of Qasim's Law 80, but explained that Iraqi public opinion would not allow the new regime to retract the law. Stewart advised IPC management that Law 80 could be subject to a "practical interpretation," but he cautioned against pushing too hard on the new government. From Stewart's standpoint, the IPC had an opportunity to work with a friendly government, and "IPC actions [were] likely to constitute a key factor in its survival."[56] Stewart recommended a modest production increase as a show of good faith and that the IPC send a high-level delegation to Iraq to begin negotiating the larger issues surrounding Law 80.

Despite Stewart's optimism, IPC managing director Geoffrey Herridge rejected Stewart's proposal, choosing instead to wait and see "how the situation shakes down" before entering into a new round of negotiations.[57] Herridge's refusal to negotiate with al-Wattari was supported by the analysis of Richard Bird, a Beirut-based IPC analyst. In contrast to Stewart's view that the company should be willing to accommodate al-Wattari's demands, Bird regarded the new oil minister as merely a "transitory figure" lacking any real power.[58] Rather than negotiating with this relatively low-level technocrat, Bird advised that "we must disengage Wattari quickly" and negotiate directly with the "soldiers and politicians" at the top of the regime. Bird was particularly encouraged by a recent press conference in which President 'Arif stated that "all laws issued by Kassem on oil affairs will be reconsidered."[59] Bird took this as evidence that the company need not accept the "rape" of its concessionary rights by the Iraqi government, and that a reversal of Law 80 was still possible.

By the time that the IPC did finally send a negotiating team to Baghdad in late April, the Iraqi position had hardened considerably. In the interim, the Iraqi government had established a three-person "small committee" within the Ministry of Oil to advise the government in its negotiations with the IPC.[60] In addition to al-Wattari, the committee was composed of Adib al-Jadir and Khair el-Din Haseeb, both of whom were economic advisers with strong Nasserist leanings, and both of whom were committed to the eventual nationalization of Iraq's oil. The IPC, for its part, was equally committed to the opposite principle. The company demanded a complete and immediate retraction of Law 80 and warned that production would not increase until this was done.[61] Al-Wattari tried to explain that this was impossible. Given Iraqi public opinion, neither "he, nor anyone else, not even the RCC [Revolutionary Command Council] could amend it . . . That would be political suicide."[62] Given the distance between the two negotiating positions, the April negotiations quickly collapsed.

The failure of the Iraq-IPC negotiations alarmed the State Department. In an effort to break the deadlock, the State Department met with British embassy officials in Washington on April 29. In the meeting, the State Department requested that the British government instruct British oil companies to be more forthcoming with the new leadership in Baghdad. For their part, British officials stressed that British shareholders in IPC had long been "prepared to negotiate with a new Iraq Government whenever Qassim were overthrown," but described the new regime as disorganized and dysfunctional and therefore impossible to deal with.[63] But the State Department was not convinced that the companies had offered "anything useful in the Iraqi view."[64] On the contrary, the State Department believed that the British were being unrealistic in what they could expect from the new regime, and attributed this lack of realism to the "old school persuasion" of BP officials in London. The State Department continued to pressure the British over the course of the spring and early summer, but to no avail; neither side was willing to compromise on the fundamental question of Law 80.

THE KURDISH INSURGENCY

The difficulties that the Ba'thist government faced in negotiating with the IPC were soon compounded by a new problem: the reemergence of the Kurdish insurgency in northern Iraq. Mullah Mustafa Barzani and the Kurdish Democratic Party (KDP) initially supported the Ba'thist coup against Qasim. On February 10, the KDP sent a congratulatory telegram to the new Ba'thist-led government and announced a ceasefire to the war (which had begun in September 1961).[65] In early March, General Tahir Yahya, chief of the general staff, traveled to Barzani's mountain stronghold in the far north of Iraq to negotiate an autonomy agreement.[66] However, Yahya found Barzani in no mood to compromise. Barzani, enjoying subsidies from both Israel and Iran, regarded the Kurdish revolt as the critical element accounting for Qasim's weakened position and the success of the February coup.[67] In Barzani's view, no regime in Baghdad could survive without his support. He therefore presented Yahya with maximalist autonomy demands including Kurdish control over Kirkuk oil fields—along with a guarantee that an autonomous Kurdish government under his leadership would receive two-thirds of Iraq's total oil revenue.[68] Yahya was given three days to comply with Barzani's demands or war would be resumed. The war was not in fact resumed in March, but tensions between the two sides continued to escalate over the course of April and May, leading senior Iraqi officials to increasingly look to a military solution to the Kurdish question.

Escalating tensions with the Kurds were a cause of concern for the Kennedy administration.[69] Komer and the CIA were particularly worried that the Soviet Union, which was denouncing the Ba'thist regime as installed and supported by the CIA, would take advantage of a new Kurdish uprising as a way to undermine the regime in Baghdad.[70] To head off this threat, the United States, in early April, agreed to an initial military aid package that included 40 tanks, 12 tank transporters, 15 combat helicopters, and 500 military trucks.[71] US military assistance to the Ba'th, however, did nothing to resolve the escalating conflict. On the contrary, Iraqi-Kurdish tensions continued to increase. The situation became so serious that in mid-May the Kennedy administration's Special Group on Counterinsurgency, a high-level group led by the president's brother Bobby that oversaw US aid to military regimes in the Third World, took up the issue in one of its weekly meetings. For the Special Group, the "prolongation of the conflict in Iraq engenders instability, and provides an opportunity for communist exploitation of the Kurdish problem in Iraq and in neighboring countries."[72] The Special Group saw "a firm Iraqi military position" as offering the best prospect for "an early end to hostilities and [the] advancement of internal stability in Iraq" and recommended providing the Ba'thist regime with increased military assistance toward this end.[73]

The suggestion that the US increase military assistance to the Ba'th elicited some resistance from those recessive elements within the State Department that had more general reservations about the Ba'th. According to one unsigned embassy report (Lakeland?), "much of Iraq's wealth in recent past has been squandered on [the] maintenance [of an] oversize military establishment [that] could be diverted to build schools, hospitals, and promote general economic situation which appeared to be static and declining rapidly."[74] Not only was the military establishment oversized already, but these officials feared that increasing US military assistance to the Ba'th would make a war with the Kurds more rather than less likely. In May, an unsigned embassy report expressed concern that the government in Baghdad seemed to "favor a 'final solution' of the Kurdish problem," and that it was advocating "a program of outright genocide in Kurdistan."[75] According to Air Force commander Hardan al-Tikriti, the "Kurds should either accept [the] 'opportunity to become Arabs,' or face 'extermination.'"[76] Such sentiments continued to increase among senior Iraqi leaders over the course of May, and on June 10, the Iraqi army sent troops into Kurdistan, initiating the "second wave" of the Kurdish War.[77]

As fighting broke out in the north, Iraqi leaders requested increased aid from the US—to include the provision of napalm weapons—ironically, a petroleum-derived defoliant used to destroy enemy food supplies.[78] As part of the effort to secure US support, the director general of security, Jamil Sabri Bayati, offered to provide the US with a Russian-made "T-54 tank and technical manuals on Soviet equipment."[79] Robert Komer strongly supported responding favorably to the Iraqi request. From his standpoint, the logic was very simple: "Soviets have come out directly in support of Kurds; ergo, we should support the Iraqis. A little ammo for the Iraqis would be a good investment, even without a delightful bonus"—the "bonus" being the T-54 manual.[80] While Komer believed that the Iraqi proposal "made sense on many counts," he expressed frustration with NEA head Phillips Talbot, whom he described as "too waffly for CIA's taste (and in this case for mine)."

What Komer described as Talbot's "waffly attitude" was concern within the State Department that providing "napalm to be used to put down the Kurdish uprising" at a time when "Soviet press and radio are initiating charges of genocide against Kurds entails some propaganda risks."[81] Moreover, the actual use "of napalm might destroy villages, but would not necessarily drive Kurds to surrender; on the contrary, it might stiffen their resistance and cause them to seek active material Soviet support." Despite these risks, the Kennedy administration agreed to supply Iraq with the requested arms (presumably including the napalm munitions), and just as the State Department warned, the harsh repressive campaign only stiffened the Kurdish resistance and prolonged the fighting.[82]

THE NASSERIST CHALLENGE

In addition to the challenges of negotiating with the IPC and countering the Kurdish insurgency, the Ba'th soon faced a new challenge from pan-Arabist officers in the military who were not members of the Ba'th party.

These officers gravitated toward President 'Abd al-Salam 'Arif and a group of high-ranking commanders around him whose orientation and relations were more directed to Egypt and Nasser than to the regional leadership of the Ba'th party in Syria. In theory, Iraqi Ba'thists and these "Nasiriyun," as the embassy described them, shared a commitment to pan-Arab unity. Indeed, both 'Arif and the Ba'th initially broke with Qasim over his refusal to join with Nasser and the UAR. But the UAR proved a rather unhappy affair that Qasim was wise to avoid.[83] The Syrian business class in particular bristled under Egyptian control and led a movement to secede from the union in September 1961. The Ba'th, for its part, had only supported the merger in 1958 out of convenience, as it sought an alliance with Egypt against the Syrian Communist Party. Once the threat of Syrian Communists was vanquished by Nasser, the Ba'th party also began to bristle under Egyptian control. As Syria withdrew from the UAR, the Syrian Ba'ths equivocated, which exacerbated tensions between Nasser and the Ba'th.

Despite inner tensions within the pan-Arabist movement, all parties involved were careful to maintain a unified public image. Nasser appeared to support a March 1963 Ba'thist coup in Syria. In truth, the Syrian Ba'th probably got more help from the CIA than from Egypt. A Syrian Ba'thist involved in the coup later recalled that "there was a push from the West and in particular from the United States for the Ba'ath to seize power and monopolize it and push away all the other elements and forces."[84] But on the surface it appeared that in the spring of 1963, the conditions were right for the long-awaited political unification of Egypt, Syria, and Iraq. Representatives of the three states met in Egypt in April and devised a "Cairo Charter" that outlined a step-by-step process for unifying the three countries.[85]

Once in power, however, the Iraqi Ba'thists proved no more willing to cede Iraqi sovereignty to Egypt than had Qasim. Nor were the Iraqi Ba'thists particularly willing to share power with Iraqi Nasserists. The Ba'th's effort to "monopolize political power," and its unwillingness to take meaningful steps toward unification, in turn, led a growing number of military officers to align with 'Arif and the Nasiryun against the Ba'th.[86] One of the earliest manifestations of this tension was a Nasserist coup attempt in late May.[87] The Ba'th discovered and suppressed the coup plot before it got off the ground, but tensions between the two factions continued to escalate and were exacerbated by events in neighboring Syria. There, negotiations over

Arab unification came to a complete halt in July when Syrians Nasserists staged a major uprising that was only put down with considerable force by the Syrian Ba'thist regime.[88] With the outbreak of violence in Syria, Egypt pulled out of any further unity negotiations and initiated a propaganda campaign against the Ba'thists, who were now demoted to the status of "fascist dogs."[89]

The growing Nasserist opposition to the Ba'thist regime, and the Ba'th's harsh measures in suppressing opposition groups, raised concern among some members of the US embassy staff in Iraq. William Lakeland, for example, filed alarming reports about frequent Ba'thist atrocities—including the use of "special rape prisons for Iraqi girls."[90] These measures succeeded in intimidating the opposition, but also shocked and alienated large sections of Iraqi opinion and weakened the regime's already thin base of popular support. Lakeland warned of the everpresent possibility of a Nasserist coup and cautioned against becoming too deeply committed to a Ba'th party that was growing increasingly isolated and unpopular. Melbourne, however, dismissed such concerns. Melbourne believed that the National Guard was a "formidable force" that would allow the Ba'th to keep its firm hold on the "machinery of government and instruments of power" in Iraq for the foreseeable future.[91]

Based in large part on Melbourne's confidence in the Ba'thist regime, the US upgraded its political representation in Baghdad and resumed formal diplomatic relations with Iraq (which had been severed since June 1961) in July. The new ambassador was Robert Strong (1963–67), who "had been in Syria when the Ba'ath Party first came to prominence and . . . had apparently gotten the idea that this was a potentially—how shall I say?—modernizing and maybe even democratizing influence," as Lakeland later recalled. As the conflict between Nasserists and Ba'thist grew more open, Strong defended his preference for the Ba'th: "Some people may think we are Baath-lovers. I prefer to think that we are trying to be realistic in evaluating a factor of importance in the area."[92] That factor was the party's demonstrated commitment to fighting Communism in Iraq.

In contrast to Lakeland's concern that the Ba'th's brutal methods were alienating large segments of Iraqi society, Strong insisted, "As a clandestine group with good intelligence experience and capabilities, Ba'thists are likely to be able to make the formation of [a] hostile, effective power grouping difficult, including in the army."[93] Strong noted that there were 1,200 Ba'thist officers—some 20 percent of the officer strength—and that the "National Guard is [an] effective power instrument [that] opposition army officers cannot overlook."[94] Strong expressed concern that failure to put down the Kurdish rebellion could cause problems for the regime, but was confident that the regime was sufficiently "tough and ruthless" to hang on to power despite the Kurdish insurgency and growing Nasserist opposition.[95]

In August, after what he described as "two months of cold, objective analysis," Strong expressed his satisfaction with the Ba'th's progress in establishing a stable regime. He acknowledged that that were things to "dislike and even fear (a bit)" about the Ba'th, but warned that the "disappearance of the Baath" would result in Iraq dropping back into "chaos, utter incompetence, and [the] breeding of communism."[96] To avoid this outcome, Strong advocated offering increasingly public support for the regime. Whereas the State Department had once instructed the embassy to "avoid creating the impression that we sired the regime," Strong now maintained that the United States need not worry about "confirming [the] charge of US sponsorship of the Baath."[97] Such charges were "already widely believed," he explained, and it was "apparent that the Baath don't mind a certain amount of evidence of our support and they are showing this in a variety of ways."[98]

According to Strong's line of reasoning, brandishing US support could help the Ba'th fend off Nasserist challengers in the army. However, subsequent events demonstrated that the Ba'th's increasingly open affiliation with the US undermined the party's credibility and legitimacy within Iraq and the larger region. Indeed, the Ba'th's apparent dependence on US support opened the regime up to criticism from Egypt. It was in this context that Nasser's confidant and *al-Ahram* editor Muhammad Hasanayn Haykal published his interview with Jordan's King Husayn in which the Jordanian king accused the Ba'th of having come to power with the assistance of the CIA.[99] Haykal continued this theme of the "Ba'th as collaborator" in November when he characterized the party as dependent on "'certain international powers' who have been persuaded that the Ba'th is the only political force in the area capable of blocking Nasser's revolutionary tide"—a clear if veiled reference to the CIA.[100]

The growing split between Nasser and the Ba'th exacerbated an emerging split within the Ba'th itself. The party had long been riven by tensions between a radical civilian wing and a military faction. The conflict with Nasser brought this tension to the surface. It was the military wing that enjoyed the confidence of Washington and that had dominated the party and government since taking power in February. But as the main leadership of the party started to falter, the civilian wing, led by party general secretary ʿAli Salih al-Saʿdi, launched a bid to seize power from the military wing. To accomplish this internal party coup, and overcome the military wing's control of the armed forces, al-Saʿdi sought to draw strength from the National Guard auxiliary force. By the fall of that year, the National Guard had grown to a mass organization by recruiting among oil workers—and indeed offering oil employment in exchange for National Guard service.[101]

Weldon Matthews's close analysis of the Iraqi labor movement provides deep insight into al-Saʿdi's organizational strategy as he sought to wrest control of the party. Matthews shows that in the immediate aftermath of the February coup, the CIA working in association with a subsidiary of the American Federation of Labor–Congress of Industrial Organizations (AFL-CIO) sought to "liquidate" Communist influence within the Iraqi labor movement by forming new Baʿthist-led, anti-Communist labor unions.[102] But in order to do this, the party had to draw strength from the "powerful radical currents that traversed the lower ranks of the party's supporters."[103] For the military leadership of the party, the Marxian concept of class conflict was anathema to Baʿthist doctrine regarding the organic unity of (pan-)Arab society. In the military Baʿthist model of development, the Arab bourgeoisie, supervised by the military, would lead the process of economic modernization. But "Baʿthist labor leaders resisted their own regime's anti-democratic labor policy, demanded autonomous and democratic unions, embraced class struggle, and pursued nonaligned international labor solidarity."[104] *Waʿi al-ʿUmmal (Consciousness of the Workers)*, the Baʿthist labor federation's newspaper, denounced US "neocolonialism" and embraced "Afro-Asian solidary."[105] The "authentic meaning of labor unity," the paper insisted, "was 'democratic, socialist, and revolutionary.' This unity could be achieved only by 'the struggle of the oppressed masses against imperialist capitalism.'"[106]

In an effort to capitalize on the radical current within the Iraqi labor movement, al-Saʿdi engineered a dramatic reorientation of party doctrine at the Sixth National Congress of the Baʿth Party held in Damascus for three weeks in October 1963.[107] At the conclusion of that conference, al-Sa'di unveiled a new manifesto that unambiguously embraced Marxist class struggle, rapid socialization of the Iraqi economy, and diplomatic rapprochement with Soviet bloc countries. In response to the party's newfound Marxism, Lakeland worried that while most Iraqis "simply ignored the Ba'th's long winded-propaganda . . . those of the business and propertied class who have studied the Manifesto seem to be generally dismayed by its tone and content."[108] Strong, on the other hand, believed that the Ba'th was simply under pressure "to go Nasser one better in the competition for the title of 'leading exponent of Arab socialism'," and that the embrace of Marxism was a "tactical ploy" rather than indicative of a fundamental shift in the party's philosophical orientation.[109]

On November 11, Strong reported that the Ba'th's tactical maneuvers were succeeding, that the "younger pro-Nasser types" in the army were sufficiently checked, and that the Ba'th faced "no immediate threat" to its control of the government.[110] However, just as Strong was filing this report, the Ba'th broke into two warring factions. On the one side stood al-Sa'di and the National Guard. On the other side stood the army nationalists led by al-Bakr. On the same day that Strong filed his report, al-Bakr's forces arrested al-Sa'di at gunpoint, placed him on a plane bound for Franco's Spain, and attempted to dissolve the National Guard.[111] What followed was a week of confused party infighting and violence in the streets.[112] On November 18, in the midst of this confusion and chaos, Nasserist army officers led by President 'Arif and Chief of Staff Tahir Yahya deposed Prime Minister al-Bakr and deployed overwhelming army force to suppress pockets of Ba'thist resistance throughout the country. For the moment, the Ba'th party in Iraq was *fini*.

APOCALYPSE NOW FROM IRAQ TO VIETNAM

With the overthrow of the Ba'th, Ambassador Strong reflected on the basis of US support for the now-defunct regime and the prospects for the party's return to power. In a report to the State Department he concluded of the Ba'th:

> They are disorganized and need to rebuild but were not destroyed by a superior political force. They are devoutly anti-communist and work at it (which is more important in Iraq than in any other Arab state); and there is no other element in Iraq any better able to organize stability or with a social and economic program which can compare with Baathi counter appeal against

communist blandishments to [the] underprivileged. This is our principal interest in Iraq.[113]

Despite the "personal ambition and indiscipline" proving that they were "still Arabs," Strong believed that al-Bakr, 'Ammash, and the military wing of the party learned valuable lessons from their experience in power and that they were working to rebuild the party to better hold power.[114]

It was likely in response to Strong's continued defense of the Ba'th that Lakeland filed a long and gruesome report that detailed Ba'th atrocities.[115] In prefacing his report, Lakeland apologized for seeming to take "undue interest in the macabre," but insisted that it was necessary to provide an extensive catalog of Ba'thist horrors so the State Department might better understand *"the popular revulsion against the Baath . . . [which] will have a more or less permanent effect on the political developments in the country—particularly on the prospects of a Baathi revival."*[116] The contents of the report are grotesque, but suffice to say that Lakeland offered a truly apocalyptic vision, in the original Greek sense of the word.[117]

Lakeland's report on Ba'thist atrocities arrived in Washington to an American capital in disarray. Amidst CIA efforts to assassinate political leaders in Congo, Cuba, the Dominican Republic, Vietnam, and God only knows where else, Americans had just watched their own president gunned down in the streets of Dallas. In his first column published after the JFK assassination, entitled "We All Had a Finger on That Trigger," journalist I. F. Stone argued that there was a direct causal link between American efforts to kill foreign leaders and the death of their own president. "Let us ask ourselves honest questions," he implored:

> How many Americans have not assumed—with approval—that the CIA was probably trying to find a way to assassinate Castro? How many would not applaud if the CIA succeeded? Have we not become conditioned to the notion that we should have a secret agency of government—the CIA—with secret funds, to wield the dagger beneath the cloak against leaders we dislike? Even some of our best young liberal intellectuals can see nothing wrong in this picture except that the 'operational' functions of CIA should be kept separate from its intelligence evaluations! . . . When the right to kill is so universally accepted, we should not be surprised if our young President

was slain. It is not just the ease in obtaining guns, it is the ease in obtaining excuses, that fosters assassination.[118]

Whatever the ultimate causes of the Kennedy assassination, the immediate consequence was to shift power in Washington to Lyndon B. Johnson, a man who shared none of his predecessor's romantic attraction to Nasser, and who would, in the coming years, grow increasingly obsessed with the effort to "cut off Ho Chi Minh's pecker" in Vietnam.[119] As Johnson took the reins of power in Washington, the United States all but disengaged from Iraq. In contrast to the efforts of Eisenhower and Kennedy to make, unmake, and remake regimes more favorable to this or that conception of American interests, Johnson leaned heavily on the regional enemies of Arab nationalism—Israel, Saudi Arabia, Iran, and the British—to contain Nasser, while the US focused its attention and resources on what Bundy, Rostow, and the lot of national security managers in Washington still called, for lack of a better concept, the effort to "bring modernity to Vietnam."

American foreign policy in Vietnam produced a horrific tragedy that killed millions of people and permanently scarred the landscape. But the diversion of America's imperial gaze to Southeast Asia also provided Iraqis with the political space needed to overthrow the Ba'th and focus their efforts on building the institutional capacity to nationalize the IPC. It is to this process of Iraqi institutional development that we now turn.

Chapter 6

THE EMERGENCE OF THE IRAQ NATIONAL OIL COMPANY

THE OVERTHROW OF THE BAʻTH IN NOVEMBER 1963 WAS HIGHLY significant to the politics of oil in the Middle East. The Nasserist officers who executed the coup brought with them into power a particular set of Arab oil experts who had spent much of the preceding decade formulating a unified regional oil policy. A leading figure in this effort to formulate a common oil policy was Abdullah Tariki, the former Saudi oil minister who had been exiled from the kingdom for his radicalism. Along with Mohammad Salman of Iraq and Francisco Parra of Venezuela, Tariki had been a driving force in organizing the oil congresses of 1959–60 that led to the formation of OPEC. But as we saw in chapter 4, progress along that path toward a unified regional oil policy was violently interrupted by the dramatic events of 1962–63. As Faysal consolidated royal authority in Saudi Arabia in the face of the Free Officers' Revolution in Yemen in September 1962, Tariki was exiled to Beirut. In February 1963, the Baʻth murdered Qasim—the most significant oil state leader since Mossadegh.

With the overthrow of Qasim the movement for oil sovereignty came to a grinding halt. The new Baʻthist regime, lacking a popular base of support and entirely dependent on covert assistance from the United States, relied heavily on the coercive instruments of government and provoked a massive popular backlash. The Baʻth ran into the Nuri al-Said problem. The more extreme and authoritarian its anti-Communist measures, the more the regime

FIGURE 8. Arab world leaders at Luxor, 1964. Algerian president Ahmed Ben Bella (left), Soviet premier Nikita S. Khrushchev (center-left), Egyptian president Gamal Abdel Nasser (center), and Iraqi president 'Abd al-Salam 'Arif (right) at the ancient Temple of Luxor following a visit to the Aswan Dam, May 21, 1964. Source: Hulton Archive, Getty Images. Reprinted with permission.

endeared itself to Washington. But the more the regime endeared itself to Washington, the more it estranged itself from its own citizens. A regime so deeply disarticulated from the general will of the society simply was not capable of organizing a grand patriotic cause like the nationalization of the IPC. In the absence of any positive agenda beyond attracting money and guns from Washington, the Ba'thist regime fell into a vacuum of leadership and ideas. Rather than unifying with Iraqi Kurds on the basis of a shared interest in nationalizing the IPC, and using diplomacy to negotiate a stable autonomy agreement, the Ba'th found it all too easy to fall back on US-supplied arms and ammunition to enforce a "final solution" to the overlapping Kurdish and Communist problems in Iraq.

The Ba'th's nine-month reign of terror represented a low point in the modern history of Iraq. And as was the case everywhere it appeared, the application of the Jakarta Method left permanent scars on Iraqi society. One can only wonder how Iraqi history might have turned out differently had Qasim been allowed to carry out his intended reforms. Something was lost in 1963 that could never be fully recovered. But the Nasserist officers who organized the overthrow of the Ba'th made a good faith effort to try.

With the advent of the Nasserist regime in Iraq, progress toward a unified regional oil policy resumed. In the years ahead, Tariki would be a frequent adviser in Baghdad. There he worked closely with Khair el-Din Haseeb and Adib al-Jadir, two Iraqi oil experts awarded high positions in the regime that emerged from the November 1963 overthrow of the Ba'th. These figures would go on to play larger-than-life roles in fundamentally transforming the energy relationships of the era. They sought to complete the work that Qasim had begun. To succeed in this, the "Haseeb group," as Tariki's Iraqi followers would come to be known, devised a political strategy centered on building transnational coalitions in opposition both to US hegemony and to the essentially colonial political economy of oil which that hegemony underwrote. Employing such a transnational strategy, the Haseeb group accomplished nothing less than a revolution in international legal norms with regard to oil concession agreements.

KHAIR EL-DIN HASEEB, TAHIR YAHYA, AND THE NASIRIYUN

The social biography of Khair el-Din Haseeb, who was in many ways the key architect of Iraq's radical oil policy, offers a useful lens through which we can view and understand the seismic forces transforming the regional political economy of oil in the 1950s and 1960s.[1] Haseeb was born in Mosul in 1929. After his father died when he was just two weeks old, he was raised by his grandfather—"a prominent Mosuli intellectual who read books on Western and Arabic literature."[2] As a child, Haseeb sat in on the weekly salons that his grandfather held for local and regional dignitaries. In the 1930s, heavy snows and poor health conspired to destroy the family's sheep herds, and the Haseebs' economic situation deteriorated dramatically. His grandfather fell ill and a cousin assumed control of the estate. The cousin "sold everything—even the chairs!" Most of Haseeb's brothers and cousins entered the army for lack of better opportunities. "We were rich and then we were poor. That was a great advantage, because I learned both situations in life. . . . This is how my value system was formed," he told me as we walked through Beirut's Hamra district in January 2016.

Seventy years earlier, in 1947, Haseeb had completed his secondary education in Mosul and moved to Baghdad to begin working in the Iraqi civil service—a clerical position in the Ministry of the Interior. His salary was not commensurate with his level of education, but he took the job to support this mother and three sisters. He soon enrolled in classes at Baghdad University's recently opened College of Commerce and Economics. He quickly distinguished himself as an exceptional student, receiving "more than a dozen" national prizes—one awarded directly by Prime Minister Nuri al-Said at his graduation ceremony in the summer of 1954.

As he neared completion of his studies in Baghdad, Haseeb wrote a letter of application addressed simply to "London University." The letter was eventually forwarded to the London School of Economics, and a qualifying exam was arranged. On the day that he graduated first in his class at Baghdad University, Haseeb received a letter of acceptance from LSE. In October 1954, he moved to London to begin coursework. At LSE Haseeb pursued an MS in economics with a specialization in statistics. After graduating in 1957, he moved to Cambridge University where he earned a PhD in statistics three years later. His PhD thesis, later published as *The National Income of Iraq, 1953–1961* (Oxford University Press, 1964), was eventually used as the basis for UN and World Bank development planning in Iraq.

Haseeb recalled that when he arrived in London in 1954, he had very little in the way of "political orientation. My only target was to study outside of Iraq." However, he soon took an interest in the ideas of Fabian (gradual reformist) socialism and joined the Arab Student Union, to which he was elected vice president.[3] As a student activist he had participated in a "few demonstrations in support of the Algerian patriots," but soon underwent "an intensification of my political consciousness" as a result of the 1956 Suez War. During the war, he helped organize demonstrations in support of Egypt, and wrote Nasser a letter of ASU support. Nasser replied in a personal letter thanking him for his support and encouraging him in his studies and efforts on behalf of the Arab world.

With the purpose of advancing the cause of Arab independence, Haseeb returned to Iraq in July 1957 to complete his PhD thesis research on the country's national income. He recalled that when he left for London in 1954, he didn't "know Iraq—only Mosul and Baghdad." It was only when he returned in 1957 that he got "a more complete picture." In his effort to compile a complete account of Iraq's earnings he traveled the country from north to south, "counting everything of value—from barrels of oil to the income of prostitutes!" But it was what he saw in Iraq's southern marshes that "shook his consciousness." The social conditions that he observed there left a deep and long-lasting impact on his worldview. One moment in particular was seared into his memory:

> It was 30 August 1957. The temperature was more than 50 degrees. I was visiting the marshes of Bera and Suda by *mashuf* [reed boat], and saw a peasant working in the hot sun—planting rice. It took me a month to recover from the sunburn on that day! But this peasant was completely naked in the sun. And there was no water! They had to boil what they drank to kill the insects. The shaykh had electricity, a shower, and a generator. But everyone else had nothing.
>
> It had a very basic effect on my future thinking.

After completing his PhD at Cambridge and returning to Iraq in 1960, Haseeb was briefly employed in the IPC's Baghdad office. However, he soon left the company (on amicable terms; the company regretted losing his service) to become Qasim's director general of the Iraqi Federation of Industries.[4] After the overthrow of Qasim, Prime Minister al-Bakr appointed Haseeb along with Adib al-Jadir to join with al-Wattari in forming a "Small Committee" to devise a coherent national oil policy.[5] It was Haseeb and

FIGURE 9. Khair el-Din Haseeb, 1957. Khair el-Din Haseeb surveying Iraq's southern marshes while conducting research for his PhD thesis at Cambridge University. Source: Courtesy of Khair el-Din Haseeb. Reprinted with permission.

al-Jadir who had prevailed on al-Wattari to withstand pressure from the IPC to retract Law 80 in the spring of 1963. After serving on the oil committee, President al-Bakr appointed Haseeb to serve as governor and chairman of the board of Iraq's Central Bank. In this capacity, Haseeb worked closely with the IMF, World Bank, and UN on development planning, and advised the Iraqi Social Security Organization on a national pension plan. All of this work was based on the national income analysis that he had completed for his PhD thesis, published by Oxford in 1964.

As impressive as was Haseeb's rise, under the Ba'thist regime, he was still just a 35-year-old economic adviser with no military ties and very little in the way of real political power. This would all change with the November 1963 coup that brought 'Abd al-Salam 'Arif to power. 'Arif had executed his coup against the Ba'th by forming an alliance with the "Nasiriyun"—the network of Nasserist army officers who had thrown their support to the Ba'th in the spring and then withdrawn it in the fall. These Nasiriyun were adherents to Nasser's general philosophy of Arab nationalism, but not partisans of the Ba'th's particular "vanguard" sect within that broader Arab nationalist movement. The leading figure among these Nasserist officers was Major General Tahir Yahya.

Born in Tikrit in 1913 (possibly of Afghan descent), Yahya emerged as a leading military officer in the 1950s. He was an early organizer of the Free Officers' movement and was among the handful of officers involved in the decision to launch the 1958 revolution.[6] During the 1958 coup he commanded the elite 20th Infantry Regiment as it seized control of the Iraqi capital. After the coup, he served as Qasim's director general of police, but was retired in December 1958 for suspected Nasserist sympathies.[7] He joined the Ba'th Party in 1962, but was regarded as a "chance Ba'thist" who was uninvolved in planning or executing the February 1963 coup. After the coup, he served as chief of the general staff but then joined with 'Arif to eject the Ba'th from power. As he had in 1958, he once again commanded the 20th Infantry Brigade as it wrested control of the streets of Baghdad from the Ba'th's National Guard. In return for this service, 'Arif appointed Yahya prime minister in place of Ahmed Hasan al-Bakr. Al-Bakr was then given the largely ceremonial post of vice president, until that position was abolished in March 1964, and al-Bakr was placed under house arrest and "retired from politics." Upon assuming control of the government, Yayha renounced ties to the Ba'th, which he had only joined in 1962, and formed a new cabinet dominated by Nasserist officers.[8]

It was Yahya, as the new power broker in Iraqi politics, who acted as Haseeb's main patron and protector within the Iraqi political system. Haseeb, in turn, provided Yahya with economic and technical expertise that was informed by a broader commitment to the philosophy of Arab nationalism. This philosophical commitment was apparent in a major address broadcast throughout Iraq in December 1963. In the speech, Yahya laid out the most elaborate and ambitious political and economic program since the 1958 revolution.[9] Yahya promised to restore the rule of law after the chaos of the Ba'thist regime, appealed to all nationalist elements to form a broad front against the forces of "imperialism and reaction," and called for a foreign policy of "positive neutrality" and nonalignment in accordance with the Bandung Charter. Yahya also introduced an ambitious program of economic development that included the modernization of agriculture, new investments in communication and transportation infrastructure, inter-Arab cooperation on development issues, and the formation of a national oil company to exploit the oil fields reclaimed under Law 80.[10]

THE AL-JADIR OIL OFFENSIVE

To advance the cause of developing oil resources reclaimed under Law 80, Adib al-Jadir, the new minister of industry, authored an important article in *al-Jumhurriyah (The Republic)*, a government newspaper published in Baghdad in January 1964.[11] In his article, al-Jadir castigated the previous regime for failing to advance the cause of oil sovereignty. As part of a more active oil policy, he reprised Sassoon Hasqail's arguments from the 1920s (see chapter 1) by calling for the training of Iraqis for managerial positions within the company, the inclusion of Iraqis on the board of directors in London, and the opportunity for the Iraqi government to purchase 20 percent of the IPC shares. None of this could be achieved, al-Jadir argued, without close cooperation with Egypt, and he cited Qasim's division with Nasser as a source of Iraqi weakness and underdevelopment. Whereas the Ba'th had been careful to ensure that oil issues were not "submitted to a public forum," al-Jadir now sought to use the press to mobilize public support for a vigorous prosecution of Iraqi claims against the companies.

Al-Jadir's article in *al-Jumhurriyah* was followed, on February 8, by Yahya's announcement of Law 11. The law formally established the Iraq National Oil Company (INOC), and vested it with the power to exploit the Law 80 territories, either on its own, or in association with other international companies—so long as INOC held a minimum 50 percent interest in any joint venture agreement.[12] While the law had no immediate effect on IPC operations, the companies saw it as a direct threat to their interests.[13] The biggest concern was that the law would allow the government of Iraq to accept competitive bids from rival companies interested in getting a foothold in Iraq.[14] This was especially worrying because of recent trends in the international oil industry—namely, the continued rise of the independent internationals. These included large formerly domestic producers interested in expanding internationally, as well as partially state-owned European and Japanese firms interesting in breaking the majors' dominance in European and Asian markets. These firms looked with envy at the profitability of the majors and were willing to offer producing countries much better concession terms than prevailed among the existing agreements.[15] Al-Jadir and

Yahya saw in these companies natural allies in their struggle with the IPC. To defend against the emerging alignment between the Nasiriyun and the independents, the IPC demanded that the dispute over Laws 80 and 11 be adjudicated in a court of international arbitration, and threatened to bring legal action against any company doing business with the INOC in the absence of a resolution.[16]

The IPC's threats of legal action were, however, largely empty. They were made against the backdrop of a revolution in international legal norms with regard to natural resources. Over the course of the previous decade, concessions such as the one that the IPC held came under sustained legal challenge. After Iran nationalized BP in 1951, BP claimed that the nationalization decree violated their existing contract rights and demanded that the case be arbitrated by the International Court of Justice (ICJ) at The Hague. In January 1952, Iranian prime minister Mohammad Mossadegh traveled to The Hague to argue against arbitration: "The decision we have taken to nationalize expresses the political will of a free and sovereign people. Understand then, we are calling on the terms of the [United Nations] Charter to ask you to refuse to intervene in the matter."[17] In July, the ICJ agreed and refused to hear the case. The ruling established an important legal precedent— the sovereign right of developing states to exercise control over their natural resources. In December, the UN General Assembly, led by Iranian Djalal Abdoh, adopted a resolution affirming this principle and established an Economic and Financial Committee to define the "legal machinery of self-determination."[18]

But, of course, "between equal rights force decides."[19] The UN could affirm whatever principle it liked, but Kermit Roosevelt and the CIA had other ideas. The overthrow of Mossadegh was a setback to the program of sovereign rights. The battle was rejoined, however, at Bandung and the Arab League in 1955. It was carried forward when Nasser successfully nationalized the Suez Canal Company in 1956. Then another step forward at the Cairo Oil Summit in 1959. And then two more with the Baghdad and Beirut oil meetings in September and October 1960. Steps had become strides. In Beirut, Tariki called on exporting countries to assert their sovereign right to unilaterally amend or abolish existing concessionary agreements. The Free Princes in Saudi Arabia demanded a constitution, natural resource sovereignty, and an end to oil company intervention into their country's domestic political affairs. Riding a reformist wind, King Saud displaced his brother Faysal and elevated Abdullah Tariki to a cabinet-level position in December. For a brief moment, the oil minister of the world's largest oil producer was a Nasserist (see chapter 3).

The winds of change moved international bodies in 1962. In June, OPEC passed Resolution IV.33, its most substantial to date. It called for a significant increase on rates of taxation applied to foreign companies. According to the "50–50 principle" that had prevailed in the region since the early 1950, total oil revenue was split equally between companies and governments. However, included in the government's share was a 12.5 percent "royalty" for the depletion of reserves. Resolution IV.33 called for the "expensing of royalties"—meaning that the royalty should be paid in addition to, rather than as a part of, the government's 50 percent take of total revenue.[20] In essence, OPEC was trying to shift from a 50–50 revenue-sharing formula to something closer to a 63–37 split favoring the producing governments. Not only would such a reform allow countries like Iraq to accumulate local capital for development, it affirmed the sovereign right of exporting countries to determine their terms of international trade. This principle was further affirmed in December when the UN passed Resolution 1803. The resolution constituted what historian Christopher Dietrich describes as an "economic bill of rights" for the Third World in that it recognized the right of postcolonial states to "permanent sovereignty over natural resources," including the right to unilaterally abrogate contracts.[21]

While the UN was affirming its postcolonial bill of rights, Gamal Abdel Nasser was testing the bounds of acceptable economic reform. In May 1962, he announced the National Charter of the Egyptian Revolution, which outlined an ambitious program of nationalization and agrarian reform. Banks, insurance companies, large shipping companies, and heavy industries were all to be converted to public control. Large agrarian estates were to be broken up and redistributed to landless peasants.[22] For a brief moment, it appeared that the entire Arab world was on the verge of a broad social revolution. The landed shaykhs and comprador industrialists were going to be expropriated while sons of postmen and landless peasants were going to enjoy electricity and indoor plumbing. Abdullah Tariki had been ejected from state power in Saudi Arabia, but exile to Beirut may have only elevated his regional influence. In Beirut, he established a private consulting business, founded the journal *Arab Oil and Gas,* and became a frequent adviser to oil-producing states—especially Iraq under 'Arif and Yayha.

IRAQ IN OPEC

In Iraq, the Tariki philosophy left a clear imprint on Prime Minister Yahya's oil policy. As Yahya came to power and announced his program of economic development and diplomacy in the spirit of Bandung, Iraq began to play a more active role in OPEC. Although Iraq had been a founding member of OPEC, it had ceased attending OPEC meetings after OPEC member states sided against Iraq in the Kuwait crisis of 1961. But as Yahya took power, Iraq resumed attending OPEC meetings and began pushing it in a more radical direction. The first indication of this was the December 1963 replacement of Fuad Rouhani, an Iranian who was a relative moderate, by 'Abd al-Rahman al-Bazzaz, a prominent Iraqi pan-Arab nationalist and former dean of the Baghdad College of Law, as OPEC secretary general.[23] Sir Geoffrey Harrison, the deputy undersecretary of state for the British Foreign Office, who knew al-Bazzaz from his time as Iraqi ambassador to England (1963–64), regarded him as an "extreme nationalist" and warned the State Department that he would lead OPEC in a more radical direction.[24] Al-Bazzaz would subsequently prove rather conservative with regard to oil issues. But in 1964, the British assessment of his ascendance within OPEC was essentially correct. As OPEC general secretary, al-Bazzaz reopened the issue of royalties expensing and pressed the matter firmly. Rather than negotiating with the companies, al-Bazzaz joined Tariki in calling on OPEC members to exercise their sovereign authority to unilaterally legislate tax code changes.[25]

The threat of unilateral legislative action was sufficient to compel the companies to compromise. Especially given that the companies had never actually expected the 50–50 formula established in the early 1950s to last as long as it had. In their view, it was only the political conservatism of Iran that had kept it in place since that time. But now, in the early 1960s, Iran faced the threat of being "expelled from OPEC" if it did not join with Iraq and other producers in calling for the readjustment of tax rates. In the face of growing pressure from Iraq, the State Department advised the companies to engage in a "searching, hard-headed review of their positions to determine whether they might not make adjusted offer which would enlist 'moderate' Arab support and set pattern of peace in industry for lengthy period."[26] The

State Department never tired in its effort to save international capitalism from and for international capitalists.

Critical self-reflection and compromise, however, were not part of the IPC's business model. Whatever the State Department might have to say, the companies were still unwilling to formally recognize the existence of OPEC. Rather than negotiating with the producers as a unified body, the companies insisted on separate negotiations in each country. But in Iraq, they were not even willing to do this. After the IPC refused to negotiate with al-Wattari, who remained Iraq's oil minister despite the fall of the Ba'th, al-Wattari asked the IPC to appoint a negotiator of its choosing. When the companies suggested Fuad Rouhani, Iraq accepted. Then all of the other producers also appointed Rouhani to represent their interests, effectively forcing the companies to negotiate with OPEC as a unified body.[27]

As OPEC gained power it became more conservative. In equal measure. It now existed, in the eyes of the companies, but was led by Rouhani, who had just been replaced by al-Bazzaz. The ground was moving in a different direction than the people walking on it. Rouhani, and behind him the shah, much to the consternation of Iraq, then negotiated a sweetheart agreement with the companies. In December 1964, OPEC announced its first collective bargaining agreement. The companies accepted a formula for phased expensing of royalties. OPEC, in turn, accepted a number of concessions. These included a "quitclaim" whereby OPEC members renounced any outstanding financial claims against the companies; an arbitration clause whereby OPEC members waived their right of sovereign action and agreed to arbitrate future disputes at The Hague; and a "most-favoured company" clause whereby existing concessionaires would be given priority over new companies seeking to enter the region.[28]

Al-Bazzaz was prepared to accept this agreement. But al-Wattari denounced the terms as "grossly unjust." Al-Wattari took particular exception to the "most-favoured company" clause. He cited "Independent and Japanese interest in contracting with INOC," and refused to foreclose Iraq's options in this regard. According to al-Wattari, the success of Iraq's independent oil policy "was evidence that the socialist view was workable" and endless capitulation to the companies was unnecessary.[29] In the face of internal OPEC divisions, it was up to individual countries to determine whether or not they were going to accept the agreement. Iran, Saudi Arabi, Kuwait, and Qatar all accepted. But Iraq, Venezuela, and Indonesia, still under the nationalist regime of Sukarno, did not.

Al-Wattari was clearly willing to push harder than al-Bazzaz. But Tariki, now running an oil consulting business in Lebanon, was willing to push harder still. At the Fifth Arab Petroleum Conference held in Cairo in April 1965, Tariki gave a major address in which he argued that all of the existing concessions in the region were legally invalid in that they had been concluded among unequal parties and had institutionalized terms of unequal exchange that were an affront to the national sovereignty of the producing countries. In his speech, he called on producers to nationalize the concessions that had been "imposed on us during the era of imperialism. . . . If we cannot nationalize today, let us prepare ourselves to do so later."[30]

Tariki's speech caused a major uproar within OPEC. In response, al-Bazzaz attacked Tariki for "provoking [an] emotional reaction rather than addressing reason."[31] Francisco Parra of Venezuela agreed. In his view, "Cold calculation will serve the interests of the producing countries better than red-hot emotion."[32] The following week, the Cairo newspaper *al-Akhbar* (*The News*) sponsored a debate between Tariki and al-Wattari on the future of Arab oil in which al-Wattari agreed with al-Bazzaz that Tariki's call for immediate nationalization was not practicable.[33] However, the differences between Tariki on the one side, and Parra, al-Bazzaz, and al-Wattari on the other, were more tactical and strategic than they were philosophical. Philosophically, all parties involved accepted the premises of the unequal exchange thesis, and that nationalization was the long-term remedy.[34] What was at issue was essentially a question of sequencing and timing. As government officials in oil-exporting states, Parra, al-Bazzaz, and al-Wattari were simply more cautious than Tariki. But ultimately, it was Tariki's handwriting on the wall.

As a sign of the times, and an indication of what lay ahead, Iraq marked the sixth anniversary of the Free Officers' Revolution in July 1964 by unveiling a broad program of socialist transformation designed to facilitate the eventual nationalization of the IPC. According to what became known as the "July Measures," Khair el-Din Haseeb announced the nationalization of all banks and insurance companies, as well as thirty-two large industrial and commercial establishments. The nationalized enterprises would now come under the authority of new Economic Organization overseen by

FIGURE 10. Khair el-Din Haseeb, 1964. Khair el-Din Haseeb as governor of the Central Bank of Iraq and director of the Economic Organization. Source: Courtesy of Khair el-Din Haseeb. Reprinted with permission.

Haseeb, who became known as Iraq's "Economic Czar."[35] The July nationalizations did not extend to oil, as the "fear of western intervention" and the "example of Iran" still loomed large in the minds of Iraqis, according to the US embassy.[36] But in announcing the socialist measures of July 1964, Haseeb made it clear that it was only a matter of time before the IPC would too be brought under state control.

STATE'S DILEMMA: DETERRING THE INDEPENDENTS

The emergence of a coherent nationalist regime in Iraq put the United States in a difficult position. A core element of that nationalist regime's political strategy was to forge transnational coalitions in opposition to the dominance of the majors. The close collaboration with Egypt and the activism in OPEC were just two aspects of this broader program of transnational coalition building. But over the course of 1964–65, a somewhat surprising coalition partner emerged: the American independent oil companies that were natural competitors to the established majors. As part of the effort to build this coalition, al-Wattari had traveled to Washington in March 1964 to meet with an "unknown oil representative."[37] That unknown representative turned out to be E. L. Steiniger, chairman of Sinclair Oil Company—a particularly aggressive American independent interested in acquiring an Iraqi concession. But Steiniger was far from alone. While in Washington several other American companies approached al-Wattari with offers to help Iraq develop the oil fields nationalized under Law 80.[38]

The sight of al-Wattari meeting with large domestic producers interested in moving into the international field (firms including Sinclair, Phillips, Pauley, Continental, and Union) touched a raw nerve at the State Department. In the wake of al-Wattari's visit, Secretary of State Dean Rusk, and high-level

FIGURE 11. Baghdad financial district, 1959. Photo by Latif al-Ani of the Central Bank of Iraq and Baghdad financial district. Source: Latif al-Ani courtesy of The Arab Image Foundation. Reprinted with permission.

adviser Averell Harriman, invested considerable effort in deterring the independents from entering Iraq while the Law 80 dispute remained unresolved. Harriman was particularly concerned with the Iraq-IPC situation because he had, in the 1940s, been a founding partner of Brown Brothers Harriman & Co., a powerful Wall Street law firm that represented several major oil companies. Harriman had led an ill-fated "Harriman Mission" to Tehran in July 1951 to negotiate a compromise settlement to the dispute arising from Iran's nationalization of the Anglo-Iranian Oil Company.[39] He therefore understood the sensitivity of the issues involved in the Iraq-IPC dispute and did everything that he could to deter the independents from complicating the delicate negotiations in Baghdad.

As it became clear that American companies were not willing to wait for a settlement with the IPC before entering Iraq, Secretary of State Rusk composed a telegram to the embassy in Iraq outlining what was at stake in the Iraq-IPC dispute. The embassy was to inform any independent oilmen turning up in Baghdad that the outcome of the dispute between Iraq and the IPC would have "broad implications" throughout the region.[40] If Iraq succeeded in securing an agreement with an American company to develop fields reclaimed under Law 80, Iraq would have

> good reason to suppose that concession agreements can be terminated unilaterally . . . whenever GOI [Government of Iraq] considers that it is in its own interest to do so. Other producing governments could draw same conclusions and concept of unilateral change of agreements which already has its adherents, e.g., Tariki, would be markedly strengthened.

The embassy was to further instruct any new company entering Iraq in the absence of a Law 80 settlement that the State Department "could not assure diplomatic support" in the event that it too found itself in a dispute with that government.

While the embassy sought to intercede with American commercial agents in Iraq, Harriman reached out to Sinclair chairman Steiniger to meet in Washington on May 6. In the meeting, Harriman recounted the Iraq-IPC dispute and outlined the State Department's position on the issue: "We would not wish governments, such as Iraq, to get the impression that American oil companies can be pushed around."[41] Steiniger "admitted the validity of this reasoning" and explained that he understood the delicacy of the situation, but he insisted that his company was "crude short" and could not afford to forego opportunities in Iraq while Sinclair's international competitors moved in to claim a share of the market. Moreover, Steiniger could not "tell a sovereign government that it must settle with [the IPC] before [Sinclair could] do business with it." In response to Sinclair's insistence on its right to move through an "open door" in Iraq, Harriman issued a lightly veiled threat:

> The USG [US Government] follows the problems of the oil companies very closely. Sometimes we can be of help and sometimes not. The relationship between the US Government and the oil companies is a two-way street. We prefer to talk about a problem as we are now doing rather than have Sinclair come around later to the US Government and take a stand in some other area demanding USG support.

Despite Harriman's warning, the State Department was unable to deter independent firms from expressing interest in Iraq. The continued interest of American independents led Arthur Dean, who succeed Foster Dulles as senior partner at Sullivan & Cromwell, to call upon Harriman to express frustration with the behavior of the American independents and request "additional efforts" to "deter American companies from making offers to the Iraq Government."[42] Arthur Dean insisted that Dean Rusk was not doing enough and that "American companies, merely by talking to the Iraqis, are giving the GOI encouragement." To this, Harriman explained that the State Department did not actually "have legal authority to prohibit American companies from entering Iraq," and that interceding with the government of Iraq "in support of the companies" would only enflame "Iraqi sensitivity."

In the face of unrelenting independent interest in Iraq, the State Department called Ambassador Strong to Washington to discuss the matter. In the meeting, George Ball, the State Department's undersecretary for political affairs who had a reputation for sympathizing with Third World nationalism, expressed frustration with the slow pace of the Iraq-IPC negotiations and expressed the opinion that the "Department had stood down the independent companies for quite a while now," and that "we should make clear to [Exxon and Mobil] that we could not hold the line in Iraq forever." Strong, in apparent agreement with Ball, stated, "He hated to see the negotiations drag on too much longer for as time passed there was increasing danger that

Iraq's political instability, together with British and Iranian activity against the present Iraqi Government, might result in a new Iraqi regime less willing and able to reach an agreement than the present Government."

In December 1961, as ambassador to Iraq, John D. Jernegan had defended Iraq's right to nationalization. But now, as a member of the NEA back in Washington, he emphasized the opposite principle that "oil producing countries should be prevented from making a success out of nationalization or other unilateral actions with respect to oil concessions legally held by foreign companies."[43] Ball agreed with this principle, but noted, "American companies which heeded the Department's advice to stay out of Iraq might eventually find themselves undercut by other American companies that chiseled. Also there were the Japanese, Italians, and other foreign oil operators to worry about." Both agreed to call Exxon and Mobil to Washington to emphasize the importance of moving rapidly toward a settlement.

THE REVOLUTION IN INTERNATIONAL LEGAL NORMS

The unrelenting interest of independent oil companies seeking new concessions in Iraq, on the one hand, and the equally unrelenting interest of the majors companies in keeping the independents out, on the other, led the State Department to examine the legal principles at issue in the Iraq-IPC dispute. To clarify the nature of the IPC's legal rights in Iraq, Ball sought the opinion of Walter J. Levy, an influential private consultant. Levy had advised numerous oil companies, producing governments, and the US government. In the 1930s, Levy had been a German-Jewish academic expert in petroleum law. With the advent of the Nazi regime, he fled to the UK where he joined the British Ministry of Economic Warfare, and then the OSS, where he used his industry expertise to advise Allied war-planners on the precise locations of German oil facilities.[44] After the war, Levy had served as Harriman's technical adviser in the July 1951 effort to mediate the dispute between Mossadegh and BP. He therefore understood the issues involved in Iraq very well.

Undersecretary Ball began the meeting by asking Levy to share his impressions of the situation in Iraq.[45] Levy explained that in addition to the American independents, a major threat to the IPC position came from foreign companies, especially partially state-owned firms in France and Italy. Given the threat of foreign competition, Levy doubted that American independents would wait for "clearance from the State Department before making any offers to the government of Iraq." When the conversation turned to the IPC legal position, Levy warned against pushing the issue too far.

> An objective historical analysis of the IPC concession would show that Iraq had not been treated fairly. A good case could be made to support Iraq's contention that vast relinquishments of territory by IPC should have taken place long ago.... In view of this background, said Mr. Levy, the Department would be well advised to keep IPC-Iraq Government oil issues from going to arbitration.

When asked what he "thought would happen in other oil producing countries if Iraq made a success of Law 80," Levy explained that

> the major companies would then have to relinquish territory elsewhere much faster than they now planned but added that he did not think the Department should shed any tears over this because the companies held fantastic oil reserves far beyond their needs. He thought the companies' reluctance to settle Law 80 issues with Iraq without getting back a sizeable portion of territory was caused particularly by their desire to avoid accelerated relinquishment demands from Saudi Arabia. Mr. Levy mentioned a figure of 200–300 billion barrels as Aramco's actual reserves but added that the companies "really didn't know what they had."

Minutes from the meeting were then forwarded to select members of the State Department with a note to treat the contents with "EXDIS," or extreme discretion, as the "Info here is too hot (commercially speaking) for wide distribution."

The State Department next met with its legal adviser, Andreas Lowenfeld, to clarify the legal issues involved. Lowenfeld prefaced his analysis by stating that "the principle issues involved [in the Iraq-IPC dispute] are at that frontier between international law and politics where no firm answer can be given by a lawyer alone."[46] He nonetheless went on to present a legal analysis which made it clear that there was very little basis for IPC's claim that Laws 80 and 11 were in violation of any US, international, or Iraqi laws, or that the company was owed *any* compensation. He rather cited a series of recent legal decisions affirming a state's sovereign right to nationalize foreign-held properties so long as "prompt, adequate, and effective compensation" was provided. In the case of Law 80, *"IPC's property as such has not been taken, and in fact IPC's operations have continued substantially unimpeded"* (emphasis added). IPC's claim was, therefore, "at most a claim for breach of contract," and it could not reasonably expect *any* compensation. Lowenfeld recounted IPC's history of "excluding or swallowing up all competitors" and suggested that there appeared to be "no effective legal remedy against the Government of Iraq. . . . While the legal issues in the IPC-Iraq dispute are numerous and complicated, law does not appear to provide solutions."

In light of the political and legal analysis provided by Levy and Lowenfeld, the State Department grew increasingly impatient with the IPC. Not only was the IPC standing on weak legal ground, but the longer the Iraq-IPC negotiations dragged on, the more likely it was that a foreign firm would acquire a concession which would represent a "set-back to our long-term interest of maximizing private American investment in foreign oil resources."[47] Moreover, the failure of the IPC to work toward a settlement "could lay the U.S. government open to charges by other U.S. oil companies that an unreasonable degree of preference has been given to the IPC shareholders having the effect of providing IPC a privileged position in respect to future oil operations in Iraq and of preventing non-IPC companies from competing for the most promising unproven areas available under current Iraqi laws."

Armed with cutting-edge legal and political analyses, the State Department finally met with the representatives of Exxon and Mobil on October 26. In the meeting, Undersecretary Ball requested a progress report on IPC negotiations, and urged the companies to come to a settlement as the "Department had no way of putting a complete quarantine on the situation."[48] The oil representatives insisted that the IPC was working diligently toward a resolution. IPC officials had engaged in thirty-five separate negotiating sessions since September 2, and "IPC negotiators often engaged in self-critical reflections to make certain that the IPC position and terms offered to the Iraqis were sound and as forthcoming as possible." However, the Iraqis appeared in no hurry to settle. They had recently asked for a recess in negotiations, and were taking their time in defining their position. "They apparently wanted to pick out the best features from a variety of international concessions and put them together in a single concession document, thus ensuring an eminently favorable concession document from the GOI point of view." In this context the majors emphasized that the presence of Sinclair representatives in Iraq offering the government more favorable terms than the IPC was prepared to offer was undermining the IPC position and delaying a settlement. Moreover, they reported progress in their talks with al-Wattari and INOC chair Ghanim al-ʿUqayli, but expressed frustration that these relative moderates were "always looking over their shoulder," and that any agreement they might reach with al-Wattari would be overturned by the prime minister. The meeting ended on the rather inconclusive note: "There was no logical limit," in the words of Mobil's Henry Moses, on how long the negotiations might last.

THE FRENCH DEFECTION

What doesn't bend, breaks. This much was true of the IPC consortium in the fall of 1964. Despite its best efforts, the State Department could not convince the IPC to yield to any of Iraq's demands. Part of the problem was the complex ownership structure of the IPC. The IPC was not one company but rather a consortium of distinct firms occupying varied and distinct market positions. Given their varied market positions, there was always the possibility of disunity and competition among the constituent firms. By the end of 1964, a clear factional split emerged within the consortium. On the one side stood Exxon and BP. Both companies held substantial reserves elsewhere in the region—BP in Iran and Kuwait, Exxon in Saudi Arabia and Kuwait—and were particularly concerned to see that the principle of resource nationalization did not spread. The other faction within the IPC was led by the French CFP, which was a relatively "crude short" company, meaning that it lacked adequate crude oil supplies to service its existing markets. CFP therefore sought an early settlement of the Law 80 dispute and an immediate increase in production. CFP was supported in this by Shell and Mobil, both of which were also relatively crude short and more interested in expanding production than they were concerned about "precedent setting."[49]

Overlaying the commercial rivalry within the IPC was a larger French political ambition. The key figure leading representing this larger political ambition was French president Charles de Gaulle (1959–69). De Gaulle was among a rising generation of world leaders who had grown impatient with the rigidities of American hegemony under the auspices of the Cold War. Enrico Mattei had been another. In Tunisia in 1960, Mattei had boldly declared that unlike the Seven Sisters cartel and the "Anglo-Saxon imperialists," he was not "afraid of decolonization." He rather stood with the aspirations of the Afro-Asian world against Anglo-Saxon imperialism.[50] Mattei's dream of a world revolution against American hegemony came to a fiery end in October 1962 (see chapter 3). But by this point, de Gaulle had taken up the mantle of Cold War nonalignment in solidarity with the Third World.

The French embrace of Third Worldism under de Gaulle represented a dramatic turnabout in French foreign policy. While the term "Third World" (*tiers monde*) was of French origin and was a reference to the Third Estate of the French Revolution, the "Fourth Republic" (1946–58) had drifted a great distance from French revolutionary ideals and was among the most reactionary of the European colonial powers. Having been overrun by Germany for most of World War II, the French conservatives who were returned to power in 1946 shifted their attention to losing the French-Indochina War (1946–54). Having lost the Indochina War, France turned its attention to losing the Algerian War of Independence (1954–62) and the Suez War (1956). Failing in four wars in rapid succession compelled many French to try another tact.[51] In the face of what revolutionary theorist Frantz Fanon described as "a *dying colonialism*," French voters elected de Gaulle prime minister in June 1958. He had been the leader of the French resistance to the Nazis in WWII and led the Provisional Government of the French Republics between 1944 and 1946, before retiring to private life.

Upon returning to power in 1958, de Gaulle commissioned a new French Constitution, and then in January became the first president of the Fifth Republic. The first order of business was extricating France from the war in Algeria. Once he had finally completed this task in 1962, de Gaulle turned his attention to remaking French relations in the Arab world. Up to this point France had been allied with Israel against Nasser and the broader force of Arab nationalism. But in 1962 de Gaulle began implementing a pro-Arab foreign policy that centered on forging close bilateral relations with Iraq.[52] A strong position in the Arab world would, in turn, support de Gaulle's broader ambition of nonalignment in the Cold War. Toward this end he issued a memorandum in 1958 that effectively declared French independence from NATO, and France left the alliance altogether in 1966.[53] To effectively win independence from NATO, de Gaulle sought to forge an economic alliance with West Germany. Iraq and the Arab world were central to this larger strategy because oil exports from Iraq, through the CFP, accounted for 20 percent of the French energy market.[54] De Gaulle hoped to increase Iraqi oil production to meet more of France's own demand as well as to provide low-cost oil to Germany.

The entirety of de Gaulle's foreign policy of Cold War nonalignment rested on CFP's ability to increase oil production in Iraq. But none of this could happen until the Iraq-IPC dispute was settled. In the interest of bringing about that settlement, Jacques Morizet of the French embassy in Washington reached out to the State Department to elicit its help in bringing Iraq-IPC negotiations to a successful conclusion in January 1965. In the meeting, Morizet pressed the State Department to prevail on Exxon and Mobil to be more forthcoming with regard to Iraqi demands. To this, Andrew Ensor, who would soon leave the State Department for a top executive position with Mobil, explained that while the department maintained a "close liaison with the American shareholders," Exxon and Mobil were, unlike CFP, private companies and that the State Department could not order them to do anything.

In their meeting with the French, State Department officials did not disclose that they had in fact been trying unsuccessfully to compel Exxon and Mobil to be more forthcoming with the Iraqis. On the contrary, the State Department insisted (despite knowing better) that it was Iraqi, not IPC, intransigence that best explained the deadlock in Baghdad. If Exxon and Mobil were to accede to Iraq's unreasonable demands, they claimed, it would set a very bad precedent throughout the region. To this, Morizet warned that if the IPC were unwilling to settle, Iraq would have no choice but to nationalize the companies, which would set a far more dangerous precedent. To this the State Department's George Bennsky responded that the fear of nationalization was overblown—the government in Baghdad was "fully aware [of the] consequences which resulted for Iran from their attempted expropriation in the early 1950s." While the reference to the fate of Mossadegh was intended to settle the issue, Morizet ended the meeting by assuring his American counterparts that they "could expect to hear more from him soon." Ten days after Morizet's call on the State Department, French representatives made the same appeal to the British Foreign Office in London.[55]

The French diplomatic offensive was a success. After much handwringing among parent companies, the IPC finally relented and allowed CFP president Jean Duroc-Danner to lead a new round of highly secret negotiations in May 1965 that was to finally bring an end to the Law 80 dispute.[56] Within a month Duroc-Danner, working in close association with Oil Minister al-Wattari, produced a far-reaching draft agreement with the government of Iraq that settled all outstanding issues. The so-called "Wattari Agreement" entailed the formation of the Baghdad Oil Company, a new INOC-IPC joint venture to develop the Rumaila field (see map 3). IPC partners (with the exception of Exxon, which sold its interest to Mobil) retained two-thirds of the ownership shares in the new company, but implicitly recognized Laws 80 and 11, and agreed to increase the total volume of Iraqi oil production, and agreed to pay Iraq £20 million to settle the royalties expensing issue.[57]

To the State Department it appeared the majors had finally relented and accommodated themselves to the changed political and legal realities of the mid-1960s. France had seemingly succeeded where the State Department had failed in the effort to drag the companies into the modern era. But neither the State Department nor any of the parent companies—including CFP—realized just how changed those circumstances were. The Wattari Agreement represented a significant revision to the IPC's previously uncompromising position, and all parties involved—the French, the majors, the US and British governments, and al-Wattari himself—believed that it would be greeted as a major victory in Iraq. But in seeing it this way, the parties to the Wattari Agreement overlooked the radicalism of Tariki's philosophy, and the extent to which that radicalism was shared among ordinary Iraqis.

THE COLLAPSE OF THE WATTARI AGREEMENT

Contrary to expectations, the proposed Wattari Agreement created a loud public uproar of opposition. Part of this was due to the way in which the agreement was negotiated. Al-Wattari had negotiated it in strict secrecy, hoping to simply present the prime minister and cabinet with a fait accompli. But when the agreement was presented to the cabinet for ratification in July, Adib al-Jadir and five other Nasserist cabinet members resigned their posts in protest and mounted a vigorous press campaign against its ratification.[58]

The most forceful critique of the agreement appeared in an anonymous editorial published in Baghdad's *al-Thawrah al-'Arabiyyah* (*The Arab Revolution*). Though unsigned, the IPC traced the authorship of "Iraq and the Oil

Companies" to Abdullah Tariki, as it tracked closely with a lecture that he gave in Baghdad in June 1963 at the invitation of al-Jadir. IPC analysts speculated that the editorial came as a result of meetings between Tariki and al-Jadir in Beirut in May.[59] The editorial critiqued the Wattari Agreement as conforming to the pattern of earlier concessionary arrangements in that it was "concluded by unequal parties" and served to reinforce the power of the IPC as a "government within a government."[60] It cited the Arthur D. Little oil accounting report showing that the IPC had used accounting tricks and complex pricing formulas to cheat Iraq out of millions of pounds annually that Tariki had referenced in his speech at the October 1960 Arab Oil Conference in Beirut. Worse yet, IPC was using its ill-gotten gains for "subversive and coup d'état purposes." Tariki described the IPC as "the prime mover in the country," and claimed that its machinations "created [the very] atmosphere of instability" that it cited as an excuse to avoid capital investment. According to Tariki's editorial, no less than the sovereignty of the Iraqi state was at stake. The "governments of civilized countries do not," he argued, "resort to negotiations but [rather] to legislation" in pursuit of social and economic objectives. As an example of "civilized governments" using the power of legislation, Tariki cited the example of the US government "imposing" income taxes on companies such as General Motors and US Steel, and British nationalizations of the health care, coal, and railroad industries.

This critique was explosive within the political context of Iraq, but was, nonetheless, relatively restrained when compared to that of the Islamist Tahrir (*Liberation*) Party. According to a Tahrir pamphlet, the agreement was in "total contradiction to Islam" which "prohibits the Moslems from allowing infidels to rule over [them]."[61] "Besides," the pamphlet added, "religious rule prohibits the ownership of oil by any company on the grounds that oil is public property and should, therefore, remain a property for all Moslems on whose behalf the State undertakes its exploitation, investment and processing."

Opposition was no less determined from what remained of the Communists. Even before the agreement was announced, the Communist publication *Sarkat al-Kadehin* (*Cry of the Workers*) denounced rumors of ongoing negotiations as an insult to Iraqi sovereignty. The paper warned that those who would "think of selling their riches at a trifling price" would eventually have to face the wrath of the people with regard to those elements who have sold themselves to the imperialists for a contaminated handful of money. We advise them that what they have received, and will receive, will never help them and never protect them against the ire of the public who understands what is being prepared for them in private.[62]

Throughout Iraq, one issue upon which Nasserists, Islamists, and Communists could agree was Iraq's sovereign right to unilaterally revise concession agreements through legislation. There was a broad national consensus in favor of keeping the IPC out of Rumaila. In the controversy that ensued, the Wattari Agreement was shelved, and al-Wattari was forced to resign in the face of popular outrage.[63]

OF PRINCES AND PRESIDENTS: THE FATE OF
OIL SOVEREIGNTY IN SAUDI ARABIA, IRAN, AND IRAQ

The Nasserist regime that came to power at the end of 1963 did a great deal to advance the cause of oil sovereignty in Iraq and beyond. In Saudi Arabia, Abdullah Tariki's embrace of oil sovereignty as a legal doctrine put him on a collision course with the oil companies that were allied with kingdom's ruling family. For his principled commitment, Tariki was exiled to Beirut, where his ideas grew only more radical. A similar dynamic prevailed in Iran. As we have seen, Iranian oil adviser and OPEC general secretary (1961–63) Fuad Rouhani was far more moderate in his dealings with the oil companies than was Tariki or al-Wattari. But for even just talking to Tariki and al-Wattari, Rouhani was "pushed aside" and "disciplined" by the shah. In the wake of Rouhani's effort to work with other oil producers on the royalties expensing issue in 1963, he was displaced in the Iranian councils of government and made to step down from OPEC.[64]

In both Saudi Arabia and Iran, US-allied monarchies blocked the efforts of their own most able citizens to advance the cause of oil sovereignty. But a wholly different political dynamic prevailed in Iraq. There, the Nasserists regime did just the opposite. Under Prime Minister Tahir Yahya, Iraq brought in the best oil experts in the region and asked them to build the institutions and relationships that would allow the government to exercise true sovereignty over its natural resources. As a result of the efforts of people like Tariki, Haseeb, and al-Jadir, Iraq succeeded in asserting and defending a new international legal norm.

Before the advent of the Nasserist regime in Iraq, the unilateral abrogation of a concessionary agreement was seen to violate the sanctity of contracts. And before 1964, violating the sanctity of contracts was seen in Washington as suspicious of Communist ties. And suspicion of Communist ties was quite often sufficient to spring the CIA into covert action to bring about regime change. But by 1965, the idea that CIA covert operations could hold back the tide of resources nationalism was appearing less and less realistic. There was a growing sense that the world was rapidly changing, and that Washington's ability to influence the course of world events was rapidly diminishing. One factor that accelerated these trends, and that exposed significant contradictions in the logic of American foreign policy, was the June 1967 Arab-Israeli War.

Chapter 7
THE ARAB-ISRAELI JUNE WAR

IN THE SECOND HALF OF THE 1960S, MANY OF THE ASSUMPTIONS upon which American foreign oil policy was based started to come undone. On one level, the problem was political and economic. Since the late 1940s, US foreign oil policy rested on a series of interlocking agreements and relations. There was the US relationship to and support for the major oil-producing states. And there was the US relationship to and support for the major oil-producing companies. As we saw in the previous chapter, both sets of relationships were strained by the nationalist movement in Iraq. Iraq challenged the oil complacency of the US-allied regimes in Iran and Saudi Arabia. And Iraq invited independent US and French oil interests into the country to compete with the majors. The US State Department was like the proverbial Dutch boy with his finger in the dike. And as the proverb suggests, the State Department would not be able to hold back the combined forces of Arab nationalism, independent American capitalism, and European (mainly French) Cold War nonalignment. Each of these forces gathered strength in the late 1960s.

But the problem was not merely political and economic. There was also a spiritual and moral dimension to the crisis. Historian Darren Dochuk interprets the economic forces at work in the late 1960s in sectarian and theological terms. In his study of the religious history of the American oil industry, he describes a distinct religious expression of the leading domestic oil and gas firms as "wildcat Christianity," which he contrasts against the "civic religion of crude" practiced by the international majors. Whereas the majors prized rational efficiency and extolled the Protestant ethic described by Max Weber, the domestics were imbued with the "charismatic" qualities that Weber associated with pre-industrial "warrior heroes."[1] Whereas the majors adhered to an ethic of good corporate citizenship and progressive developmentalism, the independents embodied the virtues of rugged individualism. They "took risks and pursued profits as if there were no tomorrow [and] held tightly to a theology premised on the power of the personal encounter with an active Creator, the mysteries of an earth whose hidden riches enchanted and eluded reason, and the need to labor tirelessly—be it drilling or evangelizing—before time ran out."[2]

Dochuk's Weberian analysis opens up new vantage points through which we can view a number of important developments in US-Iraqi relations and the economic history of the late 1960s: the limits and failures of the State Department's ability to promote economic development and political stability, the aggressive push of domestic American oil and gas companies to vastly expand US production of nontraditional sources of oil and gas (tar sands, shales, etc.), the symbolism of Jerusalem in the domestic political fights of both the US and Iraq, and the centrifugal tendencies of an international system that was increasingly exceeding the bounds of what was permissible under US hegemony. These four interrelated forces converged in the summer of 1967 as a result of the Arab-Israeli June War. The course and outcome of that war would serve to dramatically accelerate the nationalization of the Iraq Petroleum Company. Dochuk's ideal types help us to see the various forces at work in this process, but ultimately, we will need a more materialist form of analysis to explain this material outcome.[3]

THE CRISIS OF THE OFFICERS' STATE

The en masse resignation of the Nasserist ministers in July 1965 was an important turning point in Iraqi history. In November 1963, President 'Abd al-Salam 'Arif had allied with Tahir Yahya and the Nasiryun to eject the Ba'th from power. 'Arif then had to share power with Yahya and the Nasserists. But with the departure of the Nasserists, President 'Arif, supported by a group of army officers immediately loyal to him (the so-called "'Arefites"), would emerge as the dominant figure in Iraqi politics. 'Arif was much more conservative than Yayha and the Nasserists, and after July 1965, he led a marked moderation in Iraqi policy in general, but with regard to oil in particular.

No one was happier to see the advent of a conservative trend in Iraqi politics than James Akins, the main political officer in the Baghdad embassy. In Akins's view, the Nasserists' resignations reflected much more than the controversy surrounding the terms of the proposed Wattari Agreement. It was rather an admission that the whole notion of socialism in Iraq was a failure. In a series of economic portraits painted in 1965, Akins decried the "capital flight" induced by the July measures.[4] As Iraqi entrepreneurs either forwent new investments or left the country—with their capital—altogether, Haseeb's Economic Organization suffered from a shortage of competent public administrators to manage socialized enterprises. As a result, food prices and unemployment rose, while black markets emerged and overall rates of economic growth declined. In Akins's view, this was no mere economic or technical failure but rather reflective of a broader moral crisis. In the standard invective directed at whoever happened to be out of favor with the embassy at any given moment, Akins described Yahya and Haseeb as "opportunistic" and "corrupt" (while, of course, those who treated the companies with kid gloves were "principled" and "moral").

While the US embassy was quick to blame the concept of socialism and the corruption of the Nasserist regime, another important factor in explaining Iraq's economic difficulties was a new flaring of the Kurdish insurgency. The Yahya government had negotiated an uneasy ceasefire with the Kurds in February 1964, but by the winter of 1964–65 that ceasefire had begun to break down. In April 1965, curiously at the very moment that the IPC relented to French demands to enter negotiations with al-Wattari, Kurdish insurgents supported by "the Iranians and Israelis—and perhaps the British," launched a new round of fighting.[5] The combination of Iraq's economic malaise with the intractable quagmire in Kurdistan contributed to a growing disillusionment with the role of the military in Iraqi politics.

In June 1965, Akins filed a long report reflecting on popular disillusionment with the so-called "officers' state" in Iraq.[6] In his dispatch, Akins described how the image of the military had changed since the army coup of 1958:

Iraqis looked to their military officers in the 1930's and in the upheavals of 1958 and 1963 to deliver them from the corrupt civilian politicians and from civilian bickering and inefficiency. The officers, many Iraqis believed, were clean; they were honorable and ambitious only for the welfare of the country. The picture was tarnished after July 1958. November 1963 saw its complete effacement. The officers quickly proved to be at least as corrupt and far crueler and more dangerous than their civilian predecessors. They were inefficient and arrogant. The unkindest cut of all was that they were immensely expensive. The military establishment now devours a substantial proportion of the budget of the country. And its officers, often failures in school and usually drawn from the middle and lower middle classes, are paid high salaries which arouse the jealousy and disfavor of most civilians.

Despite this widespread disillusionment with military rule, Akins fantasized about a new coup that might produce a "permanent benevolent dictatorship" in Iraq. He found that while there was broad support for the "Army returning to its barracks,"

> Such a transformation of power assumes the retention of a strong military man as president or prime minister or a military clique at least for a transitional period after which two alternative paths would appear: a permanent benevolent dictatorship or a return to a parliamentary form of government. The simplest would be the retention of the leader of the next coup as dictator. If intelligent and farsighted he could then satisfy many of the aspirations of the people.

Akins believed that a "permanent benevolent dictatorship" represented the best hope for the future, but concluded his report on a rather pessimistic note: "Unfortunately Iraq is not a reasonable country. With its weak and divided nature perhaps there can never be any solutions to the problems which have plagued it since its independence."

In the fall of 1965, President 'Arif sought to exploit this sense of social and political malaise to remove, once and for all, the Nasserist officers with whom he shared power. However, checking the Nasserists could not be accomplished in one move. Rather than a frontal assault, he sought to outflank and pincer his rivals. As an opening move, he demanded Yahya's resignation in September.[7] But to avoid a Nasserist backlash, he initially replaced

Yahya with 'Arif 'Abd al-Razzaq, the radical nationalist commander of the air force. Two weeks later, al-Razzaq, sensing that he was being used as a pawn in a war of position against Nasser, organized a coup to remove 'Arif and consolidate power for himself. However, the coup was discovered and suppressed before it could get off the ground, and al-Razzaq was forced to flee to Cairo.[8]

'Arif took advantage of al-Razzaq's overreach to replace him with 'Abd al-Rahman al-Bazzaz, who had recently left OPEC to serve as 'Arif's deputy prime minister, foreign minister, and oil minister (to replace al-Wattari, who had resigned in the face of the popular opposition to the agreement he negotiated with the IPC). Al-Bazzaz, Iraq's first civilian premier since the 1958 revolution, was a close friend and ally of 'Arif and shared the president's basic worldview.[9] Both al-Bazzaz and 'Arif adhered to a strand of Arab nationalism that was more informed by socially conservative interpretations of Sunni Islamic doctrine than by socialism. Both figures were uncomfortable with the socialist trend in Iraqi politics represented by the ascendance of Yahya, Haseeb, and al-Jadir.

With the rise of al-Bazzaz, the pendulum in Iraqi politics began to shift in a more conservative direction. In this environment, Haseeb was forced out, and Iraqi policy underwent significant conservative moderation. Whereas the Yahya government had made oil issues (in OPEC and with the IPC) a central concern of Iraqi policy, al-Bazzaz now shifted focus to negotiating an agreement with Iraqi Kurds. After al-Bazzaz assumed the premiership in September 1965, he withdrew from further negotiations with the oil companies and made it clear that he would not reopen negotiations until the Kurdish issue was resolved—a condition that ensured that negotiations would not be rejoined any time soon.[10]

'Arif's efforts to consolidate power were cut short in April 1966 when he was killed in a helicopter accident while engaged in a national speaking tour.[11] With the death of 'Arif, a power vacuum developed in which there was increasing conflict for control of the government between al-Bazzaz and 'Abd al-'Aziz al-'Uqayli, the hardline minister of defense who commanded the war in the north and put himself forward as a possible successor to 'Arif.[12] Al-Bazzaz was able to prevail upon the cabinet and sovereignty council to replace 'Arif with his more moderate, less ambitious older brother

'Abd al-Rahman at the end of April.[13] For the moment, al-Bazzaz's position was secure and he used it to successfully negotiate a peace agreement with the Kurds, which was signed on June 29, 1966. However, the agreement met with a violent reaction from army hardliners who launched a new effort to overthrow al-Bazzaz the following day. The attempt was easily suppressed, but it indicated the extent of the opposition to al-Bazzaz within the military. This opposition continued to mount until 'Arif the elder was compelled to replace al-Bazzaz on August 6 with Major General Naji Talib—a consensus candidate of the army.[14]

Whereas al-Bazzaz had tabled the oil agenda, Talib sought to consolidate his tenuous position by rapidly concluding a comprehensive agreement with the IPC.[15] In November 1966, he made the IPC an offer it couldn't refuse: a 50–50 joint-venture between IPC and INOC to develop the Rumaila oilfield.[16] If the IPC did not accept his offer by January 1, 1967, Talib would exercise Iraq's sovereign right to legislate the unilateral transfer of control of the field to the INOC.

In the face of Talib's demands, the consortium faced a dilemma and was internally divided. French president Charles de Gaulle (1959–69) harbored a Napoleonic dream of a French-led European Economic Community, in which CFP would displace the Anglo-American majors in supplying European energy needs.[17] CFP was therefore willing to accede to whatever the Iraqis wanted. The British had a long tradition of Anglo-American oil imperialism to uphold. But as the Americans waded deeper and deeper into the rice paddies of Vietnam, the Labour government that had prevailed in London since October 1963 looked more and more to de Gaulle and the European Economic Community for its future than it did to Washington. It therefore fell to the Americans to hold the line in Iraq.

Exxon outlined its strategy of massive resistance to the changes in world oil in a January 1967 international company memorandum:

> We have been put on notice by the Governments of Iran and Saudi Arabia that they will expect terms similar to those agreed between IPC and Iraq. Therefore, to agree voluntarily to give INOC a 50% interest in North Rumaila would result in immediate repercussions in neighboring countries. But if Iraq seizes North Rumaila by unilateral action, it is, in our opinion, less likely that other countries will follow.[18]

In plain language Exxon acknowledged that provoking a crisis in Iraq was preferable to accepting a compromise that would undermine its interests elsewhere.

Exxon's affinity for crisis prevailed. In February 1966, the Syrian Ba'th had carried out an internal coup in which a younger and more radical faction of the party consolidated power.[19] The new regime in Damascus then claimed that the IPC owed the Syrian government some £30–40 million in unpaid transit fees for oil shipped through the three hundred miles of IPC pipeline that crossed Syrian territory en route to Mediterranean shipping terminals at Banias, Syria, and Tripoli, Lebanon (see map 2). When negotiations on the issue broke down in December (that is, just before Talib's deadline), Syria seized IPC facilities and shut down the pipeline that carried roughly one million barrels a day of Iraqi crude—65 percent of Iraq's total production—to market.[20] The shutdown deprived the already cash-strapped Iraqi government of some $600,000–800,000 in oil revenue for every day that the crisis persisted.[21] Syria's Ba'thist government called on Iraq to follow its bold action in nationalizing IPC property and pledged to restore the flow of Iraqi oil to European markets once Iraq had taken its lead. Talib accused the IPC of deliberately provoking and prolonging the dispute in order to place financial pressure on his government to concede to IPC demands.[22]

THE CRISIS OF AMERICAN CORPORATISM

The IPC-Syria crisis and its financial effect on Iraq was a source of concern for the US embassy in Baghdad. Despite 'Arif the elder's relatively weak grasp on power, US officials were generally pleased with the orientation of his government—if not the premiership of Naji Talib.[23] According to the State Department's analysis, there had "been a gradual but continuing swing of the pendulum back toward moderation" in Iraqi policy since the resignation of the Nasserist ministers, and particularly so after the emergence of 'Arif the elder.[24] The department was encouraged by indications that 'Arif was determined to "avoid overdependence on the USSR or an overly close tie with the UAR [Egypt and Yemen]."[25] In the department's analysis, the Syrian demand for increased transit dues was merely a cover for its true objective, which was to undermine 'Arif's leadership and disrupt the "moderate trend in Iraq."[26] US embassy officials were concerned that the crisis, particularly the loss of Iraqi oil revenue, was increasing conflict between the moderate 'Arif and the more radical Talib, and that 'Arif was being pulled closer to Talib by the economic hardships imposed by the shutdown.[27] The embassy in Baghdad warned that as economic pressure within Iraq mounted:

> Radicals will be able to obscure real issues and arouse emotions of people on basis of anti-Western, anti-IPC appeal to point of serious "street" action in form of mass student strikes and mob demonstrations which moderate authorities unable [to] deal with short of serious bloodletting. Extremists then would be able to take over by default. This might then lead to takeover of IPC or even control of Iraqi oil production by Communist countries; complete socialization of Iraqi economy; reversal of present policy of improving relations with Turkey, Iran and Kuwait; a renewed threat to security of Kuwait; serious prosecution of "Arab causes"; hostility to foreigners in Iraq; and drastic increase in the strength of Commies with a concomitant rise in role of Soviets in Iraq.[28]

The State Department only referred to "Commies" when it was nervous and desperate. In 1961, the department, along with rest of the American government, concluded that it really wouldn't matter, from a global supply standpoint, if Communists gained control of Iraqi oil production (see chapter 3). But now, in late 1966, the US embassy suggested that such an eventuality might portend The End of the World.

The embassy's hysterical analysis of the Syria-IPC dispute pointed to an underlying crisis of American corporatism. Central to the corporatist conception of American oil policy was the idea that American interests would be best served by a permanent benevolent dictatorship in Iraq similar to the one that prevailed in Iran. However, as the turnstile of Iraqi premiers demonstrated, establishing such an order was easier said than done. The inability of the State Department (and CIA) to replicate what it had accomplished in Iran, in turn, opened the department to criticism from its domestic opponents—most significantly, the Department of the Interior.[29] One pillar of American corporatism was the phalanx of permanent benevolent oil dictatorships in the Persian Gulf. That pillar had been unstable since Qasim's coup in 1958. A second major pillar of American corporatism was the Seven Sisters cartel. That pillar was rendered unstable (first by CFP's inclusion in the IPC consortium, but more presently) by Iraq's successful effort to attract independent investment in Iraq's reclaimed oil fields. Now, with the State Department's approach resting on these dangerously unstable foundations, the Department of the Interior went on the attack. As it did so, it mobilized the full "artillery of heaven" in its effort to facilitate capital accumulation on the part of domestic American oil and gas companies.[30]

THE PROPHETS (AND PROFITS) OF AMERICAN ENERGY INDEPENDENCE

The crisis of political stability in Iraq (and the larger region), illustrated by the Syria-IPC crisis, demonstrated, for the Department of the Interior, the validity of its long-standing argument that the "Free World" could not depend on the Middle East for "vital" supplies of energy.[31] Interior, captured as it was by domestic American energy interests, argued that the United States should—rather than bending over backwards to appease what it regarded as the unholy alliance of Oriental despots and major internationals—dramatically increase domestic oil and gas production. With any luck (and enough subsidies), the US could become the Saudi Arabia of world oil. In the fullness of time, this would come to pass (that is, November 2018).[32] But in the middle of the 1960s, those who could envision American self-sufficiency in energy production remained voices in the wilderness.

In the middle 1960s, the Prophets of American Energy Independence had yet to fully emerge.[33] But this idea of cutting ties to "Oriental despots" and subjecting the major multinationals to the market discipline of (subsidized and protected) domestic competition dovetailed neatly with growing popular enthusiasm in the United States for the belief that if Israel could extend its sovereignty over the whole of Biblical Israel, then perhaps the conditions would be right for the Second Coming of Jesus.[34] For decades, many in the American government had labored under the notion that US support for Israeli territorial expansion could undermine US oil interests in the region. But if the Prophets of American Energy Independence were to be believed, and the United States had the potential to become the Saudi Arabia of world oil, then the US was in no way dependent on Arab goodwill. If people like T. Boone Pickens, the 1964 founder of Mesa Petroleum, which specialized in technological exploitation of nontraditional oil sources in the American West, were correct, the US could stand with Israel until the end of time without fear of oil supply cutoff.[35]

Signs of the growing fervor for a Second Coming were apparent in the popular cultural phenomenon that was *Exodus*—the wildly popular 1960 film starring Paul Newman based on the 1958 book by Leon Uris.[36] Less noticed at the time but ultimately more significant, John F. Walvoord, president of the Dallas Theological Seminary (DTS)—a school of religious instruction financed by Texas oil money—wrote *Israel in Prophecy*, which held that the restoration of Biblical Israel (to include Israeli control of Greater Jerusalem) would be a precondition and imminent sign of the Second Coming.[37] In April 1967, Hal Lindsey, a student of Walvoord at DTS, predicted that Israel's conquest of Jerusalem was at hand. As this came to pass two months later, Lindsey began assembling his DTS lecture notes to author the first in his series of *Late Great Planet Earth* books that became a cult phenomenon in the 1970s.

The perfect symmetry between Lindsey's strand of eschatological thought and the ambitions of energy capitalism (call it Petrodollar Christianity) reached its logical endpoint in President Reagan's 1981 nomination of James Gias Watt, a Hal Lindsey devotee, to serve as secretary of the interior.[38] In his confirmation hearing, when questioned about ties to the oil and gas industry and whether or not he was concerned "about preserving the environment for future generations, he forthrightly replied, 'I do not know how many future generations we can count on before the lord returns.'"[39]

But it would be several decades yet before the Department of the Interior would become wholly captured by the forces of Petrodollar Christianity. In the months leading up the June 1967 Arab-Israeli War, Interior was still consumed with the more earthly task of breaking up the prevailing alliance between the State Department and the major multinational oil companies. As the specter of nationalist expropriations loomed throughout the postcolonial world, Interior took more and more interest in developing North American offshore oil resources. In so doing, it subtly undermined the "public-private partnership" in the exploitation of foreign oil.[40]

In the face of Interior's attack, the State Department mounted a spirited rearguard defense. In February 1967—that is, at the height of the IPC-Syria crisis—the State Department produced a position paper that defended its historically close relations with oil-producing states in the region.[41] In seeking to assess "The Importance of Near East Oil," the paper began by wowing its audience with some basic (and awesome) economic statistics:

- The area contains two-thirds of the Free World's oil reserves, and provides over one-third of its current production.

- Production costs are roughly a tenth of such costs in the United States.
- The area supplies over half of Western Europe's oil.
- Over 85 percent of Japan's oil comes from the Persian Gulf.

It then acknowledged some glitches in the system (the Syria-IPC shutdown, nationalism, and the like), but noted that, on balance, Middle Eastern despots were growing more enlightened by the day:

> Middle East producing countries are exhibiting signs of becoming more responsible and even more conservative in their relations with petroleum operators so as not to interrupt the flow of royalties and taxes from their oil production. The blow of the Mossadegh Madness to the Iranian treasury in 1951–54 was not lost on the other producing states, nor is Iraq's current loss of $630,000 per day because of Syria's closing of IPC pipelines unnoticed by other area oil suppliers.

Seeing the pay cut that a case of "Mossadegh Madness" could bring, most of the despotic regimes in the region were in the business of business.[42] But, as the State Department reminded its audience, it wasn't just the Middle Eastern despots who were getting rich. American stock portfolios were benefiting handsomely as well:

> Strategic significance of Mid-East oil aside, the financial aspects are of prime importance. US companies have invested $2.75 billion in the area, and from this investment $750 million in profits flows back to the US annually. About 93 per cent of the US investment in the Middle East is in the oil industry.

Clearly, Wall Street stood to make a killing by continuing to back these Middle Eastern despots. But not everyone in Washington was moved by the love of money alone. Some remained more enchanted by the idea of bringing modernity to Southeast Asia. The paper reminded these readers that the Persian Gulf provided more than 60 percent of US fuel requirements for the Vietnam War. "How are you going to drop napalm on Vietnamese villages without Arab oil?" the paper seemed to taunt American war-planners.

Having thus addressed the imperatives of both Wall Street and Grandiose Strategy, the paper then took aim at its true enemy—the Department of the Interior:

> Recovery of oil from shale and tar sands is technically feasible, but costs will be high and large investments will be required at a time when cheap petroleum

could be brought from the Middle East in great quantities. Thus, the Persian Gulf area is a prolific potential future reserve for the US itself.

Given this ease of access, the State Department warned against pressure to embark on a "crash program to obtain fuel energy from other petroleum areas and from other sources of energy (atomic power, coal, oil shale, tar sands)" designed to allow the US to "loosen political relations with Mid-East producers."

The Prophets of American Energy Independence were seductive in their appeal—indeed, "atomic power, coal, oil shale, tar sands," and the like were the wave of the future. But the State Department "Wise Men," with their cosmopolitan and global perspective, warned against being drawn in by this siren song of economic nationalism.[43]

> Perhaps a more feasible course would be to *strengthen our political ties with Iran and the Arab Middle East countries, play down our relations with Israel, and protect our fortunate access to the prolific oil resources of the area* [original emphasis]. We would hope that the countries themselves would continue to grow more responsible, interdependent among themselves, and interdependent with the West—which is, after all, the market for Mid-East oil.

When viewed from the State Department, there really was a harmony of interests among consumers and producers, and it was companies that made that harmony hum.

Elegant as it was, the State Department's position paper did not weigh in on how "playing down our relations with Israel" would affect the chances for a Second Coming. But the desert preachers close to President Johnson could certainly read the handwriting on the wall. LBJ had been reared in the Texan traditions of the Protestant Christadelphian sect, which held that "reestablishing a Jewish state in Palestine would hasten the 'Second Coming' of Christ."[44] As he took the reins of world power, LBJ fancied (indeed described) himself as a "cross between a cowboy and a Baptist preacher." The people of Vietnam came to know the fire and brimstone of his sermons better than most. But Arab regimes that might threaten the security of Israel would also know LBJ's wrath. They were, in the president's mind, the moral equivalents of Viet Cong terrorists, who were, in turn, the moral equivalents of the "merciless Indian savages" that had so long haunted the American frontier.[45] As NSC staffer Hal Saunders explained in May 1967:

The "war of national liberation" as a technique has come to the Middle East—on Israel's borders and now in South Arabia. President Johnson in Vietnam has invested much of himself in demonstrating that we will not tolerate this brand of aggression. His friends in the Middle East are asking how he can stand against terrorist attackers in Vietnam and not in Israel or South Arabia? We must find a way to contain them or risk losing the respect the President has won for his courage in Vietnam.[46]

Western Civilization was under attack from a terrorist threat that lurked from South Vietnam to South Arabia and beyond. As Middle East tensions built in the spring of 1967, that threat appeared poised to destroy Israel altogether. And if Israel's "manifest destiny" were in doubt, then what of America's own?[47]

Walvoord, Lindsey, and the Christadelphians who had formed LBJ's preconscious were all well aware of the threats that Israel faced and the promises that it foretold. From their standpoint, the Arab-Israeli war was objectively progressive—it advanced the world toward its necessary end. But the State Department appeared utterly blind to all of this. Rather than doing its part to hasten the Second Coming, the State Department sought only to uphold a doomed status quo. Hoping to change everything so that nothing might change, the State Department pressed the IPC to provide Iraq some "tide-over money" and urged the companies to bring an immediate end to the Syria-IPC crisis.[48]

In March, the oil majors finally yielded to State Department pressure and came to terms with the Syrian colonels. The IPC agreed to pay Syria higher shipping rates, and Syria reopened the pipeline.[49] A few weeks later, the IPC advanced Iraq £14 million as compensation for its lost revenue.[50] For a brief moment, it appeared that the State Department had saved the day and the Battle of Armageddon had been forestalled. Flush with IPC cash, President 'Arif denounced the failures of Arab socialism in Egypt, declared that Iraq had had enough of slogans, and sang the praises of his "brother"—the shah of Iran. This was no empty talk. In mid-May 1967, President 'Arif sacked Naji Talib and assumed the position of prime minister for himself.[51] Iraq appeared well on its way to achieving Akins's "permanent benevolent dictatorship."

A CONQUEST FORETOLD: THE ARAB-ISRAELI JUNE WAR

The best-laid plans of mice and men often go awry. State Department hopes for the emergence of a permanent benevolent dictatorship in Iraq were dashed by the events of June 1967. That month, escalating tensions between Israel on the one hand, and Syria and Egypt on the other, resulted in the second Arab-Israeli war in eleven years. The war began on June 5, when Israel launched air strikes that destroyed (a still-grounded) Egyptian air force. It ended six days later with Israeli military forces occupying all of Mandate Palestine and large portions of Egypt and Syria.[52]

The June War had a seismic impact on the regional oil order. As the threat of war loomed, Nasser called on Arab states to deploy "oil as a weapon" in the coming battle against Israel.[53] The US Department of the Interior then constructed a spreadsheet assessing the susceptibility of all of the major oil-producing regimes to "Nasserite pressure," and found that Iraq was most vulnerable.[54] And indeed, in Iraq mounting tensions with Israel paved the way for the return of Tahir Yahya, Khair el-Din Haseeb, and Adib al-Jadir.[55] Yahya had returned as deputy prime minister when 'Arif sidelined Talib in May, but took effective control of Iraqi foreign policy when the war began. As Israeli warplanes pounded Egyptian targets, al-Jadir convened an oil conference in Baghdad in which Egypt, Syria, Saudi Arabia, Kuwait, Abu Dhabi, Qatar, and Libya called on all Arab oil-producing states to withhold oil shipments to any state supporting Israel's attack on Egypt and Syria. Yahya, though quietly concerned about the financial implications of such a move, dutifully announced a total embargo on Iraqi oil exports.[56]

Striking oil workers and other acts of popular sabotage compelled other Arab states to follow Iraq's lead. Or at least say they did. All Arab oil-producing states issued tough-sounding declarations, but as Saudi oil minister Ahmad Zaki Yamani (*quietly*) made clear to diplomats in Jidda, "Of course, Saudi Arabia would permit oil shipments to go to the West, despite the announced embargo."[57] Reports from the trade press suggested that other producers were doing the same and it was really only Iraq that elected to forego oil revenue to advance a political end.[58] As Yamani put it, the Arab-Israeli struggle was really only a "cover for [a] regional conflict between 'socialist' and conservative Arab states," and "only the Iraqis are naive enough to believe what the Egyptians tell them and to do what Nasser says."[59] But even in Iraq, there were limits to Arab solidarity. There, Yahya and the cabinet, concerned about the loss of oil revenue so soon after the protracted Syria-IPC crisis, restrained what they considered al-Jadir's suicidal action.[60] At the end of June, these more pragmatic voices prevailed and Iraq resumed limited shipments to France and Turkey, provided those states did not turn around and supply the US and UK.[61] Other states made similar announcements, and, at the end of August, Arab ministers met at Khartoum to announce the formal end to an embargo that had had little to no immediately discernable effect.[62]

To the extent they have noted it at all, most historians regard the embargo as a dismal failure.[63] It seemed only to confirm the truism: "We Arabs cannot drink our oil so we must sell it."[64] Indeed, the attempted embargo appeared to backfire spectacularly on three counts: it failed to change US policy, participating states lost market share that they could not recover after the war, and, by failing in this way, the producers simply demonstrated their weakness and division on the world stage. The Arabs had played their hand and were shown to be holding nothing more than a pair of deuces.

America's desert preachers reveled in ecstatic glory. As Israel claimed sovereignty over Old Jerusalem, the Cassandras who warned that US support for Israel would result in a supply cutoff were proven wrong yet again—just as had been the case in 1948 and 1956. Now, in the summer of 1967, it was painfully obvious that the US could "green light" Israeli territorial expansion without fear of any meaningful Arab reprisal.[65] Simply put, there was no oil weapon. The threat was entirely imagined. Or so it seemed.

THE PROPHECY OF JOHN MCCONE

On one level, it is difficult to argue with the received wisdom regarding the efficacy of the 1967 embargo. Yes, the United States had more political and economic power than did Arab states (radical, conservative, or otherwise) in the 1960s. The dependence of oil-producing Arab states on Western markets for state revenue severely limited their ability to use oil as a political instrument and weapon in defense of Palestinian rights or anything else. But the spectacular failure of the 1967 embargo can obscure subtler and less immediately perceptible changes in the international petroleum economy—that is, the attempted embargo exposed cracks in the concessionary system established in the wake of World War I. The Arab-Israeli June War revealed vulnerabilities in the structure of world oil in a couple of ways: it sowed divisions among the consuming nations, and it accelerated the nationalization of the Iraq Petroleum Company.

One of the first observers to grasp the inner meaning of 1967 was John A. McCone, who had recently resigned as director of the CIA. McCone had a unique and interesting perspective on the crisis. A "rightest Catholic . . . with holy war views," as I. F. Stone described him, McCone came to the CIA in 1961 with very strongly fixed positions on two issues: the importance of making money in the oil business and the importance of American nuclear superiority.[66] After graduating from UC Berkeley with a degree in mechanical engineering in the 1920s, he formed the Consolidated Steel Corporation in 1929, which made a fortune building pipelines for Standard Oil, among other clients. Eight years later, he, with Steven Bechtel, formed the Bechtel-McCone Corporation, the petrochemical processing firm that specialized in the construction of oil refineries, pipelines, and associated industries (and whose overseas division head was murdered in Iraq on July 14, 1958—see the introduction).[67] In 1950, President Truman had made McCone undersecretary of the air force, where he played a leading role in organizing the Strategic Air Command—that is, the American nuclear arsenal. In 1951, McCone left government to form the Nuclear Power Group, a Bechtel spinoff that specialized in the construction of nuclear reactors.[68] Given McCone's background in nuclear issues, President Eisenhower, in 1957, asked him to return to government to chair the US Atomic Energy Commission (AEC), which regulated the production of civilian nuclear energy.

As AEC chair, McCone longed for the days of an American nuclear monopoly, and remained deeply invested in restricting the further diffusion of nuclear technology around the world. In the last years of the Eisenhower administration, he grew alarmed over Israeli efforts to build, with French assistance, a nuclear reactor at Dimona in the Negev Desert. In December 1960, he planted a story in the *New York Times* warning the public of the Israeli nuclear program.[69] McCone's sense of alarm was shared by outgoing secretary of state Christian Herter. In Herter's farewell briefing to the Senate Foreign Relations Committee he warned of Israeli efforts to acquire a bomb. After hearing what Herter had to say in that briefing, committee member John Hickenlooper concluded that the "Israelis have just lied to us like horse thieves on this issue."[70] This same sense of alarm was shared by incoming president Kennedy, for whom "apprehension about the Israeli bomb undoubtedly was a factor in his surprising appointment of John McCone to replace Allen Dulles as CIA director in the wake of the Bay of Pigs debacle."[71] For McCone, whose business interests in the Arab world ran deep, "an Israeli bomb would lead to escalation and then you could just cross off oil from the Middle East for years."[72]

While nuclear escalation worried the more cautious President Kennedy, visions of fire and brimstone held more of an allure for President Johnson.[73] Indeed, there was a deeply Thanatosian character to Johnson's political psychology.[74] How could it not be? His presidency was baptized in the blood of his slain predecessor and party rival. And that rival's brother was still the attorney general and chairman of the Special Group on Counterinsurgency. The country as a whole would surely judge him inadequate to the moment—just a West Texas hick where there once stood a handsome prince from Cambridge. Kennedy had stood brave and tall against Communism in Vietnam. LBJ couldn't find Vietnam on a map. Wherever it was, he was sure there wasn't any Texas oil money invested there. To make matters worse, he was challenged in 1964 by Barry Goldwater, a presidential candidate whose organic roots reached even deeper to the south and farther to the west than did Johnson's.[75] All the while JFK's brother Bobby appeared poised to accuse LBJ of squandering his martyred brother's victories and losing Vietnam to the Communists.

As demons closed in from every direction, and as an increasingly millenarian popular culture took root in the country, Johnson leaned into apocalyptic imagery and symbolism. It was in September 1964—as Goldwater called for all-out victory in Vietnam and Pentagon war-planners mobilized for exactly that—when Johnson released the infamous "Daisy Ad."[76] The ad, aired while the memory and trauma of the Cuban missile crisis was still fresh in the public mind, invited viewers to imagine the world coming to a fiery end in a nuclear Armageddon.

It was at this very moment of heightened nuclear anxiety that CIA counterintelligence chief James Jesus Angleton allowed the Israeli Mossad, a spy agency he helped to create, to smuggle American nuclear secrets out of the country, so that Israel could put the finishing touches on its own nuclear bomb.[77] In Johnson's preconscious, a nuclear-armed Israel was a prophecy fulfilled.[78] Even at a more conscious level,

> Johnson's support for Israel was almost surreal . . . [He] remembered the warnings of his Baptist relatives: "If Israel is destroyed the world will end."

And he also saw in Israel the type of courageous last stand with which he, as a Texan, was so comfortable. "Israel ... was a latter-day Alamo, surrounded on all sides by compassionless enemies and Nasser was a reincarnated Santa Ana, the Mexican general who laid siege to that fort."[79]

It is a sobering thought that those who held the nuclear launch codes understood the world in terms of something that they once saw in a movie about cowboys and Indians.[80] It is even more sobering to realize that the check on this kind of apocalyptic thinking was John McCone. McCone effectively rejected the mutually assured destruction (MAD) theory of nuclear warfare (that any use of nuclear weapons would necessarily escalate to total nuclear war on a world scale). He believed, along with the original architects of the American nuclear program, that the bomb was made to be used.[81] He adhered to the theory of tactical, or limited, nuclear warfare in which atomic weapons could be used as a rational application of politics by other means. McCone believed that the US should use its own nuclear arsenal to destroy the Chinese nuclear weapons program so that Washington could bring the war in Vietnam to a successful conclusion. But in McCone's view, Johnson simply sat passively as China successfully tested its bomb in October 1964, and with that successful test, effectively signaled the US surrender to Communism in Asia. Those were not conditions under which McCone could work. He offered his resignation in April 1965, with a scathing letter to LBJ denouncing the president's unwillingness to win the war.[82]

It was this trinity of issues—winning the war in Vietnam, nuclear nonproliferation, and making money in the oil business—that McCone brought to bear on his analysis of the 1967 Arab oil embargo. At the height of that crisis, he briefed the NSC on the grand strategic implications of the supply cutoff.[83] He began by stating, "We are getting two or three hundred thousand barrels of petroleum products daily from the Middle East for the war effort in South Vietnam." That certainly sounded like a lot. Hopefully it would be enough to get at the heartstrings of the NSC. But it didn't take McCone long to get at the issue that was nearer and dearer to his own heart: making money in the Arab world. He acknowledged that when it came to making money in the Arab world, "The subject is all too often dismissed as purely a commercial and vested interest of the oil companies." But McCone sought to situate the question in a much broader strategic context. It was not simply the profit margins of US-registered companies but the whole question of American Grandiose Strategy that was at stake.[84]

Having invited the national security managers to view oil profits in the most grandiose of terms, McCone explained that the biggest concerns with regard to the embargo were the European ingrates. The United States had just suspended antitrust regulations to allow for a coordinated oil supply lift to offset lost Arab production, and this was helping to fill the immediate shortfall. But when it came down to it, the European powers, France and West Germany in particular, but increasingly Britain as well, had grown tired of their dependence on the Seven Sisters cartel for the vast majority of their vital energy needs.

Now, with the majors over a barrel, France was trying to exploit their vulnerability. As Arab-Israeli tensions mounted over the course of that spring, de Gaulle warned against Israeli aggression. On the eve of war, de Gualle severed completely the French-Israeli arms supply relationship that had existed since Israeli's founding.[85] As the war began, in response to the announced embargo, de Gaulle, with the support of West Germany, sought to forge a common European Economic Community oil policy that would bypass the Anglo-American majors and negotiate directly with the Arab oil-producing states.[86] This was no idle threat. The previous January, the French state had organized *Entreprise de Recherche et d'Activités Pétrolières* (ERAP), a wholly state-owned oil company for this very purpose.[87]

It was this French connection that was most worrying to McCone as he briefed the national security managers in the summer of 1967. According to McCone, due to this typical French tendency to capitulate and surrender (if not collaborate) before the demands of Arab nationalism, American oil companies found themselves in dire straits. Lest the national security managers tell the companies to go drink from the sea as "serious matters" of Grandiose Strategy were at stake, McCone emphasized that "the activities of the international oil companies through their subsidiaries constitute the largest and most effective channel of contact in the relationship with the governments of the Middle East . . . [and that] the oil of the Middle East does contribute substantially to the U.S. balance of payments." Weak tea, for sure. But one can't blame McCone for playing the hand dealt.

It is very unlikely that McCone had captured the imagination of his audience with his appeal to what was in the best interest of Standard Oil. But nonetheless, he persisted.

The friendly Arab states are encountering difficulty in maintaining their position against the constant criticism of the U.S. Government by the hostile states. An example is the problem the Saudi Arabian Government is having in maintaining its position, which is essentially friendly, against the demands of such unfriendly countries as Iraq, which are urging the expulsion of Americans and the nationalization and expropriation of the American-owned companies.

Anticipating the old line about the Arabs not being able to "drink their oil," McCone insisted that this time the threat was real. The wolf was at the door:

With these trends in evidence, the dangers of expropriation, expulsion, and nationalization of American interests seem real and should not be dismissed in Washington.... The situation is very different from 1957, when none of these countries had the capability to enter the oil business, and therefore the Arab oil-producing states do not have to look back at the tragedy of Iran after Mossadeq expropriated the oil and production was shut off completely because of lack of capability.

The key difference from the Mossadeq/Suez era was Europe:

The Europeans are definitely making carefully guarded overtures to all of the oil-producing Arab countries, pointing out that should the latter be forced to take over American oil properties, they can depend on the Europeans for assistance.

So to avoid the "Europeans taking advantage of our [meaning the majors'] plight," McCone made a few specific appeals.

According to McCone's analysis, the US government needed to "emphasize a balanced position" in its public statements with regard to the Arab-Israeli conflict, so as to counteract the "brainwashing going on by the press." If the US government was interested in protecting the value of American capital investments in the Middle East, he stressed that it would have to make "clear and unequivocal statements" to the effect that Israel's "territorial aggrandizement through military action" was unacceptable under international law and was contrary to American foreign policy.

It is unclear who McCone thought he could persuade with this kind of rent-seeking dressed up as Grandiose Strategy. Hal Saunders had framed the issues in much more relevant and crystalline fashion just before the outbreak of war. Israel was under threat from the same "brand of aggression" that threatened American national security in Vietnam.[88] President Johnson had won a great of respect for his "courage in Vietnam," but now all of that was put in jeopardy by shortsighted oil companies who couldn't manage to look beyond the next quarterly earnings report. How could McCone's concern for a few barrels of oil possibly compare with the moral imperative of defending Western Civilization? Israel was putting its back into that fight, and here McCone and the oil companies were prepared to sacrifice the Jews on the Altar of Mammon.

McCone's views were totally out of step with the prevailing mood in Washington. Much more salient analysis—analysis consistent with Saunders's conceptual framing—came from Julius C. Holmes. Holmes was a retired general officer with a background in military intelligence who had served as ambassador to Iran in 1955, and again from 1961–65.[89] In the spring of 1967, he had been commissioned to lead a high-level interdepartmental review of American foreign policy in the Middle East with the intention of providing policymakers with "doctrinal guidance" for the next five years.[90] In a sense, he was unveiling a Five-Year Plan for anti-Communism in the Middle East.

The Holmes study yielded an alarming set of conclusions. It found that the United States and Israel were natural allies facing a common existential threat from an implacable Arab foe:

> It is abundantly clear that the USSR has a firm policy to achieve dominant influence in the eastern and southern Mediterranean basin. It is equally clear that the Arabs are as emotionally committed to [the] destruction of Israel as were their ancestors to elimination of the Christian Kingdom of Jerusalem. The Soviets use Arab hatred of Israel to advance their interests and the Arabs use the Soviet presence and assistance to further their objective. The result is a situation which is damaging and dangerous for United States interests.

Clearly, the Judeo-Christian West was engaged in a clash of civilizations, and the successful defense of the proverbial "Christian Kingdom of Jerusalem" would require a whole new level of existential commitment.

But in the view of Holmes and proponents of his study, an unfortunately large contingent of the US government appeared to be persuaded that the best way to defend Western Civilization was by arming and financing its enemies. Case in point was US military and economic aid to Egypt. But in light of the June War, it had become clear, to the Holmes group, that the US could no longer

> accept Egyptian efforts to resolve the Palestine question through force, eliminate Western presence or influence in the Middle East, or topple moderate Arab leaders. The foundations for long term U.S.-UAR cooperation can be laid only when Cairo signifies its willingness to develop communities of interest based on mutual trust and respect.

Rather than entertaining Nasser's audition for the part of a modern-day Saladin, the Holmes group proposed an entirely "new" approach based on strengthening US support for "conservative monarchs," and publicly withdrawing from Arab-Israeli diplomacy while insuring that "Israeli qualitative conventional arms superiority over potential Arab opponents is maintained."[91] This all made a great deal of sense to President Johnson. With a preconscious steeped in the eschatological significance of the Israeli conquest of Jerusalem, and as a seasoned veteran in domestic oil's generational war against the majors, he was in no mood to brook any nonsense from the oil majors.

As LBJ readied for a showdown with the companies, he was encouraged by former national security adviser McGeorge Bundy. As the hour approached, Bundy talked up his champion: don't let "these people . . . crowd you." Remind them that "we did our damnedest" to get concessions from Israel that "moderate Arabs could accept," but that "cooperation on these matters is a two-way street," and the Arabs would never be satisfied so long as "we are not directly arrayed against Israel." Should you get any pushback, "remind these gentlemen of the basic sentiments of the American people," as registered by a recent Harris poll showing "overwhelming support" for Israel.[92] In the face of such appeals, the majors never had a chance. McCone and their other representatives had appealed to logos and ethos, whereas domestic oil and gas, and the Israel lobby, could appeal to a much deeper pathos.

McCone had little chance of convincing Johnson, but what he said about Europe and the Middle East was essentially correct.[93] France had long since enlisted in the struggle against US hegemony. That it might receive at least some West German cooperation was expected. But the fall of Britain caught even the most astute observers in Washington by surprise. There, Harold Wilson's Labour government was weathering a financial crisis brought on by the war. Between May and September the Arab states, led by Kuwait and Saudi Arabia, dumped £236 million in British sterling on world markets (presumably in response to Nasser's call for "Arab nations to move out of sterling").[94] The wartime closure of the Suez Canal also resulted in a 400 percent increase in British shipping costs for oil exported from the Persian Gulf around Cape of Africa. The combined effect was a precipitous decline in the value of sterling and a severe economic shock in the City of London. The US briefly considered backstopping the value of sterling by refusing to allow Arab states to exchange silver for gold, but concluded that "given 'powerful economic weapons' the producers could 'use against the Atlantic nations' . . . such a bold option was 'more a gun at our head than theirs.'"[95]

In 1951–53, it was the US and Britain that held a gun to the head of Mossadegh. And now the proverbial gun was in the other hand (the hand of Mossadegh's ghost, that is; Mossadegh died under house arrest in Albroz on March 5, 1967). Staring down the barrel of Arab oil power, Britain demonstrated an increasing willingness to side with France and the ECC. In November, Britain supported French efforts at the UN to advance Resolution 242, which called on Israel to withdraw from "territories occupied" during the war. A few months later, the British announced that they would be withdrawing all military forces from the region.[96] The whole notion of stationing troops in the Middle East to guarantee security of access was beginning to appear a particularly expensive delusion. As the British foreign secretary (and soon-to-be Labour prime minister) George Brown put it: "Why should we not, like other European countries, obtain oil from the Persian Gulf by paying for it instead of maintaining forces there?"[97] But for the Johnson administration, this was just one more betrayal from America's so-called friends. When Brown explained the plan to US secretary of state Dean Rusk, Rusk "accused him of spurning global power for 'free aspirins and false teeth' at home, railing, 'For God's sake, act like Britain!'"[98]

American gnashing and wailing aside, the British were beginning to place more faith in markets than military bases. The problem is that the entirety of the oil order in the region was organized around the effort to prevent the emergence of a free market in oil. The British and French willingness to enter into market relations with Iraq's nationalist government spelled doom for the IPC.

THE SECOND YAHYA GOVERNMENT

The 1967 Arab oil embargo fundamentally altered the balance of power in world oil. Nowhere was this shift more apparent than in Iraq. There are decades when nothing happens. And then there are months when decades happen. The latter was the case in Iraq in the aftermath of the June War. In August, Yahya's government issued Law 97, which permanently barred the IPC from operating in North Rumaila. In September, Yahya issued Law 123, which purged moderates from the Ministry of Oil and from the board of the Iraq National Oil Company (INOC), and replaced them with a board led by Haseeb and al-Jadir. In October, CFP sent a delegation to Baghdad to negotiate a separate peace with the INOC to develop Rumaila independent of the other IPC partners.[99] The CFP bid, combined with indications that Mobil, Shell, and even the British government were softening their opposition to Law 80, compelled the IPC to make a competing offer. But by this point, al-Jadir was unwilling to accept either.[100] Iraq would rather draw on direct state-to-state support from France and the Soviet Union to develop its oil resources without the participation of CFP or the IPC.

In November, al-Jadir negotiated an agreement with CFP's national competitor ERAP to develop a large tract of former IPC areas in southern Iraq—though notably *not* including Rumaila. In February 1968, President 'Arif traveled to Paris to participate in an elaborate signing ceremony.[101] Rather than a traditional concession, or joint-venture agreement, ERAP offered a new type of arrangement known as a "service contract"—a short-term agreement whereby the foreign company would supply capital and technology to the INOC in exchange for supply guarantees at discount prices. Haseeb, al-Jadir, and Tariki (who resumed advising the Iraqi government) praised the agreement as offering a new model for state-company relations in the Middle East, one in which producing-state interests would dominate, and which would allow the state to develop the markets and experience to operate a wholly nationalized oil sector within a relatively short period of time.[102]

In December, al-Jadir negotiated a far-reaching agreement with the Soviet Union for open-ended capital, technical, and marketing assistance for the "direct development of the Iraqi national oil industry."[103] The agreement with the Soviet Union was followed shortly thereafter by an announcement from the INOC that it would no longer be considering joint-venture bids for Rumaila.[104] It would rather build up the technical, economic, and marketing capacity through agreements such as those concluded with ERAP and the USSR to develop the field itself. On May 6, Haseeb warned IPC negotiators that the government of Iraq would soon undertake the complete nationalization of IPC's southern operations and that the companies could not expect any compensation whatsoever.[105] On May 14, the IPC reported that the INOC was taking physical occupation of southern oil fields and was replacing IPC signs and locks with INOC signs and locks.[106] On May 16, IPC's analyst in Beirut compiled a report finding that that "inherent in the philosophy of people like Khaireddin Haseeb" was the belief that Iraq would, upon nationalizing the companies, be able to "build up a fully integrated business" in short order.[107] Iraq stood poised to claim victory in its long struggle.

Chapter 8

THE RETURN OF THE BA'TH

IN THE SPRING OF 1968, THE IRAQI REGIME, LED BY PRIME MINister Tahir Yahya, was poised to finally carry out the long-awaited nationalization of the IPC. All of the necessary preconditions for a successful nationalization were met. The INOC had established the organization and infrastructure to develop the Law 80 fields without IPC involvement. The Haseeb–al-Jadir group was in full control of INOC and had reached technical service and marketing agreements with France and the Soviet Union that assured a successful nationalization. The sword that was so long suspended over the neck of the companies appeared ready to fall.

Just when it appeared that the fate of the companies was sealed, they were, somewhat miraculously, granted a four-year reprieve, as Iraq underwent yet another change of government. In July 1968, the Ba'th party reemerged to take power under the leadership of General Ahmad Hasan al-Bakr. The second Ba'thist regime was more internally coherent than the first—there was no longer a civilian wing in competition with a military wing—but divisions remained among factions within the military wing. Understanding how, by the end of 1969, the Ba'th managed to establish a stable regime requires that we disentangle a number of conspiracies that transpired in Iraq in the wake of the July coup. Two particular conspiracies were especially significant in this period: the conspiracy of Robert Anderson, and the Tikriti Overture. It was only by mastering the politics of intrigue and defeating these conspiracies that the Ba'th was able to establish a stable "coup-proof" regime—that is, a regime impervious to internal subversion that could only be changed through full-scale military invasion, occupation, and reconstruction.[1]

THE PENROSE AFFAIR

Edith Penrose is an intriguing figure.[2] The daughter of a 1920s-era California highway engineer (the main architect of California's spectacular Highway 1), she enrolled at UC Berkeley and began studying economics in 1932. As a freshman, she married a classmate, a law student named David Burton Denhardt, in a secret (from their families) ceremony at Grace Memorial Cathedral in San Francisco. Two years later, she began attending the lectures of Ernest F. ("Pen") Penrose, a British-born economist famous for "razzing" his female students.[3] After David graduated and moved to Colusa, California, to work as a deputy district attorney, Edith remained in Berkeley to work as Pen's research assistant. Eventually, Edith joined David in Colusa where they built a home and started a family. However, Edith and Pen remained in contact through an intimate exchange of letters in 1937–38. As she confided in these letters, Edith soon found herself miserable in the role of homemaker to a country lawyer.[4] Pen was similarly unhappy in his own marriage. Just when the situation appeared most desperate, "fortunate" tragedy struck. In October 1938, David was killed in a suspicious hunting accident. A grand jury investigated the case and found that he had been shot at close range, but chose not to issue an indictment or disclose the identity of the shooter. Edith was convinced that David had been murdered by local political rivals in Williams, a nearby settlement of a few hundred scattered farmers and ranchers.[5]

The door on Edith's first marriage had closed, but the door to her second marriage was just opening. After the death of her husband, Pen invited Edith join him in a move to Geneva, Switzerland, where he was to work for the International Labor Organization. Edith leapt at the opportunity to escape California's sleepy Central Valley. (Pen's wife remained in Berkeley with their two children, and the marriage effectively ended at this point.)[6] Edith and Pen's time in Geneva was, however, cut short by the threat of Nazi invasion. After escaping the Nazis, Pen took a position as an economic adviser to the US embassy in London. After the war, Pen and Edith married and moved to Baltimore, where Edith pursued a PhD in economics at Johns Hopkins, while Pen took a position at the Center for Advanced Study at Princeton.

The Penroses' time in Baltimore was rocky. Edith excelled under the mentorship of Austrian economist Frtiz Machlup (a former student of Ludwig von Mises and Friedrich Hayek, founders of the "Austrian" or "neoliberal" school of economics), but Pen found the culture of the emerging Cold War stifling. In 1951, Senator Joseph McCarthy accused Pen's friend and colleague Owen Lattimore of being a Soviet agent. Lattimore had made the mistake of substituting his decades of experience living in China, land of his birth and first twenty-eight years, for Cold War orthodoxy when assessing the merits of Chiang Kai-shek's nationalist regime. The Penroses then played a central role in organizing Lattimore's legal defense in a case that stretched on for years. Pen was so embittered by the experience that in 1955 he applied for a research sabbatical and received a Fulbright award to teach at the Australian National University in Canberra. Edith was happy in Baltimore but dutifully followed along.

At the end of that year, the Penroses briefly returned to the United States. But by this time Pen's ideas about the US had become fixed. As he observed in his journal:

> This journey has emphatically confirmed my sharp revulsion from the American 'way of life,' notably in the last five or six years during which the whole society has been infected with the poison of witch-hunting and [in which] shocking revelations of the fundamental weakness of American culture have come to light.[7]

Surely there was a measure of sincerity in Pen's revulsion at American political culture in the 1950s. But what appears to have weighed most heavily on his consciousness was the intensified security clearance screenings that McCarthy introduced. As chief economic adviser to the American embassy in London during the war, Pen had negotiated directly with the Soviets over lend-lease aid and postwar economic reconstruction, and he was not eager to account his past associations during this period (such as his work as assistant to Harry Dexter White—the US Treasury Department official who negotiated American interests at Bretton Woods, and who also spied for the Soviets).[8]

Rather than conforming to Cold War academic culture (and McCarthy-era background checks), Pen looked for other opportunities. Johns Hopkins geographer Isiah Bowman offered him one: move to Iraq to help develop a Department of Economics at Baghdad University. In search of academic freedom, Pen moved to Nuri al-Said's Iraq in 1957. Again, Edith followed along. Although the move appeared to take her away from her work on the "theory of the firm" at Johns Hopkins, Iraq proved an ideal research environment. She began teaching courses in history and economics at Baghdad University and found in the IPC a research enigma that would occupy her imagination for decades to come: what explained the firm's phenomenal rate of profit—so far above and beyond what other firms producing primary products could hope to realize.[9] Pen, for his part, recovered from his aversion to Cold War paranoia and began quietly informing the US embassy of subversive activity on campus—"their college was a 'hotbed of communists.'"[10]

It was not Edith's choice to go to Iraq. But it was in Iraq that she found her true calling. In short order, she distinguished herself as one of the world's foremost experts on the history and economics of oil. In 1959, after two years in Iraq, she was awarded with dual appointments at the London School of Economics (LSE) and the School of Oriental and African Studies (SOAS). From Baghdad and London, she published, among other works, *The Theory of the Growth of the Firm* (Oxford, 1959), *The Large International Firm in Developing Countries: The International Petroleum Industry* (MIT, 1968), and *Iraq: International Relations and National Development* (Benn, 1978). This last was a landmark study co-authored with Pen that remains the most detailed account of Iraqi oil politics and history.[11] Pen, for his part, largely retired from academic work, though he was on the faculty of Baghdad University in 1961–62, and the couple were in Iraq at the time of the February 1963 coup.[12] He spent the next two decades traveling, lecturing, researching, and writing—increasingly for *Le Monde diplomatique*.[13]

In October 1967, the Penroses applied for travel visas to enter Iraq. But despite their long association with the country, and despite (or because of?) what Pen described as their intimate relations with some of the most prominent Iraqi families—"the Uqailis, Gailanis [Kaylanis], and al-Arawis"—their applications were held up for months. It was only thanks to the special intervention of Nasir al-Hani, the Iraqi ambassador to Lebanon, that a short-term visa was finally approved in May 1968. Their stay in Baghdad was tumultuous. Arriving on May 18, they checked into the Aliwiyah Rest House—the "elegant former residence" of one-time premier Naji Shawkwat, where they "had lived during the curfews and street fighting" of February 1963. The next day, they met with a number of their former students, including 'Abd al-Rahman al-Bazzaz, who were now in Iraqi government posts. As they conducted their business, the Penroses were followed by *mukhabarat* everywhere they went, and after just two days in the country, they were summoned to the British Regency and asked to leave Iraq immediately.

The Penroses managed to evade and delay Iraqi authorities for several days. They used this time to meet with the United Nations Economic Research Centre, which was then working with the Iraqi government on development planning. In their meeting, they made a special effort to dissuade the UN team from working with Khair el-Din Haseeb, the former director of Iraq's Central Bank now serving on the board of directors of the Iraq National Oil Company (INOC). They explained:

> Mr. Haseeb was intimately involved in Iraqi politics and that from a UN point of view it might not be wise to become too closely associated with people with special political connexions. . . . Haseeb is a competent statistician but not an economist, but he now passes in Iraq as an economist and assumes that role in discussion with the U.N. missions.

In the words of their confidant, Yusuf al-Kaylani, the head of the prestigious al-Kaylani family and mosque and a respected and retired Iraqi diplomat, Haseeb was one of "the 'young men' suddenly hoisted from nowhere into positions of power that go to their heads." The UN economists thanked the Penroses for this information (intelligence?), adding that it "was not always easy for them to find their way in the Baghdad environment."

After being expelled from Iraq, the Penroses traveled to Beirut, where Pen related the story in harrowing detail to the British embassy (which in turn shared Pen's written account with the US embassy).[14] Pen explained that while they were unable to complete their research in Iraq, they nonetheless considered the trip a success as their presence had "caused a split in the government and a see-saw struggle between two groups"—one opposed to them and one in support. It was Haseeb, in their view, who had led the group that opposed their presence in the country. Haseeb was a "dangerous man" and they resolved to do all that they could to bring about his downfall:

We shall continue the struggle on our own account through a number of channels including the Iraqi ambassador [Nasir al-Hani] here.... In my view Haseeb is a man to be avoided. He is capable of flagrant deception and it is a mistake to think that one can persuade him by direct talks, formal or otherwise. He is best kept clear of. His downfall will come and may be hastened by forcing his interference into the open through use of other channels but certainly not by attempting persuasion on him personally.

TAKING STOCK: THE IPC CONFRONTS A CHANGED WORLD

The Penrose mission to Iraq in May 1968 came toward the end of long, hot, and uncomfortable spring for the IPC. As French and Soviet assistance poured into Iraq, and as Haseeb and his colleagues pledged to use this support to carry through the complete nationalization of the Iraqi oil industry, IPC analysts "took stock" of the company's "current position" and found the situation dire.[15] Obviously, the best-case scenario for the companies would be a rightwing coup that would bring an end to Haseeb's nationalization drive and restore the companies to their position of political dominance within Iraq. Perhaps the same Ba'thist officers who had put a bullet in Qasim's temple in 1963 would be available to let Yahya, Haseeb, and al-Jadir know that there are hard-and-fast rules to the way the global economy worked. But given the public mood, who was to say that the next prime minister wouldn't be just as radical, if not more radical, than Yahya?

In a March review of the situation, IPC analysts lamented that there was little hope of "dislodging" the Haseeb–al-Jadir group in the near term.[16] While it was possible to imagine a change of government within a year, the IPC position paper did not believe that it would be possible to diminish the influence of these anti-Western "dogmatic socialists" within the Ministry of Oil. Even if a right-wing group did come to power, it was very unlikely that it would be "able to reverse nationalist decrees especially concerning Rumaila."[17] Given that the nationalization of the IPC had become a fixed idea in the official mind of Baghdad, the paper advised adopting a "soft line" in negotiations. Specifically, it called for expanding production and avoiding territorial and other final status issues in favor of patient step-by-step negotiations.

The IPC's rather pessimistic analysis of its situation in Iraq colored its perception of a Ba'thist army officers' convention that took place at the home of former prime minister al-Bakr in April.[18] The IPC thought it a good thing that the Ba'th was conspiring against Yahya. But, again, even if Yahya were removed, it seemed likely that "the hard core, (Jadir and Haseeb in Oil) would stay and, if anything, increase their power and position, while the Premiership might go to a new man of lesser strength and ability to control" the radicals.[19] As much as the IPC disliked Yahya, the company's chief representative in Baghdad believed that Yahya was the only force capable of restraining the more radical tendencies of Haseeb and al-Jadir. The companies took particular note when Haseeb warned in the Iraqi press that the UK had plans to invade an occupy Iraqi oil fields to maintain physical control of the property. Should it come to that, Haseeb threatened that the Iraqi people were prepared to "fight in a street war" to defend their sovereignty over Iraqi oil resources.[20]

Rather than engaging in a street war, Rudi Jackli, the IPC's chief representative in Baghdad, sat down with Iraqi negotiator Husayn Ghulam in May to begin those patient step-by-step negotiations recommended in the company's March position paper. In their meeting, Ghulam warned the IPC against pursuing regime change in Iraq:

> He asked whether the Oil Companies were waiting for a change of Government; whether they did not realise that these were not demands of individuals but that they were national demands which would be inherited by any Cabinet that might come in. He wondered whether we did not realise that a new Prime Minister would have to prove all over again that he was brave and successful on the Oil front and that we would have to suffer anew whilst the present Prime Minister would be in a strong enough position based on his past record to work towards a settlement with us.[21]

Jackli found Ghulam's arguments compelling. The incentive structures in Iraq suggested that any new government would be more radical than the prevailing regime. As difficult as it was to deal with Yahya and the oil radicals, Jackli actually saw their reemergence as fortuitous for the settlement of outstanding issues. In his view, the burden of official responsibilities would moderate the behavior of "extremists like Jadir." And given that there was relatively little chance of a more pro-IPC government coming to power any time soon, Jackli recommended that the companies come to terms with the Yayha government: "If we can't do business with the type of Cabinet we have now we might as well retrench (or even pack) for it is the deals with them which will stand a chance to last."[22]

From Jackli's perspective, the Yahya regime possessed something sorely lacking in many previous regimes—legitimacy. It enjoyed relatively widespread support among the Iraqi people. This fact alone meant that it would be possible to conclude an agreement that stood a "chance to last." Jackli, as the chief representative—the equivalent of an ambassador—tended to take on Baghdad's perspective as his own. But the situation looked very different from London, where important IPC decisions were made, or Beirut, where regional intelligence was collected and analyzed. While Jackli saw great promise in open diplomacy and believed that it was possible to come to terms with Yahya and Haseeb, the Penroses seem to have been bearing a different message when they departed Beirut for Iraq ten days after the Jackli-Ghulam meeting.

The Penrose interest in bringing about Haseeb's downfall grew only more urgent as the spring wore on. In June, Abdullah Tariki gave an interview with *al-Thawrah* in which he praised the recent INOC-ERAP agreement as a step toward complete nationalization and a blow against "economic imperialism and underdevelopment."[23] Moreover, Iraq's bold example was leading the way for other producing countries. Affirming this radical principle, OPEC, at its Sixteenth Conference later that month, adopted a far-reaching "Declaratory Statement of Petroleum Policy in Member Countries." The statement urged OPEC to work toward state ownership of oil-producing operations in all member countries within a relatively short period of time.[24]

All outward signs seemed to indicate that Iraq was on the verge of nationalization, and that other states in the region would follow. But outward signs can be deceiving of inner realities. Lloyd Ahlgren, for example, vice president of Booz, Allen & Hamilton, an international management consulting firm that worked very closely with the CIA, called on the State Department in mid-July with a much more upbeat assessment of the situation in Iraq.[25]

Ahlgren reported that all of the doom and gloom was misplaced, that Yahya would soon be "stepping down," and that the business climate in Iraq would soon improve markedly.[26] The biggest threat to American interests in Iraq did not, Ahlgren contended, stem from Iraqi radicalism but rather from US support for Israel. Moderate Arab leaders could be groomed for power in Iraq and beyond, but only if Israeli expansionism could be contained. He therefore urged the State Department to protect American capital investments in the region by embracing the upcoming change of government in Iraq, and limiting American support for Israel:

> The feeling among many Arabs that the US Government supports Israel ... has harmed US commercial interests badly, not only in Iraq but also in Kuwait and Saudi Arabia. It is in the interests of the American economy for the US Government to adopt a more sympathetic posture toward the Arab world, but it apparently is difficult to drum up US domestic support for American interests in the Arab world.

Clearly, there was a great deal of disagreement about what constituted American interests in the Arab world. Ahlgren believed that those interests would be best served by supporting the government that was about to take power in Iraq, but he also believed that those interests were threatened by domestic special interest groups which favored Israeli expansion and remained indifferent to the plight of the majors.

THE CONSPIRACY OF ROBERT ANDERSON

As luck would have it, Ahlgren's reading of the political tea leaves was on the mark. The day after Ahlgren met with the State Department, a group of Iraqi military officers led by Lt. Col. ʿAbd al-Razzaq al-Nayif, President ʿArif's chief of military intelligence, seized control of key government institutions, jailed Yahya, put ʿArif on a plane bound for England, and declared a new regime. Although carried out by al-Nayif, the coup was organized by al-Bakr and his deputy, Saddam Hussein. At the time, the exact relationship between the al-Nayif group and the al-Bakr group was somewhat unclear, but the State Department's intelligence bureau immediately interpreted the coup as the work of the Baʿth and were cautiously optimistic.[27] But the NSC had a very different reading of events. After the spectacular failure of the Baʿth to establish a stable regime in 1963, many around Johnson were skeptical of the party. This was particularly so after a group of radical Baʿthists seized power in Syria in 1966 and aligned their regime with the Soviet Union.[28] As the new group took power in Iraq, the NSC acknowledged that it was, as yet, unclear "how radical" they would be, but worried that as Baʿthists "their tendencies will be towards moving Iraq even closer to [the Palestinian] Fatah, the Syrians and the Soviets."[29]

While the NSC was wary of any new Ba'thist government in Iraq, the American embassy in Beirut (the principal source of political information on Iraq after the closure of the embassy in Baghdad during the June 1967 War) was much more optimistic. On July 22, the political officer in Beirut reported that Iraq's Ba'thists were *not* in league with Syria. On the contrary, the Syrian regime was reportedly describing al-Nayif and his followers as "lackies of Kuwait and the IPC."[30] From Beirut, it appeared that it was the moderate al-Nayif who had furnished the leading element of the coup, and that al-Bakr was brought in as a figurehead at the last minute.[31] After receiving the embassy's assessment, the NSC then informed the White House that "the Baathists are from the right-wing of the party," and that "the Syrians had nothing to do with the coup."[32] As the dust began to settle, the NSC concluded, "The new government could still be a little harder for us to deal with than the old ['Arif]—if we ever have a chance to deal with it—but if we had to have a Baathist government there, this is probably the best we could expect."[33] Not exactly a ringing endorsement. But also not the end of the world.

The more optimistic readings of the change in government were based on the enthusiasm of conservative media outlets in Beirut. Reporting there predicted that the al-Nayif government would soon cancel the recently concluded oil agreements with the French, and that it might even dissolve the INOC altogether.[34] Even more encouraging still was the fact that Yahya and al-Jadir had been arrested and jailed, while Haseeb had gone into hiding.[35] As the radicals were purged, "moderate technocrats" took their places, much to the satisfaction of the IPC.[36] At the end of July, the new regime invited IPC representatives to Baghdad to negotiate directly with al-Nayif over all outstanding Iraq-IPC issues.[37]

It was in this context of anticipated Iraqi moderation on oil issues that former treasury secretary Robert Anderson called upon Walt Rostow, the national security advisor.[38] Anderson was now ostensibly a businessman representing the Pan American Sulfur Company and the Gulf Sulfur Company, both of which were interested in doing business in Iraq.[39] In his July 30 phone conversation with Rostow, Anderson reported the details of his recent meeting with an Iraqi interlocutor by the name of Lutfi al-Obeidi.[40] Obeidi was formerly "employed by Anderson" and was reportedly very close to al-Bakr. Anderson conveyed the new government's interest in resuming diplomatic relations with the United States, and its request for American economic aid. Anderson suggested that Rostow respond favorably to this request, and that he intercede with World Bank chair Robert McNamara to secure development loans for Iraq. The new leadership was, in Anderson's view, moderate and well disposed to the West.[41] The new finance minister, Salih Kubba, was in Anderson's words "a good friend and a solid citizen, as is the new Foreign Minister [Nasir al-Hani]."

Anderson explained that the coup had not been directed at the moderate president 'Arif but rather against the radicals led by Yahya. "Before seizing power," the new group "tried to persuade Aref to change the PM and the Cabinet but he was too weak to do anything." After taking power they "debated about whether to shoot the old Prime Minister [Yahya] but decided it would be better not to do so. They didn't want world opinion to say that theirs was just another Iraqi blood bath." From Anderson's perspective these were all positive signs. As was Obeidi's indication that the new government would adopt a policy line which would be sufficiently independent of Egypt and Syria.

On July 30, as IPC negotiators arrived in Baghdad to negotiate with al-Nayif, and as Rostow was considering the Anderson/Obeidi proposal, al-Bakr mounted a second coup—this time against al-Nayif, who was then exiled to Switzerland as al-Bakr proclaimed himself president and commander-in-chief of the armed forces.[42] Al-Bakr claimed this move was necessary to prevent "reactionary elements" from selling out Iraqi oil interests to the IPC.[43] This may have been true to a very large extent. And it is the way that Haseeb understood what happened. As director of Iraq's Central Bank, Haseeb had clashed with al-Bakr in 1963 over political appointees to the bank's board. But Haseeb believed these minor and long-forgotten issues and that he was on "good terms" with the new president. Haseeb expected to be retained as an adviser to the new regime. But when Haseeb emerged from hiding on August 1, he too was arrested and jailed.[44] At the same time al-Bakr quietly informed the IPC that there would be no return to the radical oil policy Yahya initiated during the June War.[45]

To Haseeb the conclusion to be deduced from al-Bakr's actions was simple. From jail, Haseeb wrote a letter to al-Bakr demanding to know why he was being jailed.[46] He implored the president to "either present charges against me and prove them in court, or else it will be clear that you are acting on behalf of the oil companies."[47] The letter was then leaked to *al-Hawadith* (*Incidents*), a weekly newspaper published in Beirut and then circulated widely throughout the Arab world. Al-Bakr reacted harshly to Haseeb's defiant action. After the letter was published, Haseeb was transferred to the infamous Qasr Nihaiya prison where he was interrogated and tortured by a committee under instructions from Saddam Hussein, who accused him of being "Nasser's representative in Iraq."[48]

Haseeb's arrest and al-Bakr's consolidation appeared a positive development for many in the State Department. In their view, "the Right-wing Baʿthis will probably not press further nationalization . . . [and] may also be more businesslike and less politically hamstrung in their dealings with foreign companies than was the Arif government."[49] Equally encouraging was the Baʿth's selection of Rashid al-Rifai, a new moderate oil minister who enjoyed the confidence of the State Department.[50]

While the State Department's intelligence service was generally satisfied with the Baʿth's initial moderation on oil issues, it expressed concern that the party's "power base is still very narrow," and that it lacked sufficient military support to secure its hold on the government.[51] Likewise, the IPC worried that by striking at al-Nayif, the Baʿth had alienated conservative army elements, and would be "forced to turn to the left—in particular to the Communists," to establish a stable regime.[52] Indeed, arch-conservative Ghanim al-ʿUqayli refused the Baʿth's invitation to take over the INOC, stating that he would rather pursue opportunities as a private consultant until a more stable, right-wing government emerged.[53]

With signs of impending doom seemingly everywhere it looked, the IPC did discern a glimmer of hope when Hardan al-Tikriti, the new minister of defense, extended a peace offering to the companies. In mid-October, al-Tikriti met with BP and Mobil officials in Baghdad to discuss ways in which the companies could move forward in a spirit of cooperation with the new government.[54] "Mr. McDonald [of Mobil] was obviously very intrigued by al-Tikriti who he describes as . . . having a very commanding presence . . . [and who] had been jailed by the Communists and was clearly a very tough individual." Moreover, al-Tikriti was now "residing and working in the PM's office," which seemed to "suggest a prominent role in GOI." In their meeting, al-Tikriti laid out his dilemma to the oilmen rather plainly: "He could give them an agreement that would be pleasing to them. However, he would be dead the next day. On the other hand, he could completely stop the flow of oil and he would be a hero within Iraq." Al-Tikriti hoped the companies would proffer a face-saving agreement that would solidify his own position within the Iraqi power structure, and al-Tikriti would, in turn, ensure the companies' interests in Iraq were secure. The key sticking point of course remained US support for Israel. No face-saving agreement would be possible so long as the US continued to shield Israel from pressure to withdraw from territories occupied during the 1967 war. According to al-Tikriti, "just a word" from the US recognizing Arab concerns would make a world of difference.

CLOSING THE TIKRITI OVERTURE

The Tikriti Overture was a godsend for IPC. Here was someone with whom they could do business. All they needed was "a word" from Washington regarding the question of Palestine that would allow al-Tikriti and other moderates to carry the day against their more radical colleagues.[55] Couldn't such a word be arranged? James Akins, the Iraqi embassy official who would soon move to a new position as director of the State Department's Office of Fuel and Energy, endorsed such a proposal with the same familiar arguments that had failed to sway the Johnson administration during the June War of the previous year:

> Our vulnerability to Arab pressure lies in the possibility of nationalization of our oil interests in the Arab world. This would mean a loss of several billion dollars in direct investment, of thirty years effort in building an industry and of at least a billion dollars annually toward our balance of payments— the direct damage to the United Kingdom would be even more severe.[56]

The problem is that Akins and his allies among the oil majors spoke the language of rational economic interests, when it was visions of celestial paradise that ultimately moved Washington. Unless the international majors were able to elevate their concerns to a higher spiritual plane, their arguments would continue to fall on deaf ears. In the face of the Johnson administration's deafness to their Cassandra-like wailing, the attitudes of the oilmen grew "explosively critical" of American foreign policy.[57]

Given the depth of Johnson's animosity to the international oil majors, the Tikriti Overture was doomed from the beginning. Lest there be any doubt about the character of the new regime, on November 10 (just as al-Tikriti's proposal was being considered in Washington), President al-Bakr chose to kidnap and murder Foreign Minister Nasir al-Hani. Recall that al-Hani had been the Iraqi ambassador to Lebanon who had arranged for the Penroses' entry into Iraq in May, and whom the Americans regarded as "one of the few Iraqi officials willing and able to contribute to better understanding between US and Arab world."[58] After the coup, al-Hani would have much preferred to remain in the safe confines of Beirut, but was called back by the al-Nayif government to serve as the new foreign minister.[59] According to Barzan al-Tikriti, a key figure in the July 17 coup (who was also a brother of Saddam Hussein and the eventual director of the Iraqi Mukhabarat), al-Hani had been the "connecting link to the Americans," and the CIA in particular, and he was murdered in November 1968 to conceal the American role in the coup.[60] In light of al-Hani's murder, NEA director Talcott Seeyle highlighted "the thuggery prevalent in Iraq" under the Ba'th, and rejected the idea of sending anyone to Iraq to meet with Hardan al-Tikriti to discuss reopening relations. Moreover, Seeyle had very little "confidence in the longevity of either Tikriti or his government" and preferred to simply wait out the next change of regime.[61] As the US interests section of the Belgian embassy in Baghdad (the US still had no diplomatic representation in Iraq) observed, the murder of al-Hani showed that "anarchy and violence seem inherent in Baathism."[62]

There is a certain irony in the Johnson administration's rejection of the Tikriti Overture. In 1963, it was the US government that fell in love with the Ba'th, while the IPC could not be bothered. But five years later, it was the IPC looking to the Ba'th, and the US government that couldn't be bothered. But Johnson administration's lack of interest in reaching an accord with the Ba'th was not due to a lack of trying on the part of the State Department. The State Department responded to the Crusade of Julius C. Holmes with the same tired apologia for the moderate Arab states and the importance of US capital investments in the Arab world.[63] But the more those arguments were plied the less effect they had. Such claims held the most sway as unspoken assumptions. By the time that the argument had to be actually articulated, all hope was gone and the battle was lost.

Perhaps the clearest indication that the era of the majors' domination in Washington was rapidly coming to an end was the election of Richard Nixon in November of 1968. The financial contributions from domestic oil and gas by this time had shifted away from Johnson and toward Nixon through Goldwater. And as president, Nixon would appoint Henry Kissinger to serve as his all-powerful national security advisor, and for Kissinger, the defense of Holmes's "Christian Kingdom of Jerusalem" was an article of faith. As Salim Yaqub observes, "If a single drive motivated Henry Kissinger's entire approach to the Arab-Israeli conflict, it was to shield Israel from pressure to withdraw from all or most of the territory it had occupied in the 1967 Arab-Israeli War."[64] Over the next eight years, Kissinger worked diligently to institutionalize Israeli control over "territories occupied" during the 1967 War.[65]

As the Nixon administration fortified the American defenses around Holmes's "Christian Kingdom of Jerusalem," the Ba'thist regime in Iraq proceeded in another direction. The murder of Nasir al-Hani had been part of a broader consolidation of authority within Iraq on the part of Hasan al-Bakr and his Tikriti kinsman, Saddam Hussein—or *al-Sayyid al-Na'ib* (Mr. Deputy) as he became known.[66] The Lyndon Johnson administration looked on this development with great dread. The ominous character of the regime was only reinforced in January 1969, when al-Bakr arrested and hanged nine Iraqi Jews whom he accused of being part of an American spy ring.[67]

Despite indications of the new regime's ruthlessness, or perhaps because of it, the oil companies continued to hold out hope for the Ba'th. They remembered the Ba'th's anti-Communism in 1963 more closely than did Washington and thought that the consolidation of the right wing of the party would be good for their interests. Perhaps this new group would be willing to strike a lasting agreement.[68] The company's optimism in this regard was fed by meetings with Hardan al-Tikriti, who was still trying to convince them that "the door to North Rumaila is not shut" and "a new proposal would be welcome."[69] But the desperation in al-Tikriti's voice was growing palpable. In one such meeting he pleaded: "You are rich and we are rich and we can be rich together with all this oil to do good things for this country and for the West. This is our policy we want to work with you and not against you but you must help us."[70] This sounded good to the companies. It also sounded good to the British Foreign Office. So far as the Foreign Office could tell, an "influential and confident Group (led by [Saddam Hussein al-]Takriti, and with important party backing from President Bakr) are strongly in favor of a settlement with IPC."[71] According to the British embassy in Baghdad, Saddam, as the new "strongman" of the party, "bore no grudge against the IPC" and was "by no means opposed to reaching agreement with the IPC, provided its terms . . . could be dressed up in such a way that the regime could defend itself against any charges of going back on its word or of yielding to imperialist monopoly pressures."[72]

On the ground in Baghdad, Cocky Hahn, the IPC's new chief representative, reported that "in view of Saddam's elevation," and the general "strengthening of the right wing of the party which embraces all those who support us," the time was finally right for a settlement. He recommended that IPC "send a very senior representative," but warned:

> We must, for God's sake, not send some swollen headed spokesman who thinks IPC is a state within a state, who will make 'parliamentary' speeches for the record, but when it comes time to crunch will have to trot back to London for instructions or authority. They will be dealing with the very top here and must deal accordingly—openly and frankly in a positive spirit—man to man, eye to eye. Everything is ready here for an agreement now—time is short and long negotiations would be certain to fail. If [IPC] representatives fail to reach quick agreement with the men who will deal with them—who, including new V.P. Saddam [Hussein al-]Tikriti, want swift action—then fault will be theirs and Iraq will survive without them.[73]

IPC management in London was, however, unmoved by Hahn's appeal and remained unwilling to recognize Law 80 and relinquish control of the nationalized oil fields to the INOC.[74] Upon hearing this, 'Abd al-Karim al-Sheikhly, the Iraqi negotiator, expressed his regret that the "companies' attitude had not changed." He then informed the IPC negotiators, "The companies were now too late. . . . Arrangements had now been made with friendly countries which would enable INOC to develop North Rumaila, without relations to the companies except perhaps as commercial buyers."[75]

The breakdown of the December 1969 Iraq-IPC negotiations marked the end of an era. Having looked to the West for a negotiated settlement to the Law 80 dispute, the Iraqi Ba'th now looked in another direction. In December 1969, al-Bakr appointed Sa'dun Hammadi, a highly competent administrator with a PhD in economics from the University of Wisconsin–Madison (class of 1956), to serve as the new minister of oil and director of the Iraq National Oil Company. Although he had been a member of the Ba'th since the 1940s, Hammadi was on the left wing of the party and was an oil radical aligned with Yahya, Haseeb, and the previous regime. Under Hammadi, Iraq cut off all negotiations with the IPC and forged ahead with economic and technical cooperation with the Soviet Union.[76]

In August 1970, Hussein led a delegation to Moscow to negotiate a $142 million economic and technical aid agreement toward this end.[77] In September, al-Bakr marked the death of Nasser by releasing Haseeb and other prominent Nasserists from jail—concluding that the Nasserist threat to the Ba'th had passed. Haseeb was then allowed to resume teaching as a professor of economics at Baghdad University and began informally advising Hammadi, who was a close personal friend. Haseeb also informally advised the Ba'th in the sense that he "knew that the Ba'th had informants in all of my classes so I advised Bakr in that way, on pipeline issues and negotiations with the IPC . . . I also brought in regional experts such as Tariki as a way of advising the state on how to carry out the nationalization and settlement."

By the end of 1970, Iraqi politics had advanced all the way back to where they were in the spring of 1968. The government of Iraq was once again poised to nationalize the oil industry. And by this point, the IPC had run out of cards to play.

Chapter 9
THE NATIONALIZATION OF THE IPC

THE OIL COMPANIES SAW GREAT PROMISE IN THE RISE OF SADdam Hussein. This was no accident. Saddam allowed the companies to see what they wanted to see. And then he took what he wanted. Saddam—whose eventual overthrow required a full-scale military invasion by the world's most heavily armed state—did not rise from the dirt as a matter of chance. As he emerged through the crucible of Iraq's politics of intrigue, he mastered the principles of that game, and played it better than anyone else in the field. Two of the most bedrock elements of that game were resource nationalism and ethno-sectarian difference. Any bid to build real power in Iraq would have to harness the spiritual and moral force of resource nationalism, and harness that force in such a way that diverse communities in Iraq could see something of themselves in—and derive real material benefit from—the policies of the state.

The Iraqi state was not designed to give full and equal representation to all. It was designed to protect British imperial interests. If it was going to serve any other end, it would have to be redesigned along different principles. Qasim and Yahya had done much to reconstruct the essential functions of the Iraqi state. They did this in a socialist but non-Communist fashion that kept its distance from the Soviet Union. The problem with the non-Communist approach to economic development was that it was the Communists who had the most intelligent and farsighted vision of an inclusive

Iraqi national identity. As Communists, they cared little for differences among tribes and sects. From the Communist standpoint, all that mattered was that one was a comrade committed to the ideals of Communism.

If Saddam and the Ba'th were going to transcend ethno-sectarian difference to achieve true oil sovereignty, then they would have to draw on the strengths of Communism. Unfortunately, an earlier incarnation of the Ba'th had murdered the Communists' leaders and decimated their ranks. As powerful as the party was in the 1940s and 1950s, it was completely shattered by the trauma of 1963. Now as the Ba'th resumed power, it would have to figure out a way to put what remained of those pieces back together.

THE TRIUMPH OF THE BA'TH

The nationalization of the IPC was the centerpiece of a broad political movement on the part of the Ba'th—and particularly on the part of its leading figures, Hasan al-Bakr and Saddam Hussein. Upon coming to power in July 1968, al-Bakr and Saddam had one overriding objective: establish a stable Ba'thist-controlled regime; and they seem to have recognized from early on that this would require a double or triple movement. In the first instance, their faction within the party would have to consolidate power against its rivals—recall that it was intraparty rivalries that brought down the Ba'thist regime in 1963. At the same time that they consolidated control over their own party, they would have to consolidate the party's control over the state against rival parties and groups, and they would have to do all of this while simultaneously navigating the cross-currents of regional and international politics. Each of these objectives was integral to the others. Forging domestic, regional, and international alliances was central to securing al-Bakr's control of the party. But forging stable domestic, regional, and international alliances would not be possible without a unified and coherent leadership group at the top of the party and regime.

Solving the Iraqi political Rubik's Cube was no small order. As it came to power in July 1968, the Ba'th remained a seething cauldron of conflicting personalities competing for power. Al-Bakr's most serious rivals within the party were Salih Mahdi 'Ammash, the former defense minister (February to November 1963) who was now minister of interior, and General Hardan al-Tikriti, the former commander of the air force and now minister of defense, commander-in-chief, and chief of staff of the armed forces. Both figures commanded large personal followings among high-ranking military officers. As a check on this military wing of the Ba'th Party, al-Bakr brought his younger kinsman, Saddam Hussein, into his inner circle. Hussein had come up through the civilian wing of the party's internal security apparatus.[1] As a young man, he had participated in the October 1959 assassination attempt on Qasim. He then escaped to Cairo until the Ba'th took power in 1963. After the 1963 coup, he became a key organizer within the civilian wing of the party and was jailed in 1964 for allegedly plotting to overthrew President 'Arif. In 1966, he escaped from jail. At that point, al-Bakr, as secretary general of the Iraqi Ba'th Party, made him deputy secretary general.[2] In this capacity, Saddam organized and led the party's formidable complex of internal security apparatuses.[3]

As al-Bakr's chief deputy, Saddam proved a shrewd and ruthless tactician who skillfully employed carrots and sticks to co-opt, marginalize, or eliminate al-Bakr's rivals to power.[4] But this would take some time to achieve. As a first step toward this end, al-Bakr and Saddam reached out to the Kurdish Democratic Party (KDP) and the Iraqi Communist Party (ICP) in an effort to forge a National Patriotic Front. This would be a Ba'thist-led alliance of the most powerful and well-organized domestic political forces in the country. Toward this end, al-Bakr offered cabinet posts to representatives from each movement.[5]

Al-Bakr's opening to the ICP was particularly novel. One, because of the Ba'th's history of bloody conflict with the Communists, and two, because in the previous era, such overtures to the left were sure to invite foreign intervention. Yahya and Haseeb were taken down for simply making eyes at the French. But now the brash leadership of the Ba'th was openly courting the Communists. This overture to the Communists was necessary because the Ba'th had just allied with al-Nayif to unseat the Nasserists, and needed whatever allies on the left that it could find. The Communists, however, recalling the Ba'th's history of bloody reprisals against them in 1963, refused to enter into any alliance with the regime unless "full civil liberties were restored, political parties legalised and democratic elections held."[6] Until then, the party's central leadership adopted a position of official neutrality, while in southern Iraq, a Maoist breakaway faction waged a guerilla war that bedeviled the regime for several months in the spring of 1969.[7]

Forging an alliance with the KDP proved only slightly less perilous. Whereas the Communists flatly refused to join al-Bakr's government, the KDP initially accepted four cabinet posts.[8] However, KDP leader Mullah Mustafa Barzani soon took exception to the terms of the proposed alliance with the regime. Barzani sensed that al-Bakr and Hussein were seeking to subtly undermine and weaken his leadership of the Kurdish movement by favoring a younger, more urban, and socialist faction of the KDP led by Jalal Talabini and Ibrahim Ahmad.[9] Rather than allowing himself to be edged out of the Iraqi power structure, Barzani deepened his long-standing alliance with Iran and Israel—two traditional geopolitical rivals to Iraq that had been providing financial assistance to the KDP since the outbreak of fighting in 1961.[10] With support from Iran and Israel, Barzani launched a new uprising in December 1968—the first significant fighting in the north since the spring of 1966.[11] By February 1970, Iranian and Israeli financial assistance to the KDP amounted to more than $3.3 million per month.[12]

The outbreak of war in the north led to a recalibration of the political analysis in Baghdad. The longer the fighting lasted, the more power would flow to al-Tikriti and 'Ammash—both of whom had substantial bases of support among conservative, anti-Kurdish military officers.[13] To preempt any challenge from al-Tikriti and 'Ammash, Saddam negotiated a political settlement with Barzani and the KDP known as the March Manifesto of 1970. This was the most expansive statement of Kurdish national rights in Iraqi history. The agreement recognized Iraq as a "bi-national state," and pledged to respect Kurdish rights in all domains—including Kurdish linguistic rights, Kurdish participation in government, Kurdish administrators for Kurdish areas, agrarian reform, and a census to determine the Kurdish population of Kirkuk.[14] Barzani was not yet willing to join the National Patriotic Front, but the terms of the March Manifesto were sufficient to compel him to lay down his arms. A major obstacle in the Ba'th's road to power was well on its way to being resolved.

The next obstacle to the consolidation sought by al-Bakr and Saddam was the threat posed by al-Tikriti. That obstacle was shattered in September 1970, and the ground on which that that rock was split was the Israeli-Palestinian conflict. One of the major lessons that the Ba'th learned from its failure in 1963 was to avoid the contentious politics of pan-Arab unionism in favor of a strict adherence to Iraqi nationalism.[15] But this shift away from pan-Arabism in no way precluded the Baʻth from making radical pronouncements with regard to the Arab cause in Palestine. Al-Bakr's government rejected UN Resolution 242 and vowed to "liberate the whole of Palestine [by] armed struggle." Toward this end it positioned 17,000 Iraqi soldiers and 100 tanks in Jordan to support Palestinian guerillas operating out of Palestinian refugee camps in the country. However, after those Palestinian guerrillas hijacked four airliners and landed them in Jordan in September 1970, the Jordanian army, with the support of Israel and the West, made war on the Palestinian Liberation Organization. In what became known as "Black September," Iraqi troops under the command of al-Tikriti stood by as a Western-backed Jordanian army routed the PLO, killing hundreds of Palestinians and wounding many thousands more.[16] The outcome of the fighting in Jordan proved a fortuitous tragedy for al-Bakr and Saddam, as it provided them the "excuse they needed to remove Hardan al-Takriti and purge his leading supporters from the armed forces."[17] In the wake of "Black September," al-Tikriti was stripped of his cabinet ministries and exiled to Algeria.[18] Six months later, in March 1971, Baʻthist assassins traced him to Kuwait City and gunned him down in the street.[19]

With the March Manifesto, and the dismissal of al-Tikriti, two major obstacles in al-Bakr's path to political consolidation had been cleared. Winning Communist support and eliminating the threat posed by ʻAmmash were the next orders of business. Al-Bakr and Saddam accomplished this in a series of related moves. The first was to win Communist support by "donning the Communists' own robes."[20] That is, the Baʻth adopted the Communists' economic and diplomatic program wholesale. It forged close diplomatic relations with China, the USSR, and Soviet Bloc countries at the same time that it embarked on an ambitious program of socialist transformation of the country's economy (if not its politics). The nationalization of the IPC was only the capstone of this effort.

As early as 1969, the Baʻth introduced broad land reform measures that equalized landholdings and abolished peasant debts. A more systematic and ambitious land reform program was introduced in 1970. At the same time the regime invested—before the massive influx of oil revenue of the 1970s—unprecedented sums in the provision of healthcare and education. It introduced new laws regulating such measures as conditions of work, labour unions, pensions and social security. The new laws set minimum wages and maximum working hours, prohibited child labor and protected workers against arbitrary dismissal. A comprehensive national insurance scheme was introduced in 1971 on the basis of contributions from employees, employers, and government.[21]

These were impressive strides to the left, but the Communist Party was not yet convinced that the Ba'th had changed its stripes, and refused to join the National Patriotic Front. However, a turning point occurred in September 1971 when the party was reorganized such that 'Ammash—the last Iraqi figure sympathetic to the IPC—was removed from the scene in Baghdad by his appointment to serve as ambassador to the Soviet Union. As 'Ammash departed Baghdad, Saddam was made vice president. With 'Ammash now contemplating the snows of Moscow, IPC managing director Geoffrey Stockwell reflected on the significance of the cabinet reshuffle: "It is quite unrealistic to hope that a nice gentlemanly, rightwing collection of Sandhurst trained Colonels with a strong belief in the Capitalist system will take over and be ready to deal with us. There are none left."[22]

For a half-century, the IPC had come to depend on military officers trained at the Royal Military Academy Sandhurst in London to serve as reliable vehicles of British influence in Iraq. But those days were over. Saddam, as the new strongman, was not trained in the niceties of drill and ceremony at Sandhurst, but rather in the rough-and-tumble world of the Ba'thist security apparatus in the crucible of Iraq's postcolonial politics. As the new vice president, he assumed control of the oil portfolio and embarked on a consorted effort to win Communist support for the regime by bringing the IPC nationalization to a successful conclusion.[23]

In February 1972, Saddam Hussein visited Moscow to secure final marketing arrangements in anticipation of the pending nationalization.[24] Two months later, Soviet premier Alexi Kosygin traveled to Iraq to preside over the first export of Rumaila crude, which set sail for the Soviet Union on April 7.[25] Two days later, Iraq and the Soviet Union signed a fifteen-year Treaty of Friendship and Cooperation that assured the Iraqi regime of wide-ranging support for its nationalist oil policy.[26]

Having secured this fundamental national political objective, the Communists had no choice but to sign on to the National Patriotic Front and associate themselves with the regime.[27] In this sense, the nationalization of the IPC nationalization was more than just a victory over the international oil companies—it represented a victory over the sectarianism and political divisions that had hobbled previous Iraqi regimes.

REARGUARD COLLAPSE

As Iraq moved forward with Rumaila production, the IPC dealt a major financial blow to the regime by cutting production from Iraq's northern Kirkuk field to just 60 percent of its total capacity. The IPC claimed that the production cut was a result of a drop in tanker rates that made oil piped across Syria uncompetitive, but the move was widely interpreted as politically motivated.[28] In the face of IPC's production cut, Oil Minister Hammadi issued a final ultimatum on May 18. Hammadi gave the IPC two weeks to restore Kirkuk production to full capacity, or the company would face immediate nationalization.[29] When the company failed to comply, the Government of Iraq issued Law 69 of 1972, which unilaterally transferred ownership of the IPC to the Iraqi Company for Oil Operations—a new subsidiary of the INOC. However, under advice from Haseeb, Law 69 exempted from nationalization the Basrah Petroleum Company (BPC), the wholly owned subsidiary of the IPC that produced oil from Iraq's southern Zubair oilfields. This was done so that Iraq would retain an important source of revenue, and so that the BPC could serve as a kind of bargaining chip to compel IPC cooperation in negotiating final settlement terms. The idea was that the IPC would come to terms faster if the threat of further nationalization remained hanging over their heads. Had Iraq nationalized all at once, the IPC might have been more likely to dig in and drag out compensation negotiations. At least that was the thinking in Baghdad. This caveat notwithstanding, Law 69 represented the single-largest oil expropriation since the Iranian government nationalized its oil industry in 1951.

The world had changed since the early 1950s, but the CIA was the last to know of it. As far as it could tell, "the Iraqi government has nationalized the major part of its oil industry at a time when its negotiating position is extremely weak." Given what the CIA understood to be the realities of the world oil, the agency remained confident that Iraq would be incapable of marketing the approximately one million barrels per day of Iraqi oil normally exported from IPC fields. Marketing this volume of oil would require the "cooperation of most of the members of OPEC," and this level of transnational cooperation seemed highly unlikely.[30] This assessment was based largely on the belief of Exxon and Mobil that it would be possible to "let the Iraqis fail on their own," as there was "no way" that Iraq would be able to "market anything near full volume[s] even if companies take no overt action."[31]

As it turned out, the CIA got it wrong. It drastically underestimated the changes that had occurred in the regional politics of oil in recent years. Contrary to American expectations that Iran and Saudi Arabia would be able to prevent OPEC from supporting the Iraqi action, OPEC convened a special meeting in Beirut on June 9, in which it not only affirmed Iraq's sovereign right to nationalize the IPC but offered financial assistance and issued a ruling forbidding any member state from increasing production in an attempt to undermine the IPC nationalization.[32] Moreover, Kuwait, driven by the impulses of its "unruly National Assembly," went so far as to propose Kuwaiti cutbacks in support of "the Arab cause," while Saudi Arabia expressed its unwillingness to "betray the cause of Arabism."[33] Even Iran, America's closest ally in OPEC, and the centerpiece of the Nixon administration's regional strategy, was unwilling to oppose the Iraqi action. Iranian finance minister Jamshid Amouzegar told US embassy officials in Tehran that the IPC's approach to dealing with the government of Iraq "illustrated their stupidity and lack of understanding of how to deal with oil producing countries by acting as if negotiations were a grand poker party in which bluffing was an acceptable tactic."[34] Rather than increasing production, Iran held production steady and stood with OPEC in affirming Iraq's right to nationalize.[35]

Even more worrying for American officials was the fact that anticipated consumer solidarity failed to materialize. France, for one, sent the government of Iraq a telegram expressing its support on June 7. "According to French judicial doctrine," the telegram read, "the nationalization of the IPC cannot be contested. It is an inherent right of sovereignty for any state to engage in nationalization."[36] The following week, Saddam Hussein flew to Paris to negotiate a major purchase agreement that guaranteed CFP a 23.75 percent share of Iraq's nationalized oil.[37] The French defection was somewhat predictable. But other European states such as Italy, Spain, and Greece soon followed suit in negotiating direct state-to-state purchase agreements.[38] Even the British refused to support the American hard line on Iraq and opposed any attempt to embargo Iraqi oil.[39] As Iraq succeeded in marketing its nationalized oil over the course the summer and fall of 1972, it became increasingly clear that the IPC would have very little leverage in imposing a settlement on Iraq. By February 1973, IPC negotiators were ready to "swallow our pride" and conclude an agreement with Iraqi officials over all outstanding issues.[40]

On March 1, 1973, Iraq and the IPC reached a comprehensive settlement. According to the terms of the agreement, Iraq would provide the IPC partners with roughly $340 million worth of oil (15 million tons) as compensation for expropriated IPC facilities, while the IPC agreed to pay the government £141 (or $360 million) to settle long-standing accounting disputes.[41] According to the State Department's analysis of the deal, the IPC essentially handed over "title to its property in Iraq in exchange for [a] write-off of its bad taxes." Exxon was particularly unhappy with this outcome. In its view, the European partners were so desperate for "access to Iraqi oil" that they were prepared to accept "agreement on almost any terms."[42] While the American companies absorbed the shock of the new agreement, Iraqis celebrated with fireworks in Baghdad.[43]

It would be hard to overstate the significance of the successful IPC nationalization. It meant that when oil prices spiked in the 1970s, the government of Iraq, and not the private corporations, was the primary beneficiary. But Iraq was not simply a passive beneficiary of rising oil prices. It was rather an active agent in pushing those prices up—more directly in some ways than others. Oil prices had been gradually rising due to increasing global demand in the late 1960s and early 1970s, but spiked dramatically in response to the next round of the Arab-Israeli War in October 1973.[44]

Iraq responded to the outbreak of fighting on October 6 with the immediate and unilateral nationalization of the US and Dutch shares in the BPC (leaving only the French, British, and Gulbenkian interests momentarily intact).[45] At the same time, Iraq withdrew financial assets from US banks and pledged to make these funds available as development loans to Third World countries hurt by higher oil prices.[46] Saddam Hussein called on other Arab producers to do the same. But rather than following Iraq's radical lead, other Arab states, led by Saudi Arabia, elected instead to impose a production cut and a shipping embargo against the US and other states aligned with Israel. For its part, OPEC, as a whole, elected to raise posted prices from $3.03 to

$5.11 per barrel on October 17. This increase was then followed at the end of December by another OPEC increase to $11.65 per barrel. While Iraq did not single-handedly engineer these price increases, it did contribute to this outcome, as the increases were adopted as a face-saving but less radical alternative to Iraq's call for immediate nationalization.

Regardless of whoever—or whatever—was responsible for engineering the spectacular increase in oil prices in the early 1970s (and this was not a monocausal affair, as will be discussed below), Iraq reaped a windfall. For decades, Cold Warriors had warned that if the Soviets gained a foothold in the Middle East they would be able to use that position to cut off the West's access to the oil of the region. But of course the exact opposite happened as a result of the 1972 Iraqi-Soviet Treaty of Friendship and the IPC nationalization. Between 1972 and 1980, Iraqi oil exports doubled. In this same period, Iraq constructed a second pipeline from Kirkuk to the Mediterranean through Turkey, a new "strategic pipeline" from Haditha to Rumaila and Faw (which allowed Iraq to pump northern oil south to the Gulf, or southern oil north to the Mediterranean according to global market demand), and a fleet of state-owned tankers (see map 3).[47] In this same period (1972–80), Iraq nationalized the last foreign-owned BPC shares (the French, British, and Gulbenkian positions) and saw its oil revenue increase from $575 million to $26 billion.[48]

The Ba'th used this influx of oil wealth to build a vast social welfare state. It constructed an expansive network of state-of-the-art hospitals and clinics at which healthcare services were administered free of charge. It undertook an ambitious program to train new doctors, and the ratio of doctors in the country went from 1:4,200 in 1968 to 1:1,790 in 1980. As a result of these investments, average life-expectancy increased from 46 to 57.[49] At the same time, the regime doubled the number of primary and secondary schools in the country. Education services, from primary school through university, were similarly provided free of charge. The number of university-enrolled students in this period increased from 49,194 in 1973, to 96,301 by 1980. In that same period, the number of university professors increased from 1,721 to 6,515.[50]

In addition to social welfare spending, the Ba'th undertook massive port expansion and other domestic infrastructure projects.[51] As the state invested oil revenue in the construction of roads, bridges, offshore ports, and public buildings, the percentage of the population employed in construction grew from less than 3 percent in 1967 to more than 10 percent by 1977.[52] In this same period, the percentage of the population employed in the service sector increased from 13 percent to more than 31 percent, the percentage of the population employed in manufacturing increased by almost a third, and overall rate of government employment doubled. By 1980, almost a third of the country's urban population was employed in the public sector. As a result of these efforts, a broad, highly educated and healthy middle-class emerged.[53] In many ways the 1970s represented a "golden age" in the modern history of Iraq.

THE TREACHERY OF THE CIA

Iraq's golden age didn't last. Economic progress in Iraq invited the covert wrath of the CIA and neighboring Iran. Contrary to images of the shah as a CIA puppet, in this affair it appears that it was the CIA dancing on a string while the shah called the tune.[54] The shah had, since the announcement of the British withdrawal from region in 1968, put his country forward to serve as the successor to the British Empire. And here he played on America's imperial anxieties to his own advantage. Over the next several years, the shah successfully extracted unprecedented arms transfers from the United States and effectively co-opted and directed the world's most powerful spy agency.

As the shah sought to turn American resources to his own purposes, he enjoyed a number of decisive advantages. The first was that as a monarch, he did not have to stand for democratic election and faced no term limits. While American presidents might come and go with the wind, the shah remained. With each passing year, his mastery at manipulating the US national security bureaucracy grew more advanced.[55] Indeed, the shah had begun cultivating Richard Nixon's political career as early as 1960, and by the time that Nixon became president in 1969, the shah enjoyed an outsized influence on Nixon's understanding of the world.[56]

A second decisive advantage that the shah enjoyed in his effort to wield the levers of American power was Nixon's selection of Henry Kissinger to serve as his all-powerful national security advisor. Last chapter we saw that Kissinger was emotionally and psychologically invested in Israeli control over as much physical territory as possible. But Kissinger was also obsessed with the Soviet threat to the region after the British withdrawal. And Kissinger's anxiety in this regard was the raw material with which the shah could erect a massive military and strategic edifice. Immediately upon coming into office, the shah (who had normalized relations with the USSR in 1962) began aggressively plying Cold War narratives to maximize his own advantage. When the shah visited the White House in April 1969, he warned that "the Soviet Union wanted to penetrate the Persian Gulf area," that Baʿthist Iraq was becoming the Soviets' preferred instrument of penetration, and that only a super-armed Iran could contain the Iraqi-Soviet threat to regional order.[57]

The shah's warning touched a nerve in Washington. No fear ran deeper in the American capital than the fear of Soviet penetration.[58] In this sense, it was Greece in 1947 all over again. The British were shirking their imperial responsibilities and thereby creating a "strategic opening" for the Soviets to exploit. Without US intervention, the Soviets would be able to take over the region and deny its prolific oil resources to the world. And just as Kennan and Forrestal responded to the emergence of a "strategic vacuum" with the Truman Doctrine, so Kissinger played farce to Kennan's tragedy by authoring a new "Nixon Doctrine"—a policy of unchecked arm sales to Iran as a check on the Soviet Union. But as a strategic concept, the Nixon Doctrine failed to garner the same emotional resonance that Kennan had been able to marshal a generation earlier. Even the fear of Soviet penetration had become largely pro forma. The zeitgeist had simply shifted. In the aftermath of the Vietnam War, as the US sought détente with a USSR that was not blocking, but facilitating, Western access to Middle East oil, "Red Scare" was a much more difficult sell than it had been in the 1920s or the 1940s.

That the Nixon Doctrine made no sense proved no impediment to its successful implementation. In September 1970, after nearly two years of the shah's careful cultivation of Nixon and Kissinger, the US formalized this policy of Iranian military primacy with National Security Decision Memorandum 92.[59] The substance of this new policy was worked out in May 1972, in the wake of the Iraqi-Soviet Treaty of Friendship and Cooperation. At the end of that month, Nixon and Kissinger visited Tehran to meet with the shah, and it was in that meeting that the shah secured an American commitment to provide Iran with unrestricted access to the American arsenal and to covertly finance a new wave of fighting in Iraqi Kurdistan.[60]

The State Department rejected both of the initiatives discussed in the Tehran meeting. A massive increase in arms sales to Iran would only drive up oil prices—as the shah would demand new hikes to finance his appetite for US guns—and lead to pressure on the companies to concentrate regional production in Iran, where American companies held only a minority interest in the operating consortium. As a consequence, a "substantial portion of the profits" from this production "would go to non-American companies."[61] Moreover, as Exxon tried to impress upon the administration, there was no reason to believe that a heavily armed Iran would have "a stabilizing influence in the Middle East and point[ed] to the wise use of oil revenues by other states such as Saudi Arabia and Kuwait."[62] On the contrary, the vast influx of arms into the region only made "fresh wars likely, if not inevitable."[63] The oil companies therefore lobbied the State Department to maintain an equally balanced approach to Iran and Saudi Arabia as the "twin pillars" of American regional strategy, and to discourage Iran from upsetting that balance by "overbuying" US military equipment.[64]

That the State Department would try to discourage arms sales to Iran in favor of a closer relationship with Saudi Arabia demonstrated the extent to which it was fundamentally out of step with the dominant mood in Washington. The whole notion of moving closer to Saudi Arabia was suspect so far as Kissinger was concerned. Saudi Arabia was of course led by King Faysal—"a firm believer in the anti-Semitic 'Protocols of the Elders of Zion,' which he had published and distributed, and never tired of telling his American interlocutors that the Zionists and the Communists were conspiring together to drive a wedge between the United States and the Arab world."[65] The shah's narrative regarding the threat of Soviet penetration through Ba'thist Iraq was much more in line with Kissinger's own worldview than were Faysal's diatribes against the Zionist-Communist global conspiracy. As the shah put it: "Faisal! He does not live in the same world as the rest of us. All he does is mouth about Jerusalem and insist that Jews drink the blood of non-Jews once a year."[66]

Given Faysal's attitude toward "the Jews," Kissinger was markedly unsympathetic to oil company lobbying on Saudi Arabia's behalf. On the contrary, Kissinger rejected the oil companies preference for Faysal over the shah as little more than rent-seeking on the part of a special interest group. Whereas the shah was focused on the paramount issues of world order (defeating Communism and the like), the oil companies were concerned only with their own bottom line. And that bottom line was conflicting ever more sharply with the reigning conception of the national interest. As Hal Saunders of the NSC put it:

> What interest does the US, as a nation, have in the maintenance of the oil companies in their present form in the producing countries? A cruder way of putting this is: How would it affect the national interest—in contrast to the companies' interest—if they were reduced to distributing oil after buying it from the producers on a contract basis?[67]

Core to the corporatist thesis that had once governed American foreign oil policy was the notion that what's good for Aramco is good for the US and vice versa. Clearly, that thesis no longer held sway in Washington.

The Nixon administration may not have seen a clear and compelling national interest in indulging the demands of Aramco, but it did see a clear and compelling national interest in meeting the shah's demand for new arms deliveries. In the face of State Department warnings about overdependence on the shah, Saunders emphasized that England, France, and Italy were all competing aggressively to supply Iran with weapons, and there was "no reason for us to lose the market."[68] And that market was not insignificant. The Grumman Corporation, for example, was teetering on the edge of bankruptcy as the Vietnam War ran down, and the Iran deal could remake the company's fortunes for a generation to come.[69] And the fortunes of the Grumman Corporation might, in turn, shape the fortunes of the Nixon administration's 1972 reelection campaign, as the company was an important employer in the electorally significant New York–Long Island region.[70] Given such considerations, Kissinger let it be known throughout the bureaucracy that "decisions on the acquisition of military equipment should be left primarily to the government of Iran."[71] As purchasing decisions were left to the shah, Iranian demand for US arms increased. And as Iran's demands for US arms increased, so too did the shah's demand for the oil price increases that were implemented under the cover of the October War.[72]

The second major item discussed at the May 1972 meeting between Nixon and the shah—the notion of the United States providing covert assistance to the Kurds—struck the State Department as even more ill-conceived than the policy of unlimited arms sales to Iran. Not only would arming an opposition group in a Soviet-aligned state threaten the fledgling policy of détente with the USSR, but State Department analysts noted that the whole enterprise of backing Barzani was a fool's errand. "Time was against" the 69-year-old Barzani, as power within the KDP movement was beginning to shift to the "younger, reformists and leftist faction" led by Jalal Talabani. Moreover, the

State Department worried that many of Barzani's "war-weary followers may be reluctant to take up arms again so soon after the long, wearing struggle of the 1960's."[73] In its analysis, the Kurdish people,

> who have had a little over five years of relative peace . . . cannot be eager to take up arms again. A correspondent for Le Monde who explored Kurdish views early in April 1972 found younger, urban Kurds saying that they have already won better conditions than any of the neighboring Kurdish groups, even if not all they wished, and that to go to war now would risk missing out on Soviet-aided development plans which are already beginning to accelerate the economy in the rest of Iraq.

Iraq was experiencing a golden age of intercommunal harmony, and it didn't make any sense to try to tear this down. Even if the "added strain of another Kurdish war" did bring down the Ba'thist government, the Kurds would not be "able to determine the composition of the next regime. Nor would any likely Iraqi successors be more stable, stronger, or very much less dependent on the USSR than the present government."[74] Even the two CIA officers in the field who were tasked with administering US covert aid considered the operation the "dumbest thing we'd done in our careers" and warned that "this effort is not going to rebound to the benefit of the United States, or the Kurds, or the Iranians."[75]

The State Department, and behind it the oil companies, might raise this or that objection, but ultimately, it was the shah, working in and through Kissinger, who called the shots. After receiving instructions from Tehran, Kissinger in July 1972 authorized $5 million in covert assistance to the Kurds—a down payment in what would eventually total more than $20 million in secret aid by 1975.[76] In December, Richard Helms moved from his position as director of the CIA to Tehran where he assumed the ambassadorship and carried out the shah's instructions to a T.[77]

MULLAH MUSTAFA'S REBELLION

The Nixon administration's commitment to support the Kurdish insurgency represented the culmination of Barzani's life and work. Barzani and his KDP had once been associated with the left. After the failure of Barzani's 1946 revolution, he received exile in the USSR, where he remained until the 1958 revolution. After he returned to Iraq, Barzani had always been careful to maintain correct relations with Moscow and the Iraqi Communist Party.

But now that he had Nixon and Kissinger in his pocket, Barzani was feeling a newfound confidence.[78] Flush with American cash funneled through the shah, Barzani broke decisively with the USSR and the Ba'th in the summer of 1972. He purged Communists from the KDP movement and initiated sporadic attacks on Iraqi government positions. With the outbreak of the 1973 October War, Israel stepped up pressure on Barzani to launch a full-scale offensive that would draw Iraqi forces away from the Israeli-Syrian front. For the moment, the shah vetoed a full-scale Kurdish offensive, but with Israel's firm backing, Barzani demanded what "amounted to an independent Kurdish state that would include Kirkuk and its oil."[79] Tensions between Iraq and the Kurds continued to mount, and by the summer of 1974, Iraq and the KDP were engaged in a full-scale war.

The outbreak of fighting in the north forced the Ba'th to remain in alliance with the Soviet Union and the Iraqi Communist Party longer than it would have otherwise liked.[80] The Ba'thist-Communist alliance had always been a marriage of convenience, and by the mid-1970s, the Ba'th was looking for an opportunity to leave. By the mid-1970s, the marriage had served its purpose. Iraq was now an oil-rich state in full control of its own resources. It was no longer a supplicant nation looking for barter agreements with the Soviet Union for essential technical aid. The regime rather looked with envy on the high-tech armaments that the United States was supplying Iran.[81] But as long as Iraq remained allied with the left against the Kurds, its road to an arms supply agreement with the US was blocked. If the Ba'th could liquidate its partnership with the Communists, then it would be free to cut out social welfare spending altogether and spend all of its money on military imports from the West.

To realize his longer-term objectives, Saddam sought to bring the fighting in the north to an end as soon as possible. To this end, he reached out to Iran with a deal that the shah could not refuse: Iraq would yield contested territory in the southern Shatt al-Arab waterway in exchange for an end to Iranian and CIA support for the Kurdish insurgency.[82] The shah leapt at the opportunity to revise a humiliating border that had been imposed on his father by British "colonialist diktat" in 1937.[83] It was also clear to the shah by this point that the Kurds were going to lose unless the full weight of the Iranian army came to their defense. The shah was also worried that the longer the uprising lasted, and the worse it went, the more likely it was that Kurdish unrest would spread to the Iranian side of the border. He therefore immediately cut off aid to the Kurds (and ordered the CIA to do the same), sealed the border between the two countries, and threatened to send his army into the field to cut down any Kurds unwilling to abide by the terms of what became known as the Algiers Agreement of March 1975.

Without support from Iran and the CIA, the culmination of Barzani's life and work collapsed. In the spring and summer of 1975, Iraqi tanks and fighter jets rolled through Iraqi Kurdistan, exacting a grisly revenge. Barzani and a hundred thousand followers escaped to Iran before the border was sealed in March, but those Kurds who remained on the Iraqi side were subjected to harsh authoritarian control.[84] Over the next several years, the Ba'th razed some fourteen hundred Kurdish villages and deported more than a half-million Kurds to concentration camps in the south, while moving Arab families into what were now formerly Kurdish regions in the north. In this way the Ba'th sought to establish new demographic facts on the ground in the north—a policy that would generate immense bloodshed in subsequent years.[85]

THE TRAGEDY OF THE BA'TH

By the time that the Ba'th crushed the Kurdish insurgency, military expenditures consumed nearly 30 percent of the budget, and Iraq was well on its way to becoming a garrison society ruled by a highly authoritarian regime that was now sufficiently autonomous from the broad national social movements that had driven Iraqi politics since the 1930s.[86] The government had become "coup-proof," in the term of art. Dissent was severely repressed and promotion and advancement through public bureaucracies was determined by loyalty to the regime rather than professional competence. This was a far cry from the secular, democratic, and socialist Iraq that Ibrahim, Haseeb, and al-Jadir had originally envisioned.

Given circumstances that prevailed in Iraq by the mid-1970s, Haseeb and al-Jadir were forced to flee the country—Haseeb to Lebanon and al-Jadir to Switzerland. Both continued to work with the United Nations on development and human rights issues, and both were involved in founding the Center for Arab Unity Studies—an independent, nonpartisan research center in Beirut in 1981. But both remained permanently exiled from the country of their birth, and the country for which they had long endured and sacrificed so much. Their movement had been co-opted and their stories—to the extent they were ever known—were lost entirely to the United States.[87]

But it could have been worse. Whereas al-Jadir and Haseeb were jailed for one and two years respectively, Yahya spent the remainder of his days in an Iraqi prison, subjected to special cruelties by Saddam Hussein. And then many years after his death in a dark and forgotten prison cell, when his name was nowhere else remembered in the English language, it was drafted into service in support of an American argument for regime change:

> Cruelty is the tyrant's art. He studies and embraces it. His rule is based on fear... But lost among the most outrageous atrocities are smaller acts that shed light on his personality. Tahir Yahya was the Prime Minister of Iraq when the Baath Party took power, in 1968. It is said that in 1964, when Saddam was in prison, Yahya had arranged for a personal meeting and tried to coerce him into turning against the Baathists and cooperating with the regime. Yahya had served Iraq as a military officer his whole adult life, and had at one time even been a prominent member of the Baath Party, one of Saddam's superiors. But he had earned Saddam's enduring scorn. After seizing power, Saddam had Yahya, *a well-educated man whose sophistication he resented*, confined to prison. On his orders Yahya was assigned to push a wheelbarrow from cell to cell, collecting the prisoners' slop buckets. He would call out "Rubbish! Rubbish!" The former Prime Minister's humiliation was a source of delight to Saddam until the day Yahya died, in prison. He still likes to tell the story, chuckling over the words "Rubbish! Rubbish!"...
>
> This, ultimately, is why Saddam will fail. His cruelty has created great waves of hatred and fear, and it has also isolated him.... In Iraq itself he is universally hated.... The forces that protect him... [are] governed by fear and self-interest, and will tilt decisively if and when an alternative appears. The key to ending Saddam's tyranny is to present such an alternative. It will not be easy. Saddam will never give up. Overthrowing him will almost certainly mean killing him. He guards his hold on the state as he guards his own life. There is no panic in his fight.[88]

In seeking to persuade readers to support an American military invasion of Iraq, the writer speaks of Yahya's well-educated sophistication, which represented such a threat to Saddam's tyranny. That Yahya—who did so much to advance the independence of his country—would be marshalled in support for a US invasion is perhaps the cruelest irony of all. History is a merciless teacher.

NEON LIGHTS IN THE VALLEY OF DARKNESS AND THE MAJESTY OF MUIR WOODS

Yahya's sad end recalls a different beginning and suggests an alternative history that might have been. In September 1952, the State Department hosted an Iraqi royal visit.[89] The royal party, consisting of King Faysal II, the Regent 'Abd al-Ilah, and their entourage of servants and aides, enjoyed a tour of the US from sea to shining sea. The purpose of the visit, Roger Davies explained at the time, was to "fashion a cadre of excellent contacts and good friends who will [no longer] visualize the United States solely through the [lens] of Hollywood." Davies noted that while the true significance of the visit could not be "evaluated properly" for many years, from "an intermediate standpoint" it was clear that the visit was a success, as it "awakened a searching interest in our country and people on the part of the royal party." And this interest was the "first step toward a sympathetic understanding" between the two governments.

Davies's memo describing the royal visit and its potential long-term significance merits deeper analysis for what it reveals about the nature of the US-Iraqi relationship in the early 1950s, and what it suggests about the different potential historical trajectories that the relationship could have taken. Particularly significant is what it reveals about how Davies understood his own country, and what he imagined that the royal party saw in it:

> ... Throughout the journey maps were in great demand, and that the stretch of territory from New York to San Francisco could all be under one flag was almost beyond the royal party's powers of comprehension.
>
> Our guests saw slums and they saw mansions. They passed by deserts and abandoned farmsteads, and they witnessed the accomplishment of irrigation in rich valleys and extensive land holdings. It was *manifest* to them that poverty and privation exist here as elsewhere in the world, yet they did not point to these facts as would [Jewish Bolshevik writer] Mr. Ilya Ehrenburg. Rather they marveled at a small landowner's house and barn, and the fact that he owns his land outright. At no time did the royal visitors exhibit any sign of envy or sense of inferiority; instead they seemed to accept our accomplishments as potentially within their grasp for the development of Iraq. [Emphasis added.]

The passage is deeply revealing.[90] It connects the story of America's involvement in the Iraq Petroleum Company to the centuries-long spiritual tradition of manifest destiny. All of the providential themes of American continental conquest were manifest in the Davies memo. There was the sublime awe at the sheer expanse of physical territory. There was the silent presence of a multitude of Indigenous societies removed to make way for the story of individual freedom writ large on the built environment—from mansions to abandoned farmsteads as choice and covenant might decide.[91] There was a certain way of seeing the visiting Iraqis as the noble savages of a subordinate tribe—these were not sullen Bolsheviks compensating for their own inferiority with a Ghost Dance of property equalization.[92] These were men who could accept their position within the hierarchy of a man and then ascend that scale. These were people who could be civilized and taught the virtues of irrigation in the desert.

Even "the Jewish question" could be successfully navigated. While the regent refused to be in "attendance at receptions where persons of Jewish faith were to play the role of host . . . elsewhere and otherwise, the royal party mixed freely and pleasantly with Americans of every race and creed," and even showed a "preference for the dark-eyed beauty of Jewish girls to that of gentile." Moreover, Abe Schiller, a mob-connected Jewish casino magnate, who "gave the King a .45 revolver at Las Vegas, indelibly impressed His Majesty[,] not with his ancestry but with his lavender stetson, his green string tie and his rainbow shirt with pearl buttons." If Iraqi royals could make eyes at Jewish girls and the king could receive a classically phallic symbol as a gift from colorful and flamboyant Jewish casino magnate, then perhaps all things were possible. After all, as it says in the *Qu'ran: wa ja'alnikum shu'fiban wa-qaba'ila li-ta'draffu* (And I have created peoples and tribes so that they could get to know each other).[93]

The fate of the Iraqi royals is relayed in grisly detail in the introduction to this book. Davies himself was cut down by an assassin's bullet while serving as ambassador to Cyprus in 1974.[94] But traveling with the royal party in 1952 were two young colonels—the description of whom evoked a different voice in Davies. Whereas the royals were depicted as comical figures fascinated with fast cars, strong drinks, shiny pistols, and pretty girls, the colonels are depicted in a more somber, almost tragic tone. Davies noted ruefully that "[Colonel] Jassam alone showed any interest in politics."

> Jassam was impressed with the political and economic social democracy practiced in the United States and asked for a detailed explanation of our

presidential electoral system, marveling when assured that neither Mr. Stevenson nor Mr. Eisenhower contemplates bribing the voters or stuffing the ballot boxes. The system of 'checks and balance' left him muttering.

He launched occasionally into tirades against the 'independent' voter who weakens effectiveness of a two party system, cursed the bureaucracy in Baghdad, and at Hoover Dam remarked darkly that "THEY have the oil royalties, THEY have the water, and if THEY don't do something like this in Iraq, something will happen."

Indeed something happened. One can almost envision Davies seeing it happen before it happened. One can discern through the arrogance and racism of interdepartmental prose a kind of tragic sensibility. One gets the sense that if only Jassam and his friends might have taken just a little more care in making a carbon copy of American democracy to bring back to Iraq—then perhaps the whole bloody affair could have been avoided.[95]

This was clearly the wrong lesson for Davies to draw. American democracy in the 1950s was very much a work in progress. To get it right, the possibility exists that perhaps American democracy had much to learn from Iraq. As much is suggested by Davies's description of the other officer accompanying the royal party:

> Colonel Yahya was the esthete [one who has a special appreciation for art and beauty] of the royal party, composing poetry, singing classical songs and drawing caricatures. He was most impressed with the beauty of the Rocky Mountains, and the majesty of Muir Woods.

An offhand comment in an obscure diplomatic record. But perhaps it carries a hidden meaning for us all. It tantalizes the imagination. It tugs at the heart. What would it mean to transcend the illusion of freedom peddled on the Vegas strip, to forego oil royalties, and to emerge from the shadow of the Hoover Dam? What would it mean to put the beauty of the Rocky Mountains and the majesty of Muir Woods (and other such sacred spaces) at the center of our global relationships? What would it mean for the people of America and the people of Iraq to really get to know one another? We better find out. Time is short.[96]

CONCLUSION

SINCE BEFORE WORLD WAR I, THE AMERICAN STATE DEPARTMENT has claimed to uphold the principles of national self-determination and open diplomacy. By examining the history of the Iraqi effort to nationalize the IPC, a very different picture has emerged. In this history, we see that the American commitment to these values has always been more rhetorical and apparent than real. From the 1920s through the 1950s, the United States played a supporting role as the British constructed an authoritarian client regime in Baghdad that would protect British oil and other imperial interests. In this period, the US stood on the side of an "Anglo-Saxon world order" against Iraqi demands for national self-determination.

When General 'Abd al-Karim Qasim emerged to challenge this colonial hierarchy and establish a pluralistic national identity with true sovereignty over Iraq's natural resources, the CIA conspired to murder him. But the CIA was not content to simply murder Qasim and his closest aides. On the contrary, Iraq served as a kind of laboratory setting for the counterinsurgency gurus grouped around the Kennedy administration. It was in Iraq (among other places) that the CIA, working in close collaboration with the Ba'th Party, developed what would become known as the "Jakarta Method"— that is, the systematic mass murder of suspected Communists as a root-and-branch approach to removing the impediments to capitalist development.

US intervention left deep scars on Iraqi society—as it did in so many other places in the 1960s. But that society proved remarkably resilient. Against tremendous odds, reformist army officers led by General Tahir Yahya stood up to Washington and its local Ba'thist clients, to resume the work begun under Qasim. Yahya, more than anyone else near state power in the mid-1960s, brought in the best minds from across the region to devise a strategy that could overcome the immense advantages enjoyed by the world's major multinational oil corporations. These revolutionaries established and built up Iraqi state institutions. They engaged in a transnational discourse of sovereign rights that, in time, transformed international legal norms. They formed partnerships across national boundaries—with American independent oil companies, with de Gaullist France, and finally, when all else failed, with the Soviet Union—to realize that objective.

As was the case with Qasim, Yahya paid dearly for daring to be bold. For all that he had done to build the state capacity to nationalize the oil industry, Yahya was locked away in a Ba'thist dungeon, as the oil companies once again conspired with whoever would further their business interests. But the idea of nationalizing oil was so much bigger than Qasim, Yahya, or any one person. It was the material analog to a multicultural conception of Iraqi national identity. If the Ba'th's was to be anything more than just another in the turnstile of regimes that came and went in the 1960s, it would have to take on the cause of oil sovereignty as its own.

In a perfect world, it would have been a government constituted upon Ibrahimian principles that would have carried through the historical task of oil nationalization. Something very close to this could have happened in 1961 without any real harm to anyone and with a great deal of benefit to the world. But between that world and this, lays American power. And in this world, it was al-Sayyid al-Na'ib who carried through the historic task of nationalization. In this world, only such a figure was sufficiently adapted to wield the levers of state power. Who could withstand the immense pressure coming from Washington but a kind of Arab Stalin backed by the Soviet Union?

But this world built in the exchange between American Grandiose Strategists and coup-proof oil states is not sustainable. The apocalyptic imagination of a hyper-armed American state generates a whole raft of self-fulfilling prophecies. Many Americans, official and otherwise, took on the crusade against Communism as their own in the 1960s, and they were willing to follow that line to the ends of the earth. But other Americans took inspiration, direction, and leadership from the rising currents of *tiers monde*—from the tireless activism of the Abdullah Tarikis, Khair el-Din Haseebs, and Adib al-Jadirs of the world—and committed themselves to what Huey P. Newton described as the "sterner stuff of politics." They did this fully aware that before one can build a new world, one first has to imagine it. That work remains unfinished. As we pick through the still-smoldering, bombed-out rubble of the world they tried to build, we would do well to remember the history recounted in this book, and remember in particular the resilience of an Iraqi society that refused to accept the world as determined by Washington.

Acknowledgments

This book was a long time in the making. It began as an argument with a sergeant on top of a Bradley Infantry Fighting Vehicle under the hot summer sun of a Fort Hood motor pool: Who created these weapons and why? Then it was a set of notes in a community college classroom about the impending US invasion of Iraq. Then it was the outrage and frustration of seeing American troops march off to yet another senseless and destructive war. Still later it was the bitterness of seeing the perpetrators of a great crime escape justice.

As this project moved from an argument on an army base to finished book, I have accrued intellectual and financial debts that no honest person could ever hope to fully recount, let alone repay. First and foremost, I want to thank my wife and kids for sharing me with this project for so long, and my wife in particular for helping me think through the argument and narrative as a whole. I also want thank my parents and older brother for encouraging me to explore the world and teaching me to understand it. I also want to thank Joel Beinin for being such a tremendous source of moral and intellectual inspiration. Joel saw promise in this project before anyone else, and with incredible patience and generosity helped me to bring the ideas into greater clarity and focus. I want to thank him especially for his willingness to support me in taking intellectual risks.

Joel also helped connect me with a network of scholars, each of whom has left a determining imprint in the final product. At Stanford, Joel introduced me to Barton Bernstein and Gordon Chang, who taught me the craft of diplomatic history; to Robert Crews and Priya Satia, who taught me how to think more deeply and critically about empires and cultures; and to Ramzi Salti and Salim Alweiss, who were ever patient in teaching me the Arabic language.

I also want to thank Joel for introducing me to Bob Vitalis, whose influence on my thinking would be impossible to overstate. *America's Kingdom*, an early draft of which I read at a very formative stage in my intellectual development, continues to serve as the model and inspiration for this book in its final form. I want to thank Bob especially for helping me think through common misperceptions about the international political economy of oil, and for encouraging me to tell a new and different story.

As I developed the core arguments for this book, I had the good fortune to present key findings at MESA and SHAFR, at NYU's Hagop Kevorkian Center for Near Eastern Studies, and at the Center for American Studies and Research at the American University of Beirut. Each of those events yielded very constructive feedback, and I would like to thank Osamah Khalil, Arang Keshavarzian, Begum Adalet, and Waleed Hazbun for their respective roles in organizing them. I would also like to thank the Academic Research Institute in Iraq for providing support for travel to Lebanon and the UK.

As I neared completion of this manuscript, I received very valuable feedback on drafts of the work from Joel Beinin, Bob Vitalis, Nathan Citino, Chris Dietrich, David Painter, Kevin Kim, Osamah Khalil, Priya Satia, Weldon Matthews, Roger Stern, Sayres Rudy, Mike Tumolo, and Jennifer Biedendorf. Everyone who read in part or whole offered valuable feedback to make the book stronger and better. Most of what I've done here is just to assemble the good ideas of others, and I am eternally grateful for all of those good ideas.

At Cal State Stanislaus, I would like to thank the Department of History and the College of Arts, Humanities, and Social Sciences for providing such a collegial work environment, and for generous support in the form of the course releases that allowed me to complete the work. I would also like to thank my Stan students for teaching me how to speak to a nonspecialist audience. The book is largely written in my "lecture voice," and without those students I wouldn't have that voice.

At Stanford University Press, I want to thank Kate Wahl and her editorial team for their expertise in bringing this project into final form. Kate, in particular, cultivated this project over a long period of time and offered me invaluable advice on how to make the arguments accessible to the broadest possible audience. In production, I want to thank Clémence Cottard Hachem of the Arab Image Foundation in Beirut for locating, and making available to me, Latif al-Ani's photography to illustrate the manuscript. I discovered al-Ani's work rather late in the process, and there is definitely more to be said about the world as it appears through al-Ani's lens (see Jala Makhzoumi and Mona Damluji, "Baghdad through Latif al-Ani's Lens," *Jadaliyya*, April 17, 2016). Thankfully the AIF still stands, through it all, so that this work can continue. Godspeed to whoever might take it up.

Last, but far from least, I would like to thank As'ad AbuKhalil and Khalil Issa for introducing me to Khair el-Din Haseeb. Haseeb is a key figure in the story recounted in this book, and this story would be impossible to recount without Haseeb's remarkable generosity, searing intellect, and impeccable memory. I first met Haseeb in the archival materials of the State Department and Iraq Petroleum Company. The Haseeb in those archives bore little resemblance to the Haseeb who I have gotten to know by phone and email since 2015, and who I had the good fortune to extensively interview in Beirut in January 2016. Since that time, Haseeb has read a complete draft manuscript and offered invaluable corrections and research materials. This book is in many ways dedicated to Haseeb and to what he tried to do in Iraq in the 1960s.

Notes

INTRODUCTION

1. Details of what transpired at the New Baghdad Hotel remain sketchy. The relevant volume of *Foreign Relations of the United States*, the State Department's official documentary history of American foreign policy, only mentions the incident in a brief footnote. See Baghdad to State, July 14, 1958, *Foreign Relations of the United States* [*FRUS*], *1958–1960*, v. 12, doc. 112, n. 1 [hereafter, for example, *FRUS, 1958–1960*, 12, 112n1]. All *FRUS* documents are available here: https://history.state.gov/historicaldocuments. For additional details see Elizabeth Bishop, "'Blown Away by the Winds Like Ashes': Biopower in Egypt's #25 Jan. and Iraq's 14 Tammuz," *Alternatives: Turkish Journal of International Relations* 12, no. 3 (Fall 2013): 53–57; Sally Denton, *The Profiteers: Bechtel and the Men Who Built the World* (New York: Simon & Schuster, 2016), 76; Laton McCartney, *Friends in High Places: The Bechtel Story—The Most Secretive Corporation and How It Engineered the World* (New York: Ballantine Books, 1998), 70, 79, 117; "Baghdad Reports Americans Slain; Californians Believed to Be Iraq Mob Victims, State Department Says," *New York Times*, July 16, 1958, 15; "Eugene Burns Reported Victim of Iraq Mob," *Bend Bulletin* (Bend, Ore.), July 16, 1958; Stan Carter, "How Iraq Mob Slew Americans," *Associated Press*, July 22, 1958; "In One Swift Hour," *Time*, July 28, 1958; "After the Bloodbath," *Time*, August 4, 1958.

2. "Eugene Burns Reported Victim of Iraq Mob," *Bend Bulletin*.

3. Leonard Mosley, *Dulles: A Biography of Eleanor, Allen and John Foster Dulles and Their Family Network* (New York: Dial Press, 1978), 469.

4. Bishop, "'Blown Away,'" 56.

5. The initial embassy reporting only listed two missing Americans (Colley and Burns); Alcock was not reported missing until much later. "In its formal note, Iraq's Ministry of Foreign Affairs stated no documentation had been found of Alcock's entry." See Bishop, "Blown Away," 57.

6. Bishop, "Blown Away," 56.

7. Bishop, "Blown Away," 56–57.

8. Bishop, "Blown Away," 57.

9. Bishop, "Blown Away," 57.

10. Geoff Simons, *Iraq: From Sumer to Saddam* (New York: Palgrave Macmillan, 2004), 252.

11. Denton, *The Profiteers*, chaps. 1–12; McCartney, *Friends in High Places*, chaps. 1–12.

12. "Bechtel—History," www.bechtel.com/about-us/history/.

13. "Warren A. Bechtel," www.bechtel.com/about-us/warren-a-bechtel/.

14. In deriving meaning from these records, I draw on the methodology described in Frank Costigliola, "Reading for Meaning: Theory, Language, and Metaphor," in *Explaining the History of American Foreign Relations*, ed. Michael J. Hogan and Thomas G. Patterson, 2nd ed. (Cambridge: Cambridge University Press, 2004), 279–303. I also draw methodological insight from Michel-Rolph Trouillot, *Silencing the Past: Power and the Production of History* (Boston: Beacon Press, 1995).

15. Robert Vitalis, *America's Kingdom: Mythmaking on the Saudi Oil Frontier* (Stanford: Stanford University Press, 2007); Timothy Mitchell, *Carbon Democracy: Political Power in the Age of Oil* (London: Verso, 2011); Roger J. Stern, "Oil Scarcity Ideology in US Foreign Policy, 1908–97," *Security Studies* 25, no. 2 (2016): 222–27; Robert Vitalis, *Oilcraft: The Myths of Scarcity and Security That Haunt U.S. Energy Policy* (Stanford: Stanford University Press, 2020).

16. This problem was first identified and analyzed by Karl Marx, *Capital*, vol. III, chap. 13.

17. Mitchell, *Carbon Democracy*, 39–42.

18. On the state as a "unitary actor," see Ole R. Holsti, "Theories of International Relations," in *Explaining the History of American Foreign Relations*, ed. Michael J. Hogan and Thomas G. Patterson, 2nd ed. (Cambridge: Cambridge University Press, 2004), 54.

19. See Timothy Mitchell, "The Limits of the State: Beyond Statist Approaches and Their Critics," *American Political Science Review* 85, no. 1 (March 1991): 77–96.

20. Christopher R. W. Dietrich, *Oil Revolution: Anti-Colonial Elites, Sovereign Rights, and the Economic Culture of Decolonization* (New York: Cambridge University Press, 2017).

21. See Dietrich, *Oil Revolution*, 42–46.

22. Orit Baskhin, *The Other Iraq: Pluralism and Culture in Hashemite Iraq* (Stanford: Stanford University Press, 2009). See also Ussama Makdisi, *Age of Coexistence: The Ecumenical Frame and the Making of the Modern Arab World* (Oakland: University of California Press, 2019).

23. For a more traditional or "orthodox" interpretation of US-Iraqi relations in this same period (1958–75), see Bryan Gibson's *Sold Out? US Foreign Policy, Iraq, the Kurds, and the Cold War* (New York: Palgrave Macmillan, 2015). Gibson rejects the notion that American foreign policy was driven by economic motives. He argues that American foreign policy in Iraq, including US covert operations, constituted a rational and coherent strategy of Soviet containment. In Gibson's analysis, "US decisions and actions were based on a single unifying perception: the Soviet Union posed a threat to Iraq's sovereignty" (xxii). In contrast to this traditional interpretation, I argue that the Soviet danger was systematically overstated for rhetorical purposes throughout the period under analysis. Rather than seeing American foreign policy as part of a rational and coherent strategy, I focus on the ad hoc nature of American foreign policy-making and the ways in which the rhetoric of national security was used as a cover for ulterior, often economic, motives.

24. William Appleman Williams, *The Tragedy of American Diplomacy*, 50th Anniversary Edition (New York: W.W. Norton, 2009). On the significance of Williams's epistemological synthesis, see Peter Novick, *That Noble Dream: The "Objectivity Question" and the American Historical Profession* (Cambridge: Cambridge University Press, 1988), 446–48.

25. William Appleman Williams, *Empire as a Way of Life: An Essay on the Causes and Character of America's Present Predicament, along with a Few Thoughts about an Alternative* (New York: Ig, 2007 [first published 1980]).

26. Williams, *Tragedy of American Diplomacy*, 37–38.

27. On American imperialism as sublimated theology, see Anders Stephanson, *Manifest Destiny: American Expansion and the Empire of Right* (New York: Hill and Wang, 1995); Eugene McCarraher, "The Heavenly City of Business," in *The Short American Century: A Postmortem,* ed. Andrew J. Bacevich (Cambridge, MA: Harvard University Press, 2012), 187–230; Edward Rhodes, "Onward, Liberal Soldiers? The Crusading Logic of Bush's Grand Strategy and What Is Wrong with It," in *The*

New American Empire: A 21st Century Teach-In on U.S. Foreign Policy, ed. Lloyd C. Gardner and Marilyn B. Young (New York: New Press, 2005), 227–52. For a broader theoretical discussion of the sublimation of theology, see Talal Asad, *Formations of the Secular: Christianity, Islam, and Modernity* (Stanford: Stanford University Press, 2003).

28. On "business privilege," see David S. Painter, *Oil and the American Century: The Political Economy of U.S. Foreign Oil Policy, 1941–1954* (Baltimore: Johns Hopkins University Press, 1986), 209.

29. Jack Snyder, *Myths of Empire: Domestic Politics and International Ambition* (Ithaca, NY: Cornell University Press, 2013).

CHAPTER 1

1. On Iraq's quasi-sovereignty, see Susan Pedersen, "Getting Out of Iraq—in 1932: The League of Nations and the Road to Normative Statehood," *American Historical Review* 115, no. 4 (October 2010): 975–1000.

2. The US-British relationship in Iraq was more cooperative than was the case in Egypt and Iran. See William Roger Louis and Ronald Robinson, "The Imperialism of Decolonization," *Journal of Imperial and Commonwealth History* 22, no. 3 (1994): 462–511; Nicholas G. Thacher, "Reflections on US Foreign Policy towards Iraq in the 1950s," in *The Iraqi Revolution of 1958: The Old Social Classes Revisited*, ed. Robert Fernea and William Louis, 62–76 (London: I. B. Tauris, 1991); Frederick W. Axelgard, "US Support for the British Position in Pre-Revolutionary Iraq," in Fernea and Louis, *Iraqi Revolution of 1958*, 77–94; Simon Davis, *Contested Space: Anglo-American Relations in the Persian Gulf, 1939–1947* (Boston: Brill, 2009); Christopher D. O'Sullivan, *FDR and the End of Empire: The Origins of American Power in the Middle East* (New York: Palgrave Macmillan, 2012); Nathan Citino, "Defending the 'Postwar Petroleum Order': The U.S., Britain, and the 1954 Saudi-Onassis Tanker Deal," *Diplomacy & Statecraft* 11 (July 2000): 137–60.

3. Mary C. Wilson, "The Hashemites, The Arab Revolt, and Arab Nationalism," in *The Origins of Arab Nationalism*, ed. Rashid Khalidi, Lisa Anderson, Muhammad Muslih, and Reeva S. Simon (New York: Columbia University Press, 1991), 204–21.

4. William Ochsenwald, "Ironic Origins: Arab Nationalism in the Hijaz, 1882–1914," in Khalidi et al., *Origins of Arab Nationalism*, 189–203.

5. On the often-exaggerated role of Lawrence, see Priya Satia, *Spies in Arabia: The Great War and the Cultural Foundations of Britain's Covert Empire in the Middle East* (Oxford: Oxford University Press, 2008), 11–12.

6. See Muhammad Muslih, "The Rise of Local Nationalism in the Arab East," in Khalidi et al., *Origins of Arab Nationalism*, 167–85; Elizabeth F. Thompson, *How the West Stole Democracy from the Arabs: The Syrian Arab Congress of 1920 and the Destruction of Its Historic Liberal-Islamic Alliance* (New York: Atlantic Monthly Press, 2020).

7. "Anglo-French Joint Statement of Aims in Syria and Mesopotamia," November 8, 1918, https://wwi.lib.byu.edu/index.php/Anglo-French_Joint_Statement_of_Aims_in_Syria_and_Mesopotamia.

8. Peter J. Sluglett, *Britain in Iraq: Contriving King and Country* (New York: Columbia University Press, 2007), 29; Muhammad Y. Muslih, *The Origins of Palestinian Nationalism* (New York: Columbia University Press, 1988), 128.

9. Charles Tripp, *A History of Iraq* (Cambridge: Cambridge University Press, 2002), 40; Sara Pursley, "'Lines Drawn on an Empty Map': Iraq's Borders and the Legend of the Artificial State" (Parts 1–2), *Jadaliyya* (June 2–3, 2015), www.jadaliyya.com/pages/index/21759/lines-drawn-on-an-empty-map_iraq's-borders-and-the.

10. *Treaty of Versailles*, June 28, 1919, 55–56, www.loc.gov/law/help/us-treaties/bevans/m-ust000002-0043.pdf.

11. Mahmoud Haddad, "Iraq before World War I: A Case of Anti-European Arab Ottomanism," in Khalidi et al., *Origins of Arab Nationalism*, 120–50.

12. David McDowall, *A Modern History of the Kurds*, 3rd rev. ed. (New York: I. B. Tauris, 2004), 119, 156–59.

13. Muslih, *Origins of Palestinian Nationalism*, 128.

14. Sluglett, *Britain in Iraq*, 34.

15. On the revolt and British suppression, see Abbas Kadhim, *Reclaiming Iraq: The 1920 Revolution and the Founding of the Modern State* (Austin: University of Texas Press, 2012); Sami Zubaida, "The Fragments Imagine the Nation: The Case of Iraq," *International Journal of Middle East Studies* 34 (2002): 205–15; Sluglett, *Britain in Iraq*, 52–55; Priya Satia, "The Defense of Inhumanity: Air Control and the British Idea of Arabia," *American Historical Review* 111, no. 1 (February 2006): 16–51; Toby Dodge, *Inventing Iraq: The Failure of Nation-Building and a History Denied* (New York: Columbia University Press, 2003), 135–36; Tripp, *Iraq*, 41–44.

16. Sluglett, *Britain in Iraq*, 17–21; Dodge, *Inventing Iraq*, 5–42.

17. Sluglett, *Britain in Iraq*, 40.

18. Sluglett, *Britain in Iraq*, 38.

19. Very closely paraphrased from Sluglett, *Britain in Iraq*, 37.

20. George E. Gruen, "The Oil Resources of Iraq: Their Role in the Policies of the Great Powers," in *The Creation of Iraq, 1914–1921*, ed. Eleanor H. Tejirian (New York: Columbia University Press, 2004), 113.

21. Timothy Mitchell, *Carbon Democracy: Political Power in the Age of Oil* (London: Verso, 2011), 48.

22. Mitchell, *Carbon Democracy*, 49–59; Daniel Yergin, *The Prize: The Epic Quest for Oil, Money, and Power* (New York: Free Press, 2008), 131–32.

23. Marian Kent, *Oil and Empire* (New York: Palgrave Macmillan, 1976).

24. Mitchell, *Carbon Democracy*, 60–65; Yergin, *The Prize*, 124–25, 131–48.

25. On the origins of the TPC, see Marian Kent, "Agent of Empire? The National Bank of Turkey and British Foreign Policy," *Historical Journal* 18, no. 2 (June 1975): 367–89; Edith and Ernest F. Penrose, *Iraq: International Relations and National Development* (Boulder, CO: Westview Press, 1978), 20–29; Gregory P. Nowell, *Mercantile States and the World Oil Cartel, 1900–1939* (Ithaca, NY: Cornell University Press, 1994), 90–94; Sluglett, *Britain in Iraq*, 65–75.

26. Yergin, *The Prize*, 145.

27. Sluglett, *Britain in Iraq*, 70.

28. David Styan, *France and Iraq: Oil, Arms and French Policy Making in the Middle East* (London: I. B. Tauris, 2006), 21–24; Nowell, *Mercantile States*, 94, 135–41; Anand Toprani, review of Luigi Scazzeri, "Britain, France, and Mesopotamian Oil, 1916–1920," *H-Diplo* 593 (March 2, 2016).

29. American Petroleum Institute, "Memorandum on Mesopotamia, and Other Oil-Bearing Regions, Affected by the Recent Peace Settlement," September 1919, in US Senate Subcommittee on Multinational Corporations, *Multinational Corporations and United States Foreign Policy*, part 8, (Washington, DC: Government Printing Office, 1975), 516–17.

30. On the application of the US "open door" policy in Iraq, see Stern, "Oil Scarcity Ideology," 222; Douglass Little, *American Orientalism: The United States and the Middle East*, 3rd ed. (Chapel Hill: University of North Carolina Press), 45–48; William Stivers, *Supremacy and Oil: Iraq, Turkey and the Anglo-American World Order, 1918–1930* (Ithaca, NY: Cornell University Press, 1982), 110.

31. Sluglett, *Britain in Iraq*, 71; Stivers, *Supremacy and Oil*, 30–32, 91; Yergin, *The Prize*, 187–89.

32. James Bamberg, *The History of the British Petroleum Company*, vol. 2, *The Anglo-Iranian Years 1928–1954* (Cambridge: Cambridge University Press, 2009); G. S. Gibb and E. H. Knowlton, *History of the Standard Oil Company of New Jersey*, vol. 2, *The Resurgent Years, 1911–1927* (New York: Joanna Cotler Books, 1956); H. M. Larson, E. H. Knowlton, and C. S. Popple, *History of the Standard Oil Company of New Jersey*, vol. 3, *New Horizons, 1927–1950* (New York: Harper & Row, 1971).

33. Penrose and Penrose, *Iraq*, 23, 60, 63–64; Sluglett, *Britain in Iraq*, 51–52, 73; Gruen, "Oil Resources of Iraq," 113.

34. Penrose and Penrose, *Iraq*, 6, 57–80, 137–48.

35. Edmund A. Ghareeb, with the assistance of Beth K. Dougherty, *Historical Dictionary of Iraq* (Lanham, MD: Scarecrow Press, 2004), 337–38.

36. Memorandum by J. Skliros to IPC groups, December 9, 1937, quoted in US Senate, *Multinational Corporations*, 531. See also John M. Blair, *The International Petroleum Cartel*, quoted in John M. Blair, *The Control of Oil* (New York: Vintage, 1976), 83–84. On the effect of these layoffs on intercommunal violence in Iraq, see Arbella Bet-Shlimon, *City of Black Gold: Oil, Ethnicity, and the Making of Modern Kirkuk* (Stanford: Stanford University Press, 2019), 84–87.

37. Letter from J. Skliros, general manager of the IPC, to F. Lewisohn, secretary of the IPC, June 27, 1938, US Senate, *Multinational Corporations*, 531.

38. Pedersen, "Getting Out of Iraq—in 1932."

39. Phoebe Marr, *The Modern History of Iraq* (Boulder, CO: Westview, 2004), 50–51; Hana Batatu, *The Old Social Classes and the Revolutionary Movements of Iraq: A Study of Iraq's Old Landed and Commercial Classes and of Its Communists, Ba'athists, and Free Officers* (Princeton, NJ: Princeton University Press, 1978), 342–44.

40. Davis, *Contested Space*, 47–52; Marr, *Modern History of Iraq*, 59–60.

41. Davis, *Contested Space*, 47.

42. Tripp, *A History of Iraq*, 99.

43. Bashkin, *The Other Iraq*, 2, 17, 35–36, 63.

44. Marr, *Modern History of Iraq*, 53–55.

45. Peter L. Hahn, *Missions Accomplished? The United States and Iraq since World War I* (New York: Oxford University Press, 2012), 7; Davis, *Contested Space*, 53; Marr, *Modern History of Iraq*, 54.

46. Marr, *Modern History of Iraq*, 52–57.

47. Batatu, *The Old Social Classes*, 345.

48. David S. Painter, "The Marshall Plan and Oil," *Journal of American History* 9, no. 2 (May 2012): 161; Bamberg, *British Petroleum and Global Oil, 1950–1975*, 1–2.

49. On the "greatest material prize," see Report by the Coordinating Committee of the Department of State, August 1945, *FRUS, 1945*, 8, 45. On largest overseas investment, see Vitalis, *America's Kingdom*, 9.

50. Painter, "Marshall Plan and Oil," 164–65.

51. Painter, "Marshall Plan and Oil," 163; Mitchell, *Carbon Democracy*, 27–31; Yergin, *The Prize*, 391–412.

52. Painter, "Marshall Plan and Oil," 164.

53. Joe Stork, *Middle East Oil and the Energy Crisis* (New York: Monthly Review Press, 1975), 47–49.

54. David S. Painter, *Oil and the American Century: The Political Economy of U.S. Foreign Oil Policy, 1941–1954* (Baltimore: Johns Hopkins University Press, 1986), 129–34; Yergin, *The Prize*, 415–19; Giuliano Garavini, *The Rise and Fall of OPEC in the Twentieth Century* (Oxford: Oxford University Press, 2019), 54–62.

55. Painter, *Oil and the American Century*, 129–34.

56. Painter, *Oil and the American Century*, 134.

57. Painter, *Oil and the American Century*, 169–71.

58. Painter, *Oil and the American Century*, 271; Stork, *Middle East Oil*, 47.

59. Ervand Abrahamian, "The 1953 Coup in Iran," *Science & Society* 65, no. 2 (Summer 2001): 185.

60. Mary Ann Heiss, "The International Boycott of Iranian Oil and the Anti-Mosaddeq Coup of 1953," in *Mohammad Mosaddeq and the 1953 Coup in Iran*, ed. Mark J. Gasiorowski and Malcolm Byrne (Syracuse, NY: Syracuse University Press, 2004), 178–200.

61. Iraq Petroleum Company, "Brief Study: Iraq Exports," n.d., IPC Negotiations, Folder 136002, British Petroleum Archive, Warwick University, Coventry, UK [hereafter IPC followed by folder number].

62. For IPC production figures, see IPC, *The Oil Industry in 1951: Statistical Review*, August 29, 1952, www.bp.com/content/dam/bp/pdf/Energy-economics/statistical-review-2015/statistical-review-1951.pdf; Penrose and Penrose, *Iraq*, 148.

63. Joe Stork, "Oil and the Penetration of Capitalism in Iraq," in *Oil and Class Struggle*, ed. Petter Nore and Terisa Turner (London: Zed Books, 1980), 176; Daniel Silverfarb, "The Revision of Iraq's Oil Concession, 1949–52," *Middle Eastern Studies* 32, no. 1 (1996): 69–95.

64. Stork, "Oil and Capitalism," 176.

65. Stork, "Oil and Capitalism," 178.

66. Bashkin, *The Other Iraq*, 57–58.

67. Bashkin, *The Other Iraq*, 249–53; Makdisi, *Age of Coexistence*, 154–56.

68. Makdisi, *Age of Coexistence*, 149–51.

69. Dodge, *Inventing Iraq*.

70. Makdisi, *Age of Coexistence*, 154–56; Sara Pursely, *Familiar Futures: Time, Selfhood, and Sovereignty in Iraq* (Stanford: Stanford University Press, 2019), 79–106.

71. Bashkin, *The Other Iraq*, 2, 17, 35–36.

72. Bashkin, *The Other Iraq*, 61–69; Batatu, *The Old Social Classes*, 301–05.

73. Bashkin, *The Other Iraq*, 64–66.

74. Bashkin, *The Other Iraq*, 64.

75. Bashkin, *The Other Iraq*, 63.

76. Bashkin, *The Other Iraq*, 77–79.

77. Batatu, *The Old Social Classes*, chaps. 11–35.

78. Batatu, *The Old Social Classes*, 743.

79. On the New Deal current of thought in the US State Department, see Leo Panitch and Sam Gindin, *The Making of Global Capitalism: The Political Economy of American Empire* (New York: Verso 2013), 103–5; James L. Gelvin, "American Global Economic Policy and the Civic Order in the Middle East," in *Is There a Middle East? The Evolution of a Geopolitical Concept*, ed. Michael E. Bonne, Abbas Amnat, and Michael Ezekiel Gaspar (Stanford: Stanford University Press, 2012), 191–206; Christopher O'Sullivan, *FDR and the End of Empire: The Origins of American Power in the Middle East* (New York: Palgrave Macmillan, 2012); Davis, *Contested Space*; Paul W. T. Kingston, "The 'Ambassador for the Arabs': The Locke Mission and the Unmaking of U.S. Development Diplomacy in the Near East, 1952–1953," in *The Middle East and the United States: A Historical and Political Reassessment*, ed. David W. Lesch, 30–50 (Boulder, CO: Westview Press, 2003); Robert Vitalis and Steven Heydemann, "War, Keynesianism, and Colonialism: Explaining State-Market Relations in the Postwar Middle East" in *War, Institutions, and Social Change in the Middle East*, ed. Steven Heydemann (Berkeley: University of California Press, 2000), 100–148; Nicholas Thacher, "Reflections on US Foreign Policy towards Iraq in the 1950s," in *Iraqi Revolution of 1958*, 75; Niel M. Johnson, "Oral History Interview with Nicholas G. Thacher," May 28, 1992, www.trumanlibrary.org/oralhist/thachern.htm.

80. On the conservative, pro-British current of thought in US foreign policy, see John T. McNay, *Acheson and Empire: The British Accent in American Foreign Policy* (Columbia: University of Missouri Press, 2001); Axelgard, "US Support for the British Position in Pre-Revolutionary Iraq," 77–94. On the role of race and its relationship to notions of "business privilege" in conservative thought, see Robert Vitalis, *White World Order, Black Power Politics: The Birth of American International Relations* (Ithaca, NY: Cornell University Press, 2015), 151–57; Matthew Connelly, "Taking Off the Cold War Lens: Visions of North-South Conflict during the Algerian War for Independence," *American Historical Review* 105, no. 3 (June 2000): 739–69; Stivers, *Supremacy and Oil*, 64–73.

81. Mitchell, *Carbon Democracy*, 120.

82. Robert J. McMahon, "Eisenhower and Third World Nationalism: A Critique of the Revisionists," *Political Science Quarterly* 101, no. 3 (1986): 457. On the centrality of racial and religious anxiety to this worldview, see Connelly, "Taking Off the Cold War Lens," 741–43.

83. Mitchell, *Carbon Democracy*, 118–23; Kingston, "The 'Ambassador for the Arabs'"; Axelgard, "US Support for the British Position in Pre-Revolutionary Iraq," 77–94.

84. Elie Podeh, "The Perils of Ambiguity: The United States and the Baghdad Pact," in Lesch, *The Middle East and the United States*, 107.

85. See Little, "Sympathy for the Devil? America, Nasser, and Arab Revolutionary Nationalism," in *American Orientalism*, 157–92; David W. Lesch, "'Abd al-Nasser and the United States: Enemy or Friend?" in *Rethinking Nasserism: Revolution and Historical Memory in Modern Egypt*, ed. Elie Podeh and Onn Winckler (Gainesville: University of Florida Press, 2004), 205–29; Malik Mufti, "The U.S. and Nasserist Pan-Arabism," in Lesch, *The Middle East and the United States*, 168–90.

86. Robert Vitalis, "The Midnight Ride of Kwame Nkrumah and Other Fables of Bandung (Ban-doong)," *Humanity* 4, no. 2 (2013): 264–65.

87. Little, *American Orientalism*, 168–69.

88. Little, *American Orientalism*, 167–73; Robert R. Bowie, "Eisenhower Dulles and the Suez Crisis," in *Suez 1956: The Crisis and Its Consequences*, ed. William Roger Louis and Roger Owen (Oxford: Clarendon Press, 1989), 189–214.

89. William Roger Louis, "Dulles, Suez, and the British," in *John Foster Dulles and the Diplomacy of the Cold War*, ed. Richard H. Immerman (Princeton, NJ: Princeton University Press, 1990), 147.

90. Louis, "Dulles, Suez, and the British," 147.

91. Mordechai Bar-On, "David Ben-Gurion and the Sèvres Collusion," in Louis and Owen, *Suez 1956*, 147.

92. Bar-On, "David Ben-Gurion and the Sèvres Collusion," 148–50.

93. Bar-On, "David Ben-Gurion and the Sèvres Collusion," 148–50; Maurice Vaisse, "France and the Suez Crisis," in Louis and Owen, *Suez 1956*, 131–43.

94. British Foreign Secretary Selweyn Lloyd quoted in Vaisse, "France and the Suez Crisis," 139; Keith Kyle, "Britain and the Crisis, 1955–1956," in Louis and Owen, *Suez 1956*, 103–30; Ivan L. Pearson, *In the Name of Oil: Anglo-American Relations in the Middle East, 1950–58* (Brighton: Sussex Academic Press, 2010), 66–67; Stephen G. Galpern, *Money, Oil, and Empire: Sterling and Postwar Imperialism, 1944–197* (Cambridge: Cambridge University Press, 2009) 166–78; Louis and Robinson, "The

Imperialism of Decolonization," *Journal of Imperial and Commonwealth History* 22, no. 3 (1994): 465–67.

95. Pearson, *In the Name of Oil*, 74; Little, *American Orientalism*, 174–75; Bowie, "Eisenhower, Dulles, and the Suez Crisis," 199, 214; Louis and Robinson, "The Imperialism of Decolonization," 478.

96. Little, *American Orientalism*, 179.

97. Diane B. Kunz, "The Importance of Having Money: The Economic Diplomacy of the Suez Crisis," in Louis and Owen, *Suez 1956*, 229–32; Galpern, *Money, Oil, and Empire*, 178–92.

98. Rashid Khalidi, "Consequences of the Suez Crisis in the Arab World," in Louis and Owen, *Suez 1956*, 377–92.

99. Dulles quoted in Louis, "Dulles, Suez, and the British," 147. See also Pearson, *In the Name of Oil*, 74, 78–79.

100. Eisenhower quoted in Little, *American Orientalism*, 169–70.

101. Dwight Eisenhower, Special Message to the Congress on the Situation in the Middle East, January 5, 1957, www.presidency.ucsb.edu/ws/?pid=11007; Salim Yaqub, *Containing Arab Nationalism: The Eisenhower Doctrine and the Middle East* (Chapel Hill: University of North Carolina Press, 2004).

102. Malcolm H. Kerr, *The Arab Cold War: Gamal 'Abd al-Nasir and His Rivals, 1958–1970*, 3rd ed. (Oxford: Oxford University Press, 1971).

103. Tripp, *A History of Iraq*, 109, 118.

104. Rashid Khalidi, "Perceptions and Reality: the Arab World and the West," in *A Revolutionary Year: The Middle East in 1958*, ed. William Roger Louis and Roger Owen (London: I. B. Tauris, 2002), 181–208.

105. Malik Mufti, *Sovereign Creations: Pan-Arabism and Political Order in Syria and Iraq* (Ithaca, NY: Cornell University Press), 71–98; Kerr, *The Arab Cold War*, 7–16.

106. Vitalis, *America's Kingdom*, 192–93.

107. Irene L. Gendzier, "Oil, Politics, and US Intervention," in Louis and Owen, *A Revolutionary Year*, 101–42.

108. Telegram from US Embassy Iraq to the Department of State, October 14, 1958, *FRUS, 1958–1960*, 12, 138.

CHAPTER 2

1. For the CIA's own more expansive definition (including the collection, analysis, and operationalization of secret information), see Martin T. Bimfort, "A Definition of Intelligence," *Studies in Intelligence* 2, no. 4 (February 1958): 75–78, www.cia

.gov/library/center-for-the-study-of-intelligence/kent-csi/vol2no4/html/v02i4a08p_0001.htm.

2. Michael J. Hogan, *A Cross of Iron: Harry S. Truman and the Origins of the National Security State, 1945–1954* (Cambridge: Cambridge University Press, 1998), 24.

3. Hogan, *Cross of Iron*, 32–33.

4. Hogan, *Cross of Iron*, 56.

5. Hogan, *Cross of Iron*, 61, 63.

6. The National Security Act, July 26, 1947, NARA, https://catalog.archives.gov/id/299856.

7. CIA legal counsel quoted in Peter Grose, *Gentleman Spy: The Life of Allen Dulles* (Amherst: University of Massachusetts Press, 1994), 282–83.

8. Frank Costigliola, "'I React Intensely to Everything': Russia and the Frustrated Emotions of George F. Kennan, 1933–1958," *Journal of American History* 102, no. 4 (March 2016): 1092; Grose, *Gentleman Spy*, 282.

9. Executive Secretary of the National Security Council to Director of Central Intelligence, NSC 4-A, December 17, 1947, *FRUS, 1945–1950, Emergence of the Intelligence Establishment*, 247. Emphasis added.

10. National Security Council Directive on Office of Special Projects, NSC 10/2, June 18, 1948, *FRUS, 1945–1950, Emergence of the Intelligence Establishment*, 292. Emphasis added.

11. Senate Select Committee (Church Committee) to Study Governmental Operations with Respect to Intelligence Activities, *Interim Report: Alleged Assassination Plots Involving Foreign Leaders* (Washington, DC: Government Printing Office, 1975), 3.

12. J. R. R. Tolkien, *The Hobbit* (London: George Allen & Unwin, 1937). For a Foucauldian analysis of the "One Ring" as a metaphor for secrecy, knowledge, and power, see Jane Chance, *Lord of the Rings: The Mythology of Power* (Lexington: University of Kentucky Press, 2001), 21–22, 45–48.

13. On the Dulles family background, see Stephen Kinzer, *The Brothers: John Foster Dulles, Allen Dulles, and Their Secret World War* (New York: St. Martin's Griffin, 2013).

14. Grose, *Gentleman Spy*, 311–14.

15. Grose, *Gentleman Spy*, 281–87, 290–95.

16. Grose, *Gentleman Spy*, 283–84.

17. See Walter Millis and E. S. Duffield, eds., *The Forrestal Diaries* (New York: Viking Press, 1951); Townsend Hoopes and Douglass Brinkley, *Driven Patriot: The Life and Times of James Forrestal* (New York: Knopf, 1992).

18. Hoopes and Brinkley, *Driven Patriot*, 107.

19. Hoopes and Brinkley, *Driven Patriot*, 390.

20. Hoopes and Brinkley, *Driven Patriot*, 395.

21. Hoopes and Brinkley, *Driven Patriot*, 395–96.

22. Hoopes and Brinkley, *Driven Patriot*, 392, 398–99.

23. Hoopes and Brinkley, *Driven Patriot*, 392, 398–99.

24. Hoopes and Brinkley, *Driven Patriot*, 431.

25. This psychological profile is drawn from Jerrold M. Post and Robert S. Robins, *When Illness Strikes the Leader: The Dilemma of the Captive King* (New Haven, CT: Yale University Press, 1995), 107–8. Post and Robins are both academic political psychologists long associated with CIA's Center for the Analysis of Personality and Political Behavior, which was founded and directed for twenty-one years by Post.

26. Post and Robins, *When Illness Strikes the Leader*, 113. Post and Robins attribute the suicide to a failure of Bethesda doctors to administer "electro-convulsive therapy (ECT)," which they describe as a "treatment modality [that] can be a lifesaving therapy for a suicidal patient suffering from involutional melancholia" (111).

27. Kinzer, *The Brothers*, 52.

28. Kinzer, *The Brothers*, 54.

29. Grose, *Gentleman Spy*, 299; Kinzer, *The Brothers*, 93–94.

30. Robert Divine, *Eisenhower and the Cold War* (New York: Oxford University Press, 1981), 19–20; Kai Bird, *The Chairman: John J. McCloy—The Making of the American Establishment* (New York: Simon and Schuster, 1992), 386–87; Grose, *Gentleman Spy*, 332–33.

31. Grose, *Gentleman Spy*, 332; John Foster Dulles, "A Policy of Boldness," *Life*, May 14, 1952.

32. Grose, *Gentleman Spy*, 332–33.

33. Grose, *Gentleman Spy*, 337.

34. Robert Griffith, "Dwight D. Eisenhower and the Corporate Commonwealth," *American Historical Review* 87, no. 1 (February 1982): 87–122; Fred I. Greenstein, *The Hidden-Hand Presidency: Eisenhower as Leader* (Baltimore: Johns Hopkins University Press, 1994).

35. For an insightful review of the vast literature on the relationship between Eisenhower and Foster Dulles, see Nathan J. Citino, *From Arab Nationalism to OPEC: Eisenhower, King Sa'ud, and the Making of US-Saudi Relations* (Bloomington: Indiana University Press, 2002), 13.

36. See McMahon, "Eisenhower and Third World Nationalism"; Douglas Little, "Mission Impossible: The CIA and the Cult of Covert Action in the Middle East," *Diplomatic History* 28, no. 5 (November 2004).

37. See McMahon, "Eisenhower and Third World Nationalism."

38. C. W. Mills, *The Power Elite* (New York: Oxford University Press, 2000 [first published 1956]), 356.

39. Graham Greene, *The Quiet American* (New York: Penguin Books, 2002 [first published 1955]). Also reflecting an increasingly paranoid cultural milieu of the era, Tolkien, in 1954–55, published the *Lord of the Rings* trilogy, in which the "One Ring" of invisibility takes on increasingly sinister tones. Indeed, the plot revolves around the effort to destroy the ring. See *The Fellowship of the Ring*; *The Two Towers*; *The Return of the King* (London: Allen and Unwin, 1954–55).

40. See Landsdale's proposals for "Operation Northwoods" in Cuba in March 1962. These include potential false-flag attacks to justify a US invasion. See James Bamford, ed., "Pentagon Proposed Pretexts for Cuba Invasion in 1962," *National Security Archive* (April 30, 2001), https://nsarchive2.gwu.edu/news/20010430/.

41. H. Bruce Franklin, "By the Bombs' Early Light; Or, The Quiet American's War on Terror," *The Nation* (February 3, 2003).

42. Grose, *Gentleman Spy*, 444.

43. Loch K. Johnson, *A Season of Inquiry Revisited: The Church Committee Confronts America's Spy Agencies* (Lawrence: University Press of Kansas, 2015), 12i.

44. Frank J. Smist Jr., *Congress Oversees the United States Intelligence Community 1947–94*, 2nd ed. (Knoxville: University of Tennessee Press, 1994), 6; Ranelagh, John, *The Agency: The Rise and Decline of the CIA* (New York: Simon and Schuster, 1996), 283–85; CIA, "How Intelligence-Sharing with Congress Has Evolved," *Center for the Study of Intelligence* (March 19, 2007), www.cia.gov/library/center-for-the-study-of-intelligence/csi-publications/books-and-monographs/sharing-secrets-with-lawmakers-congress-as-a-user-of-intelligence/1.htm#ft4.

45. There is a great deal of mystery surrounding the Bruce-Lovett Report. There are references to it in virtually all published histories of the CIA, and in numerous diary entries in the Eisenhower Library. But the report itself seems to have disappeared. Harvard historian Arthur M. Schlesinger, Jr., claims to have discovered the document, along with transcripts of Senate testimony associated with the report, while conducting research in the Robert F. Kennedy Papers for his biography, *Robert Kennedy and His Times* (Boston: Houghton Mifflin, 1978), 455–59. He claims to have viewed the documents before they were deposited in the Kennedy Library under

restricted access. However, subsequent researchers have been unable to locate the report in the Kennedy Library, and neither the Eisenhower nor Kennedy Library acknowledges any such document in its possession. On efforts to track down the original report (and associated documents) see Grose, *Gentleman Spy*, 589. Grose was the deputy director of the State Department Policy Planning Staff during the Carter administration. He went on to be foreign and diplomatic correspondent for the *New York Times* and executive editor of *Foreign Affairs*. His detailed analysis of the Bruce-Lovett Report (444–49) is based on Schlesinger's research notes as well as interviews with key intelligence figures including Kermit Roosevelt, Robert Amory, Robert Komer, Gordon Gray, Herman Phleger, Loy Henderson, and Norman Paul.

46. Schlesinger, *Robert Kennedy and His Times*, 455.

47. Schlesinger, *Robert Kennedy and His Times*, 455.

48. Schlesinger, *Robert Kennedy and His Times*, 457.

49. For this interpretation, see Hugh Wilford, *America's Great Game: The CIA's Secret Arabists and the Shaping of the Modern Middle East* (New York: Basic Books, 2013), 282. (The section heading "American Spies in Arabia" borrows from Satia, *Spies in Arabia*.)

50. Greene mocked the Third Force concept: "You've got the Third Force and National Democracy [blood] all over your right shoe." *The Quiet American*, 154.

51. Grose, *Gentleman Spy*, 433.

52. Foster Dulles outlined the OMEGA strategy in Dulles to Eisenhower, Near East Policies, March 28, 1956, *FRUS, 1955–1957*, 15, 223. For analysis of OMEGA, see Wilford, *America's Great Game*, 218, 222. For Eisenhower's response, see Little, *American Orientalism*, 169–70.

53. Wilford, *America's Great Game*, 282.

54. On Nasser and the Egyptian Communist Party, see Joel Gordon, *Nasser's Blessed Movement: Egypt's Free Officers and the July Revolution* (Oxford: Oxford University Press, 1992), 92–98, 149–51. On support for Nasser within US intelligence agencies, see Mufti, *Sovereign Creations*, 87, 100.

55. Wilford, *America's Great Game*, 283–84.

56. Wilford, *America's Great Game*, 284.

57. On Paul's background, see Wilford, *America's Great Game*, 285; "Norman S. Paul Dies," *New York Times* (June 1, 1978). OSS/CIA historian Robert Harris Smith conducted an oral history interview with Paul. That interview, located in Smith's personal files, was provided to Peter Grose for use in preparing *Gentleman Spy*.

58. Wilford, *America's Great Game*, 285.

59. Grose, *Gentleman Spy*, 455–56.

60. On the shift from Dulles to Bissel, see Grose, *Gentleman Spy*, 449.

61. Jeffrey G. Karam, "Missing Revolution: The American Intelligence Failure in Iraq, 1958," *Intelligence and National Security* 32, no. 6 (2017): 693–709.

62. Gliden to Cumming, July 16, 1958, *FRUS, 1958–1960*, 12, 120.

63. Karam, "Missing Revolution," 702.

64. On the concept of imperial anxiety, see Satia, *Spies in Arabia*, 69, 236.

65. Briefing Notes by Director of Central Intelligence Dulles, July 14, 1958, *FRUS, 1958–1960*, 12, 110.

66. Irene L. Gendzier, "Oil, Politics, and US Intervention," in Louis and Owen, *A Revolutionary Year*, 101–42; Eisenhower and Dulles Telcon, July 15, 1958, *FRUS, 1958–1960*, 12, 115.

67. Editorial Note, *FRUS, 1958–1960*, 12, 20.

68. 373rd Meeting of the NSC, July 24, 1958, *FRUS, 1958–1960*, 12, 31. Emphasis added.

69. The phrase is repurposed from Richard Hofstadter, "The Paranoid Style in American Politics," *Harper's Magazine*, November 1964, 77. The concept of paranoia employed in this chapter owes more to C. W. Mills's notion of "crackpot realism" and to Satia's analysis of "Official Conspiracy Theories" and "Covert Empire" than it does to Hofstadter's 1964 essay. Whereas Hofstadter focused on "unofficial conspiracy theories" at the margins of political life, Mills and Satia focus on "official conspiracies" that spring from the very centers of American power. See Mills, *The Power Elite*, 356; Satia, *Spies in Arabia*, 201–3. On the distinction between official and unofficial conspiracy theories, see also Kathryn S. Olmsted, *Real Enemies: Conspiracy Theories and American Democracy, World War I to 9/11* (New York: Oxford University Press, 2009), 6.

70. Qasim broadcast quoted in Roger Owen, "The Dog That Neither Barked Nor Bit: The Fear of Oil Shortages," in Louis and Owen, *A Revolutionary Year*, 280; Minutes of the Cabinet Meeting, July 25, 1958, *FRUS, 1958–1960*, 4, 13.

71. Minutes of the Cabinet Meeting, July 25, 1958, *FRUS, 1958–1960*, 4, 13.

72. For a critique of the "decisive weapon" theory of oil (the notion that the Soviets could wield a decisive weapon against the free world by seizing control of Middle Eastern oil), see Stern, "Oil Scarcity Ideology," 236.

73. Yergin, *The Prize*, 510.

74. Blair, *Control of Oil*, 173.

75. Dwight D. Eisenhower, Proclamation 3279—Adjusting Imports of Petroleum and Petroleum Products into the United States, March 10, 1959, www.presidency.ucsb.edu/ws/index.php?pid=107378.

76. Stone quoted in Kinzer, *The Brothers*, 107.

77. Philby quoted in David Talbot, *The Devil's Chessboard: Allen Dulles, the CIA, and the Rise of America's Secret Government* (New York: Harper, 2015), 2.

78. In 1958, Mills elaborated on his concept of "crackpot realism," when he argued, in *The Causes of World War Three*: "They [crackpot realists] know of no solutions to the paradoxes of the Middle East and Europe, the Far East and Africa except the landing of Marines." Mills quoted in Alexander Cockburn, "The Triumph of Crackpot Realism," *The Nation*, July 27, 2006.

79. Grose, *Gentleman Spy*, 449.

80. Peter Sluglett, "The Pan-Arab Movement and the Influence of Cairo and Moscow," in Louis and Owen, *A Revolutionary Year*, 209–21; Carol R. Savietz, "The Soviet Union and the Middle East, 1956–58," in Louis and Owen, *A Revolutionary Year*, 221–44; Joe Stork, "The Soviet Union, the Great Powers and Iraq," in Fernea and Louis, *Iraqi Revolution of 1958*, 95–105.

81. Nathan Citino, "Middle East Cold Wars: Oil and Arab Nationalism in US-Iraqi Relations, 1958–1961," in *The Eisenhower Administration, the Third World, and the Globalization of the Cold War*, ed. Kathryn C. Statler and Andrew L. Johns (Lanham, MD: Rowman and Littlefield, 2006), 252.

82. For a more nuanced analysis of the various and competing strands of Iraqi nationalism, see Nathan Citino, *Envisioning the Arab Future: Modernization in U.S.-Arab Relations, 1945–1967* (Cambridge: Cambridge University Press, 2016), 178.

83. Sami Zubaida, "Community, Class and Minorities in Iraqi Politics," in Fernea and Louis, *Iraqi Revolution of 1958*, 197–201.

84. On the conflict between 'Arif and Qasim, see Batatu, *The Old Social Classes*, chap. 42, "Sole Leader," 808–60; Citino, "Middle East Cold Wars," 252; Mufti, *Sovereign Creations*, 115; Marion Farouk-Sluglett and Peter Sluglett, *Iraq since 1958: From Revolution to Dictatorship* (London: I. B. Tauris, 2003), 58–60.

85. NSC 5820/1, "US Policy toward the Near East," November 4, 1958, *FRUS, 1958–1960*, 12, 51. For analysis, see Roland Popp, "Accommodating to a Working Relationship," *Cold War History* 10, no. 3 (August 2010): 399–403; Citino, "Middle East Cold Wars," 252–53; Mufti, "The U.S. and Nasserist Pan-Arabism," 168–90; Mufti, *Sovereign Creations*, 99–102.

86. Baghdad to State, December 11, 1958, *FRUS, 1958–1960*, 12, 357.

87. Cairo to State, December 15, 1958, *FRUS, 1958–1960*, 13, 229; Richard John Worrall, "'Coping with a Coup d'Etat': British Policy towards Post-Revolutionary Iraq, 1958–63," *Contemporary British History* 21, no. 2 (2007): 183; Citino, "Middle East

Cold Wars," 253; Mufti, *Sovereign Creations*, 115–16; Farouk-Sluglett and Sluglett, *Iraq since 1958*, 60–62.

88. Tels. 1753 and 1754 from Baghdad to State, December 3, 1958, summarized in *FRUS, 1958–1960*, 12, 145n1.

89. Baghdad to State, December 11, 1958, *FRUS, 1958–1960*, 12, 147n2.

90. Editorial Note, *FRUS, 1958–1960*, 12, 149; Biographical Sketch of J. D. Jernegan, n.d., Country Files, Box 117, Iraq 1961, John F. Kennedy Presidential Library [JFKL].

91. Cairo to State, December 15, 1958, *FRUS, 1958–1960*, 13, 229; Editorial Note, *FRUS, 1958–1960*, 12, 156; Rountree Conference with Eisenhower, December 23, 1958, *FRUS, 1958–1960* 13, 230.

92. Rountree/Lakeland to Dillon, December 22, 1958, *FRUS, 1958–1960*, 12, 154.

93. Baghdad to State, December 16, 1958, *FRUS, 1958–1960*, 12, 150; 392d Meeting of the NSC, December 23, 1958, *FRUS, 1958–1960*, 12, 155.

94. 392d Meeting of the NSC, December 23, 1958, in *FRUS, 1958–1960*, 12, 155

95. Briefing prepared for the NSC, December 19, 1958, *FRUS, 1958–1960*, 12, 153. See also 391st Meeting of the NSC, December 18, 1958, *FRUS, 1958–1960*, 12, 151.

96. Rountree/Lakeland to Dillon, December 22, 1958, *FRUS, 1958–1960*, 12, 154.

97. 392d Meeting of the NSC, December 23, 1958, *FRUS, 1958–1960*, 12, 155.

98. 393d Meeting of the NSC, January 15, 1959, *FRUS, 1958–1960*, 12, 157.

99. Grose, *Gentleman Spy*, 461.

100. Citino, *Envisioning the Arab Future*, 187–88

101. Batatu, *The Old Social Classes*, 866–89; Mufti, *Sovereign Creations*, 126–27; Farouk-Sluglett and Sluglett, *Iraq since 1958*, 66–69.

102. Dana Adams Schmidt, "CIA Head Warns of Danger in Iraq," *New York Times*, April 29, 1959, 1.

103. 401st Meeting of the NSC, April 2, 1959, *FRUS 1958–1960*, 12, 170.

104. 402d Meeting of the NSC, April 17, 1959, *FRUS, 1958–1960*, 12, 176.

105. General Records of the U.S. State Department, Record Group 59 (RG59), NEA Lot Files, 1958–1963, Box 3, Inter-Agency Group on Iraq, US National Archives II, College Park, Maryland [hereafter IAGI].

106. "Preventing a Communist Takeover in Iraq" (Secret), September 24, 1959, IAGI.

107. On the "madman" trope, see Citino, "Middle East Cold Wars," 246; R. Stephen Humphreys, "The Shaping of Foreign Policy: The Myth of the Middle East Madman," in *Between Memory and Desire: The Middle East in a Troubled Age*, ed. R. Stephen Humphreys (Berkeley: University of California Press, 1999), 83–112.

108. "Preventing a Communist Takeover in Iraq" (Secret), September 24, 1959, IAGI.

109. Many believe that Lakeland was a "quiet American." His relationship to the CIA is discussed in greater detail in the next chapter.

110. William Lakeland Oral History Interview with Michael Doran, April 4, 2010, Seeley G. Mudd Manuscript Library, Princeton University, 9–13, 16, 18. See also Michael Doran, "Who's Bill?" *Princeton Alumni Weekly*, October 2010; Michael Thornhill, "Bringing It All Together," *Al-Ahram Weekly*, October 21, 2004.

111. Halla summarizing Lakeland remarks of September 24, quoted in Citino, *Envisioning the Arab Future*, 193.

112. 420th Meeting of the NSC, October 1, 1959, *FRUS, 1958–1960*, 12, 204.

113. Editorial Note, *FRUS, 1958–1960*, 12, 205.

114. Citino, "Middle East Cold Wars," 256–57; "NSC Meeting Concerning Iraq," October 1, 1959; CIA to Jones, October 13, 1959, "Contingency Planning Regarding Iraq"; Meyer to Jones, October 16, 1959; Eilts to Jones, "CENTO Discussion of Iraq," October 14, 1959, all in IAGI; Baghdad to State, A-654, January 1, 1960, JFK National Security Files, University Publications of America (Frederick 1987), Microfilm Reel 1, Frames 125–26 [hereafter JFKMF 1:125–26].

115. For IAGI analysis of the Ba'th, see Meyer to Jones, "Suggested Agenda for Meeting of Inter-Agency Group on Iraq, December 4," December 3, 1959; Washburn to Jones, "NIE on Iraq," December 17, 1959; Meyer to Jones, December 26, 1959; Jones to Meyer, "Items Suggested by [CIA] for Discussion at Iraq Inter-Agency Group Meeting This Afternoon," December 28, 1959.

116. SNIE 36.2-5-59, "Short-Term Prospects for Iraq," December 15, 1959, *FRUS, 1958–1960*, 12, 210. For background on the Special National Intelligence Estimate and criticism of its conclusions, see also Washburn to Jones, "NIE on Iraq," December 17, 1959, IAGI.

117. See Critchfield Interview, "The Survival of Saddam," *PBS Frontline*, January 2000, www.pbs.org/wgbh/pages/frontline/shows/saddam/interviews/critchfield.html; Adam Bernstein, "CIA Official James Critchfield Dies at 86," *Washington Post*, April 24, 2003.

118. See Nicholas Thacher, "Reflections on US Foreign Policy towards Iraq in the 1950s," in Fernea and Louis, *Iraqi Revolution of 1958*, 75. See also Niel M. Johnson, "Oral History Interview with Nicholas G. Thacher," May 28, 1992, www.trumanlibrary.org/oralhist/thachern.htm.

119. "Suggested Comments on Special National Intelligence Estimate on Iraq" (Secret, drafted by Thacher), December 22, 1959, IAGI.

120. Meyer to Jones, "Meeting of Inter-Agency Group on Iraq: Some Points Supporting Our Present Hands Off Policy towards Iraq," December 22, 1959, IAGI.

121. See Memo for the Record, Washington, "Project Clean Up" (Top Secret), January 12, 1960, *FRUS, 1958–1960*, 12, 212. The document published in *FRUS* remains redacted in full, but an only partially declassified copy that I acquired through an FOIA request indicates that the IAGI discussed CIA proposals. All details of the proposals remain classified. See also Meyer to Jones, December 26, 1959, IAGI.

122. "IAGI Meeting" (hand-marked 2–27), IAGI.

123. For the NEA's marginal notes, see "Proposed Report to the NSC by the IAGI," n.d. I have edited the syntax of the marginal notes at the bottom of page 2 for readability. See also Meyer to Jones, "Iraq Inter-Agency Group Meeting January 12" (Secret Memo), January 11, 1960.

124. Wilford, *America's Great Game*, 283.

125. Beirut to State, no. 539 (Secret Air Pouch), "Views on Middle East Politics by Two Private American Experts," March 7, 1960 (drafted "early February"), RG59, Box 2030, Folder 780.00/1–460. In a cover letter accompanying the report, Robert McClintock, the US ambassador to Lebanon, explains that the document represented the culmination of their work for "Kim's office," suggesting that Kim Roosevelt was still (or once again) serving the CIA in some official capacity.

126. Church Committee, *Interim Report*.

127. Parenthetical references to testimony dates are omitted for readability.

128. Stephen Kinzer, *Poisoner in Chief: Sidney Gottlieb and the CIA Search for Mind Control* (New York: Henry Holt, 2019), 224.

129. Kinzer, *Poisoner in Chief*, 36–40, 48.

130. Kinzer, *Poisoner in Chief*, 40.

131. Kinzer, *Poisoner in Chief*, 11–13, 20–22.

132. Kinzer, *Poisoner in Chief*, 76, 141.

133. Kinzer, *Poisoner in Chief*, 187–90.

134. Kinzer, *Poisoner in Chief*, 205.

135. Citino, *Envisioning the Arab Future*, 205.

136. Citino, *Envisioning the Arab Future*, 180.

137. Citino, *Envisioning the Arab Future*, 180–81.

138. On how ideas about color affected US foreign policy, see, for example, Vitalis, *White World Order*; Michael Krenn, *The Color of Empire: Race and American Foreign Relations* (Washington, DC: Potomac Books, 2006); Thomas Borstelmann, *The Cold War and the Color Line* (Cambridge, MA: Harvard University Press, 2003);

Penny M. Von Eschen, *Race against Empire: Black Americans and Anticolonialism, 1937–1957* (Ithaca, NY: Cornell University Press, 1998).

139. Kinzer, *Poisoner in Chief*, 192–93, 203, 231.

CHAPTER 3

1. Kerr, *The Arab Cold War*, 17.

2. Batatu, *The Old Social Classes*, 912; Farouk-Sluglett and Sluglett, *Iraq since 1958*, 70–71; Mufti, *Sovereign Creations*, 128.

3. Batatu, *The Old Social Classes*, 922; Tareq Y. Ismael, *The Rise and Fall of the Communist Party of Iraq* (Cambridge: Cambridge University Press, 2007), 99.

4. Batatu, *The Old Social Classes*, 940; Penrose and Penrose, *Iraq*, 238n6.

5. Ghareeb, *Historical Dictionary of Iraq*, 228.

6. Memcon with Ambassador Sulaiman, Washington, DC, February 9, 1960, JFKMF 2:317.

7. Baghdad to State, no. 1920, February 20, 1960, JFKMF 13:564.

8. Baghdad to State, no. 797, March 3, 1960, JFKMF 13:603.

9. State to Various Posts, CW-9766, "Guidelines for Policy and Operations in Iraq," May 3, 1962, JFKMF 13:662. On the reorientation in the Eisenhower administration's approach to Iraq, see Citino, "Middle East Cold Wars," 247.

10. Farouk-Sluglett and Sluglett, *Iraq since 1958*, 76.

11. Batatu, *The Old Social Classes*, 835–38; Penrose and Penrose, *Iraq*, 240–52.

12. Batatu, *The Old Social Classes*, 839–40.

13. Stork, "Oil and Class Struggle," 176; Peter Sluglett, "Progress Postponed: Iraqi Oil Policy, Past, Present and Future," in *Oil and the New World Order*, ed. Kate Gillespie and Clement M. Henry (Gainesville: University of Florida Press, 1995), 232.

14. Penrose and Penrose, *Iraq*, 257–60.

15. Heiss, "International Boycott of Iranian Oil and the Anti-Mosaddeq Coup of 1953," 178–200.

16. For an analysis of the ways in which the conflict between Nasser and Qasim undermined unity on oil issues, see Citino, "Middle East Cold Wars."

17. Dietrich, *Oil Revolution*, 68–69; Garavini, *Rise and Fall of OPEC*, 90, 100.

18. Dietrich, *Oil Revolution*, 68–69; Garavini, *Rise and Fall of OPEC*, 100.

19. Cairo to State, no. 481, "Mohammed Salman–Iraqi Minister of Petroleum Affairs," November 20, 1960, JFKM 5:453.

20. Vitalis, *America's Kingdom*, 133–35; Garavini, *Rise and Fall of OPEC*, 94–96; "Abdullah al-Tariki: A Profile from the Archives," *Jadaliyya*, May 17, 2014, www

.jadaliyya.com/Details/30680; Stephen Duguid, "A Biographical Approach to the Study of Social Change in the Middle East: Abdullah Tariki as a New Man," *International Journal of Middle East Studies* 1 (July 1970): 195–220; Muhammad ibn 'Abd Allah Sayf, *'Abd Allah al-Tariqi: Sukhur al-Naft wa-Rimal al-Siyyasah* [*Abdullah Tariki: The rocks of oil and the sands of policy*] (Beirut: Riyad al-Rayyis lil-Kutub wa'l-Nashr, 2007).

21. Vitalis, *America's Kingdom*, 145–57; Rosie Bsheer, "A Counter-Revolutionary State: Popular Movements and the Making of Saudi Arabia," *Past & Present* 238, no. 1 (February 2018): 255–57.

22. Madawi al-Rasheed, *A History of Saudi Arabia* (Cambridge: Cambridge University Press, 2002), 109–14; Vitalis, *America's Kingdom*, 168; Bsheer, "A Counter-Revolutionary State," 266–68.

23. Murphy to Dillon, March 12, 1959, *FRUS, 1958–1960*, 12, 59; "Middle East Oil," March 18, 1959, *FRUS, 1958–1960*, 12, 60.

24. Vitalis, *America's Kingdom*, 199; Dietrich, *Oil Revolution*, 94; Garavini, *Rise and Fall of OPEC*, 113.

25. Hendryx quoted in Pierre Terzian (trans. Michael Pallis), *OPEC: The Inside Story* (London: Zed Books, 1985), 25. For IPC responses to Hendryx's speech, see Qatar (QPC) to London, "Cairo Oil Congress and Exhibition," May 10, 1959, IPC 161753.

26. Ghareeb, *Historical Dictionary of Iraq*, 349; Batatu, *The Old Social Classes*, 301–5.

27. Majid Khadduri, *Republican 'Iraq: A Study in 'Iraqi Politics since the Revolution of 1958* (Oxford: Oxford University Press, 1969), 134.

28. Khair el-Din Haseeb Oral History Interview, Beirut, Lebanon, January 18, 2016.

29. Cairo to State, no. 481, "Mohammed Salman–Iraqi Minister of Petroleum Affairs," November 20, 1960, JFKMF 5:453.

30. Darren Dochuk, *Anointed with Oil: How Christianity and Crude Made Modern America* (New York: Basic Books, 2019), 328, 338–43.

31. In her important book, *The Global Interior: Mineral Frontiers and American Power* (Cambridge, MA: Harvard University Press, 2018), historian Megan Black demonstrates the extent to which the Department of the Interior, over the course of the twentieth century, was a critical agent in "capitalism's expansive unfolding" across the globe (9). She documents the many ways in which the agency's regulatory functions were effectively captured by corporate interests. But she does not draw a distinction between domestic and international capitalism. She does not, therefore, note the competition between domestic and international American energy firms.

Nor the consequent tension between State (allied with the majors) and Interior (allied with the independents).

32. Jay Hakes, *A Declaration of Energy Independence: How Freedom from Foreign Oil Can Improve National Security, Our Economy, and the Environment* (New York: J. Wiley, 2008), 13–14.

33. Yergin, *The Prize*, 410–12.

34. Burton I. Kaufman, *The Oil Cartel Case: A Documentary Study of Antitrust Activity in the Cold War Era* (Westport, CT: Greenwood Press, 1978), 29; Nancy Lisagor and Frank Lipsius, *A Law unto Itself: The Untold Story of the Law Firm Sullivan & Cromwell* (New York: Paragon House, 1989), 202.

35. Department of Justice to Attorney General, June 24, 1952, in Kaufmann, *The Oil Cartel Case*, 123.

36. Lisagor and Lipsius, *A Law unto Itself*, 202.

37. Blair, *The Control of Oil*, 73; Kaufmann, *The Oil Cartel Case*, 30; Yergin, *The Prize*, 457.

38. Yergin, *The Prize*, 456; Kaufmann, *The Oil Cartel Case*, 31–32; Blair, *The Control of Oil*, 72

39. Harry S. Truman to the Attorney General, January 12, 1953, in Kaufmann, *The Oil Cartel Case*, 158.

40. Departments of State and Interior, January 1953, in Kaufmann, *The Oil Cartel Case*, 145–47.

41. Special Assistant Robert Cutler to Dulles (ca. January 1953), in Blair, *The Control of Oil*, 73.

42. Blair, *The Control of Oil*, 76.

43. Eric Pace, "Robert B. Anderson, Ex-Treasury Chief, Dies at 79," *New York Times*, August 16, 1989.

44. Wilford, *America's Great Game*, 206.

45. Blair, *The Control of Oil*, 173.

46. R. O. Kellam, "Regulation of Oil Imports," *Duke Law Journal* (Spring 1961): 192–93.

47. Blair, *The Control of Oil*, 173.

48. Paul Richter, "Former Treasury Secretary Faces Prison," *Los Angeles Times*, March 27, 1987.

49. Haykes, *Energy Independence*, 15

50. Robert Caro, *The Path to Power: The Lyndon Johnson Years I* (New York: Vintage, 1981), 841–49. Caro discussed the extent to which LBJ sought to conceal his oil

industry ties in "The Secrets of Lyndon Johnson's Archives: On a Presidential Paper Trail," *New Yorker,* January 21, 2019.

51. Jones to Hager, April 20, 1959, *FRUS, 1958–1960,* 12, 83. Blair, *The Control of Oil,* 76; Kaufmann, *The Oil Cartel Case,* 96–97; Lisagor and Lipsius, *A Law unto Itself,* 212.

52. 444th NSC, May 9, 1960, *FRUS, 1958–1960,* 4, 307; Editorial Note, *FRUS, 1958–1960,* 12, 86.

53. Jones to Hager, April 20, 1959, *FRUS, 1958–1960,* 12, 83.

54. 444th NSC, May 9, 1960, *FRUS, 1958–1960,* 4, 307; Editorial Note, *FRUS, 1958–1960,* 12, 86.

55. Yergin, *The Prize,* 484

56. NSC 5411/2, December 10, 1958, *FRUS, 1958–1960,* 7.2, 229.

57. Yergin, *The Prize,* 486.

58. Cuming to Herter, August 20, 1957, *FRUS, 1955–1957,* 12, 403.

59. Memorandum of Conversation, Rome, December 23, 1958, *FRUS, 1958–1960,* 7.2, 232.

60. Memorandum of Conversation, Rome, November 3, 1960, *FRUS, 1958–1960,* 7.2.

61. Memorandum of Conversation, Rome, November 3, 1960.

62. Memorandum of Conversation, Rome, November 3, 1960.

63. Rome to State, May 27, 1962, *FRUS, 1961–1963,* 13, 303.

64. Peter Shadbolt, "Autopsy Performed on Italian Oil Chief," *United Press International,* June 23, 1995; Donato Firrao and Graziano Ubertalli, "Was There a Bomb on Mattei's Aircraft?" *Convegno Nazionale,* IGF 20, Turin, June 24–26, 2009, 18–30; Yergin, *The Prize,* 512.

65. Journalist Said K. Aburish claims that William McHale was a CIA agent who helped to "mastermind" the 1963 coup in Iraq. See *Saddam Hussein: The Politics of Revenge* (London: Bloomsbury, 2000), 58–59. The question of McHale's involvement in Iraq is taken up in the next chapter.

66. Shadbolt, "Autopsy Performed on Italian Oil Chief."

67. Penrose and Penrose, *Iraq,* 257–58.

68. Penrose and Penrose, *Iraq,* 258; Samir Saul, "Masterly Inactivity as Brinksmanship: The Iraq Petroleum Company's Road to Nationalization," *International History Review* 29, no. 4 (2007): 756.

69. Anthony Sampson, *The Seven Sisters: The Great Oil Companies and the World They Shaped* (New York: Viking Press, 1975), 189.

70. Yergin, *The Prize*, 503.

71. Sampson, *The Seven Sisters*, 188.

72. Statement by Dr. Tala'at Al-Shaibani on the success of the first OPEC conference, undated, outlining principal decisions taken, in A. Burdett, ed., *OPEC: Origins and Strategy 1947–1973*, vol. 2 (Cambridge: Cambridge Archive Editions, 2004), 87–91.

73. On Tariki's paper, "The Pricing of Crude Oil and Refined Products," see PRA Ensor (Head of IPC Delegation), Second Arab Pet Congress, Beirut, October 17–22, 1960, IPC Negotiations, File 161754, British Petroleum Archive, Warwick University [hereafter IPC 161754]; Cottom to Strong, International Cartel Case, May 10, 1961, RG59 NEA Lot Files, 1958–1963, Box 3, 1961 Chron Inter-Office Memorandum (2 of 2).

74. Memorandum of Conversation, Standard Oil Company (New Jersey) views on the Organization of Petroleum Exporting Countries, October 19, 1960, *FRUS, 1958–1960*, 12, 92.

75. British Embassy, Tehran to British Eastern Dept, 20 September 1960, in Burdett, ed., *OPEC*, vol. 2, 92.

76. Martin to Merchant, May 3, 1960, *FRUS, 1958–1960*, 12, 85n2.

77. 460th NSC, September 21, 1960, *FRUS, 1958–1960*, 12, 91.

78. NIE 30–60, Middle East Oil, December 13, 1960, *FRUS, 1958–1960*, 95.

79. Caro, *The Path to Power*, 25. See also Ann, Markusen, Peter Hall, Scott Campbell, and Sabina Deitrick, eds., *The Rise of the Gunbelt: The Military Remapping of Industrial America* (New York: Oxford University Press, 1991).

80. Stern, "Oil Scarcity Ideology," 236; Hoopes and Brinkley, *Driven Patriot*, 395–96.

CHAPTER 4

1. See Daniel Bell, *The End of Ideology: On the Exhaustion of Political Ideas in the Fifties* (New York: Free Press, 1960).

2. Lloyd Gardner, "Harry Hopkins with Hand Grenades? McGeorge Bundy in the Kennedy and Johnson Years," in *Behind the Throne: Servants of Power to Imperial Presidents, 1898–1968*, ed. Thomas J. McCormick and Walter LaFeber (Madison: University of Wisconsin Press, 1993), 209–10.

3. On the influence of Keynesian economic theories on Kennedy advisers, see Michael E. Latham, *Modernization as Ideology: American Social Science and "Nation Building" in the Kennedy Era* (Chapel Hill: University of North Carolina Press, 2000), 42. On Keynesian macroeconomic management as a form of "counterinsurgency"

designed to preempt more radical forms of economic change, see Mitchell, *Carbon Democracy*, 123–43.

4. Latham, *Modernization as Ideology*, 114.

5. Gardner, "Harry Hopkins with Hand Grenades," 209.

6. Frank L. Jones, *Blowtorch: Robert Komer, Vietnam, and American Cold War Strategy* (Annapolis, MD: Naval Institute Press, 2013).

7. Jones, *Blowtorch*, 18–23.

8. Jones, *Blowtorch*, 52.

9. Jones, *Blowtorch*, 25.

10. Citino, *Envisioning the Arab Future*, 216–21.

11. Citino, *Envisioning the Arab Future*, 214.

12. NIE 36–61, Nasser and the Future of Arab Nationalism, June 27, 1961, *FRUS, 1961–1963*, 17, 68; Komer to Rostow, June 30, 1961, *FRUS, 1961–1963*, 17, 74.

13. Elwood to Strong, June 26, 1961, *FRUS, 1961–1963*, 17, 66.

14. State to Kuwait, June 27, 1961, *FRUS, 1961–1963*, 17, 67; Editorial Note, *FRUS, 1961–1963*, 17, 73.

15. Home to Rusk, June 28, 1961, *FRUS, 1961–1963*, 17, 70; Home to Rusk, June 29, 1961, *FRUS, 1961–1963*, 17, 72; Editorial Note, *FRUS, 1961–1963*, 17, 73.

16. On US-UK tensions over Iraq and Kuwait, see Gregory Winger, "Twilight on the British Gulf: The 1961 Kuwait Crisis and the Evolution of American Strategic Thinking in the Persian Gulf," *Diplomacy & Statecraft* 23 (2012): 665; Richard John Worrall, "'Coping with a Coup d'Etat': British Policy towards Post-Revolutionary Iraq, 1958–63," *Contemporary British History* 21, no. 2 (2007): 173–99; W. Taylor Fain, "John F. Kennedy and Harold Macmillan: Managing the 'Special Relationship' in the Persian Gulf Region, 1961–63," *Middle Eastern Studies* 38, no. 4 (October 2002): 95–122; Galpern, *Money, Oil, and Empire in the Middle East*, 246–47.

17. Baghdad to State, December 28, 1961, *FRUS, 1961–1963*, 17, 154.

18. HMG Econ Dept, "Iraq's Revised Threats against Kuwait," December 18, 1961, IPC 135979.

19. Mufti, *Sovereign Creations*, 121–25; Kerr, *The Arab Cold War*, 21–25.

20. Farouk-Sluglett and Sluglett, *Iraq since 1958*, 83.

21. Batatu, *The Old Social Classes*, 778–79, 974–82; Farouk-Sluglett and Sluglett, *Iraq since 1958*, 77, 83; Eric Davis, *Memories of the State: Politics, History, and Collective Identity in Modern Iraq* (Berkeley: University of California Press, 2005), 116–20.

22. Legislation in Iraq: Joint Opinion, November 27, 1961; Translation from the French of the Interview given to M. Empis, Editor of *La Revue Pétroliér*, by

M. Mohamed Salman, Iraqi Minister of Oil, November 15, 1961; Draft IPC to Min Oil, November 24, 1961; Ekserdjian-Salman, Memcon, December 5, 1961, IPC 135979.

23. Frank Hendryx, Tomorrow's Concession Agreement, December 5, 1961, IPC 135979.

24. INR-25, Consequences of Breakdown of Oil Negotiations, Komer Files, November 20, 1961, Box 426, Iraq 1961–1962, JFKL.

25. INR-25, November 20, 1961.

26. Reasons Justifying Law No. 80 of 1961: Defining the Exploitation Districts for the Oil Companies, *Iraqi Government Gazette* no. 616, December 12, 1961, IPC 135979.

27. Baghdad to State, no. 294, December 30, 1961, Country Files, Box 117, Iraq 1961–1962, JFKL. See also Baghdad to State, December 28, 1961; and Talbot to McGhee, December 29, 1961, *FRUS, 1961–1963*, 17, 154–55.

28. Baghdad to State, no. 294, December 30, 1961, Country Files, Box 117, Iraq 1961–1962, JFKL.

29. Komer to Bundy, December 29, 1961, *FRUS, 1961–1963*, 17, 156.

30. The report was compiled in response to Komer's oral request. See Talbot to Ball, December 18, 1961, *FRUS, 1961–1963*, 17, 150n1.

31. Jones, *Blowtorch*, 52–53.

32. Komer to Bundy, December 29, 1961, *FRUS, 1961–1963*, 17, 156.

33. Komer to Bundy, December 29, 1961.

34. Komer to Bundy, December 29, 1961, n. 3.

35. See, for example, the lengths to which the president went to avoid leaving his fingerprints on plots to assassinate both Diem and Castro. On Diem see John Prados, ed., "JFK and the Diem Coup," *National Security Archive Electronic Briefing Book* 101, November 5, 2003: www2.gwu.edu/~nsarchiv/NSAEBB/NSAEBB101/index.htm.

36. Schlesinger to President, "Protection of the President," April 10, 1961, *FRUS, 1961–1963*, 10, 86. For discussion of the controversy surrounding this memo, see Dan Morgan, "Schlesinger, Moyers Trade Volleys on Anti-Castro Plots," *Washington Post*, July 21, 1977.

37. NIE 36.2–62, January 31, 1962, *FRUS, 1961–1963*, 17, 183.

38. Baghdad to State, no. 621, March 29, 1962, JFKMF 3:161–62.

39. Baghdad to State, no. 513, "Opponents of Qasim Regime [Hashemites] Urge Intervention," January 31, 1962, JFKMF 3:108. Emphasis added.

40. Quoted in Gardner, "Harry Hopkins with Hand Grenades," 213.

41. Critchfield, "The Survival of Saddam."

42. Grant to McGhee, May 3, 1962, *FRUS, 1961–1963*, 17, 262.

43. Brubeck to Bundy, June 20, 1962, *FRUS, 1961–1963*, 17, 303.

44. Basra to State, no. 93, June 4, 1962, JFKMF 13:683.

45. Biographical Sketch of John. D. Jernegan, Country Files, Box 117, Iraq 1961–1962, JFKL.

46. Komer to Talbot, June 4, 1962, JFKMF 13:687. The brackets around "is" indicate the omission of a parenthetical reference to a recent cable. Emphasis added.

47. See the 1964 film *Becket*, quoted in Peter E. Dans, *Christians in the Movies: A Century of Saints and Sinners* (Lanham, MD: Rowman & Littlefield, 2009), 169.

48. On this dynamic, see James C. Thomson, "How Could Vietnam Happen? An Autopsy," *The Atlantic* (April 1968). Thomson was an East Asian specialist in the State Department and on the NSC from 1961 until he resigned in opposition to the war in Vietnam in 1966.

49. This resume is taken from Roy Melbourne, *Conflict and Crises: A Foreign Service Story* (Lanham, MD: University Press of America, 1993). His arrival in Baghdad is discussed on 215.

50. On endemic coup plotting: Baghdad to State, no. 592, June 25, 1962; Baghdad to State [tel. no. not declassified], July 15, 1962; Baghdad to State, no. 40, July 18, 1962; Baghdad to State, no. 46, July 20, 1962; Baghdad to State, no. 79, August 9, 1962, Country Files, Box 117, Iraq 1961–1962, JFKL.

51. John R. Starkey, "A Talk with Philip Hitti," *Aramco World* (July/August 1971), https://archive.aramcoworld.com/issue/197104/a.talk.with.philip.hitti.htm.

52. On Davies's early appointments, see Notable Names Database (NNDB), "Rodger P. Davies," www.nndb.com/people/403/000121040/.

53. Baghdad to State, no. 40, July 18, 1962. See also Worrall, "British Policy towards Post-Revolutionary Iraq, 1958–63."

54. Baghdad to State, no. 40, July 18, 1962.

55. Baghdad to State, no. 40, July 18, 1962.

56. List of Persons, *FRUS, 1961–1963*, 17.

57. On Akins's series of reports, see Baghdad to State, A-291, "Support for Qasim among the Lower Classes," September 17, 1962, JFKMF 3:560–62; Baghdad to State, A-320, "Sarifa Population of Baghdad," September 24, 1962, JFKMF 3:570–72; Baghdad to State, no. 156, September 26, 1962, JFKMF 3:576–77; Baghdad to State, A-452, "Shi'a Muslim Attitudes toward Qasim Regime," October 29, 1962, JFKMF 3:633.

58. Baghdad to State, A-291, September 17, 1962.
59. Baghdad to State, A-291, September 17, 1962.
60. Baghdad to State, A-320, September 24, 1962.
61. Baghdad to State, no. 156, September 26, 1962.
62. Baghdad to State, A-452, October 29, 1962.
63. Ismet Sheriff Vanly, "Kurdistan in Iraq," in *A People without a Country: The Kurds and Kurdistan*, ed. Gerard Chaliand, trans. Michael Pallis (New York: Olive Branch Press, 1991), 139–93; Edgar O'Ballance, *The Kurdish Struggle 1920–94* (New York: St. Martin's Press, 1996), 37–44, 47–63; David McDowall, *A Modern History of the Kurds*, 3rd rev. ed. (New York: I. B. Tauris, 2004), 302–13; Sa'ad Jawad, *Iraq and the Kurdish Question, 1958–1970* (London: Ithaca Press, 1981), 36–106.
64. Baghdad to State, no. 949, March 6, 1961, JFKMF 2:354–58.
65. Manning Marable, *Race, Reform, Rebellion: The Second Reconstruction in Black America, 1945–1982* (London: Macmillan Press), 62–63.
66. Alvandi, *Nixon, Kissinger, and the Shah*, 71–72.
67. Tabriz to State, no. 31, "Some Aspects of the Revolt in Kurdistan," September 19, 1961, JFKMF 2:748–50; Baghdad to State, no. 162, September 19, 1961, JFKMF 2:762; Baghdad to State, no. 168, September 25, 1961, JFKMF 2:785–86; Baghdad to State, no. 245, "Qassim Accuses British and Americans of Complicity in Kurdish Revolt; Exonerates USSR; Dissolves KDP," September 29, 1961, JFKMF 2:791.
68. See Baghdad to State, A-353, "Kurdish Representatives Petition Qassim," September 14, 1960, JFKMF 2:20–21; State to Tabriz, Tehran, Baghdad, CW-2436, "Approaches by Kurdish Nationalist Elements," September 18, 1961, JFKMF 2:747; Baghdad to State, no. 258, October 4, 1961, JFKMF 2:812. For analysis see Douglas Little, "The United States and the Kurds: A Cold War Story," *Journal of Cold War Studies* 12, no. 4 (Fall 2010): 63–98.
69. Baghdad to State, no. 108, August 28, 1962, JFKMF 3:507.
70. Baghdad to State, no. 233, November 5, 1962, JFKMF 3:646; Ankara to State, A-492, "Assistance to the Kurds of Iraq," November 27, 1962, JFKMF 3:696–97.
71. Baghdad to State, no. 150, September 20, 1962, JFKMF 3:565.
72. Schmidt later recorded his experiences as *Journey among Brave Men* (Boston: Little Brown, 1964).
73. See New York to State, no. 1344, October 18, 1962, JFKMF 3:620; Baghdad to State, A-476, "Communist-Kurdish Exchange on Schmidt's *New York Times* Articles," November 6, 1962, JFKMF 3:657.

74. On the Kennedy administration and oil, see Citino, *Envisioning the Arab Future*, 56–96, 235; Vitalis, *America's Kingdom*, 229–32, 246–48; Bird, *The Chairman*, 517–18.

75. Richard Slotkin, *Gunfighter Nation: The Myth of the Frontier in Twentieth-Century America* (New York: Athenaeum, 1992), 1–3.

76. Richard Goodwin, *Remembering America: A Voice from the Sixties* (New York: Little Brown, 1988) [Open Road Media, Kindle Edition, loc. 8031–39].

77. Melbourne to Strong, December 11, 1962, RG59, NEA Lot Files, 1958–63, Box 6, Baghdad 1962.

78. Melbourne to Strong, December 11, 1962.

79. Vitalis, *America's Kingdom*, 192–93, 230–34; Asher Orkaby, *Beyond the Arab Cold War: The International History of the Yemen Civil War, 1962–68* (New York: Oxford University Press, 2017), 30–37.

80. Vitalis, *America's Kingdom*, 220. On the Free Princes, see also Madawi al-Rashid, *A History of Saudi Arabia* (Cambridge: Cambridge University Press, 2002), 108–20; Bsheer, "A Counter-Revolutionary State," 255–57.

81. Vitalis, *America's Kingdom*, 238–39.

82. Citino, *Envisioning the Arab Future*, 232, 236.

83. Editorial Note, *FRUS 1961–1963*, 1, 89; Jones, *Blowtorch*, 51–70; Fain, "John F. Kennedy and Harold Macmillan," 108–16; Citino, *Envisioning the Arab Future*, 235–37.

84. Komer to Bundy, October 6, 1963. Many thanks to Nathan Citino for sharing this document from JFKL.

85. Memcon, "Round-Table Discussion of Recent Near East Developments," January 11, 1963, RG59, Central Files, 1960–1963, Box 2030, 780.00/1–662.

86. Komer-Roosevelt memcon, January 28, 1963, *FRUS, 1961–1963*, 18, 145.

87. Rusk to Baghdad, CA-1318, January 1963, JFKMF 3:844.

88. Baghdad to State, no. 293, December 17, 1962, JFKMF 3:735. See also Baghdad to State, January 15, 1963, JFKMF 3:801; Baghdad to State, no. 362, January 22, 1963, JFKMF 3:837–39; Baghdad to State, no. 352, January 19, 1963, Country Files, Box 117, Iraq 1961–1962, JFKL; Baghdad to State, February 5, 1963, *FRUS, 1961–1963*, 18, 149.

89. Baghdad to State, no. 293, December 17, 1962, JFKMF 3:735.

90. Qasim's Press Conference of January 31, 1963, as recorded by the BBC Foreign Broadcast Monitoring Service, IPC 135984. See also Baghdad to State, A-747, February 5, 1963, RG59 Central Files, 1963, Box 3943, POL 2–1 Joint Weeka Iraq 2/1/63.

91. See, for example, the US Nationality Act of 1790, which restricted naturalization as a US citizen to "free white persons." Various iterations on the theme followed in subsequent years. See James Q. Whitman, *Hitler's American Model: The United States and the Making of Nazi Race Law* (Princeton, NJ: Princeton University Press, 2017), 11–12, 39–41.

92. Whitman, *Hitler's American Model*, 11–12, 39–41.

93. Inaugural Address of Governor George C. Wallace, January 14, 1963, Montgomery, Alabama, http://digital.archives.alabama.gov/cdm/ref/collection/voices/id/2952; Thomas Noer, "Segregationists and the World: The Foreign Policy of White Resistance," in *Window on Freedom: Race Civil Rights and Foreign Affairs, 1945–1988*, ed. Brenda Gayle Plummer, 141–62 (Chapel Hill: University of North Carolina Press, 2003).

94. See Lothrop Stoddard, *The Rising Tide of Color against White World-Supremacy* (New York: Charles Scribner's Sons, 1922). Political scientists Robert Strausz-Hupé and Stefan Possony reprised the idea for a new era in *International Relations in the Age of Conflict between Democracy and Dictatorship* (New York: McGraw Hill, 1954). For analysis of Strausz-Hupé and Possony, see Vitalis, *White World Order*, 151–55.

95. London to State, no. 2992, February 6, 1963, RG59 Central Files, 1963, Box 3621, Pet 6 Companies 2/1/63.

96. Baghdad to State, no. 362, January 22, 1963. See also Baghdad to State, January 15, 1963.

97. Batatu, *The Old Social Classes*, 974–82.

98. Batatu, *The Old Social Classes*, 978.

99. Baghdad to State, A-[?], Weeka 6, February 12, 1963, RG 59 Central Files, 1963, Box 3943, POL 2–1 Joint Weeka Iraq 2/1/63.

CHAPTER 5

1. Batatu, *The Old Social Classes*, 985–87.

2. Husayn in *al-Ahram* (Cairo), September 27, 1963, quoted in Batatu, *The Old Social Classes*, 985–86; Mufti extends the quote to include the last sentence. See Mufti, *Sovereign Creations*, 144.

3. See Kate Doyle and Peter Kornbluh, eds., "CIA and Assassinations: The Guatemala 1954 Documents," National Security Archive Electronic Briefing Book No. 4, https://nsarchive2.gwu.edu/NSAEBB/NSAEBB4/ciaguat2.html.

4. Jeremy Kuzmarov, "Modernizing Repression: Police Training, Political Violence, and Nation-Building in the 'American Century,'" *Diplomatic History* 33, no. 2 (2009): 191–221; Stuart Schrader, *Badges without Borders: How Global Counterinsurgency Transformed American Policing* (Berkeley: University of California Press, 2019).

5. Deterrence of Guerilla Warfare, p. 52, Komer Files, CI Special Group 2/61–4/62 and undated, JFKL.

6. See Vincent Bevins, "How 'Jakarta' Became the Codeword for US-Backed Mass Killing," *New York Review of Books*, May 18, 2020, www.nybooks.com/daily/2020/05/18/how-jakarta-became-the-codeword-for-us-backed-mass-killing/.

7. Weldon Matthews, Malik Mufti, Douglas Little, William Zeman, and Eric Jacobsen have all drawn on declassified American records to largely substantiate the plausibility of Batatu's account. Peter Hahn and Bryan Gibson (in separate works) argue that the available evidence does support the claim of CIA collusion with the Baʻth. However, each makes this argument in the course of a much broader study, and neither examines the question in any detail. See Weldon C. Matthews, "The Kennedy Administration, Counterinsurgency, and Iraq's First Baʻthist Regime," *International Journal of Middle East Studies* 43, no. 4 (2011): 635–53; Weldon C. Matthews, "The Kennedy Administration, the International Federation of Petroleum Workers, and Iraqi Labor under the Baʻthist Regime," *Journal of Cold War Studies* 17, no. 1 (2015): 97–128; Weldon C. Matthews, "The Kennedy Administration and Arms Transfers to Baʻthist Iraq," *Diplomatic History* 43, no. 3 (2019): 469–92; Mufti, *Sovereign Creations*, 144; Little, *American Orientalism*, 63; Little, "Mission Impossible," 696; William J. Zeman, "U.S. Covert Intervention in Iraq 1958–1963: The Origins of US Supported Regime Change in Modern Iraq," MA thesis, California State Polytechnic University, Pomona, 2006; Eric Jacobsen, "A Coincidence of Interests: Kennedy, U.S. Assistance, and the 1963 Iraqi Baʻth Regime," *Diplomatic History* 37, no. 5 (May 2013): 1029–58; Hahn, *Missions Accomplished?* 48; Gibson, *Sold Out?* 45, 57–58.

8. Aburish, *Saddam Hussein*, 55–56.

9. Aburish, *Saddam Hussein*, 55–58.

10. ʻAli Karim ʻAbdullah Saʻid, *ʻIraq 8 Shubat 1963: Min Hiwar al-Mafahim ila Hiwar al-Damm—Murajaʻat fi Dhakirat Talib Shabib* [*Iraq, February 8, 1963: From a dialogue of understanding to a dialogue of blood—Reflections on Talib Shabib's memory*] (Beirut: Dar al-Kanuz al-ʻArabia, 1999), 273.

11. Michael Thornhill, "Bringing It All Together," *Al-Ahram Weekly*, October 21, 2004.

12. William Lakeland Oral History (Telephone) Interview with Michael Doran, April 4, 2010, Seeley G. Mudd Manuscript Library, Princeton, NJ, 20.

13. Lakeland Oral History, 44.

14. Lakeland Oral History, 44, 46.

15. Baghdad to State, no. 659, "Who's Who of Iraqi Communists," April 11, 1962. Akins added to the list the following month. See Baghdad to State, A-777, May 31, 1962. Many thanks to Nathan Citino for sharing these documents.

16. On the Communist purge, see Ismael, *Rise and Fall of the Communist Party of Iraq*, 107–13.

17. Melbourne to Davies, February 12, 1963, RG59 NEA Lot Files, 1958–1963, Box 7, Letters from the Field, January–June 1963.

18. T. Rees Shapiro, "Arthur E. Callahan, CIA Officer, Dies at 92," *Washington Post*, May 8, 2010; Zeman, "U.S. Covert Intervention in Iraq 1958–1963," nn. 130–34.

19. Melbourne to Davies, February 26, 1963, RG59 NEA Lot Files, 1958–1963, Box 7, Letters from the Field, January–June 1963.

20. Friedrich Nietzsche, *Beyond Good and Evil*, chap. 4, no. 68, www.marxists.org/reference/archive/nietzsche/1886/beyond-good-evil/ch04.htm.

21. On Strong's background in Syria, see Lakeland Oral History, 44; "Robert Strong," Persons, State Department Office of the Historian, https://history.state.gov/departmenthistory/people/strong-robert-campbell.

22. Robert Kaplan, *The Arabists: The Romance of an American Elite* (New York: Free Press, 1995), 172–73.

23. Baghdad to State, A-777, May 31, 1962. Many thanks to Nathan Citino for sharing this document.

24. Akins interview, "The Survival of Saddam," PBS Frontline, January 2000.

25. Michel Despratx and Barry Lando, "Iraq: Crimes and Collusions: 40 Years of Western Support for the Baathists," *Le Monde diplomatique*, English ed., November 2004.

26. US Army Attaché Baghdad to State, no. cx-24–63, February 10, 1963, RG59 Central Files, 1963, Box 3943, POL 2–4 Politico-Military Reports Iraq.

27. US Army Attaché Baghdad to State, no. cx-24–63, February 10, 1963; Baghdad to State, no. 410, February 10, 1963, RG59 Central Files, 1963, Box 3943, POL Iraq.

28. Matthews, "Kennedy Administration, Counterinsurgency, and Iraq's First Ba'thist Regime," 636.

29. See "Kubark Counterintelligence Interrogation," July 1963, in Tom Blanton, ed., "The CIA in Latin America," National Security Archive Electronic Briefing Book

No. 27 (2000), https://nsarchive2.gwu.edu/NSAEBB/NSAEBB27/docs/doc01.pdf. The Kubark torture program represented the culmination of the work that began under the direction of Sidney Gottlieb as part of the MK-ULTRA project. In short, by 1960 Gottlieb had concluded that while mind control did not work because LSD's effects were unpredictable, personality regression through sensory depravation does. See Kinzer, *Poisoner in Chief*, 195, 274–75.

30. Komer to JFK, February 8, 1963, Country Files, Box 117, Iraq 1962–1963, JFKL.

31. Telegram, February 1963 [date and all other identifying information classified], "Biographic Information on the President and Prime Minister of the New Government of Iraq." Many thanks to Nathan Citino for sharing this document.

32. "Biographic Information on the President and Prime Minister of the New Government of Iraq."

33. Baghdad to State, November 14, 1963, Country Files, Iraq 9/63–11/63, JFKL.

34. See James M. Cypher, "The Origins and Evolution of Military Keynesianism in the United States," *Journal of Post Keynesian Economics* 38 (2015): 449–76; Walter S. Salant, "The Spread of Keynesian Doctrines and Practice in the US," in *The American Economic History Reader: Documents and Readings*, ed. John W. Malsberger and James N. Marshall (New York: Routledge, 2008), 399–412. In fairness to Keynes, the military-Keynesianism of the Kennedy administration was a gross misrepresentation of Keynes's actual philosophy, which was strongly opposed to militarism. On Keynes's actual philosophy, see Zachary Carter, *The Price of Peace: Money, Democracy, and the Life of John Maynard Keynes* (New York: Random House, 2020).

35. Campbell Craig and Frederick Logevall, *America's Cold War: The Politics of Insecurity* (Cambridge, MA: Harvard University Press, 2009), 196–99; William Stivers, *America's Confrontation with Revolutionary Change in the Middle East, 1948–1983* (New York: Macmillan, 1986), 38–40; Gabriel Kolko, *Confronting the Third World: United States Foreign Policy, 1945–1980* (New York: Pantheon, 1988); John Lewis Gaddis, *Strategies of Containment: A Critical Appraisal of American National Security Policy during the Cold War* (New York: Oxford University Press, 1982), 197–99.

36. Matthews, "Arms Transfers," 471; Michael T. Klare, *American Arms Supermarket* (Austin: University of Texas Press, 1984), 27–29, 59.

37. Matthews, "Arms Transfers," 472.

38. Matthews, "Arms Transfers," 473.

39. Matthews, "Arms Transfers," 473–74

40. Mitchell, "Ten Propositions about Oil," in *A Critical Political Economy of the Middle East and North Africa*, ed. Joel Beinin, Bassam Haddad, and Sherene Seikaly (Stanford: Stanford University, 2020), 80–82.

41. "Biographical Information, February 8 Government," Komer Files, Box 426, Iraq 1961–1963, JFKL.

42. Baghdad to State, no. 437, February 14, 1963, RG59 Central Files, 1963, Box 3621, Pet 6 Companies 2/1/63.

43. Baghdad to State, no. 437, February 14, 1963.

44. Memcon with Oil Reps (Mobil and Esso), "Recent Developments in Iraq—Effect on IPC," February 14, 1963, RG59 Central Files, 1963, Box 3943, POL Iraq.

45. Ekserdjian to IPC S, "Ba'ath Party Proclamations on Oil Negotiations in Iraq," G/583, February 11, 1963, IPC 135984.

46. Kerr, *The Arab Cold War*, 21–25; Mufti, *Sovereign Creations*, 121–25.

47. Baghdad to State, A-777, "New Government Bans Printing and Sale of Arab Personalities ['Arif and Nasser]," February 14, 1963, RG59 Central Files, 1963, Box 3943, POL Iraq.

48. "Biographic Information on the President and Prime Minister of the New Government of Iraq."

49. Memcon with Oil Reps (Mobil and Esso), "Recent Developments in Iraq—Effect on IPC," February 14, 1963, RG59 Central Files, 1963, Box 3943, POL Iraq.

50. Memcon with Russell Dorr (Washington Rep of the Chase National Bank), "New Regime in Iraq," February 25, 1963, RG59 Central Files, 1963, Box 3943, POL Iraq.

51. Baghdad to State, A-1101, May 28, 1963, Iraq 3/63–5/63, Country Files, Box 117A, JFKL.

52. Memcon, State (Blackiston) with Lindenmuth (Mobil), "IPC-GOI Negotiations," February 20, 1963, RG59 Central Files, 1963, Box 3621, PET 6 Companies 2/1/63. On BP and the Ba'th, see also Davies to Eilts, March 30, 1963, RG59 NEA Lot Files, 1958–1963, Box 7, Baghdad 1963.

53. See George F. Hiller to Allen, April 19, 1963, and Allen to Hiller, April 25, 1963, in Hamid Bayati, *Al-Inqilab al-Dami: al-Khafaya al-Dakhiliyah wa-Mawafiq al-Duwal al-Inqlimiyah wa Dawr al-Mukhabarat al-Gharbiyah* [*The bloody coup: Internal mysteries, regional political positions and the role of Western intelligence*], 2nd ed., trans. Hamid Bayati (London: Mu'assasat al-Rafid, 2000), 79–80.

54. Memcon (Blackiston) with Mobil (Gross), April 26, 1963, "IPC-GOI Negotiations," RG59 Central Files, 1963, Box 3621, PET Iraq 2/1/63.

55. Stewart to Herridge, February 12, 1963, IPC 135984.

56. Stewart to Herridge, February 15, 1963, A/384, IPC 135984

57. Stewart to Herridge, February 19, 1963, A/390, IPC 135984.

58. Bird to Chairman, March 1, 1963, IPC 135985.

59. 'Arif is quoted in "Iraq—Law 80," March 12, 1963, IPC 135985. 'Arif's comments were reported in *Tayyar*, a Beirut daily on February 23.

60. Ekserdjian to IPC, April 8, 1963, IPC 135985.

61. Memcon Wattari, Uqaili, Murphy, Stewart, Road, Ministry of Oil, Baghdad, April 22, 1963, IPC 135985.

62. Memcon Wattari, Uqaili, Murphy, Stewart, Road, Ministry of Oil, Baghdad, April 22, 1963, IPC 135985.

63. Memcon with British Officials, April 29, 1963, RG59 Central Files, 1963, Box 3621, PET 6 Companies 2/1/63.

64. Memcon with Moses (Mobil) and Christian Herter, Jr. (Mobil Company Government Relations), May 3, 1963, RG59 Central Files, 1963, Box 3621, PET 6 Companies 2/1/63.

65. Jawad, *Iraq and the Kurdish Question*, 113.

66. Jawad, *Iraq and the Kurdish Question*, 132–45.

67. Roham Alvandi, *Nixon, Kissinger, and the Shah: The United States and Iran in the Cold War* (New York: Oxford University Press, 2016), 71–72.

68. Jawad, *Iraq and the Kurdish Question*, 135.

69. Komer to Bundy, March 1, 1963, *FRUS 1961–1963*, 18, 173.

70. See Bagdad to State, A-1101, May 28, 1963, Country Files, Box 117A, Iraq 3/63–5/63, JFKL. The PRC leveled similar accusations as well. See Komer to Bundy, February 14, 1963, Komer Files, Box 426, Iraq 1961–1963, JFKL; ACCRA to State, A-538, February 15, 1963, Country Files, Box 117, Iraq 1962–63, JFKL; Hilsman to State, INR Research Memo, "Implications of Iraqi Coup for Soviet Policy," February 15, 1963, Country Files, Box 117, Iraq 1962–1963, JFKL; Hong Kong to State, no. 1400, February 18, 1963, RG59 Central Files, 1963, Box 3943, POL Iraq; Moscow to State, no. 2617, April 16, 1963, RG59 Central Files, 1963, Box 3943, POL Iraq.

71. Saunders to Bundy, April 2, 1963, *FRUS 1961–1963*, 18, 204.

72. Special Group on Counterinsurgency Meeting, May 16, 1963, *FRUS 1961–1963*, 18, 251.

73. Special Group on Counterinsurgency Meeting, May 16, 1963.

74. Secret Memcon Director General of Security Jamil Sabri Bayati, April 26, 1963, RG59 NEA Lot Files, 1958–1963, Box 7, Baghdad 1963.

75. Baghdad to State, A-1039, "Iraqi Attitudes toward Kurds and Kurdish Revolt," May 7, 1963, RG59 Central Files, 1963, Box 3943, POL Iraq.

76. Baghdad to State, A-1039, "Iraqi Attitudes toward Kurds and Kurdish Revolt," May 7, 1963.

77. Jawad, *Iraq and the Kurdish Question*, 142–48.

78. Edwin Martini, "Hearts, Minds, and Herbicides: The Politics of Chemical War in Vietnam," *Diplomatic History* 37, no. 1 (2013): 58–84.

79. Davies to Talbot, "Provision of Arms to Iraq," June 20, 1963, RG59 NEA Lot Files, 1958–63, Box 7, Baghdad 1963. For deliberations and controversies with the Baʻth, see the memoirs of Foreign Minister Talib Shabib (February–November 1963), Saʻid, *Murajaʻat fi Dhakirat Talib Shabib*, 274.

80. Komer to Bundy, June 19, 1963, Iraq-Kurdish Rebellion, June 13, 1963, Country Files, Box 117A, Iraq 6/63–8/63, JFKL.

81. Davies to Talbot, "Provision of Arms to Iraq," June 20, 1963.

82. For a detailed discussion of the differences between the Departments of State and Defense regarding arms deliveries to Iraq, including a discussion of the napalm controversy, see Matthews, "Arms Transfers," 469–92; Jacobsen, "A Coincidence of Interests," 1049–54.

83. Kerr, *The Arab Cold War*, 21–25; Mufti, *Sovereign Creations*, 121–25.

84. Jamal Atasi quoted in Mufti, *Sovereign Creations*, 144.

85. See Mufti, *Sovereign Creations*, 149–52. On Barzani Kurdish's opposition to the Cairo Charter, see Jawad, *Iraq and the Kurdish Question*, 113–22. On Shiʻite opposition to the Cairo Charter, see Baghdad to State, no. 501, March 1, 1963, Country Files, Box 117A, Iraq 3/63–5/63, JFKL; Baghdad to State, A-74, May 14, 1963, "Public Demonstrations in Basra," RG59 Central Files, 1963, Box 3943, POL Iraq.

86. See Baghdad to State, no. 621, April 5, 1963, Country Files, Box 117A, Iraq 3/63–5/63, JFKL.

87. USARMA Baghdad to State, CX 107–63, May 26, 1963, Country Files, Box 117A, Iraq 3/63–5/63, JFKL.

88. INR Research Memo, RNA-34, August 7, 1963, Komer Files, Box 408, Arab Unity, 1961–1963, JFKL.

89. Cairo to State, no. 524, August 30, 1963, RG59 Central Files, 1963, Box 3943, POL 7 Visits and Meetings 2/1/63.

90. Baghdad to State, A-1083, May 21, 1963, RG59 Central Files, 1963, POL Iraq, Box 3943,
USNA.

91. Baghdad to State, A-118, "Statement by NDP on Arab Union," June 18, 1963, RG59 Central Files, 1963, Box 3943, POL 12 Political Parties 2/1/63.

92. Strong to Jernegan, November 29, 1963, RG59 NEA Lot File, 1958–1963, Box 7, Letters from the Field, 7/63–12/63.

93. Baghdad to State, no. 32, July 8, 1963, RG59 Central Files, 1963, Box 3621, PET 6 Companies 2/1/63.

94. Baghdad to State, no. 32, July 8, 1963.

95. Baghdad to State, no. 32, July 8, 1963.

96. Strong to Killgore, August 28, 1963, RG59 NEA Lot File, 1958–1963, Box 7, Letters from the Field, 7/63–12/63. On instructions to "avoid creating the impression that we sired the regime," see Brubeck to Bundy, February 13, 1963, *FRUS 1961–1963, 18*, 157.

97. Strong to Davies, September 30, 1963, RG59 NEA Lot File, 1958–1963, Box 7, Letters from the Field, 7/63–12/63.

98. Strong to Davies, September 30, 1963.

99. See Batatu, *The Old Social Classes*, 985–86.

100. Cairo to State, A-372, "Haikal Believes Baath Has Longer Life Expectancy Than Some Suppose," November 16, 1963, RG59 Central Files, 1963, Box 3943, POL 12 Political Parties 2/1/63.

101. Matthews, "International Federation of Petroleum Workers," 123–24.

102. Matthews, "International Federation of Petroleum Workers," 98.

103. Batatu quoted in Matthews, "International Federation of Petroleum Workers," 101.

104. Matthews, "International Federation of Petroleum Workers," 101.

105. Matthews, "International Federation of Petroleum Workers," 110.

106. Matthews, "International Federation of Petroleum Workers," 111.

107. Matthews, "International Federation of Petroleum Workers," 115.

108. Baghdad to State, A-402, "Comments on the Baath Party Manifesto," November 16, 1963, RG59 Central Files, 1963, Box 3943, POL 12 Political Parties 2/1/63.

109. Baghdad (Lakeland) to State, A-402, November 16, 1963.

110. Baghdad to State, no. 498, November 11, 1963, RG59 Central Files, 1963, Box 3943, POL 12 Political Parties 2/1/63.

111. Mufti, *Sovereign Creations*, 162–64; Batatu, *The Old Social Classes*, 1025–26.

112. State to Posts, CA-908, November 15, 1963, RG59 Central Files, 1963, Box 3943, POL 12 Political Parties 2/1/63. These events are detailed in INR Report, "Dissension Shakes the Baath in Iraq and Syria," November 13, 1963, Country Files, Box 117A, Iraq 9/63–11/63, JFKL; CIA to [classified], November 18, 1963, Country Files, Box 117A, Iraq 9/63–11/63, JFKL; Baghdad to State A-416, November 26, 1963, RG59 Central Files, 1963, Box 3943, POL 2–1 Joint Weeka Iraq 2/1/63.

113. Baghdad to State, A-444, "Status of the Baath Party in Iraq," December 3, 1963, RG59 Central Files, 1963, Box 3943, POL 12 Political Parties 2/1/63.

114. Baghdad to State, A-492, December 17, 1963, RG59 Central Files 1963, Box 3943, POL 12 Political Parties 2/1/63.

115. Baghdad to State, A-553, "National Guard Brutality," January 7, 1964, RG59 Central Files, 1964–1966, Box 2338, POL 12 Political Parties Iraq 1/1/64.

116. The underlining for emphasis appears in the original document. It appears to have been drawn by hand by the end reader at the State Department.

117. The modern word "apocalypse" comes from the Greek *apo* for "un" or "without" and *kalupsis* for "cover" or "mask." In this sense, an apocalypse refers to the removing of a cover or mask to reveal a truth hidden below or beneath.

118. Stone quoted in Max Holland, "After Thirty Years: Making Sense of the Assassination," *Reviews in American History* 22 (1994): 193.

119. This is how Johnson described US policy objectives in Vietnam at an August 1964 press conference. See Michael Hunt, *Lyndon Johnson's War: America's Cold War Crusade in Vietnam, 1945–1968* (New York: Hill and Wang, 2011), 85.

CHAPTER 6

1. On "social biography" as a method of analysis, see the introduction to Edmund Burke III and David Yaghoubian, eds., *Struggle and Survival in the Modern Middle East*, 2nd ed. (Berkeley: University of California Press, 2005).

2. Haseeb Oral History Interview, January 18, 2016.

3. Haseeb was also deeply influenced by the social democratic philosophy expressed in *Al-Hubz w'al-Karama (Bread and Dignity)*, a book published by Iraqi poet Yusuf Sayigh in 1960. Oral History Interview, January 2016.

4. Ekserdjian to IPC, April 8, 1963, IPC 135985.

5. Baghdad to State, A-996, "UAR-Iraq Presidential Council: Talib; Jadir; al-Hussain," June 9, 1964, RG59 Central Files, 1964–1966, Box 2340, POL 15–1 Head of State Executive Branch, Iraq 1/1/64.

6. Ghareeb, *Historical Dictionary of Iraq*, 245. Yahya's ancestry would have been Afghan if he was related to Brigadier Ahmad Muhmmad Yahya (of Mosul). On Ahmad Muhmmad Yahya, see Khadduri, *Republican 'Iraq*, 140.

7. Batatu, *The Old Social Classes*, 780, 1003.

8. Baghdad to State, A-495, December 1, 1964, RG59 Central Files, 1964–1966, Box 2340, POL 15–1 Head of State Executive Branch, Iraq 1/1/64.

9. Khadduri, *Republican 'Iraq*, 219.

10. PM's Broadcast of December 24, 1963, IPC 135986. On Egyptian-Iraqi cooperation on oil issues, see Haykal, 'Al-Ahram' Article on Oil, Voice of the Arabs, June 19, 1964, in Burdett, ed., *OPEC*, vol. 3, 365–67.

11. 'Adib al-Jadir, "Our Oil and the Policy of the Status Quo," *Al-Jumhurriyah*, January 22, 1964, IPC 135986.

12. Dalley to Ekserdjian, A/531, February 6, 1964, IPC 135986. In September 1962, Qasim issued a draft legislation forming the Iraq National Oil Company (INOC). See "Draft Law Establishing the INOC," September 29, 1962, IPC 135983.

13. Stewart to IPC, February 12, 1964. See also Dalley to Ekserdjian, A/531, February 6, 1964; Stewart to Dalley, A/532, February 10, 1964, IPC 135986.

14. CM Dalley, "Some Points on IPC's Position Regarding Negotiations," February 27, 1964, IPC 135987.

15. Stork, *Middle East Oil and the Energy Crisis*, 56–73.

16. Stewart to IPC, February 12, 1964, in IPC 135986.

17. Dietrich, *Oil Revolution*, 36.

18. UN General Assembly Resolution No. 626, December 21, 1952. For analysis, see Dietrich, *Oil Revolution*, 36–37.

19. Karl Marx, *Capital*, vol. 1, chap. 10, sec. 2, www.marxists.org/archive/marx/works/1867-c1/ch10.htm.

20. Penrose and Penrose, *Iraq*, 384.

21. Dietrich, *Oil Revolution*, 134–35.

22. Baha Abu-Laban, "The National Character in the Egyptian Revolution," *Journal of Developing Areas* 1, no. 2 (1967): 179–98; Patrick O'Brien, *The Revolution in Egypt's Economic System* (New York: Oxford University Press, 1966); Batatu, *The Old Social Classes*, 1036–37.

23. While Rouhani was moderate compared to al-Bazzaz, his mere association with OPEC was highly controversial in Iran. The shah forced him to back down against the companies in December 1963; Garavini, *Rise and Fall of OPEC*, 146–53.

24. US-UK Memcon, Washington, January 29, 1964, *FRUS, 1964–1968*, 34, 176.

25. Penrose and Penrose, *Iraq*, 385.

26. Jidda to State, April 12, 1964, *FRUS, 1964–1968*, 34, 178.

27. Penrose and Penrose, *Iraq*, 384.

28. Penrose and Penrose, *Iraq*, 385.

29. "Grossly Unjust: Wattari on Iraq's Rejection of Oil Companies' Offer," December 30, 1964; see also Tomkya (BFO) to Willcocks (BP), February 12, 1965, in Burdett, *OPEC*, vol. 3, 523–30, 605–6.

30. Dietrich, *Oil Revolution*, 116.

31. Dietrich, *Oil Revolution*, 119.

32. Dietrich, *Oil Revolution*, 120.

33. Dietrich, *Oil Revolution*, 121.

34. Dietrich, *Oil Revolution*, 118–23.

35. Batatu, *The Old Social Classes*, 1031; Penrose and Penrose, *Iraq*, 461–70.

36. Baghdad to State, A-71, "Estimate of Factors Iraqi Government Would Consider in Determining Whether or Not to Nationalize IPC," July 28, 1964, RG59, Central Files, 1964–1966, Box 1391, PET 6 Companies Iraq, 1/1/64.

37. Ekserdjian, "Wattari in Washington," March 20, 1964, IPC 135987; Memcon, Jernegan with Cornelius G. Willis, "General Exploration Co. of Ca. Interest in Iraq," March 18, 1964, RG59, Central Files, 1964–1966, Box 1391, PET 6 Companies Iraq, 1/1/64.

38. Baghdad to State, no. 831, April 4, 1964, RG59, Central Files, 1964–1966, Box 1391, PET 10 Resources, Oil Fields Iraq, 1/1/64.

39. Painter, *Oil and the American Century*, 176–79.

40. State to Baghdad, April 13, 1964, *FRUS, 1964–1968, 34*, 179.

41. Memcon, Harriman, Jernegan Lowenfeld with E. L. Steiniger (Sinclair), "Sinclair Interest in Iraqi Oil Concession," May 6, 1964, RG59, Central Files, 1964–1966, Box 1391, PET 10 Resources, Oil Fields Iraq, 1/1/64.

42. Memcon, Harriman, Lowenfeld, Ensor with Dean, "IPC Negotiations," July 2, 1964, RG59, Central Files, 1964–1966, Box 1391, PET 10 Resources, Oil Fields Iraq, 1/1/64.

43. Memcon, "Iraqi Oil Situation," September 23, 1964, *FRUS 1964–1968, 34*, 182.

44. "As an Oil Consultant, He's without Like or Equal," *New York Times*, July 27, 1969, and associated materials, Walter J. Levy Papers, American Heritage Center, University of Wyoming, Laramie.

45. Memcon, Levy with Ball et al., "Iraqi Oil Situation," October 5, 1964, RG59, Central Files, 1964–1966, Box 1391, PET 10 Resources, Oil Fields Iraq, 1/1/64.

46. Andreas Lowenfeld, "Memorandum for the Under Secretary," October 24, 1964, US Senate, *Multinational Corporations and US Foreign Policy*, 537–39.

47. Jernegan to Ball, October 23, 1964, RG59, Central Files, 1964–1966, Box 1391, PET 6 Companies Iraq, 1/1/64.

48. State Department Memcon with Exxon and Mobil, October 26, 1964, RG59, Central Files, 1964–66, Box: 1391, PET 6 Companies Iraq, 1/1/64.

49. Boyer to IPC Managers, May 19, 1964, IPC 135987; Memcon, Talbot, Ensor, Oliver, Blackiston with Moses (Mobil), Owen (ARAMCO), "IPC-GOI Negotiations," June 29, 1964, RG59, Central Files, 1964–1966, Box 1391, PET 10 Resources, Oil Fields

Iraq, 1/1/64; Moses to Grove, August 17, 1964, IPC 135897; Morris to Dalley, July 27, 1964, IPC 135987.

50. Garavini, *Rise and Fall of OPEC*, 111.

51. Maurice Vaisse, "Post-Suez France"; and Adam Watson, "The Aftermath of Suez: Consequences for French Decolonization," in Louis and Owen, *Suez 1956*, 335–40, 341–46.

52. Styan, *France and Iraq*, 48–58.

53. Styan, *France and Iraq*, 55–56. See also Garret Joseph Martin, *General de Gaulle's Cold War: Challenging American Hegemony, 1963–1968* (Oxford: Berghahn, 2013); Thomas J. McCormick, *America's Half-Century: United States Foreign Policy in the Cold War and After*, 2nd ed. (Baltimore: Johns Hopkins University Press, 1995), 130–32.

54. Styan, *France and Iraq*, 75.

55. BFO to Washington, February 1, 1965, in Burdett, *OPEC*, vol. 3, 592–93. See also Saul, "Masterly Inactivity," 770.

56. On CFP-IPC relations, see *The Times* (London), June 10, 1965, IPC 135991; Powell to HMG, "Middle East Oil," June 20, 1964, in Burdett, *OPEC*, vol. 3, 369–71. See also Saul, "Masterly Inactivity," 767–72.

57. "1965 Unsigned Agreements," September 25, 1967, IPC 161758. For analysis, see Stork, "Oil and the Penetration of Capitalism in Iraq," 185–86; Penrose and Penrose, *Iraq*, 387–89; Saul, "Masterly Inactivity as Brinksmanship," 770–72; Styan, *France and Iraq*, 79.

58. Letter to the Editor, *Arab Petroleum Review* (Baghdad), June 7, 1965, IPC 135991. See also IPC Digest, July 7–8, 1965; Cordai to Bird, July 18, 1965; IPC Press Extracts, August 9, 1965, IPC 135992.

59. Road to Managers, August 13, 1965, IPC 135992.

60. ['Abdullah al-Tariki] "Iraq and the Oil Companies," *al-Thawrah al-'Arabiyyah*, August 8, 1965, IPC 195992.

61. "Statement by the Tahreer Party Exposing the Danger of the Recent Oil Agreement" [n.d., ca. October 1, 1965], IPC 135992.

62. *Sarkat al-Kadehin* [*Cry of the Workers*], "What Is Happening behind the Scenes? More Oil Flows into Enemies' Bellies," December 1964, IPC 135989.

63. Penrose and Penrose, *Iraq*, 330.

64. Garavini, *Rise and Fall of OPEC*, 151.

CHAPTER 7

1. Dochuk, *Anointed with Oil*, 12.
2. Dochuk, *Anointed with Oil*, 13.
3. On ideal typical analysis as a methodology, see Richard Swedberg, "How to Use Max Weber's Ideal Type in Sociological Analysis," *Journal of Classical Sociology* 18, no. 3 (2018): 181–96. For a general critique of Weberian sociology, see Paul M. Sweezy, "Power Elite or Ruling Class?" in *C. Wright Mills and the Power Elite*, ed. William Domhoff and Hoyt B. Ballard (Boston: Beacon, 1968), 115–32.
4. For economic reports and statistics, see Baghdad to State, A-1048, June 2, 1965, RG59 Central Files, 1964–1966, Box 725, E2 Gen Reports and Stats Iraq 1/1/64; Baghdad to State, A-17, July 3, 1965, RG59 Central Files, 1964–1966, Box 725, E1 Gen Policy, Plans, Programs Iraq 1/1/64; Baghdad to State, A-119, August 3, 1965, RG59 Central Files, 1964–66, Box 725. For analyses see Batatu, *The Old Social Classes*, 1032–33; Penrose and Penrose, *Iraq*, 341–42, 460–68; Mufti, *Sovereign Creations*, 183–87; Stork, "Oil and the Penetration of Capitalism in Iraq," 184–85.
5. Tehran to State, January 20, 1966, *FRUS, 1964–1968, 21*, 179. See also State to Baghdad, October 26, 1965; Baghdad to State, October 30, 1965, *FRUS, 1964–1968, 21*, 176–77. On the Kurdish war see Jawad, *Iraq and the Kurdish Question*, 146–47, 177–80; Edgar O'Ballance, *The Kurdish Struggle 1920–94* (New York: St. Martin's Press, 1996), 65–76; McDowall, *Modern History of the Kurds*, 315–20.
6. Baghdad to State, A-980, "Thoughts on Past and Future Revolutions—Not a Policy Paper," May 15, 1965, RG59 Central Files, 1964–1966, Box 2339, POL 15 Government Iraq.
7. Baghdad to State, A-270, "New Iraqi Cabinet—Sept 6, 1965," September 11, 1965, RG59 Central Files, 1964–1966, Box 2339, POL 15 Government Iraq.
8. Baghdad to State, A-270, September 11, 1965. See also Penrose and Penrose, *Iraq*, 328–30; Batatu, *The Old Social Classes*, 1034.
9. Penrose and Penrose, *Iraq*, 329–46; Batatu, *The Old Social Classes*, 1064–65; Khadduri, *Republican 'Iraq*, 249–84; Ghareeb, *Historical Dictionary of Iraq*, 48.
10. Baghdad to State, A-737, "Status of Draft IPC Agreement," February 22, 1966, RG59 Central Files, 1964–1966, Box 2339, POL 15 GOV IRAQ; Bird to Managers, April 7, 1966, IPC 135993.
11. Penrose and Penrose, *Iraq*, 337; Khadduri, *Republican 'Iraq*, 263–66.
12. Jawad, *Iraq and the Kurdish Question*, 193–94.
13. State to Baghdad, CA-2030, April 15, 1966, RG59 Central Files, 1964–1966, Box 2339, POL 15 Gov Iraq; Khadduri, *Republican 'Iraq*, 264–66; Jawad, *Iraq and the*

Kurdish Question, 177–80; Penrose and Penrose, *Iraq*, 337–46; Batatu, *The Old Social Classes*, 1063.

14. See Memo, "Change of GOI," May 11, 1967; Baghdad to State, A-70, May 18, 1967, RG59 Central Files, 1967–1969, Box 2221, POL 15 Iraq 1/1/67. See also Jawad, *Iraq and the Kurdish Question*, 197–200.

15. Baghdad to State, A-737, "Status of Draft IPC Agreement," February 22, 1966.

16. Saul, "Masterly Inactivity as Brinkmanship," 773.

17. Styan, *France and Iraq*, 48–58.

18. NEDC Memo, "Iraq Negotiations," January 16, 1967, International Oil, Box 1, 37, John J. McCloy Papers, Amherst College, Amherst, MA [hereafter McCloy Papers 1:37].

19. Saul, "Masterly Inactivity as Brinkmanship," 774; Penrose and Penrose, *Iraq*, 390–94.

20. NEDC Memo, "Syria and Iraq: The Transit Dispute with Iraq Petroleum Co., LTD," January 24, 1967, McCloy Papers 1:37; "The Dispute between the Syrian Government and the IPC," in *Selected Documents of the International Petroleum Industry*, ed. Nameer Ali Jawdat (Organization of the Petroleum Exporting Countries, 1968), 385–86.

21. "Dispute between the Syrian Government and the IPC."

22. NEDC Memo, "Syria and Iraq," January 24, 1967.

23. On US attitudes toward 'Arif the elder, see Baghdad to State, May 17, 1966; Atherton to Hare, November 1, 1966; Draft Message from President Johnson to President 'Arif; Baghdad to State, November 30, 1966; Rostow to LBJ, January 21, 1967, *FRUS 1964–1968, 21*, 180, 185–88.

24. Atherton to Hare, November 1, 1966.

25. Atherton to Hare, November 1, 1966.

26. Handley to State, "Effect of IPC Pipeline Crisis on Economy of Iraq," January 10, 1967; Atherton to Davies, January 13, 1967; "IPC Crisis," January 16, 1967, RG59 NEA Lot Files, 1966–1972, Box 7, PET 6 IPC; Kingsolving to Davies, January 25, 1967; "IPC-Syrian Pipeline Agreement," March 8, 1967, RG59 NEA Lot Files, 1966–1972, Box 7, PET 6 IPC-Syria; Cairo to State, December 16, 1966, *FRUS, 1964–1968, 34*, 196.

27. See "IPC Crisis," January 16, 1967; Kingsolving to Davies, January 25, 1967; Damascus to State, January 25, 1967, *FRUS, 1964–1968, 34*, 201.

28. Baghdad to State, December 17, 1966, *FRUS, 1964–1968, 34*, 197.

29. On tensions between State and Interior, see Editorial Note, *FRUS, 1964–1968, 34*, 184; Yergin, *The Prize*, 410–12, 517–22, 536–40; Stephen J. Randall, *United States*

Foreign Oil Policy since World War I: For Profits and Security (Montreal: McGill-Queen's University Press, 2005), 272–80. On Interior's interest in developing the continental shelf as an alternative to reliance on unstable sources of supply, see Black, *The Global Interior*, 12, 166–70.

30. The phrase is borrowed from Ussama Makdisi, *Artillery of Heaven: American Missionaries and the Failed Conversion of the Middle East* (Ithaca, NY: Cornell University Press, 2009).

31. Yergin, *The Prize*, 410–12.

32. Valerie Richardson, "Obama Takes Credit for U.S. Oil-and-Gas Boom: 'That Was Me, People'," *Washington Times*, November 28, 2018.

33. Jay Hakes, *A Declaration of Energy Independence: How Freedom From Foreign Oil Can Improve National Security, Our Economy, and the Environment*, for example, would not be published until 2008 (New York: Wiley).

34. Dochuk, *Anointed with Oil*, 413, 441–44.

35. On Pickens's development of new technologies, see Yergin, *The Prize*, 709–11, 716–24.

36. On *Exodus* as popular cultural phenomenon, see Melanie McAlister, *Epic Encounters: Culture, Media, and U.S. Interests in the Middle East since 1945* (Berkeley: University of California Press, 2001), 159–78; Gershom Gorenberg, *The End of Days*, 55, 120–21; Boyer, *When Time Shall Be No More*, 141.

37. On Walvoord and Lindsey, see Gorenberg, *The End of Days*, 55, 120–21. On DTS financing, see Dochuk, *Anointed with Oil*, 487–88.

38. Gilles Kepel, *Jihad: The Trial of Political Islam*, trans. Anthony F. Robert (Cambridge, MA: Harvard University Press, 2003), chap. 3, "Petrodollar Islam."

39. Boyer, *When Time Shall Be No More*, 141.

40. Black, *The Global Interior*, 12, 166–70.

41. "Near East Oil: How Important Is It?" February 8, 1967, *FRUS, 1964–1968*, 21, 19.

42. On the concepts of "enlightened" and "Oriental" despotism, see Betty Behrens, "Enlightened Despotism," *Historical Journal* 18, no. 2 (1975): 401–8; H. M. Scott, "Whatever Happened to the Enlightened Despots?" *History* 68, no. 223 (1983): 245–57; Karl Wittfogel, *Oriental Despotism; A Comparative Study of Total Power* (New Haven, CT: Yale University Press, 1957).

43. On the Wise Men, see Walter Isaacson and Evan Thomas, *The Wise Men: Six Friends and the World They Made* (New York: Simon & Schuster, 1986).

44. See Olivia Sohns, "The Future Foretold: Lyndon Baines Johnson's Congressional Support for Israel," *Diplomacy & Statecraft* 28, no. 1 (2017): 60.

45. The final complaint against the British Crown in the US Declaration of Independence: "He has excited domestic Insurrections amongst us, and has endeavoured to bring on the Inhabitants of our Frontiers, the merciless Indian Savages, whose known Rule of Warfare, is an undistinguished Destruction, of all Ages, Sexes and Conditions."

46. Saunders to Rostow, May 16, 1967, *FRUS, 1964–1968*, 20.

47. On the centrality of manifest destiny in the Providential thought of LBJ with regard to Israel, see Sohns, "The Future Foretold," 63.

48. Handley to State, January 10, 1967.

49. "IPC-Syrian Pipeline Agreement," March 8, 1967; Handley to State, January 10, 1967.

50. "Dispute between the Syrian Government and the IPC," 385–86; "IPC-Syrian Pipeline Agreement," March 8, 1967; "Iraq Negotiations," McCloy Papers 1:37. See also Saul, "Masterly Inactivity as Brinksmanship," 774.

51. See Baghdad to State, no. 1913, "New Aref Cabinet," May 11, 1967; "Change of GOI," May 11, 1967; Baghdad to State, A-70, May 18, 1967, RG59 Central Files, 1967–1969, Box 2221, Folder POL 15 Iraq 1/1/67.

52. Tripoli to State, June 30, 1967; Tripoli to State, July 6, 1967; Editorial Note, *FRUS, 1964–1968, 34*, 253, 255, 263.

53. Dietrich, *Oil Revolution*, 142.

54. Oliver to Fried, May 23, 1967, *FRUS 1964–1968, 34*, 228.

55. Baghdad to State, June 6, 1967; Baghdad to State, June 8, 1967, *FRUS, 1964–1968*, 21, 194–95. Yahya quoted in Pawson to Managers, August 3, 1967, IPC 136000.

56. Baghdad to State, June 6, 1967, *FRUS, 1964–1968, 34*, 232.

57. Yamani quoted in White House Memcon, July 18, 1967, *FRUS, 1964–1968, 34*, 258.

58. Tripoli, Libya to State, June 30, 1967, *FRUS, 1964–1968, 34*, 253; Dietrich, *Oil Revolution*, 146.

59. Yamani quoted in Editorial Note, *FRUS, 1964–1968, 34*, 260.

60. Smallcom, August 3, 1967, IPC 161758.

61. Tripoli to State, June 30 and July 6, 1967, *FRUS, 1964–1968, 34*, 253, 255.

62. Editorial Note, *FRUS, 1964–1968, 34*, 263.

63. Yergin, *The Prize*, 454–58; Dietrich, *Oil Revolution*, 146–49. For an alternative interpretation, see M. S. Dajani and M. S. Daoudi, "The 1967 Oil Embargo Revisited," *Journal of Palestine Studies* 13, no. 2 (1984): 65–90; Dietrich, *Oil Revolution*, 166–70.

64. Haykal quoted in Robert McNamara, *Britain, Nasser and the Balance of Power in the Middle East, 1952–1977: From the Egyptian Revolution to the Six Day War* (London: Routledge, 2003), 270.

65. William B. Quandt, *Peace Process: American Diplomacy and the Arab-Israeli Conflict* (Berkeley: Universtity of California Press, 2001), 36–41; Joe Stork, "Review of Quandt *Peace Process*," *Middle East Journal* 48, no. 3 (1994): 553–56. Richard Parker, *The Politics of Miscalculation in the Middle East* (Bloomington: Indiana University Press, 1993), 3–122, 245–46.

66. On McCone's "Holy War views," see *IF Stone's Weekly*, November 7, 1960, www.ifstone.org/weekly/IFStonesWeekly-1960nov07.pdf.

67. Denton, *The Profiteers*, 48–49.

68. Denton, *The Profiteers*, 10.

69. Seymour Hersh, *The Samson Option: Israel's Nuclear Arsenal and American Foreign Policy* (New York: Random House, 1991), 72. Hersh's story in the *New York Times* was published on December 19, 1960.

70. Hersh, *The Samson Option*, 80.

71. Hersh, *The Samson Option*, 105; see also "Diplomacy under the Nuclear Shadow: Kennedy, Nasser, and Dimona," *Diplomatic History* (author and article forthcoming); Sohns, "The Future Foretold," 58; Avner Cohen, *Israel and the Bomb* (New York: Columbia University Press, 2003); Avner Cohen, *The Worst-Kept Secret: Israel's Bargain with the Bomb* (New York: Columbia University Press, 2012); Matteo Gerlini, "Waiting for Dimona: The United States and Israel's Development of Nuclear Capability," *Cold War History* 10, no. 2 (2010): 143–61.

72. Hersh, *The Samson Option*, 105–6; David M. Barrett, "Explaining the First Contested Senate Confirmation of a Director of Central Intelligence: John McCone, the Kennedy White House, the CIA and the Senate, 1962," *Intelligence and National Security* 31, no. 1 (January 2016): 74–87.

73. This paragraph represents a general interpretive synthesis of a feud between Kennedy and Johnson, from the perspective of Kennedy loyalists. See Richard N. Goodwin, *Remembering America: A Voice from the Sixties* (Open Road Media, Kindle edition), chap. 22; Arthur M. Schlesinger, Jr., *Robert F. Kennedy and His Times* (Boston: Houghton Mifflin, 1978). See also a 2013 psychological study that found that of the forty-two presidents up to George W. Bush, Lyndon Johnson scored the highest on the scales for "narcissistic personality disorder" and "grandiose narcissism." See Ashley L. Watts et al., "The Double-Edged Sword of Grandiose Narcissism: Implications for Successful and Unsuccessful Leadership among U.S. Presidents,"

Psychological Science 24, no. 12 (2013): 2379–89. For an LBJ counterperspective, see Robert A. Caro, *The Passage of Power: The Years of Lyndon Johnson IV* (New York: Knopf, 2012).

74. On Thanatos, or the psychological tendency toward repetitive self-sabotaging behaviors (or the "death drive," as Freud described it), see Maria Kli, "Eros and Thanatos: A Nondualistic Interpretation: The Dynamic of Drives in Personal and Civilizational Development from Freud to Marcuse," *Psychoanalytic Review* 105 (2018): 67–89.

75. Dochuk, *Anointed with Oil*, 423–27.

76. Robert Mann, *Daisy Petals and Mushroom Clouds: LBJ, Barry Goldwater, and the Ad That Changed American Politics* (Baton Rouge: Louisiana State University Press, 2011).

77. Joel Beinin, "The US-Israeli Alliance," in *A Critical Political Economy of the Middle East and North Africa*, ed. Joel Beinin, Bassam Haddad, and Sherene Seikaly (Stanford: Stanford University Press, 2021), 197–98; Jefferson Morley, *The Ghost: The Secret Life of CIA Spymaster James Jesus Angleton* (New York: St. Martin's, 2017), 176–81; Michael Holzman, *The CIA, and the Craft of Counterintelligence* (Amherst: University of Massachusetts Press, 2008), 162–69.

78. Hersh, *The Samson Option*, 119, 135, 143, 150–51.

79. Dochuk, *Anointed with Oil*, 437.

80. On the power of the Alamo myth to shape American historical consciousness, see Michel-Rolph Trouillot, *Power and the Production of History* (Boston: Beacon Press 1995), 1–2, 9–10.

81. On the bomb being made to be used, see Barton J. Bernstein, "The Atomic Bombings Reconsidered," *Foreign Affairs* 74, no. 1 (January/February 1995): 135–52.

82. McCone to LBJ, April [28,] 1965, *FRUS, 1964–1968*, 2, 234.

83. McCone Briefing, June 29, 1967, *FRUS, 1964–1968*, 34, 252.

84. To be clear, in my usage, Grandiose Strategy is to grand strategy as crackpot realism is to realism, and as military Keynesianism is to Keynesianism. That is to say, the latter of each is refracted through the lens of McCarthyism to produce the former.

85. Styan, *France and Iraq*, 59–67.

86. State to Berlin, June 19, 1967; Paris to State, June 27, 1967, *FRUS, 1964–1968*, 34, 246, 250.

87. Saul, "Masterly Inactivity as Brinksmanship," 772–73; Styan, *France and Iraq*, 82.

88. Saunders to Rostow, May 16, 1967, *FRUS, 1964–1968*, 21, 20.

89. Of the group's fifteen members, eight were military officers, two were from the CIA, four from the State Department, and one from the Department of the Interior. On Holmes's background, see Biographical Notes, Arlington National Cemetery, www.arlingtoncemetery.net/jcholmes.htm (accessed September 17, 2014).

90. Holmes Study, July 17, 1967, *FRUS 1964–1968*, 21, 22.

91. On Nasser as Saladin, see the 1963 Egyptian film *Al Nasser Salah Ad Din (Saladin the Victorious)*.

92. Bundy to LBJ, July 10, 1967, *FRUS 1964–1968*, 34, 256.

93. See also Memo, May 24, 1967; McCloy to Rusk, June 5, 1967, *FRUS 1964–1968*, 34, 229, 231.

94. Galpern, *Money, Oil, and Empire in the Middle East*, 269.

95. Dietrich, *Oil Revolution*, 170.

96. Simon Davis, "'A Bloody Unpleasant Meeting': The United States and Britain's Retreat from East of the Suez in the 1960s," *Diplomatic History* 34, no. 1 (2010): 230; Robert McNamara, "Britain, Nasser and the Outbreak of the Six-Day War," *Journal of Contemporary History* 35, no. 4 (2000): 619–39; Alan Dobson, "The Years of Transition: Anglo-American Relations 1961–1967," *Review of International Studies* 16 (1990): 239–58; Arieh Kochavi, "George Brown and British Policy toward Israel in the Aftermath of the Six-Day War," *Israel Studies* 22, no. 1 (2017): 1–23; W. Taylor Fain, *American Ascendance and British Retreat in the Persian Gulf Region* (New York: Palgrave Macmillan, 2008); Tore Tingvold Petersen, *The Decline of the Anglo-American Middle East 1961–1969: A Willing Retreat* (Brighton, UK: Sussex Academic Press, 2006).

97. Galpern, *Money, Oil, and Empire*, 264.

98. Davis, "'A Bloody Unpleasant Meeting,'" 230.

99. Bass to Davies, September 15, 1967; Bass to Davies, September 22, 1967; Houghton to Battle, "Iraq Oil Negotiations and Reported French Plans to Sell Arms," December 12, 1967, RG59 NEA Lot Files, 1966–72, Box 7, Folder PET 6 IPC, 4/1/67. See also Saul, "Masterly Inactivity as Brinksmanship," 775–76.

100. Memcon with Barnes (Mobil), "Iraq Oil," December 1, 1967, RG59 NEA Lot Files, 1966–72, Box 7, PET 6 IPC, 4/1/67; Bass to Files, "Resumption of Relations between Iraq and the UK," January 18, 1968, RG59 NEA Lot Files, 1966–72, Box 7, Memos w/in NEA 1968 2/3. See also Saul, "Masterly Inactivity as Brinksmanship," 775–77.

101. "Iraq Raises the Ante," November 1967, IPC 136001. For analysis of the agreement, see Styan, *France and Iraq*, 85–89; Paul Stevens, "Iraqi Oil Policy: 1961–1976,"

in *Iraq: The Contemporary State*, ed. Tim Niblock (London: Croom and Helm, 1982), 183–87; Saul, "Masterly Inactivity as Brinksmanship," 777.

102. "Sayid Jadir's Lecture on the Recent Oil Agreement," December 7, 1967; "The Greatest Expert in Oil Affairs in the Arab Homeland Says: Iraqi Oil Is Near Nationalization after the ERAP Agreement," *Al-Thawrah al-Arabiyyah, June 18, 1968*; "The Importance of Iraq's Oil Policy," *Al-Jumhurriyah*, June 18, 1968; Road to Jackli, June 19, 1968, IPC 136001–136002.

103. S. A. Skachkov to Jadir, December 24, 1967, Jawdat, *Selected Documents of the International Petroleum Industry*, 269–70.

104. Penrose and Penrose, *Iraq*, 396.

105. Notes on Small Committee Meeting Held on May 6, 1968, IPC 136002.

106. Jackli to Dalley, May 14, 1968, IPC 136002.

107. Bird, "The Prospects for Success of the Nationalisation of Iraq Oil," 16 May 1968, IPC 136002.

CHAPTER 8

1. "Coup-proof" is a term that originated among intelligence professionals. See James T. Quinlivan, "Coup-Proofing: Its Practice and Consequences in the Middle East," *International Security* 24, no. 2 (Fall 1999): 131–65. A basic model of how to coup-proof a state was put forward by CIA officer James Eichelberger in the early 1950s in a paper titled "Power Problems of a Revolutionary Government." CIA officer Miles Copeland claimed that the CIA's provision of this study to Nasser allowed Nasser to develop a coup-proof regime in Egypt. The study is included as an appendix to Copeland's *The Game of Nations: The Amorality of Power Politics* (New York: Simon & Schuster, 1969), 284–300. On the CIA's provision of the study to Nasser in the early 1960s, see Copeland, *The Game of Nations*, 85–89. Surely, Copeland exaggerated Nasser's dependence on this study.

2. This resume is drawn mainly from Angela Penrose, *No Ordinary Woman: The Life of Edith Penrose* (Oxford: Oxford University Press, 2017). Penrose is the daughter-in-law of Edith and Pen. See also C. Levallois, "Why Were Biological Analogies in Economics 'A Bad Thing'? Edith Penrose's Battles against Social Darwinism and McCarthyism," *Science in Context* 24, no. 4 (2011): 465–85; Perran Penrose and Christos Pitelis, "Edith Elura Tilton Penrose: Life, Contribution, and Influence," *Contributions to Political Economy* 18 (1999): 3–22.

3. Pen's exploits were celebrated in *The Razzberry Press*, an annual scandal sheet (published on pink newsprint) by Berkeley sophomores. Edith's name was

included in the publication's *Who's Scrooey* list for 1936. See Penrose, *No Ordinary Woman*, 20.

4. Penrose, *No Ordinary Woman*, 28.

5. Penrose, *No Ordinary Woman*, 35–40.

6. Penrose, *No Ordinary Woman*, 47.

7. Penrose, *No Ordinary Woman*, 147.

8. Pen recounted his experiences negotiating with the Soviets (and defended White against charges of spying for the Soviets) in his book *Economic Planning for the Peace* (Princeton, NJ: Princeton University Press, 1953). On his defense of White, see 291. On his aversion to McCarthy-era background checks, see Penrose, *No Ordinary Woman*, 126, 133–40. On White as a Soviet spy, see Benn Steil, *The Battle of Bretton Woods: John Maynard Keynes, Harry Dexter White, and the Making of the New World Order* (Princeton, NJ: Princeton University Press, 2013).

9. This is how she framed her research interests in her private letters to Machlup. See Penrose, *No Ordinary Woman*, 172.

10. Penrose, *No Ordinary Woman*, 164.

11. *Iraq: International Relations and National Development* is a masterpiece of political economy. Few works match its depth of research, clarity of analysis, and lucidity of writing. Although Pen was originally commissioned to write the book, Edith eventually stepped in to bring the project to completion and appears to have done the lion's share of the work. See Penrose, *No Ordinary Woman*, 229–31.

12. Penrose and Penrose, *Iraq*, author bio.

13. Penrose, *No Ordinary Woman*, 215–20.

14. Beirut to State, A-1116, June 17, 1968, RG59 NEA Lot Files, 1966–1972, Box 2, Pol 7 Visits and Meetings Iraq 1968.

15. Note on Position of IPC/BPC in Iraq, March 22, 1968, IPC 136002.

16. Note on Position of IPC/BPC in Iraq, March 22, 1968, IPC 136002.

17. Note on Position of IPC/BPC in Iraq, March 22, 1968, IPC 136002.

18. IPC Memo, April 4, 1968, IPC 161758; Jackli to Dalley, April 3, 1968, IPC 136002.

19. Jackli to Dalley, April 3, 1968, IPC 136002.

20. "Britain Threatens to Occupy the Oil Areas in Iraq," *Nahar,* April 10, 1968, IPC 136002.

21. Jackli to Dalley, May 7, 1968, IPC 136002.

22. Jackli to Dalley, May 7, 1968, IPC 136002.

23. "The Greatest Expert in Oil Affairs in the Arab Homeland Says: Iraqi Oil Is Near Nationalization after the ERAP Agreement," *Al Thawrah*, June 18, 1968, IPC 136002.

24. Penrose and Penrose, *Iraq*, 400.

25. On Booz, Allen & Hamilton links to the CIA, see Wilford, *America's Great Game*, 150.

26. Memcon with Mr. Ahlgren, July 16, 1968, RG59 NEA Lot Files, 1967–1972, Box 2, Memcons Misc 1968, 2/4.

27. DIR no. 541, "Iraqi Ba'thists Take over Government; Get Feet Wet Again," July 17, 1968, RG59 Central Files, 1967–69, Box 2221, POL 15 Iraq 1/1/67.

28. Beirut to State, no. 11235, "Iraq," July 22, 1968, RG59 Central Files, 1967–1969, Box 2221, POL 15 Iraq 1/1/67.

29. Foster to Rostow, July 17, 1968, *FRUS, 1964–1968*, 21, 199.

30. Beirut to State, no. 11235, "Iraq," July 22, 1968, RG59 Central Files, 1967–1969, Box 2221, POL 15 Iraq 1/1/67.

31. Beirut to State, A-1199, "The New Iraqi Regime," July 22, 1968, RG59 Central Files, 1967–1969, POL 15 Iraq 1/1/67.

32. Foster to Rostow, July 22, 1968, *FRUS, 1964–1968*, 21, 200.

33. Foster to Rostow, July 22, 1968.

34. Beirut to State, A-1209, "Iraq—No Immediate Change in Oil Policy Foreseen as a Result of July 17 Coup," July 24, 1968; DIR, Intel Note 618, "Right-Wing Ba'thi Takeover in Iraq: Near Term Outlook," August 6, 1968, RG59 Central Files, 1967–1969, Box 2221, POL 15 Iraq 1/1/67.

35. Wiley to Battle, "Proposed Memo to Mr. Rostow Regarding Relations with Iraq," Action Memorandum, August 1, 1968, RG59 NEA Lot Files, 1966–1972, Box 4, Memos within NEA 1968, 2/3.

36. Memcon with Iskandar, "Petroleum: Iraq—Dilemma of Iraqi Oil Technocrats," August 6, 1968, RG59 NEA Lot Files, 1966–1972, Box 2, Memcons Misc 1968 2/4; Jackli to Dalley, July 23, 1968, IPC 136003.

37. Memcon with Barnes, "Iraqi Desires to Negotiate with IPC," July 30, 1968, RG59 NEA Lot Files, 1966–1972, Box 1, Memcons NEA/ARN 1968.

38. On Anderson's "crypto-diplomacy" in the 1950s, see Wilford, *America's Great Game*, 206. For claims that Anderson was working with or for the CIA, see Aburish, *Saddam Hussein*, 73–74; Hamid Bayati, *Saddam Husayn wa al-Mu'amar al-Kubra: 'Asrar Inqilab 17 Tammuz 1968 fi al-'Iraq fi al-Watha'iq al-Sirriyah al-Amrikiyah* [Saddam Hussein and the great conspiracy: Secrets of the 17 July 1968 coup in Iraq in American secret documents] (London: Mu'assasat al-Rafid, 2000), 24.

39. On Anderson's sulfur interests see Beirut Embassy memcon with Mobil Reps, "Petroleum: Iraq, Tapline, Medreco Refinery, Iranian/Saudi Relations,"

February 8, 1968, RG59 NEA Lot Files, 1966–1972, Box 2, Memcons Misc 1968, 2/4; Brussels to State, September 27, 1968, RG59 NEA Lot Files, 1966–1972, Box 1, Correspondence with misc. posts 1968.

40. Wiley to Battle, "Proposed Memo to Mr. Rostow Regarding Relations with Iraq," Action Memorandum, August 1, 1968, RG59 NEA Lot Files, 1966–1972, Box 4, Memos within NEA 1968, 2/3.

41. Avneri reports that McNamara, along with Ford Foundation president McGeorge Bundy and World Bank president John J. McCloy, were all "present in the Middle East during the coup," and suggests that all three may have supported the coup in some way. Unfortunately, Avneri provides very little detail or documentation regarding the purpose of their visit to the region. See Avneri, "Iraqi Coups," 654–55. On McCloy's 1967 travels in the Middle East and views on the conflict, see Bird, *The Chairman*, 604–5; McCloy to Rusk, June 5, 1967, *FRUS 1964–1968*, 34, 231.

42. Wiley to Battle, "Recent Political Developments in Iraq," July 31, 1968, RG59 NEA Lot Files, 1966–1972, Box 2, POL 2–2 Political Summaries and Reports; Wiley to Battle, "New Iraq Cabinet," August 1, 1968, RG59 NEA Lot Files, 1966–1972, Box 4, Memos w/in NEA 1968 2/3; DIR, Intel Note 618, "Right-Wing Ba'thi Takeover in Iraq: Near Term Outlook," August 6, 1968.

43. RCC communiqué no. 27, July 31, 1968, quoted in Batatu, *The Old Social Classes*, 1076–77n13.

44. Haseeb Oral History Interview, January 18, 2016; Tehran to State, A-872, October 19, 1968, RG59 Central Files, 1967–1969, Box 2221, Pol 15 Iraq 1/1/67.

45. Jackli to CMD, July 31, 1968, IPC 136003.

46. Tehran to State, A-872, October 19, 1968, RG59, Central Files, 1967–1969, Box 2221, Pol 15 Iraq 1/1/67.

47. Haseeb Oral History Interview, January 18, 2016. See also Mohammad Hadid's memoirs: "Muthakkarati—The Struggle for Democracy in Iraq," title trans. Haseeb (London: Al-Saqi, 2006), 485–90. Many thanks to Dr. Haseeb for sharing the chapter on 1968.

48. Haseeb Oral History Interview, January 18, 2016.

49. DIR, Intel Note 618, "Right-Wing Ba'thi Takeover in Iraq," August 6, 1968.

50. Bass to Files, "Dr. Rashid al-Rifai, Iraq Oil Minister," August 15, 1968; RG59 NEA Lot Files, 1966–72, Box 4, Memos w/in NEA 1968 2/3; Memcon with Iskandar, "Petroleum: Iraq—Dilemma of Iraqi Oil Technocrats," August 6, 1968.

51. "Right-Wing Ba'thi Takeover in Iraq: Near Term Outlook," August 6, 1968. See also Memcon with Wolgast (Esso), "Developments in Iraq," August 27, 1968, RG

59 NEA Lot Files, 1966–1972, Box 1, Memcons NEA/ARN 1968; Briefing Paper for US-UK Talks, "Iraqi Internal Situation," September 6, 1968, RG59 NEA Lot Files, 1966–1972, Box 1, Briefing papers 1968; Memcon with Moses (Mobil), "Petroleum: Iraq—Review of Current Developments," October 4, 1968, RG 59 NEA Lot Files, 1966–72, Box 1, Memcons Misc 1968 1/4.

52. Dalley to IPC Groups, August 26, 1968, IPC 161758.

53. Memcon with Iskandar "Petroleum: Iraq—Dilemma of Iraqi Oil Technocrats," August 6, 1968.

54. Memcon with McDonald (Mobil), "Iraqi Government Feeler to US," November 1, 1968, RG59 NEA Lot Files, 1966–72, Box 3, Memos within NEA 1968.

55. State to Jidda, October 15, 1968, *FRUS 1964–1968*, 34, 264.

56. Akins quoted on August 9, in State to Jidda, October 15, 1968, *FRUS 1964–1968*, 34, 264n3.

57. Jidda to State, October 29, 1968, *FRUS 1964–1968*, 34, 225.

58. Penrose and Penrose, *Iraq*, 455; Batatu, *The Old Social Classes*, 1099; State to Beirut, November 18, 1968; Brussels to State 10651 (Confidential 282), "Further Details on Al-Hani Assassination," November 19, 1968, RG59 Central Files, 1967–1969, Box 2221, POL 15 1/1/67.

59. Beirut to State, no. 11235, "Iraq," July 22, 1968, 100–0523; Brussels to State, no. 7592, November 20, 1968, RG59 Central Files, 1967–69, Box 2221, POL 15 Iraq 1/1/67.

60. Barzan al-Tikriti, "Diary of Barzan al-Tikriti: The Sweet Years and the Bitter Years (Part I)," January 2001, 11, in US Department of Defense, Conflict Records Research Center, File SH-MISC-D-001–919. Many thanks to Khair el-Din Haseeb for sharing this record.

61. Seeyle to Davies, November 15, 1968, "Tikriti Overture"; RG59 NEA Lot Files, 1966–1972, Box 3, Memos within NEA 1968.

62. Brussels to State, no. 10651, November 19, 1968.

63. Critchfield, "Discussion of Holmes Study," August 16, 1967, *FRUS 1964–1968*, 21, 24; "U.S. Policy in the Middle East," July 19, 1968, *FRUS 1964–1968*, 21, 30.

64. Salim Yaqub, "The Weight of Conquest: Henry Kissinger and the Arab-Israeli Conflict," in *Nixon in the World: American Foreign Relations, 1969–1977*, ed. Fredrik Logevall and Andrew Preston (New York: Oxford University Press: 2008), 227.

65. On Christian Zionism, see Geoffrey P. Levin, "Culture, Communities, and Early U.S.-Israel Relations," *H-Diplo*, Essay 160, July 18, 2018.

66. See CIA, Directorate of Intelligence, Office of Political Research, "Iraq under Baath Rule, 1968–1976," November 1976, CIA Records Search Tool, USNA II (CREST).

67. RNA-6, February 14, 1969, *FRUS, 1969–1976, E-4*, 251; CIA, "Iraq under Baath Rule, 1968–1976."

68. Dalley, "General Summary of Political Situation and Company/Government Relations," February 20, 1969, RG59, NEA Lot Files, 1966–1972, Box 5, PET 2 General Reports and Statistics 1969; Untitled Report, June 8, 1969, IPC 136004.

69. Untitled Report, June 8, 1969, IPC 136004.

70. Record of Some Conversations in Iraq, July 18–30, August 8, 1969, IPC 136004.

71. Dalley to IPC, October 28, 1969, IPC 136004.

72. British Embassy Baghdad to Foreign and Commonwealth Office, "Saddam Hussein," December 20, 1969, www.gwu.edu/~nsarchiv/NSAEBB/NSAEBB107/index.htm.

73. I have edited the grammar and tense in this quotation to enhance its readability. See Hahn to Dalley, November 19, 1969, IPC 136005.

74. Discussions in Baghdad, December 2–6, 1969, IPC 136005.

75. Discussions in Baghdad, December 2–6, 1969, IPC 136005.

76. See Small Committee, January 9, 1970, IPC 136005; Biographical Note: Saadoun Hammadi, February 7, 1973, IPC 1616430; Ba'th Party (Iraq), "Economic Independence," *Revolutionary Iraq, 1968–1973*, 89–100, IPC 136019; Hammadi, *Mudhakirat wa 'Ara'a fi Sha'aun al-Naft;* Smolansky and Smolansky, *The USSR and Iraq*.

77. Paris to State, August 8, 1970; Moscow to State, August 13, 1970; CIA Cable, August 24, 1970, *FRUS, 1969–1976, E-4*, 272, 274, 275; Penrose and Penrose, *Iraq*, 427–28; Smolansky and Smolansky, *The USSR and Iraq*, 47; Michael E. Brown, "The Nationalization of the Iraq Petroleum Company," *International Journal of Middle Eastern Studies* 10, no. 1 (1979): 107–24.

CHAPTER 9

1. Batatu, *The Old Social Classes*, 1084; Farouk-Sluglett and Sluglett, *Iraq since 1958*, 121; Penrose and Penrose, *Iraq*, 360; Efraim Karsh and Inari Rautsi, *Saddam Hussein: A Political Biography* (New York: Grove Press, 2007), 127.

2. Farouk-Sluglett and Sluglett, *Iraq since 1958*, 110.

3. Farouk-Sluglett and Sluglett, *Iraq since 1958*, 120.

4. Joseph Sassoon, *Saddam Hussein's Ba'th Party: Inside an Authoritarian Regime* (Cambridge: Cambridge University Press, 2011), 163–65.

5. Farouk-Sluglett and Sluglett, *Iraq since 1958*, 113; Batatu, *The Old Social Classes*, 1098.

6. Farouk-Sluglett and Sluglett, *Iraq since 1958*, 117.

7. Farouk-Sluglett and Sluglett, *Iraq since 1958*, 122–23; Batatu, *The Old Social Classes*, 1099; Beirut to State, A-1469, "Bakr's First Hundred Days," November 21, 1968, RG59 Central Files, 1967–69, Box 2221, POL 15 Iraq 1/1/67.

8. Farouk-Sluglett and Sluglett, *Iraq since 1958*, 113; Batatu, *The Old Social Classes*, 1098.

9. Farouk-Sluglett and Sluglett, *Iraq since 1958*, 123, 126–29.

10. Alvandi, *Nixon, Kissinger, and the Shah*, 71–72.

11. Alvandi, *Nixon, Kissinger, and the Shah*, 73–75; Farouk-Sluglett and Sluglett, *Iraq since 1958*, 122, 129; Batatu, *The Old Social Classes*, 1093; Tripp, *A History of Iraq*, 199; McDowell, *A Modern History of the Kurds*, 326–330; Jawad, *Iraq and the Kurdish Question 1958–1970*.

12. Alvandi, *Nixon, Kissinger, and the Shah*, 76.

13. Farouk-Sluglett and Sluglett, *Iraq since 1958*, 129.

14. Farouk-Sluglett and Sluglett, *Iraq since 1958*, 131; Tripp, *A History of Iraq*, 199; McDowell, *A Modern History of the Kurds*, 327–29.

15. Sassoon, *Saddam Hussein's Ba'th Party*, 10–11.

16. Farouk-Sluglett and Sluglett, *Iraq since 1958*, 133.

17. Farouk-Sluglett and Sluglett, *Iraq since 1958*, 135.

18. Beirut to State, October 16, 1970, *FRUS, 1969–1976*, E–4, 278.

19. Beirut to State, October 16, 1970, n. 1.

20. The metaphor is borrowed, if slightly modified, from Farouk-Sluglett and Sluglett, *Iraq since 1958*, 149.

21. Farouk-Sluglett and Sluglett, *Iraq since 1958*, 138–39.

22. Stockwell to IPC, September 22, 1971, IPC 136011.

23. See Small Committee, January 9, 1970, IPC 136005; Biographical Note: Saadoun Hammadi, February 7, 1973, IPC 1616430; Ba'th Party (Iraq), "Economic Independence," *Revolutionary Iraq, 1968–1973: Political Report Adopted by the Eighth Regional Congress of the Arab Ba'th Socialist Party-Iraq*, 89–100, IPC 136019; Sa'dun Hammadi, *Mudhakirat wa 'Ara'a fi Sha'aun al-Naft* [Memories and opinions concerning oil] (Beirut: Dar al-Tali'a lil Tab'iyah wa al-Nashr, 1980); Oles M. Smolansky and Bettie M. Smolansky, *The USSR and Iraq: The Soviet Quest for Influence* (Durham, NC: Duke University Press, 1991).

24. Smolansky and Smolansky, *The USSR and Iraq*, 53.

25. Smolansky and Smolansky describe this as another case of "a client-state influencing the behavior of the patron." *The USSR and Iraq*, 61–62; Penrose and Penrose, *Iraq*, 433–34.

26. Elliot to Kissinger, April 13, 1972, *FRUS, 1969–1976, E-4*, 305.

27. Farouk-Sluglett and Sluglett, *Iraq since 1958*, 147.

28. Vienna to State, no. 3757, "OPEC Support Iraq vis-à-vis IPC Oil Production Drop," May 31, 1972, RG59 Central Files, 1970–1973, Box 1484, PET 3 OPEC 5/1/72.

29. See Hammadi to IPC, MPC, BPC, May 18, 1972; Macpherson to IPC, May 23, 1972; Milne to Stockwell, May 24, 1972, IPC 136014.

30. "Some Implications of Iraq's Oil Nationalization," June 1972, *FRUS, 1969–1976, E-4*, 311. See also Katz to Armstrong, June 5, 1972; State to London, Paris, Amsterdam, June 9, 1972, *FRUS, 1969–1976, E-4*, 312, 314; Seeyle to Sisco, "Essential Elements of IPC Nationalization Action," June 13, 1972, RG59 NEA Lot Files, 1966–72, Box 13, PET 2 Petroleum General Reports and Stats IRAQ 1972.

31. See Jungers (ARAMCO) to Ensor (Mobil), circulated by Ensor at SmallCom, June 6, 1972, IPC 136014.

32. Tehran to State, no. 3378, "Iran's Reaction to IPC Nationalization," June 6, 1972; Tehran to State, A-125, "Iran and the Iraqi Nationalization," July 24, 1972; Vienna to State, A-482, "OPEC: Iran, Iraq, and Participation Problems," July 8, 1972, RG59 Central Files, 1970–1973, Box 1484, Box 1484, PET 3 OPEC 5/1/72.

33. On the "unruly National Assembly," see Metelski to Jungers to Macpherson, June 8, 1972, IPC 136014. On Saudi Arabia's commitment to the "Arab cause," see Vienna to State, A-482, "OPEC: Iran, Iraq, and Participation Problems," July 8, 1972, R959 Central Files, 1970–1973, Box 1484, PET 3 OPEC 5/1/72.

34. Amouzegar quoted in Tehran to State, no. 3320, "Iranian Attitude toward Iraq-IPC Dispute," June 2, 1972, R959 Central Files, 1970–1973, Box 1484, PET 3 OPEC 5/1/72.

35. Tehran to State, no. 3378, "Iran's Reaction to IPC Nationalization," June 7, 1972, 1484: PET 3 OPEC 5/1/72; Cairo to State, no. 1669, "IPC Nationalization," June 7, 1972, RG59, Central Files, 1970–1973, Box 2382, POL IRAQ-Yemen 7/26/71.

36. Moscow to State, no. 5409, "Iraqi Foreign Minister Received by Kosygin," June 7, 1972, RG59 Central Files, 1970–1973, Box 2382, POL IRAQ-Yemen 7/26/71.

37. De Lilliac–Saddam Meeting, June 19, 1972, IPC 136015; "Iraq Oil Shipments Agreed with France," *Financial Times*, February 6, 1973; Meeting Exxon Board Room, New York, February 12, 1973, IPC 136016; CFP to Editor, *Sunday Telegraph*, April 3, 1973, IPC 136017.

38. Brussels to Baghdad, no. 32/B-92, "Oil Contract with Brazilian Company," August 8, 1972; Brown to Atherton, "Iraqi Oil: Latest Developments," June 29, 1972, RG59 NEA Lot Files, 1966–1972, Box 13, PET 2 Petroleum General Reports and Stats IRAQ 1972; Aide Memoire, February 26, 1973, IPC 136017; CIA, Directorate of Intelligence, Office of Political Research, "Iraq under Baath Rule, 1968–1976," November 1976, CREST.

39. London to State, no. 5326, "Iraq Oil: FCO View of IPC Nationalization," June 8, 1972; see also London to State, no. 5671, June 22, 1972, RG59 Central Files, 1970–1973, Box 1485, PET6 1/1/70; Memcon with British officials, "British Concern about Possible Break-down in OPEC-Oil Company Negotiations," March 9, 1972, RG59 Central Files, 1970–1973, Box 1484, PET 3 OPEC 2/18/72.

40. Danner and Jan Joost De Liefde to Stockwell, March 3, 1973, IPC 136017.

41. Korn to Sisco, "Summary of Terms of the IPC/Iraqi Package Settlement," April 5, 1973, RG59, NEA Lot Files, 1973–1975, Box 1, PET-6 IPC, Iraq 1973.

42. Korn to Sisco, "Summary of Terms of the IPC/Iraqi Package Settlement," April 5, 1973, RG59, NEA Lot Files, 1973–1975, Box 1, PET-6 IPC, Iraq 1973.

43. IPC Press Release, March 1, 1973; Bakr's BBC Radio Address, February 28, 1973, IPC 136017.

44. On oil and the October War, see Stork, *Middle East Oil and the Energy Crisis*, 210–56; Penrose and Penrose, *Iraq*, 502–11; Yergin, *The Prize*, 606–9; Abbas Alnasrawi, *Arab Nationalism, Oil and the Political Economy of Dependency* (New York: Greenwood Press, 1991), 89–108; Mitchell, *Carbon Democracy*, 173–99; Vitalis, *Oilcraft*, 57–82.

45. Penrose and Penrose, *Iraq*, 509.

46. Penrose and Penrose, *Iraq*, 509.

47. Marr, *The Modern History of Iraq*, 161, 443–48.

48. Marr, *The Modern History of Iraq*, 161.

49. Marr, *The Modern History of Iraq*, 164.

50. Marr, *The Modern History of Iraq*, 312.

51. Marr, *The Modern History of Iraq*, 164.

52. Marr, *The Modern History of Iraq*, 311.

53. Marr, *The Modern History of Iraq*, 166–67.

54. Alvandi, *Nixon, Kissinger, and the Shah*, 55, 81.

55. This is a central point in Ben Offiler, *US Foreign Policy and the Modernization of Iran: Kennedy, Johnson, Nixon, and the Shah*, (Hampshire, UK: Palgrave Macmillan, 2015).

56. Alvandi, *Nixon, Kissinger, and the Shah*, 39.

57. Alvandi, *Nixon, Kissinger, and the Shah*, 42.

58. On the fear of penetration, see Frank Costigliola "'Unceasing Pressure for Penetration': Gender, Pathology, and Emotion in George Kennan's Formation of the Cold War," *Journal of American History* 83, no. 4 (1997): 1309–39; Gary K. Wolfe, "Dr. Strangelove, Red Alert, and Patterns of Paranoia in the 1950's," *Journal of Popular Film* 5 (1976): 57–67; Scarlett Higgins, "Purity of Essence in the Cold War: Dr. Strangelove, Paranoia, and Bodily Boundaries," *Textual Practice* 32, no. 5 (2018): 799–820.

59. Alvandi, *Nixon, Kissinger, and the Shah*, 54.

60. Memcon Nixon, Kissinger, and Shah, *FRUS, 1969–1976*, E-4, 200n1; Alvandi, *Nixon, Kissinger, and the Shah*, 81.

61. Flanigan to Kissinger, January 10, 1970, Robert E. Lester (Project Coordinator), Richard M. Nixon National Security Files, 1969–1974, Middle East (Bethesda: University Publications of America, 2002), microform reel 9 [hereafter RMNMF 9]; Tore T. Petersen, *Richard Nixon, Great Britain and the Anglo-American Alignment in the Persian Gulf and Arabian Peninsula: Making Allies Out of Clients* (Brighton, UK: Sussex Academic Press, 2009), 82–83, 92–93.

62. Hoskinson to Saunders, October 17, 1969, RMNMF 9.

63. Adelman, "Politics, Economics, and World Oil," *American Economic Review* 64, no. 2 (1974): 62.

64. Saunders to Kissinger, July 14, 1972, *FRUS, 1969–1976*, E-4, 212.

65. Alvandi, *Nixon, Kissinger, and the Shah*, 52

66. Helms to Kissinger, February 14, 1973, RMNMF 10.

67. Saunders to Scowcroft, February 5, 1973, RMNMF 10.

68. Saunders to Kissinger, July 14, 1972.

69. Klare, *American Arms Supermarket*, 13–14, 33; Mitchell, *Carbon Democracy*, 186–87.

70. Andrew Scott Cooper, *The Oil Kings: How the U.S., Iran, and Saudi Arabia Changed the Balance of Power in the Middle East* (New York: Simon & Schuster, 2011), 71.

71. Kissinger to Rogers and Laird, July 25, 1972, *FRUS, 1969–1976*, E-4, 214.

72. Tehran to State, December 21, 1973, RMNMF 11; Petersen, *Richard Nixon, Great Britain and the Anglo-American Alignment*, 92–96.

73. RNAS-10, May 31, 1972, *FRUS, 1969–1976*, E-4, 310.

74. RNAS-10, May 31, 1972.

75. Alvandi, *Nixon, Kissinger, and the Shah*, 91.

76. Kissinger Memorandum, *FRUS, 1969–1976*, E-4, 322; Gibson, *Sold Out?*, 181.

77. Tehran to State, December 27, 1972, *FRUS, 1969–1976*, E-4, 241.

78. Farouk-Sluglett and Sluglett, *Iraq since 1958*, 159; Alvandi, *Nixon, Kissinger, and the Shah*, 81–87; Gibson, *Sold Out?*, 141–42.

79. Alvandi, *Nixon, Kissinger, and the Shah*, 99.

80. Farouk-Sluglett and Sluglett, *Iraq since 1958*, 160.

81. Marr, *The Modern History of Iraq*, 168–70; Tripp, *A History of Iraq*, 215; Barry Rubin, "United States–Iraq Relations: A Spring Thaw?," in Niblock, *Iraq*, 109–24.

82. Farouk-Sluglett and Sluglett, *Iraq since 1958*, 170; Alvandi, *Nixon, Kissinger, and the Shah*, 113; Gibson, *Sold Out?*, 187

83. Alvandi, *Nixon, Kissinger, and the Shah*, 111.

84. Tripp, *A History of Iraq*, 212–13;

85. Tripp, *A History of Iraq*, 214; Farouk-Sluglett and Sluglett, *Iraq since 1958*, 187–90.

86. Marr, *The Modern History of Iraq*, 166.

87. As an important exception, Ussama Makdisi describes Haseeb as the surviving embodiment of the broad secular and democratic "ecumenical" project that emerged in the latter phases of the Ottoman Empire. See *Age of Coexistence*, 213.

88. Mark Bowden, "Tales of the Tyrant," *The Atlantic,* May 2002. Emphasis added.

89. NEA Memo, Iraqi Royal Visit, September 23, 1952. Many thanks to Osamah Khalil for sharing this document.

90. As with all of the records analyzed in this book, my interpretation of this document's meaning draws on the methodology described in Costigliola, "Reading for Meaning: Theory, Language, and Metaphor."

91. Stephanson argues that essential to the eschatology of manifest destiny was the notion that the "Anglo-Saxon" race had been chosen by God to enact His plan in a Promised Land. So long as that race chose (and reaffirmed this choice on a daily basis) to live in accordance with His divine covenant, they could have faith that "He will lead them to a predetermined spot of land, clear it of enemies, and allow His people a future of endless milk and honey." Stephanson, *Manifest Destiny*, 5–7.

92. This is to say that progressive developmentalist policy advisers (such as Davies) saw in many Third World elites educable pupils in a unilineal process of modernization. That vision of modernization was based on a highly idealized, indeed mythologized, account of American political and economic development during

the nineteenth century. In this sense, the Iraqis who toured the United States in 1952 were not unlike the cadets from the Carlisle School for Indians who marched in Theodore Roosevelt's presidential inaugural parade in 1905. By contrast, those same progressive developmentalist advisers saw Communists in the Third World (and beyond) as the moral equivalents of the "merciless Indian savages" who Jefferson complained of in the *Declaration of Independence* (see chapter 7, note 44), and who participated in the Ghost Dance Movement of the 1890s. On Roosevelt's inaugural, see Jesse Rhodes, "Indians on the Inaugural March," *Smithsonian Magazine*, January 2009, www.smithsonianmag.com/history/indians-on-the-inaugural-march-46032118/.

On the various ways in which twentieth-century Americans imagined the Indigenous past and its relationship to the present, see Philip J. Deloria, *Indians in Unexpected Places* (Lawrence: University Press of Kansas, 2004). On the origins of this cosmology of noble and ignoble savagery, see Jill Lepore, *The Name of War: King Philip's War and the Origins of American Identity* (New York: Vintage, 1999).

93. Qur'an, xlix.13, in Fred Halliday, "'Orientalism' and Its Critics," *British Journal of Middle Eastern Studies* 20, no. 2 (1993): 163.

94. Telcon between Kissinger and Glafkos Clerides, August 19, 1974, *FRUS 1969–1976*, 30, 139.

95. See Mitchell, *Carbon Democracy*.

96. Mitchell suggests what this would entail by invoking efforts of the Iraqi environmental organization Save the Rivers. See Mitchell, "Ten Propositions about Oil," 84.

Index

'Abd al-Ilah, Prince, 16, 18, 43, 222
'Abd Allah, 10, 11, 12
Abdoh, Djalal, 143
Aburish, Said K.: *Saddam Hussein: The Politics of Revenge*, 113
'Aflaq, 'Aflaq, 47
AGIP (Azienda Generali Italiana Petroli), 76
Ahali Group, 69, 70
Ahlgren, Lloyd, 194–95
Ahmad, Taha Shaikh al-, 109, *111*
Akins, James: diplomatic career, 116–17, 164; education of, 86, 116; reports on situation in Iraq, 100–101, 106, 117, 164–65, 199
Alcock, Robert, 1, 234n5
Algerian War of Independence, 156
Algiers Agreement (1975), 220
Aliwiyah Rest House, 191
Allen, Roger, 99–100
Allende, Salvador, 56

American Federation of Labor–Congress of Industrial Organizations (AFLCIO), 131
Amin, Ahmad, 118
'Ammash, Salih Mahdi, 108, 119, 205–6, 208, 209
Amory, Robert, 247n45
Amouzegar, Jamshid, 211
Anderson, Robert: conspiracy of, 187, 196–97; Eisenhower and, 82; foreign policy, 73–74; private investments of, 45
Angleton, James Jesus, 178
Anglo-Iranian Oil Company, 150
Arabian American Oil Company (Aramco), 20, 35
Arab independence movement, 10–11
Arab-Israeli diplomacy, 73
Arab-Israeli June War: Arab oil embargo and, 175–76; de Gaulle and, 180; impact on regional oil policy,

Arab-Israeli June War (*continued*)
175, 176–77; occupation of Palestine, 175; outbreak of, 161, 175
Arab League, 67
Arab nationalism, 99–100, 104
Arab Oil Congress, 67, 68, 70
Arab oil embargo, 179–80, 185
Arab Petroleum Conference in Beirut, 79–80
Arbenz, Jacobo, 38, 111
'Arif, 'Abd al-Salam: 14 July Revolution and, 29; al-Bazzaz and, 166; alliance with Yahya and the Nasserists, 163–64, 165; arrest of, 48; conservatism of, 164; death of, 48, 166; dictatorship of, 174; foreign policy of, 122, 174, 185; military supporters of, 128, 163; November 1963 coup, 140; oil policy, 168; photographs of, *47*, *136*; political views of, 166; promotion of pan-Arab unity, 47; Qasim and, 46–48; release from prison, 91; removal from power, 48, 197; trial of, 57; US official's view of, 168–69
Awqati, Jalal al-, 108

Baghdad, Iraq: al-Rasheed Street, *65*; financial district, *149*; US embassy in, *112*
Baghdad Oil Company, 158
Baghdad Oil Conference, 79, 175
Baghdad Pact, 25, 41, 43, 102, 107
Bakr, Ahmad Hasan al-: consolidation of power, 195, 197, 201, 206, 207–8; Haseeb and, 139, 197–98; Hussein and, 206; as leader of Ba'th party, 187; murder of Nasir al-Hani, 200; nationalization policy, 198, 205; November 1963 coup d'état and, 132; persecution of Iraqi Jews, 201; political career of, 119, 141; release of Nasserists, 203; support of Palestine, 208
Ball, George, 151, 152, 154
Bandung Charter, 141, 143
Bandung Conference, 66
Barzani, Mustafa: demands for Kurdish autonomy, 125, 126; escape to Iran, 220; foreign affairs, 207, 218, 219; political settlement with Ba'thist regime, 207; power shift, 217–18; rebellion against Qasim, 101, 102
Bashkin, Orit, 7
Basrah Petroleum Company (BPC), 210, 212, 213
Batatu, Hanna, 108
Batista, Fulgencio, 87
Bayati, Jamil Sabri, 127
Bazzaz, 'Abd al- Rahman al-: conflict with al-'Uqayli, 166; negotiation with IPC, 146; oil policy, 145, 147; opposition to, 167; pan-Arab nationalism of, 145; peace agreement with Kurds, 166–67; Penrose and, 191; political views of, 166
Ba'thist regime in Iraq: authoritarian nature of, 129–30, 137, 201, 220–21; commitment to pan-Arabic unity, 131; Communists and, 206, 219; credibility of, 130; domestic infrastructure projects, 213–14; foreign affairs of, 122, 208, 209, 213, 215; KDP

INDEX   297

and, 206–7; Kurdish insurgency and, 219–20; land reforms of, 208–9; leading figures of, 205; military budget, 220; oil policy, 137, 198, 211–12, 213–14; political alliances of, 206–7, 208, 209–10; political stability of, 130, 198, 220; popular support of, 135; promotion of Iraqi nationalism, 207–8; socialist rhetoric of, 122, 213; struggle for power within, 205; support of Palestinian guerillas, 208; US relations with, 125, 126, 130, 137, 201

Baʻthist revolution of 1963, 113–14, 117–18

Baʻth party: al-Bark leadership of, 187; anti-Communist campaign, 110, 115; atrocities of, 110, 112–13, 133; CIA support of, 53–54, 96–97, 110–11; coup against Qasim's government, 106, 108, 119; disorganization of, 132–33; formation of, 24, 99; Iraqi branch of, 24; Kurdish uprising and, 126–27; military wing, 133; Nasser and, 91, 128; opposition to, 127–29; pan-Arabism and, 46, 48, 122, 128, 207–8; Sixth National Congress of, 131–32; split within, 130–31, 132; in Syria and Lebanon, 116

Bechtel, Steven, 177
Bechtel, Warren A., 2
Bechtel-McCone Corporation, 2, 177
Bell, Gertrude, 12
Bella, Ahmed Ben, *136*
Ben-Gurion, David, 26
Bennsky, George, 157

Bird, Richard, 124
Bissell, Richard, 42
Black, Megan, 254n31
"Black September," 208
Bowman, Isiah, 190
Bridgeman, Maurice, 79
British Petroleum Company (BP): formation of, 13; government investment in, 13–14; IPC consortium and, 103–4, 123, 143; Iran's nationalization of, 20–21; meeting with al-Tikriti, 198–99; oil reserves, 155
Brown, George, 184
Bruce, David A., 41
Bruce-Lovett Report, 40–41, 246n45
Bundy, McGeorge, 88, 94, 97, 183, 285n41
Burns, Eugene, 1
Buscetta, Tommaso, 78

Cairo Charter, 128
Cairo Conference (April 1921), 12
Cairo Oil Summit of 1959, 143
Callahan, Art, 116
Carabia, Jose, 1
Caro, Robert, 82
Castro, Fidel, 87, 96
Center for Arab Unity Studies, 220
Central Intelligence Agency (CIA): Baʻth's relations with, 53–54, 96–97, 110–11, 116; conspiracy against Qasim, 110–11, 114–16, 225; contingency planning, 97; covert operations, 33, 39–41, 42–43, 56–58, 87, 100, 133–34, 161; creation of, 31, 32; "Dark Sorcerer" of, 56; Kubark

Central Intelligence Agency (*continued*)
torture program, 266n29; perception of Iraqi oil industry, 210–11; poisoned handkerchief operation, 56, 57, 58–59, 60, 61, 62; Project Clean Up, 54–55, 61; Senate investigation of, 56; Special National Intelligence Estimate, 54; tasks of, 32–33
Chamoun, Camille, 28, 44
Chase National Bank, 122–23
Church, Frank, 55, 56, 57
Churchill, Winston, 12, 13
Citino, Nathan, 57
Cleveland, Grover, 34
Cold War: Middle East politics and, 24–25; oil boom and, 19
Colley, George, Jr., 1, 2
Communist Party of Iraq (CPI): 14 Ramadan Revolution and, 108; Baʿthist regime and, 110, 115, 206, 207, 209–10; economic agenda of, 204–5; emergence of, 23; influence of, 61, 62; militia of, 48; opposition to British imperialism, 24; Qasim's regime and, 60, 61–62; UAR and, 48; Wattari Agreement and, 159–60
Compagnie Françoise des Pétroles (CFP), 14, 155, 157, 158, 185, 211
Consolidated Steel Corporation, 2, 177
Copeland, Miles, 42, 55, 61, 62, 119
Copeland & Eichelberger consultancy firm, 55
coup-proof regimes, 220, 282n1
"crackpot realism," 38, 248n69, 249n78, 280n84
Critchfield, James, 54, 96–97, 113

Dallas Theological Seminary (DTS), 171
Davies, Rodger: assassination of, 223; career of, 99, 100; on Iraqi royal visit to the US, 222–24; language training of, 99; meeting with Roger Allen, 99; Melbourne's letter to, 116; views of the Baʿth, 99–100
Dayan, Moshe, 26
Dean, Arthur, 151
Denhardt, David Burton, 188
Deutsche Bank, 13
Dewey, Thomas, 34, 36
Dietrich, Christopher, 6, 144
Dochuk, Darren, 162, 163
Dulles, Allen: career of, 33–34, 36, 37, 38, 42; covert methods of, 37–38; foreign policy of, 30, 46; Komer and, 88; response to the Iraqi coup, 43, 46; view on Nasser, 41, 42, 51
Dulles, John Foster: anti-Communism of, 37, 45–46, 73; criticism of, 46; foreign policy of, 30–31, 36, 37, 44; illness and death of, 46, 51; Komer and, 88; meeting with Eden, 26, 27; as partner at Sullivan & Cromwell, 34, 36, 38; personality of, 45; political career of, 36–37, 72; response to Iraqi coup, 44; Suez crisis and, 26, 27; view on Nasser, 41, 51
Duroc-Danner, Jean, 158

Eden, Anthony, 26, 27
Egypt: anti-Baʿthist propaganda campaign, 129; Aswan Dam project, 25; ban of Communist Party, 42; Free Officers' coup, 24; Israel's invasion

of, 27; Kuwait crisis and, 89, 90; political regime, 282n1; Soviet arms deal with, 25; US aid to, 105; Yemen revolution and, 105

Eichelberger, James, 55, 61, 62, 119, 282n1

Eisenhower, Dwight D.: defense budget, 120; Dulles brothers and, 37–38; election of, 37; farewell address of, 87; foreign policy of, 9, 25, 30–31, 38, 63, 83, 85, 87; formation of OPEC and, 81, 82; oil quotas, 45; political appointments of, 73; pro-Nasser policy, 50, 51; public image of, 37; response to Iraqi coup, 46; review of intelligence activities, 39; Suez crisis and, 27

Eisenhower Doctrine, 27–28, 30, 41–42, 48–49, 88

ENI (Ente Nazionale Idocarburi), 76

Entreprise de Recherche et d'Activités Pétrolières (ERAP), 180, 185

European Economic Community, 167

Exxon: Ba'th Party and, 121–22; international company memorandum, 167; Iraqi-IPC settlement and, 123, 212; oil prices reduction, 78–79; oil reserves of, 155; OPEC and, 80; partnership with IPC, 34, 103; Soviet oil problem and, 77; State Department meeting with, 154

Faisal, King of Saudi Arabia, 104, 106, 144, 216

Faisal II, King of Iraq, 222, 223

Falle, Sam, 80, 81

Fanon, Frantz, 156

Faysal I, King of Iraq. *See* Hashemi, Faysal ibn Husayn al-

Faysal II, King of Iraq, 2, 16

Federal Trade Commission (FTC): *The International Petroleum Cartel* report of, 71–72

Fifth Arab Petroleum Conference, 147

Forrestal, James V.: career of, 35; creation of CIA and, 32, 36; illness and death of, 36, 46, 245n26; legacy of, 58; political views of, 34–35, 58, 215; removal from office, 35–36; views on national security, 32–33, 34

Foster, John Watson, 34

France: Algeria crisis, 156; foreign policy of, 17; mandate regime, 10; political development of, 156; struggle against US hegemony, 183; in World War II, 17

Franz Ferdinand, Archduke of Austria, 14

French-Indochina War (1946–54), 25, 156

Gallman, Waldemar J., 29, 49

Gaulle, Charles de: European Economic Community project, 167; foreign policy of, 156–57, 180; new constitution of, 156; political ambitions of, 155

Gehlen Organization, 54

Ghulam, Husayn, 193–94

Gibson, Bryan, 235n23

Goldwater, Barry, 178

Goodwin, Richard, 103

Gottlieb, Sidney, 56–57, 58, 59, 60, 266n29
Gray, Gordon, 247n45
Greene, Graham: *The Quiet American*, 38–39
Grobba, Fritz, 17
Grumman Corporation, 217
Gulbenkian, Calouste, 13

Hadid, Muhammad, 69–70
Hahn, Cocky, 202
Hall, Harry, 102
Hammadi, Sa'dun, 202–3, 210
Hani, Nasr al-, 197, 200, 201
Harriman, W. Averell, 150–51
Harrison, Geofffrey, 145
Haseeb, Khair el-Din: al-Bakr and, 197; civil service of, 138; education of, 138–39; exile to Lebanon, 220; imprisonment of, 197–98, 221; interrogation of, 198; IPC negotiations and, 124, 186; member of INOC board, 185, 191; ministerial post, 139–40; *The National Income of Iraq, 1953–1961*, 138; nationalization program, 147–48, 192–93; oil policy, 139–40; Penrose on, 191–92; photograph of, *140, 148*; political activism of, 139; release from jail, 203; return to power, 175; social biography of, 137–38; travel across Iraq, 139
Hashemi, Faysal ibn Husayn al- (Faysal I, King of Iraq), 10–11, 12, 16, 22
Hashemi, Ghazi ibn Husayn al-, 16
Hashemi, Husayn al-, 10
Hashemite Monarchy, 10, 18, 29

Hasqail, Sassoon, 14–15
Hassouna, Abdel Khalek, 66
Hawadith al- (Incidents) (weekly newspaper), 198
Hayek, Friedrich, 189
Haykal, Muhammad Hasanayn, 53, 130
Helms, Richard, 218
Henderson, Loy, 247n45
Hendryx, Frank, 69, 70, 92
Herridge, Geofffrey, 123, 124
Herter, Christian, 49, 63, 177
Hillenkoetter, Roscoe H., 32, 33
Hitti, Philip K., 99
Hogan, Michael J., 31
Holmes, Julius C., 182–83, 200, 201
Hopkins, Johns, 190
Husayn, King of Jordan, 28, 110, 130
Husayni, al-Hajj Amin al-, 17
Husri, Sati' al-, 21, 22
Hussein, Saddam: al-Bakr's coup and, 195; interrogation of Haseeb, 198; Kurdish insurgency and, 219–20; March Manifesto negotiations, 207; oil policy, 205, 211, 212; personality of, 201–2, 221; political opponents of, 207; Qasim assassination plot, 53; rise to power, 201, 204, 209; role in Ba'th Party, 206; visit to Moscow, 203, 209; visit to Paris, 211

Ibn Saud, King of Saudi Arabia, 28, 67, 144
Ibrahim, 'Abd al-Fattah, 22–23, 69, 107
Interim Report: Alleged Assassination Plots Involving Foreign Leaders, 56
International Court of Justice (ICJ), 143

INDEX   301

International Petroleum Cartel, The (report), 72
International Petroleum Company of Peru, 103
Iran: assistance to Iraqi Kurdish rebels, 102, 207; international embargo against, 20–21; Mossadegh's government, 65–66; oil industry, 21, 65, 86, 92, 143, 160; Saudi Arabia and, 216; taxation policy, 65; US relations with, 214–16, 217
Iraq: 14 Ramadan Revolution, 108–9; 1958 coup d'état, 28–29; al-Bakr's regime, 195, 196, 197; Arab-Israeli war and, 175–76; arms deal, 120–21; British colonial order, 4, 9, 11–12, 16, 17, 22, 225; China's relations with, 208; Communist threat, 54; decolonization of, 9; economic development, *xvii*, 15, 164, 169; education system of, 21–22; Eisenhower Doctrine and, 28; end of old regime, 28–29; fate of oil sovereignty, 160–61; food shortages, 17; France's relations with, 192; Free Officers' Revolution, 1–2, 8, 9, 24, 30, 42–43, 147; German influence in, 13, 17; Golden Square colonels, 16, 17; international aid to, 192; Israel's relations with, 175; Kurdish uprising, 101–2, 126–27; labor movement, 131; League of Nations and, 16; mandate period, 4, 16; National Front, 28; November 1963 coup d'état, 119, 120, 125; opposition public square, 22; political regime, 174–75, 204–5; "Rashid 'Ali coup," 17–18; religious groups, 11; Revolution of 1920, 12; second Yahya government, 185–86, 187; Soviet relations with, 60, 192, 213, 215; state-building class, 4; Syria-IPC crisis and, 172; territorial claims, 89; during World War II, 17–18. *See also* US-Iraqi relations
Iraqi Communist Party. *See* Communist Party of Iraq (CPI)
Iraqi Company for Oil Operations, 210
Iraqi Development Board, 21
Iraqi national identity, 7, 47–48, 101, 107–8, 204–5, 226
Iraqi oil industry: American oil companies and, 78, 149, 150; British control of, 3–4; map of operations, *xvi, xvii*; nationalization of, 4, 5; oil supplies, 12–13; OPEC and, 145–48; revenue, 21, 120–21, 168
Iraq-IPC negotiations, 101–2, 123–25, 150–55, 157, 193, 196, 202, 210–12
Iraqi-Soviet Treaty of Friendship and Cooperation (1972), 213, 215
Iraq National Oil Company (INOC): al-Nayif government and, 196; board of, 185; ERAP agreement with, 194; establishment of, 135, 142, 187; IPC joint venture with, 158; state control of, 187
Iraq Petroleum Company (IPC): America's involvement in, 5, 34, 222–23; British influence of, 5, 123; business model of, 146; concession agreement, 15–16; factional split in, 155; foreign threat to, 152; formation of, 3–4, 14; Iraqi government and,

Iraq Petroleum Company (*continued*) 15–16, 146, 174, 192–94, 197, 206; Law 11 and, 142–43, 153–54; Law 80 and, 86, 93, 143, 153–54; management practices, 7; nationalization efforts, 3, 90, 92, 137, 148, 163, 186, 205, 209, 225; North Rumaila operations, 185; ownership structure of, 155; production cut, 210; profit-sharing, 21; prospects of, 192; subsidiary companies of, 210; Talib's agreement with, 167; Tikriti Overture and, 201–2. *See also* Iraq-IPC negotiations

Israel: aid to Kurdish rebels, 102, 207; nuclear program, 177–78; sovereignty over Old Jerusalem, 176; territorial expansionism, 170, 171, 194; US support for, 170, 176, 178–79

Israeli Mossad, 178

Italy: energy market, 76; import of Soviet oil, 77; in World War II, 17

Jackli, Rudi, 193–94

Jadir, Adib al-: announcement of Law 11, 142; control of INOC, 187; diplomacy of, 158–59, 160, 175–76, 185; exile in Switzerland, 220; imprisonment of, 221; ministerial post, 142; oil policy, 142–43, 193; resignation of, 158; as "Small Committee" advisor, 124, 137, 139–40

Jadirs, Adib al-, 227

Jakarta Method, 112, 137, 225

Jawad, Hashim, 62, 63

Jawad, Hazim, 119–20

Jernegan, John D., 50, 63, 93, 94, 97–98, 152

Johnson, Louis, 35

Johnson, Lyndon B.: "Daisy Ad," 178; foreign policy of, 134, 173–74, 178–79, 182, 183, 201; oil and gas industry and, 103; personality disorder of, 279n73; political career of, 74; political psychology of, 178; rejection of the Tikriti Overture, 199; relations with JFK, 279n73; religious views of, 173; vice presidential nominee, 82–83

Kassem, Abd al-Karim, 53, 91

Kaylani, Rashid 'Ali al-, x, 17–18, 23, 49–50, 53, 57, 91

Kaylani, Yusuf al-, 191

Kennan, George, 33, 36, 71, 215

Kennedy, Bobby, 103, 126, 178

Kennedy, John F.: assassination of, 133; oil and gas industry and, 103; popularity of, 87–88; presidential nomination, 82; relations with Lyndon Johnson, 279n73

Kennedy administration: covert operations, 96, 111; defense spending, 120; economic policy, 120; foreign policy, 85–86, 89–90; Iraq policy, 84, 106, 123, 127; Israeli nuclear program and, 177–78; Kurdish policy, 126; Nasser and, 106; oil policy, 105; vision for the Middle East affairs, 104

Kerr, Malcolm, 60

Kesey, Ken, 57

Khrushchev, Nikita, *136*

Kirkuk oil field, 210
Kissinger, Henry, 201, 214–15, 216, 218
Knabenshue, Paul, 18
Komer, Robert: CIA career of, 88–89, 99; concern over Soviet influence, 98, 126, 127; influence within Kennedy administration, 104–5; memo on Ba'thist regime, 100, 118–19, 120; response to Law 80, 93, 94, 95; on security of world's energy, 86–87; support of Nasser, 89, 105; Vietnam mission, 88
Kosygin, Alexi, 209
Kubba, Salih, 197
Kurdish Democratic Party (KDP), 125, 206–7
Kurdish rebels: Algiers Agreement, 220; demand for oil profit sharing, 125–26; genocide against, 127; international aid to, 102, 127, 207, 217, 218–20; Iran's policy toward, 219–20; negotiation of peace agreement, 164, 166–67; political demands of, 125–26; Qasim's regime and, 101; war with Ba'thist regime, 219–20
Kuwait: British protectorate, 89; oil policy, 211; territorial claims, 89–90

Lakeland, William: association with the Ba'th, 114–15, 116; career of, 86, 95, 113; connection with CIA, 113–14; Nasser and, 53; personality of, 115; reports on situation in Iraq, 95–96, 100, 101, 129–30, 132, 133; "Who's Who" of Iraqi Communists list, 115, 117

Lansdale, Edward, 39
Lansing, Robert, 34
Lattimore, Owen, 189
Law 11, 142–43, 153–54, 158
Law 69, 210
Law 80: British opposition to, 185, 202; claims of oil reserves under, 101; Iraq-IPC dispute over, 121, 123–24, 140, 150, 153–54, 155, 158; practical application of, 142, 187; promulgation of, 86, 92–93
Law 97, 185
Lawrence, T. E., 10
League of Nations, 11, 16
Levy, Walter J., 152–54
Lindenmuth, William, 103, 123
Lindsey, Hal, 171
Little, Arthur D., 80, 159
Loudon, John, 79
Lovett, Robert, 40, 41
Lowenfeld, Andreas, 153, 154
Luce, Henry, 36

Machlup, Frtiz, 189
Macmillan, Harold, 89
Mahdawi, Fadl 'Abbas al-, 48, 57–58, 62, 109, *111*
Mansfield, Mike, 39
March Manifesto, 207, 208
Marshall, George C., 31–32, 58, 71
Marshall Plan, 19–20, 24, 25, 31–32
Marx, Karl, 108
Mattei, Enrico: anti-imperialism of, 155–56; death of, 77–78; energy policy, 76–77
Matthews, Weldon C., 111, 118, 131

Maysalun, Battle of, 11, 12
McCarthy, Joseph, 39, 189
Mccarthyism, 189
McClintock, Robert, 252n125
McCloy, John J., 285n41
McCone, John A.: analysis of Arab oil-producing states, 179–81; background and education of, 177; career of, 2–3, 177, 178; criticism of, 182; on Israeli nuclear program, 177–78; resignation of, 179; view of nuclear warfare, 179
McGhee, George, 105
McHale, William, 78, 113
McNamara, Robert, 120, 197, 285n41
Mehmet Ali Pasha, Governor of Egypt, 89
Melbourne, Roy, 98–99, 103–4, 108, 109, 116, 117
Mesa Petroleum, 170
Middle East: despotic regimes of, 172; oil production, 5, 19, 73–74; Soviet influence in, 86; US policy in, 30–31, 38, 45, 85, 86, 87
Middle East Development Company, 14
Middle Eastern Supply Centre, 17
Mills, C. Wright, 38, 39, 248n69, 249n78
Mitchell, Richard P., 53
Mitchell, Timothy, 5
Mobil, 34, 77, 121–22, 154, 198–99
Mohammad Reza Pahlavi, Shah of Iran, 214–16, 217
Monroe, Paul, 22
Monroe Committee, 22
Morizet, Jacques, 157
Moses, Henry, 155

Mossadegh, Mohammad: conspiracy against, 38; death of, 184; oil policy of, 65–66, 86, 92; removal from power, 87, 99, 143
multicultural populism, 107
Murphy, Audie, 39
mutually assured destruction (MAD) theory, 179

Na'ib, al-Sayyid al-, 226
Nasser, Gamal Abdel: Algerian rebels and, 26; anti-Communist policy of, 42, 48, 50; Ba'thist coup in Syria and, 128; British relations with, 49; Czech arms deal with, 41; diplomacy of, 66; economic reform of, 144; Iraqi Ba'thist government and, 122, 128; at Luxor, *136*; pan-Arab socialism of, 122; as regional leader, 27; rise to power, 24; US relations with, 30, 31, 48–50, 87, 89
National Guard auxiliary force, 131, 132
National Intelligence Estimate (NIE), 81, 83, 95
National Oil Company, 93, 108
National Security Council (NSC): analysis of US oil policy, 75; Ba'thist regime in Iraq and, 195–96; block of the FTC case, 75; establishment of, 31; expansion of the CIA mandate, 33; policy directive 5820/1, 49, 50; "Preventing a Communist Takeover in Iraq" study, 52–53, 55; pro-Nasser policy, 50–51; "Special Inter-Agency Working Group," 52

natural resource sovereignty principle, 6
Nayif, 'Abd al-Razzaq al-, 195, 196, 197
Newman, Paul, 171
Ngo, Dinh Diem, 87
Nixon, Richard, 200–201, 214, 217, 218
Nixon Doctrine, 215
Nuclear Power Group, 177

Obeidi, Lutfi al-, 196
oil companies: American foreign policy and, 7–8, 121–22; business interests of, 83; independent internationals, 45, 150; as international actors, 4–5; Iraqi government and, 152–53; multinational, 19; ownership links between, 19; revenue, 172
oil industry: competition in, 6; concession agreements, 6–7, 14, 15, 66–67, 69; overproduction, 5–6, 44–45; postwar boom, 19–20; religious element of, 162–63; royalties, 144, 145–46; taxation, 144
oil prices: rise of, 212–13
OMEGA Project, 41
OPEC (Organization of Petroleum Exporting Countries): collective bargaining agreement, 146; "Declaratory Statement of Petroleum Policy in Member Countries," 194; formation of, 61, 79, 85, 135; influence of, 145; internal division, 146–47; Iraq's role in, 145–48, 211; leadership, 146; rise of oil prices, 212–13; royalty policy, 144; US oil policy and, 81–82, 148; world oil politics and, 80–81

"open door" principle, 14
Ottoman Empire, *xv*, 10

Palestine: after World War I, status of, 10, 35; Arab-Jewish conflict in, 16
Palestinian Liberation Organization, 208
pan-Arabism, 48, 91
Parra, Francisco, 135, 147
Paul, Norman, 54, 247n45
Penrose, Edith: on American 'way of life,' 189; career of, 188; departure from Beirut, 194; expulsion from Iraq, 190–91; Lattimore's legal defense and, 189; life in Baltimore, 189; marriages, 188, 189; move to Geneva, 188–89; teaching position, 190; view of Haseeb, 191–92; works of, 190
Penrose, Ernest F., 188, 189, 191, 194
Penrose affair, 188–92
People's Resistance Force (PRF), 48
Pérez Alfonzo, Juan Pablo, 79
Petrodollar Christianity, 171
Philby, Kim, 45
Phleger, Herman, 247n45
Pickens, T. Boone, 170
plausible deniability doctrine, 33
Polk, William, 86, 89, 105
populist democracy, 23, 70
Prebisch, Raúl, 6
President's Board of Consultants on Foreign Intelligence Activities, 39
"Preventing a Communist Takeover in Iraq" study, 52, 55

Prophets of American Energy Independence, 170, 173
Protestant ethic, 163
Proudfit, Arthur, 79

Qasim, 'Abd al-Karim: American policy toward, 52; 'Arif and, 46–48; arrest of Ba'th leaders, 108; assassination attempt, 53, 62, 119; Ba'ath-CIA conspiracy against, 62, 113–16, 225; Communists and, 48, 54, 55, 60–61, 62; conception of Iraqi national identity, 101, 107, 108; coup against, 49–50, 52, 55, 102, 106, 108–9, 110; creation of Oil Ministry, 70; development projects, 64–65; foreign affairs, 47, 60–61, 63, 83–84, 89, 97–98, 128, 225; Kurdish minority policy, 62, 101; land reform program, 63–64; murder of, 109, 111, 135; oil policy, 44, 78, 86, 90–93, 97, 102, 106; opposition to, 97; photograph of, 47; reorganization of Iraq's institutional structure, 69; rise to power, 29; support base of, 100–101; system of moral values, 91–92; view of American imperialism, 106–7
Qasr Nihaiya prison, 198
"Quit Mesopotamia" campaign, 12

Rashid 'Ali. *See* Kaylani, Rashid 'Ali al-
Rayburn, Sam, 74
Razzaq, 'Arif 'Abd al-, 166
Rifai, Rashid al-, 198
Rikabi, Fu'ad al-, 47
Robertson, Edward V., 32

Rockefeller, David, 103
Rogers, William, 74
Roosevelt, Archie, 42
Roosevelt, Kermit ("Kim"), 42, 58, 106, 143, 247n45, 252n125
Rostow, Walt W., 88, 89, 196
Rouhani, Fuad, 145, 146, 160
Rountree, William, 50–51
Royal Dutch Shell (Shell), 13
Rumaila oil field, 158, 167, 185, 210
Rusk, Dean, 95, 149, 150, 151, 184

Said, Nuri al-: Eisenhower Doctrine and, 28; foreign relations, 43; government of, 135, 137; Haseeb and, 137; murder of, 2, 29; rise to power, 16, 18, 23
Salman, Mohammad, 66, 67, 68, 78, 90, 135
Samarra'i, Fadil al-, 118
San Remo conference, 14
Sarkat al- Kadehin (Cry of the Workers), 159
Saudi Arabia: Arab-Israeli war and, 175; Free Princes' movement, 68, 104; oil policy, 20, 160, 212; reforms, 67–68; US support of, 105–6; Yemen revolution and, 105
Saunders, Hal, 174, 181, 216
Sa'di, 'Ali Salih al-, 108, 131–32
Schiller, Abe, 223
Schlesinger, Arthur M., Jr., 94–95, 246n45
Schmidt, Dana Adams, 102
Seeyle, Talcott, 200
Sert, Josep Lluís, 112

Seven Sisters cartel, 66, 76, 169
Shabib, Talib al-, 113
Shawkwat, Naji, 191
Shawwaf, 'Abd al-Wahhab al-, 52
Sheikhly, 'Abd al-Karim al-, 202
Shirazi, Muhammad, 11
Sinclair Oil Company, 149, 151
Sirri, Rif'at al-Hajj, 52
Snow, Harold, 79
Soviet-ENI deal, 77
Soviet Union: influence in the Arab world, 30, 195; oil production, 44–45; relations with Iraq, 185–86, 203, 208, 209, 213, 215; sale of oil to the West, 83
Sparkman, John, 72
Standard Oil, 14, 71
State Department's Office of Near Eastern Afffairs (NEA), 34, 74–75, 152
Steiniger, E. L., 149, 150–51
Stephanson, Anders, 292n91
Stern, Roger, 5
Stewart, W. W., 123–24
Stockwell, Geofffrey, 209
Stone, I. F., 45, 133, 177
Strong, Robert, 103, 116, 122, 129, 130, 132–33, 151
Suez Canal Company, 25–26, 143
Suez War, 24, 28, 30, 41, 87, 139, 156, 184
Sukarno, Ahmad, 66
Sulaiman, 'Ali Haidar, 63
Sullivan & Cromwell law firm, 34, 36, 38, 72
Sykes-Picot Agreement, *xv*, 10, 11, 14
Syria: Ba'thist coup in, 128–29, 168; mandate regime, 10; seizure of IPC facilities, 168; Soviet relations with, 195
Syria-IPC crisis, 168, 169, 170, 174
Syrian Communist Party, 91, 128
Syrian General Congress, 11

Tabachali, Nazim al-, 52
Taft, Robert, 37
Tahrir (*Liberation*) Party, 159
Talabani, Jalal, 207, 217
Talbot, Phillips, 93–94, 105, 121, 122, 127
Talib, Naji, 167, 168
Tariki, Abdullah: Beirut exile, 144–45, 160; career of, 67–68, 80, 104, 227; "Iraq and the Oil Companies" editorial, 158–59; legal adviser of, 69, 92; oil policy of, 69, 79, 135, 147, 160, 185, 194; photograph, *68*; rise to power, 144
Teagle, Walter, 14
Thacher, Nicholas, 54
Thawrah al-'Arabiyyah al- (*The Arab Revolution*) newspaper, 158–59
Third World, 156, 292–93n92
Thomson, James C., 260n48
Tikriti, Barzan al-, 200
Tikriti, Hardan al-: assassination of, 208; career of, 205; exile of, 208; on Kurdish insurgency, 127; negotiations with oil companies, 198–99, 201; popular support of, 207
Tikriti Overture, 188, 199–200
Truman, Harry S.: Chinese affairs, 87; Point Four program, 25; presidential election campaign, 72; Soviet Containment policy, 37

Truman Doctrine, 27
Turkish Petroleum Company (TPC), 13, 14. *See also* Iraq Petroleum Company

United Arab Republic (UAR), 28, 46–47, 48, 50–51, 91, 119
United Fruit Company, 26
United Kingdom: Emergency Powers Defence Act, 16–17; financial crisis, 184; foreign policy of, 12, 26, 27, 49, 184–85, 193; Kuwait crisis and, 89–90; labour government, 184; mandate regime, 10
United Nations Resolution 1803, 144
United States: aid to Kurds, 102; Arab-Israeli conflict and, 183, 201; Baʿthist regime and, 137; British alliance with, 25; corporate culture, 169–70; diplomacy of, 7, 44, 248n69; domestic oil and gas production, 71, 170; Foreign Assistance Act, 120; foreign oil policy, 70–73, 82–84, 162, 216–17; Grandiose Strategy, 172, 180, 181, 280n84; idea of empire, 7, 223; invasion of Lebanon, 44; Middle East policy, 1, 24, 30–31, 74–75; national security policy, 31, 32, 215; New Deal initiatives, 24; oil import quota scheme, 73–74; oil revenue sharing, 20; opposition to OPEC, 80; protectionism of, 73; racial tension in, 101, 107–8; reaction to Law 80, 92–93, 94–96; relations with Iran, 214, 215–16, 217; security agencies, 31–32; support of Saudi regime, 105–6; synthetic fuels industry, 71; UAR and, 119; Vietnam policy, 134, 167
ʿUqayli, Ghanim al-, 155, 198
ʿUqayli, ʿAbd al-ʿAziz al-, 166
US Atomic Energy Commission (AEC), 2, 177
US Department of the Interior, 71, 170, 171, 172–73, 175, 254n31
US-Egyptian relations, 30, 31, 48–49, 87, 105
US-Iraqi relations: decline of, 98, 106–7, 211–12; economic interests and, 4–5, 7–8, 194–95, 196, 198; evolution of, 163, 222, 226–27; historiography of, 235n23; Iraqi politics and, 42, 94–98; Qasim's regime and, 48, 49–51, 52–53
USS Forrestal, 58
US State Department: Chase National Bank's meeting with, 122–23; Department of the Interior's rivalry with, 172–73; French diplomatic offensive, 157–58; oil companies and, 121–22, 157; open diplomacy principle, 225; pressure on the British officials, 125; study of Iraqi-IPC oil negotiations, 92, 169; Syria-IPC crisis and, 174; "The Importance of Near East Oil" paper, 171–73

Ventures, Ltd., 73
Versailles, Treaty of, 11
Vietnam: American policy in, 134, 167; CIA operations in, 56, 87

Vietnam War, 58, 172, 174, 215
Vitalis, Robert, 5
Von Mises, Ludwig, 189

Wallace, George, 107–8
Wall Street Crash of 1929, 15
Walvoord, John F.: *Israel in Prophecy*, 171
Watt, James Gias, 171
Wattari, 'Abd al-'Aziz al-: career of, 121; meeting with American oil companies, 148–49; negotiations with IPC, 123–24, 146; oil policy of, 140, 146, 147; resignation of, 160; "Small Committee" member, 139; Stewart's meeting with, 123
Wattari Agreement, 158–60, 164
Weber, Max, 163
White, Harry Dexter, 189
Williams, Robert, 101
Williams, William Appleman, 7
Woodrow, Wilson, 34
Woods, Bretton, 189

Yahya, Tahir: al-Bark's coup against, 195, 197; career of, 141, 221; death of, 221, 226; defeat of Ba'thist resistance, 132; economic policy of, 141–42; Iraqi royal visit to the US and, 224; Law 97, 185; negotiations with the Kurds, 125, 126; oil policy of, 142–43, 145, 148–49, 155, 160, 193, 206, 226; political opponents of, 193–94; political views of, 141; popular support of, 194; "positive neutrality" policy of, 141; power sharing of, 163–64; resignation of, 165; return to power, 175
Yamani, Ahmad Zaki, 175
Yarmouk housing complex in Baghdad, 64
Yemen revolution, 104, 105
Yusuf, Yusuf Salam, 23

Zhou Enlai, 25
Zubair oil field, 210

Stanford Studies *in* Middle Eastern
and Islamic Societies *and* Cultures

Joel Beinin and Laleh Khalili, editors

EDITORIAL BOARD

Asef Bayat, Marilyn Booth, Laurie Brand, Timothy Mitchell, Jillian Schwedler, Rebecca L. Stein, Max Weiss

Dear Palestine: A Social History of the 1948 War 2021
SHAY HAZKANI

A Critical Political Economy of the Middle East and North Africa 2021
JOEL BEININ, BASSAM HADDAD, AND SHERENE SEIKALY, EDITORS

Archive Wars: The Politics of History in Saudi Arabia 2020
ROSIE BSHEER

Showpiece City: How Architecture Made Dubai 2020
TODD REISZ

Between Muslims: Religious Difference in Iraqi Kurdistan 2020
J. ANDREW BUSH

The Optimist: A Social Biography of Tawfiq Zayyad 2020
TAMIR SOREK

Graveyard of Clerics: Everyday Activism in Saudi Arabia 2020
PASCAL MENORET

Cleft Capitalism: The Social Origins of Failed Market Making in Egypt 2020
AMR ADLY

The Universal Enemy: Jihad, Empire, and the Challenge of Solidarity 2019
DARRYL LI

Waste Siege: The Life of Infrastructure in Palestine 2019
SOPHIA STAMATOPOULOU-ROBBINS

Heritage and the Cultural Struggle for Palestine 2019
CHIARA DE CESARI

Iran Reframed: Anxieties of Power in the Islamic Republic 2019
NARGES BAJOGHLI

Banking on the State: The Financial Foundations of Lebanon 2019
HICHAM SAFIEDDINE

Familiar Futures: Time, Selfhood, and Sovereignty in Iraq 2019
SARA PURSLEY

Hamas Contained: The Rise and Pacification of Palestinian Resistance 2018
TAREQ BACONI

Hotels and Highways: The Construction of Modernization Theory in Cold War Turkey 2018
BEGÜM ADALET

Bureaucratic Intimacies: Translating Human Rights in Turkey 2017
ELIF M. BABÜL

Impossible Exodus: Iraqi Jews in Israel 2017
ORIT BASHKIN

Brothers Apart: Palestinian Citizens of Israel and the Arab World 2017
MAHA NASSAR

Revolution without Revolutionaries: Making Sense of the Arab Spring 2017
ASEF BAYAT

Soundtrack of the Revolution: The Politics of Music in Iran 2017
NAHID SIAMDOUST

Copts and the Security State: Violence, Coercion, and Sectarianism in Contemporary Egypt 2016
LAURE GUIRGUIS

Circuits of Faith: Migration, Education, and the Wahhabi Mission 2016
MICHAEL FARQUHAR